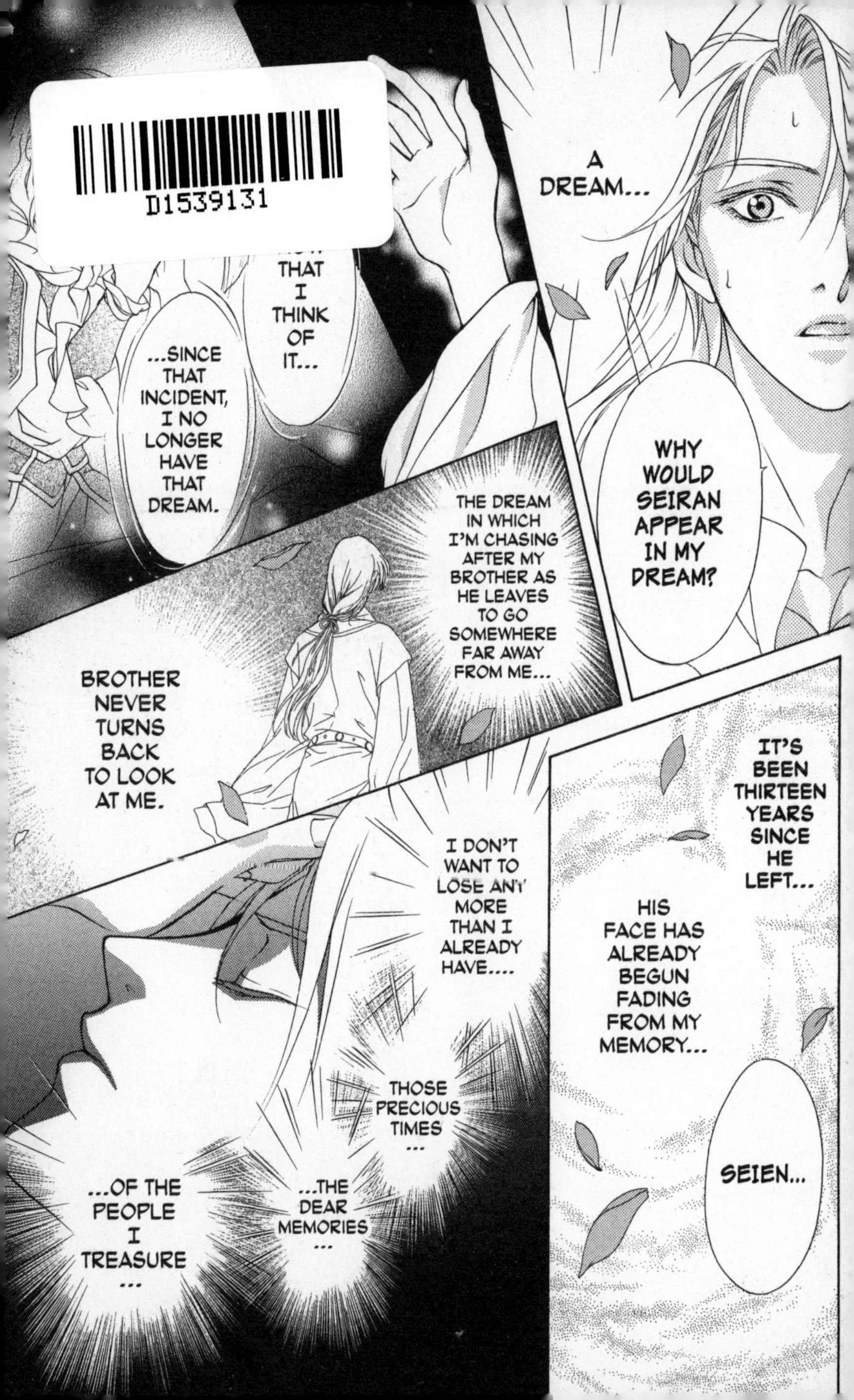
A DREAM...
WHY WOULD SEIRAN APPEAR IN MY DREAM?
THAT I THINK OF IT...
...SINCE THAT INCIDENT, I NO LONGER HAVE THAT DREAM.
THE DREAM IN WHICH I'M CHASING AFTER MY BROTHER AS HE LEAVES TO GO SOMEWHERE FAR AWAY FROM ME...
BROTHER NEVER TURNS BACK TO LOOK AT ME.
IT'S BEEN THIRTEEN YEARS SINCE HE LEFT...
HIS FACE HAS ALREADY BEGUN FADING FROM MY MEMORY...
SEIEN...
I DON'T WANT TO LOSE ANY MORE THAN I ALREADY HAVE....
THOSE PRECIOUS TIMES...
...THE DEAR MEMORIES...
...OF THE PEOPLE I TREASURE...

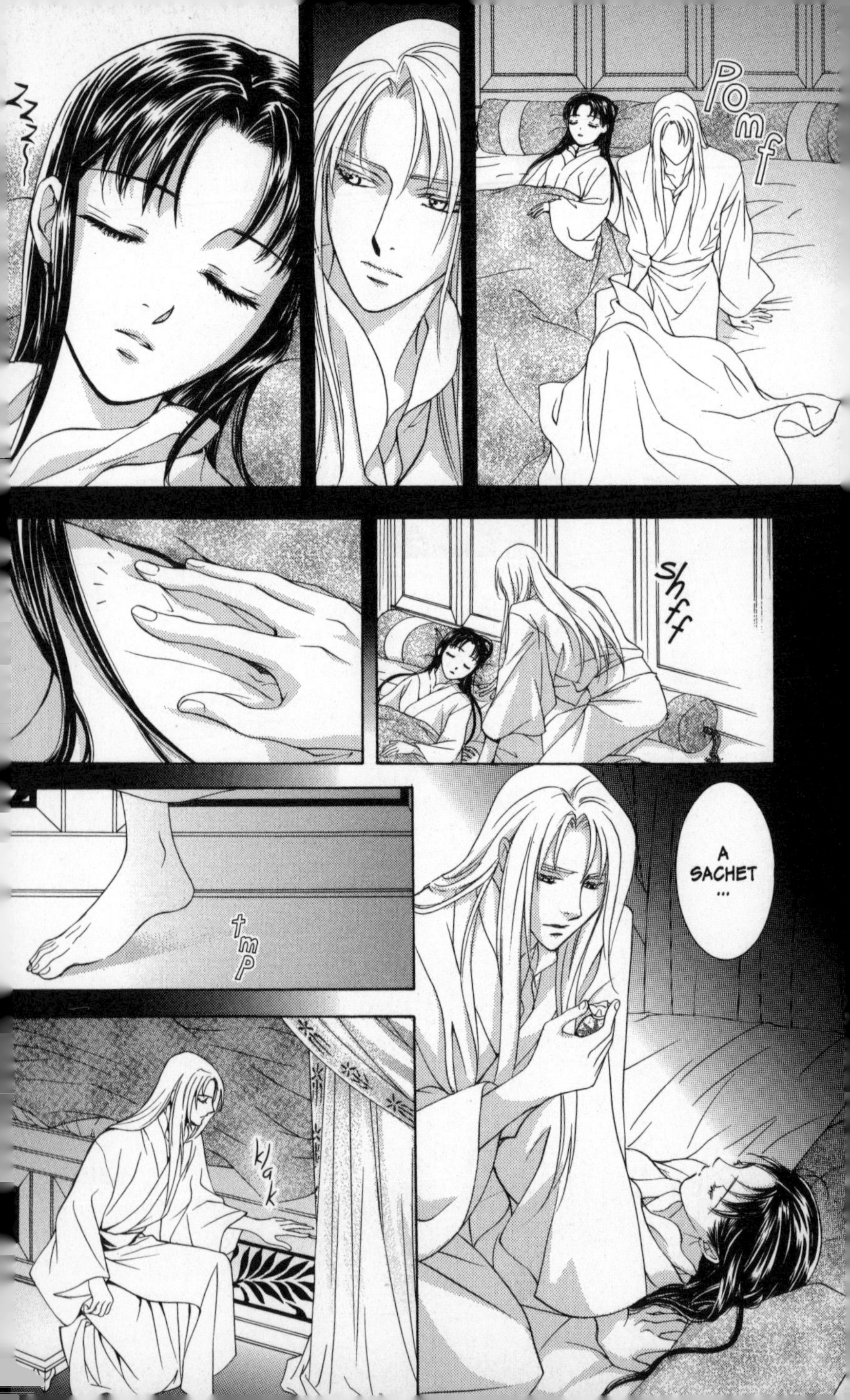
Pomf
Zzz~
shff
A SACHET ...
tmp
klak

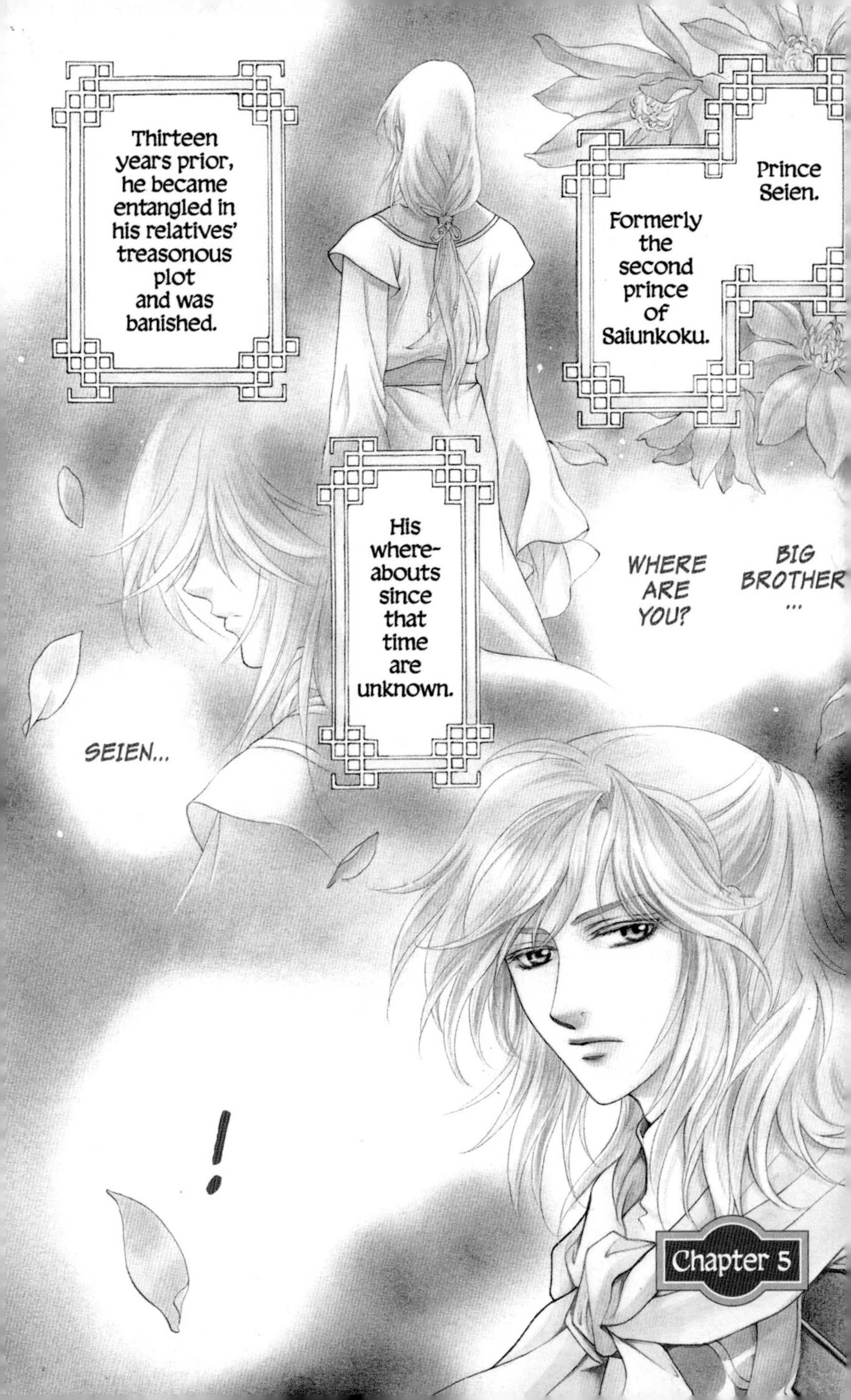
Prince Seien.
Formerly the second prince of Saiunkoku.
Thirteen years prior, he became entangled in his relatives' treasonous plot and was banished.
His whereabouts since that time are unknown.
BIG BROTHER...
WHERE ARE YOU?
SEIEN...
!
Chapter 5

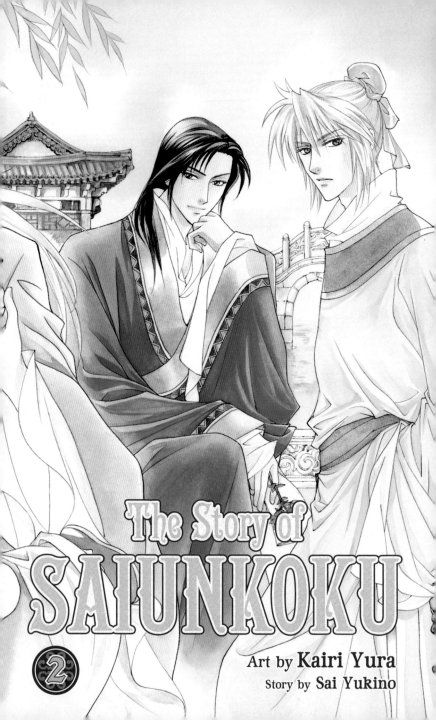

The Story of
SAIUNKOKU

2

Art by **Kairi Yura**
Story by **Sai Yukino**

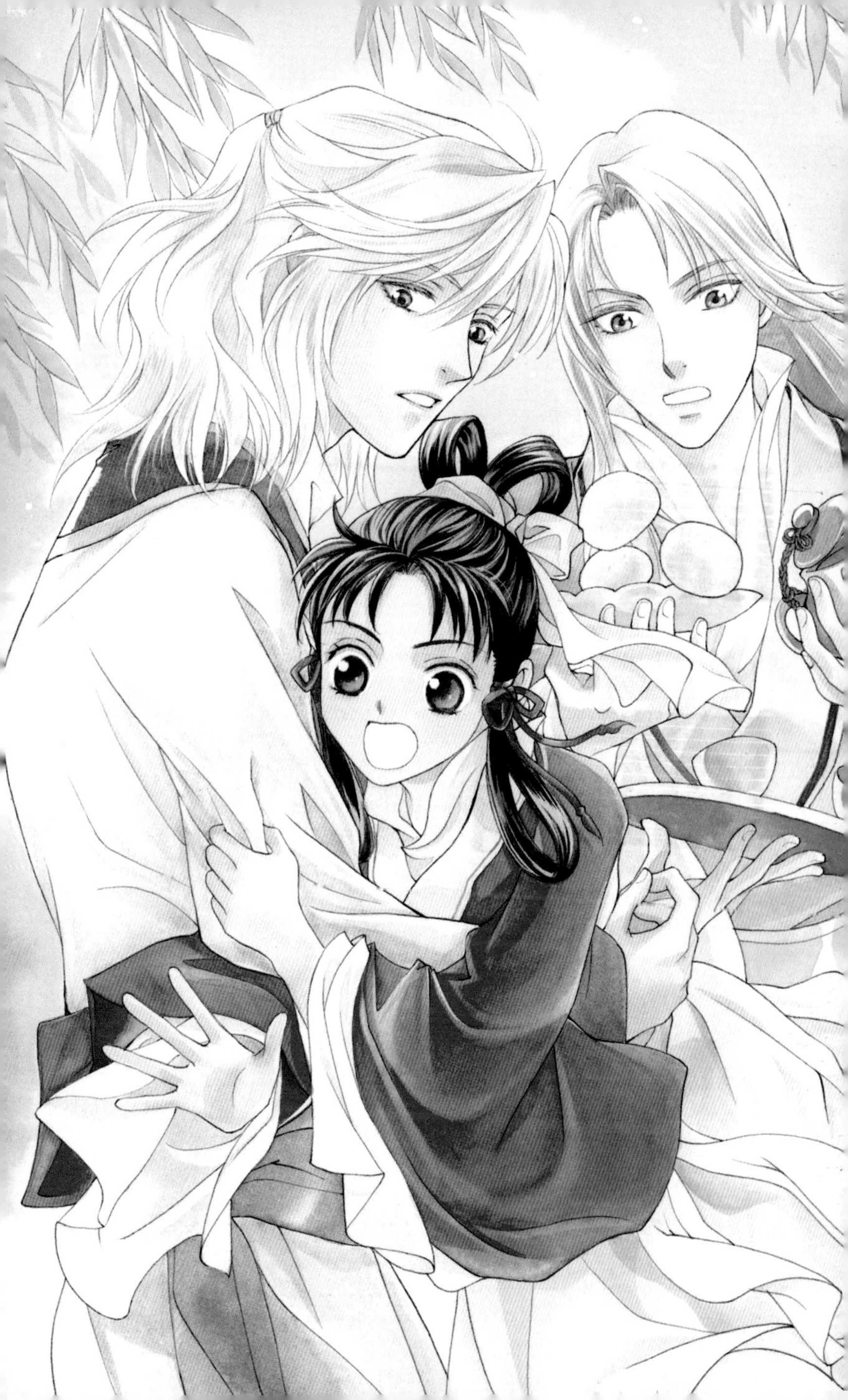

Volume 2
Contents

Story Thus Far

Upon starting a new life in the imperial court, all Lady Shurei has to do is babysit the emperor—in other words, serve as his tutor and be his Noble Consort. Despite Shurei's exasperation at the frivolous Emperor Ryuki's willful lifestyle, the two gradually come to know one another and discover a growing kinship between them. However, strange occurrences begin happening around Shurei. Getting wind of a treasonous plot, Koyu and Shuei start hunting secretly for the perpetrator...

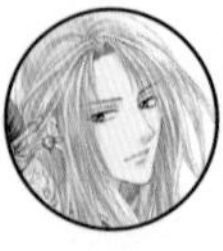

Ryuki Shi
The young emperor of Saiunkoku. He is widely known as an "idiot ruler," but it seems he has his reasons for appearing so.

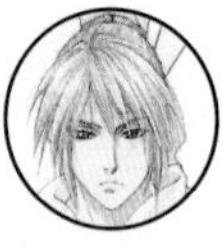

Koyu Ri
A civil servant renowned throughout the court as a genius, currently stuck in a frivolous position (perhaps?) serving Ryuki. He has a hopelessly bad sense of direction.

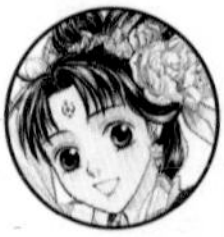

Shurei Hong
A young noblewoman of the prestigious but impoverished Hong Clan. She recently entered the Inner Court as Ryuki's tutor and erstwhile Noble Consort.

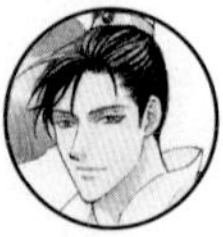

Shuei Ran
A military officer. He is a general of the Yulin Guard, a squad of soldiers charged with protecting the emperor. He is inseparable from Koyu (much to his friend's ire).

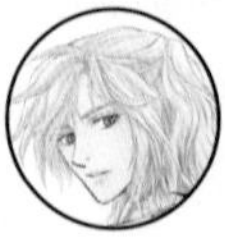

Seiran Shi
After being taken in by Shurei's father Shoka, Seiran has served the Hong household as its faithful retainer ever since. He is Shurei's protector.

The Three Great Excellencies
Since the time of the previous emperor, three elderly advisors have served the throne: Lord Advisor Sho, Lord Advisor Sou and Lord Advisor Sa. They are scheming to advance Ryuki's education.

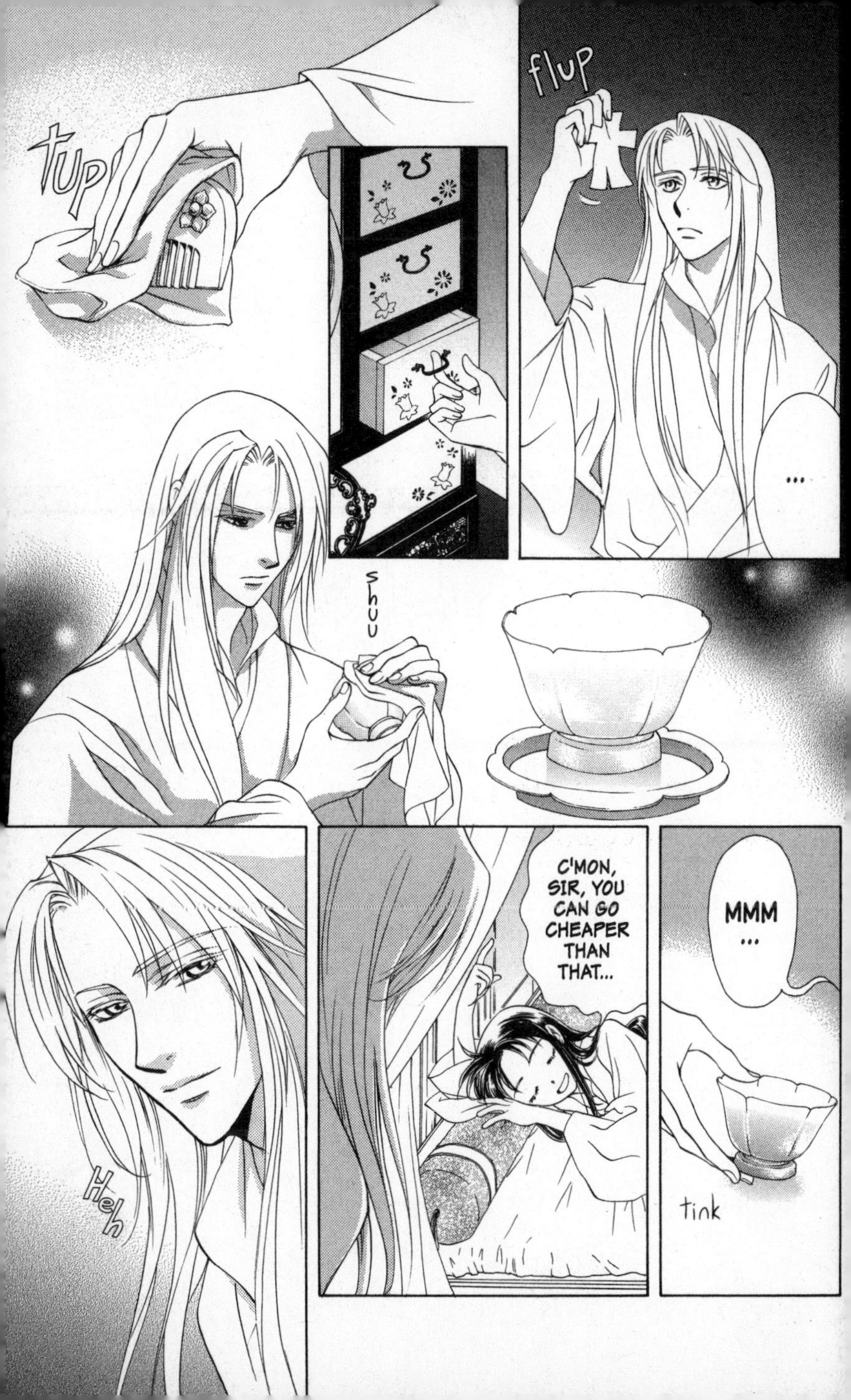
flup
...
tup
shuu
MMM...
tink
C'MON, SIR, YOU CAN GO CHEAPER THAN THAT...
Heh

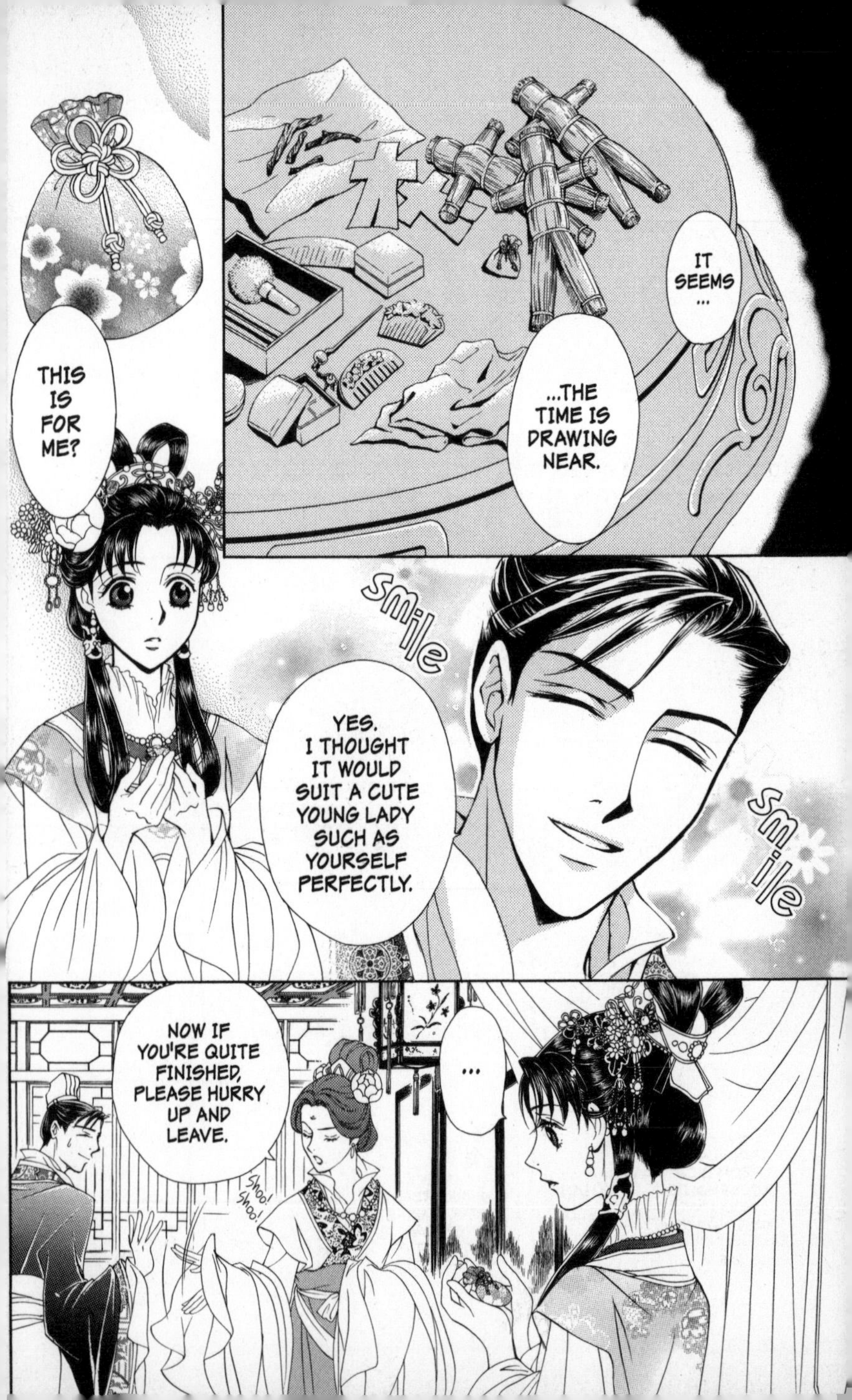
IT SEEMS...
...THE TIME IS DRAWING NEAR.
THIS IS FOR ME?
Smile
YES. I THOUGHT IT WOULD SUIT A CUTE YOUNG LADY SUCH AS YOURSELF PERFECTLY.
Smile
...
NOW IF YOU'RE QUITE FINISHED, PLEASE HURRY UP AND LEAVE.
Shoo! Shoo!

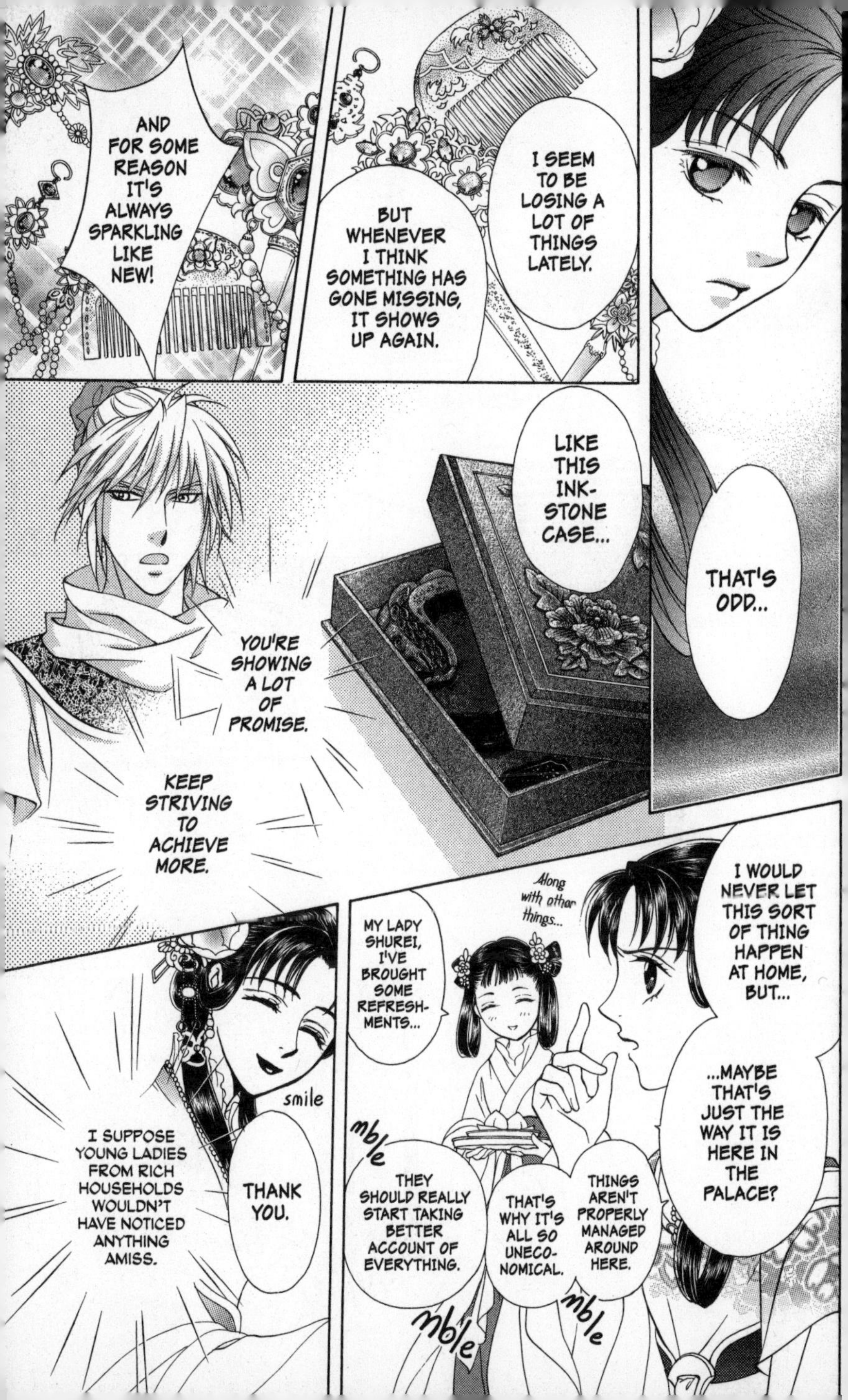
THAT'S ODD...
I SEEM TO BE LOSING A LOT OF THINGS LATELY.
BUT WHENEVER I THINK SOMETHING HAS GONE MISSING, IT SHOWS UP AGAIN.
AND FOR SOME REASON IT'S ALWAYS SPARKLING LIKE NEW!
LIKE THIS INK-STONE CASE...
YOU'RE SHOWING A LOT OF PROMISE.
KEEP STRIVING TO ACHIEVE MORE.
I WOULD NEVER LET THIS SORT OF THING HAPPEN AT HOME, BUT...
...MAYBE THAT'S JUST THE WAY IT IS HERE IN THE PALACE?
Along with other things...
MY LADY SHUREI, I'VE BROUGHT SOME REFRESHMENTS...
THINGS AREN'T PROPERLY MANAGED AROUND HERE.
THAT'S WHY IT'S ALL SO UNECONOMICAL.
THEY SHOULD REALLY START TAKING BETTER ACCOUNT OF EVERYTHING.
mble
mble
mble
smile
THANK YOU.
I SUPPOSE YOUNG LADIES FROM RICH HOUSEHOLDS WOULDN'T HAVE NOTICED ANYTHING AMISS.

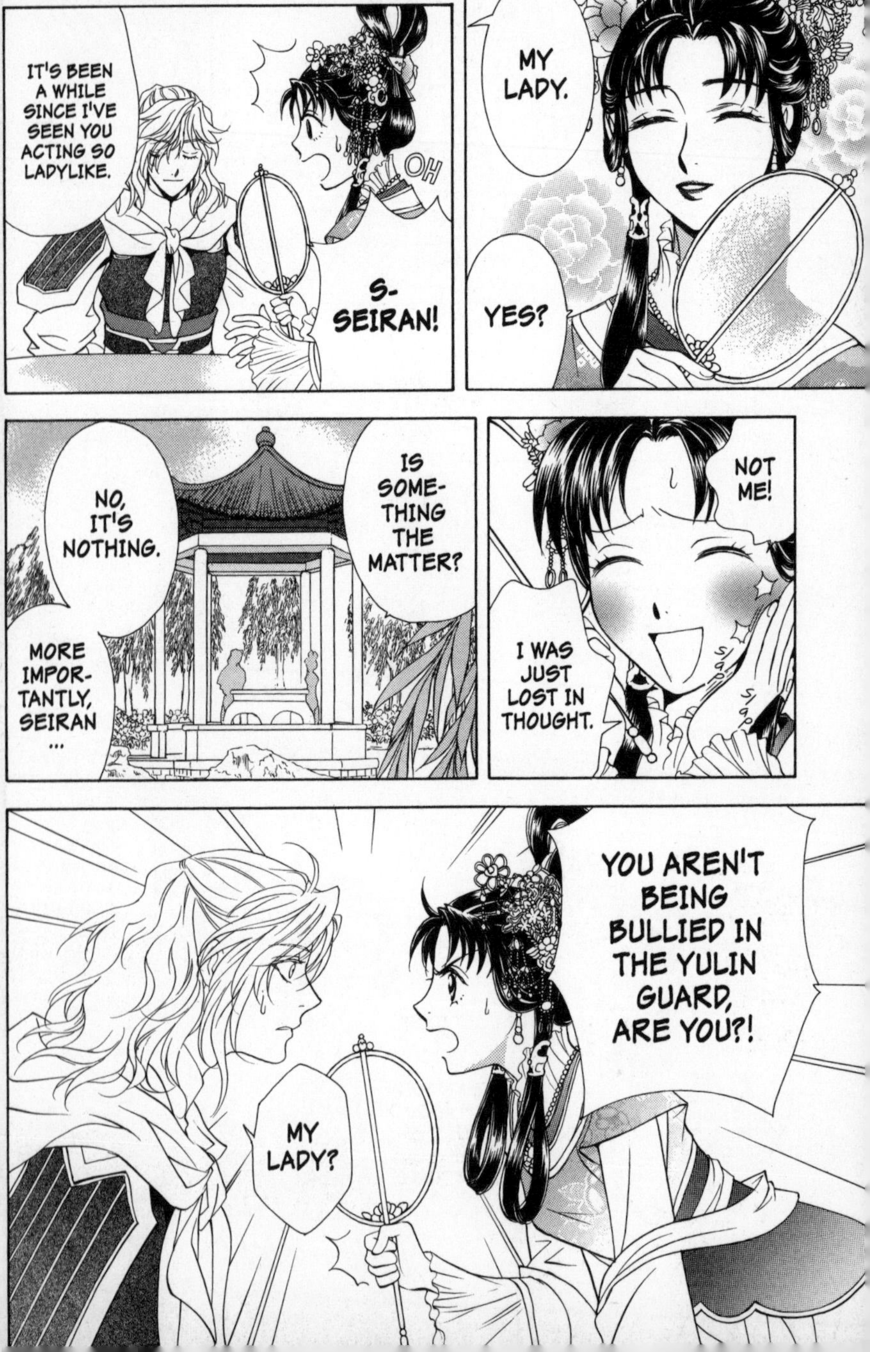
MY LADY.
YES?
IT'S BEEN A WHILE SINCE I'VE SEEN YOU ACTING SO LADYLIKE.
OH
S-SEIRAN!
NOT ME!
I WAS JUST LOST IN THOUGHT.
slap slap
IS SOMETHING THE MATTER?
NO, IT'S NOTHING.
MORE IMPORTANTLY, SEIRAN ...
YOU AREN'T BEING BULLIED IN THE YULIN GUARD, ARE YOU?!
MY LADY?

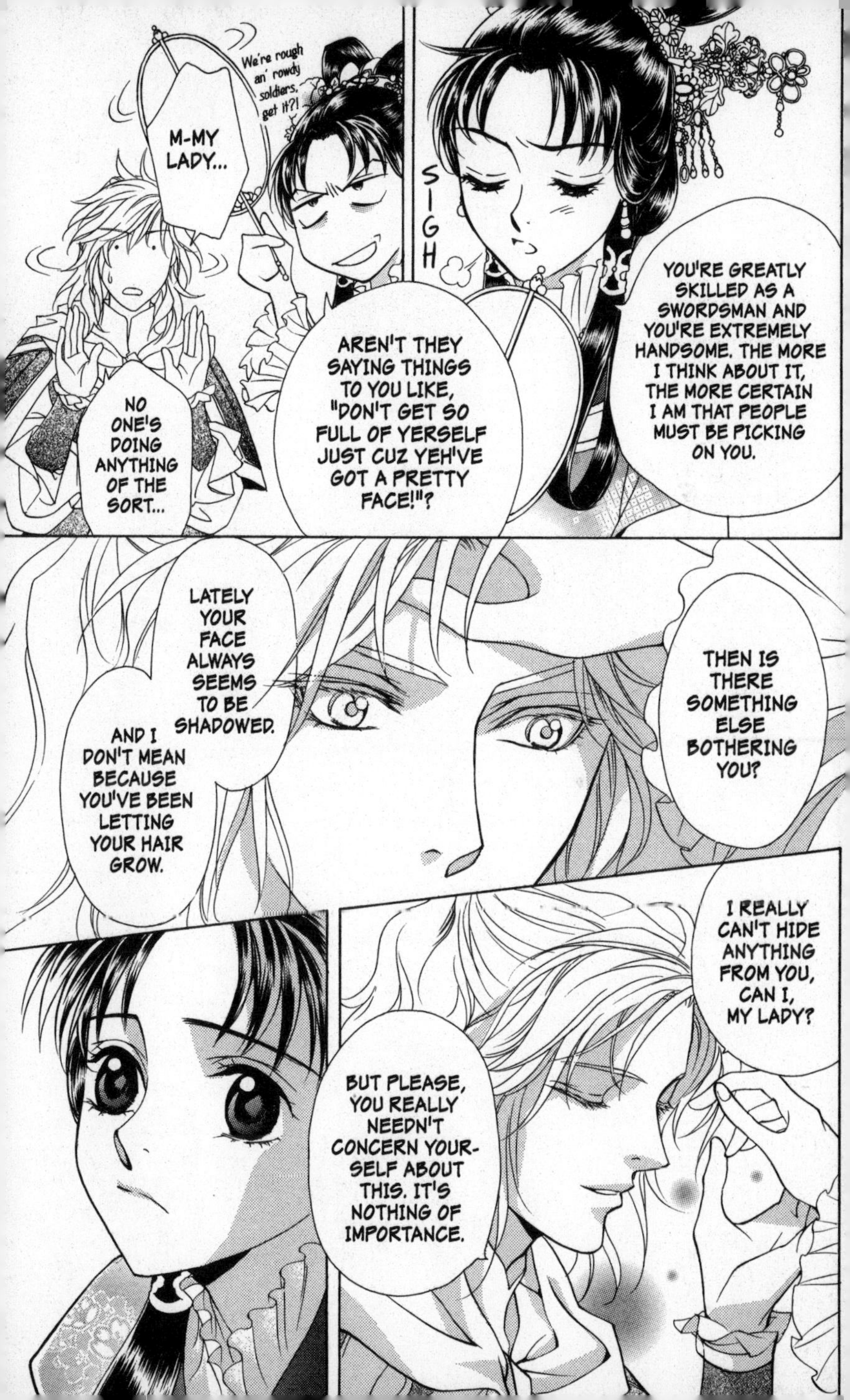
SIGH
YOU'RE GREATLY SKILLED AS A SWORDSMAN AND YOU'RE EXTREMELY HANDSOME. THE MORE I THINK ABOUT IT, THE MORE CERTAIN I AM THAT PEOPLE MUST BE PICKING ON YOU.
AREN'T THEY SAYING THINGS TO YOU LIKE, "DON'T GET SO FULL OF YERSELF JUST CUZ YEH'VE GOT A PRETTY FACE!"?
We're rough an' rowdy soldiers, get it?!
M-MY LADY...
NO ONE'S DOING ANYTHING OF THE SORT...
THEN IS THERE SOMETHING ELSE BOTHERING YOU?
LATELY YOUR FACE ALWAYS SEEMS TO BE SHADOWED.
AND I DON'T MEAN BECAUSE YOU'VE BEEN LETTING YOUR HAIR GROW.
I REALLY CAN'T HIDE ANYTHING FROM YOU, CAN I, MY LADY?
BUT PLEASE, YOU REALLY NEEDN'T CONCERN YOURSELF ABOUT THIS. IT'S NOTHING OF IMPORTANCE.

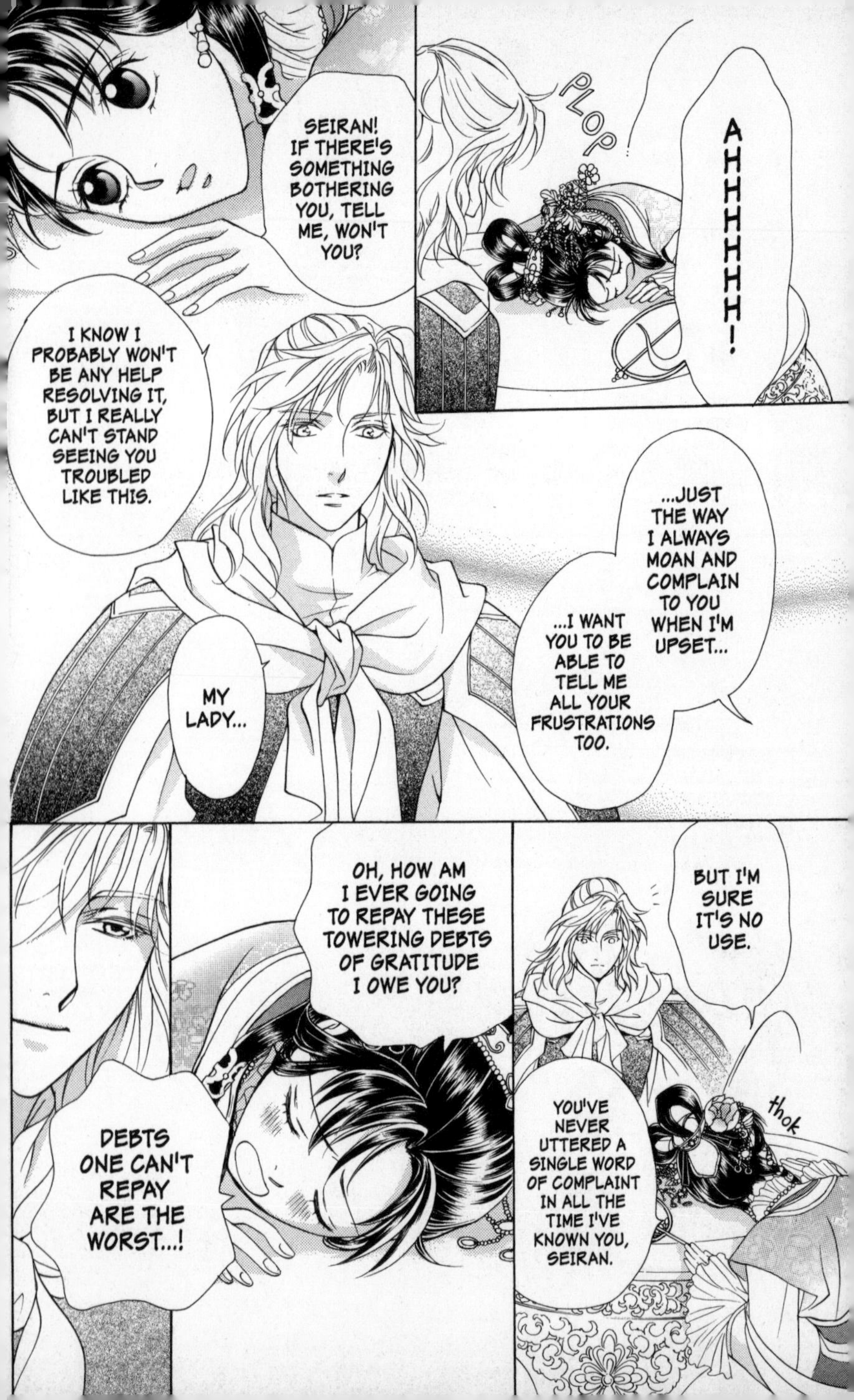
PLOP
AHHHHHH!
SEIRAN! IF THERE'S SOMETHING BOTHERING YOU, TELL ME, WON'T YOU?
I KNOW I PROBABLY WON'T BE ANY HELP RESOLVING IT, BUT I REALLY CAN'T STAND SEEING YOU TROUBLED LIKE THIS.
...JUST THE WAY I ALWAYS MOAN AND COMPLAIN TO YOU WHEN I'M UPSET...
...I WANT YOU TO BE ABLE TO TELL ME ALL YOUR FRUSTRATIONS TOO.
MY LADY...
BUT I'M SURE IT'S NO USE.
thok
YOU'VE NEVER UTTERED A SINGLE WORD OF COMPLAINT IN ALL THE TIME I'VE KNOWN YOU, SEIRAN.
OH, HOW AM I EVER GOING TO REPAY THESE TOWERING DEBTS OF GRATITUDE I OWE YOU?
DEBTS ONE CAN'T REPAY ARE THE WORST...!

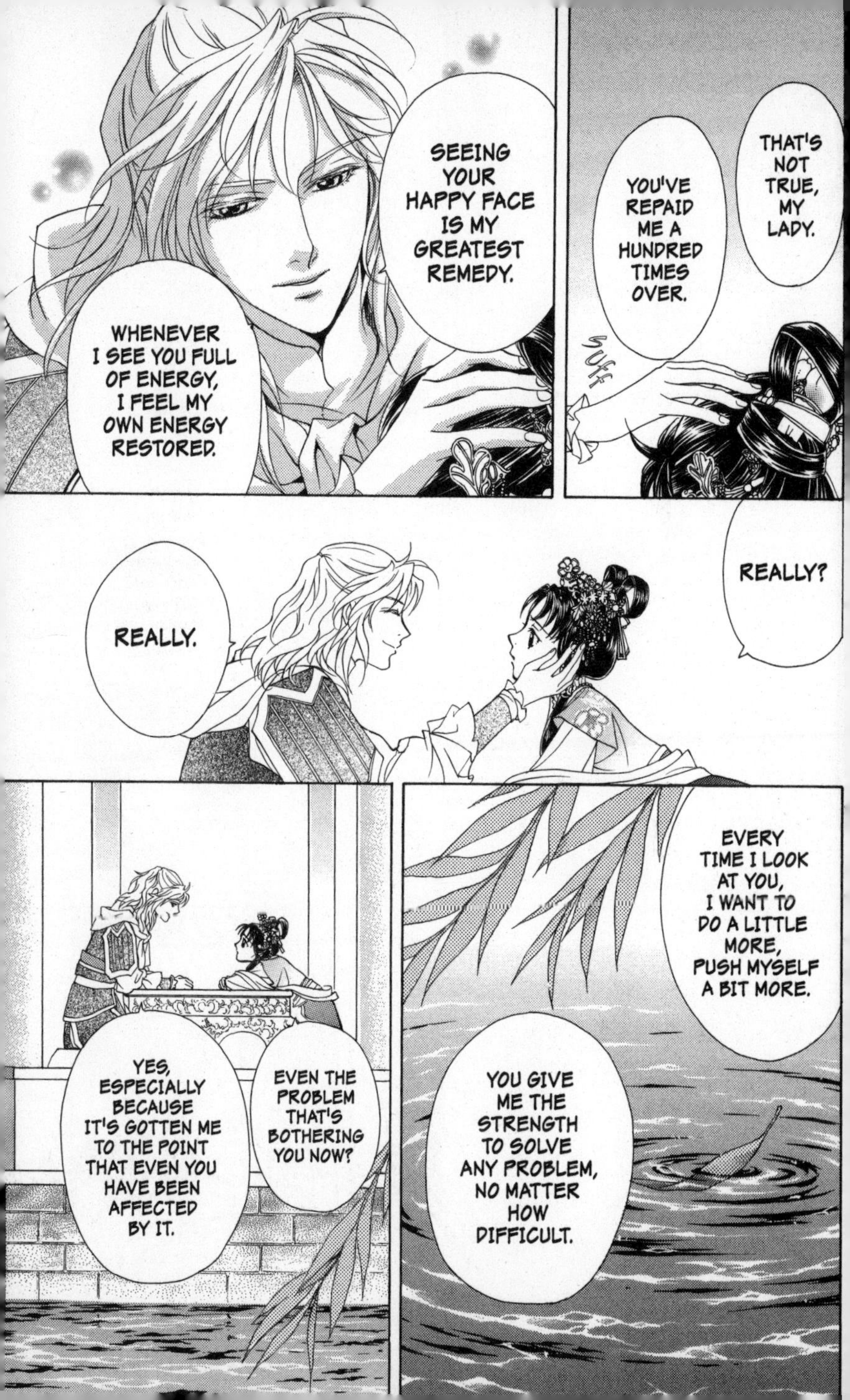
THAT'S NOT TRUE, MY LADY.
YOU'VE REPAID ME A HUNDRED TIMES OVER.
SUFF
SEEING YOUR HAPPY FACE IS MY GREATEST REMEDY.
WHENEVER I SEE YOU FULL OF ENERGY, I FEEL MY OWN ENERGY RESTORED.
REALLY?
REALLY.
EVERY TIME I LOOK AT YOU, I WANT TO DO A LITTLE MORE, PUSH MYSELF A BIT MORE.
YOU GIVE ME THE STRENGTH TO SOLVE ANY PROBLEM, NO MATTER HOW DIFFICULT.
EVEN THE PROBLEM THAT'S BOTHERING YOU NOW?
YES, ESPECIALLY BECAUSE IT'S GOTTEN ME TO THE POINT THAT EVEN YOU HAVE BEEN AFFECTED BY IT.

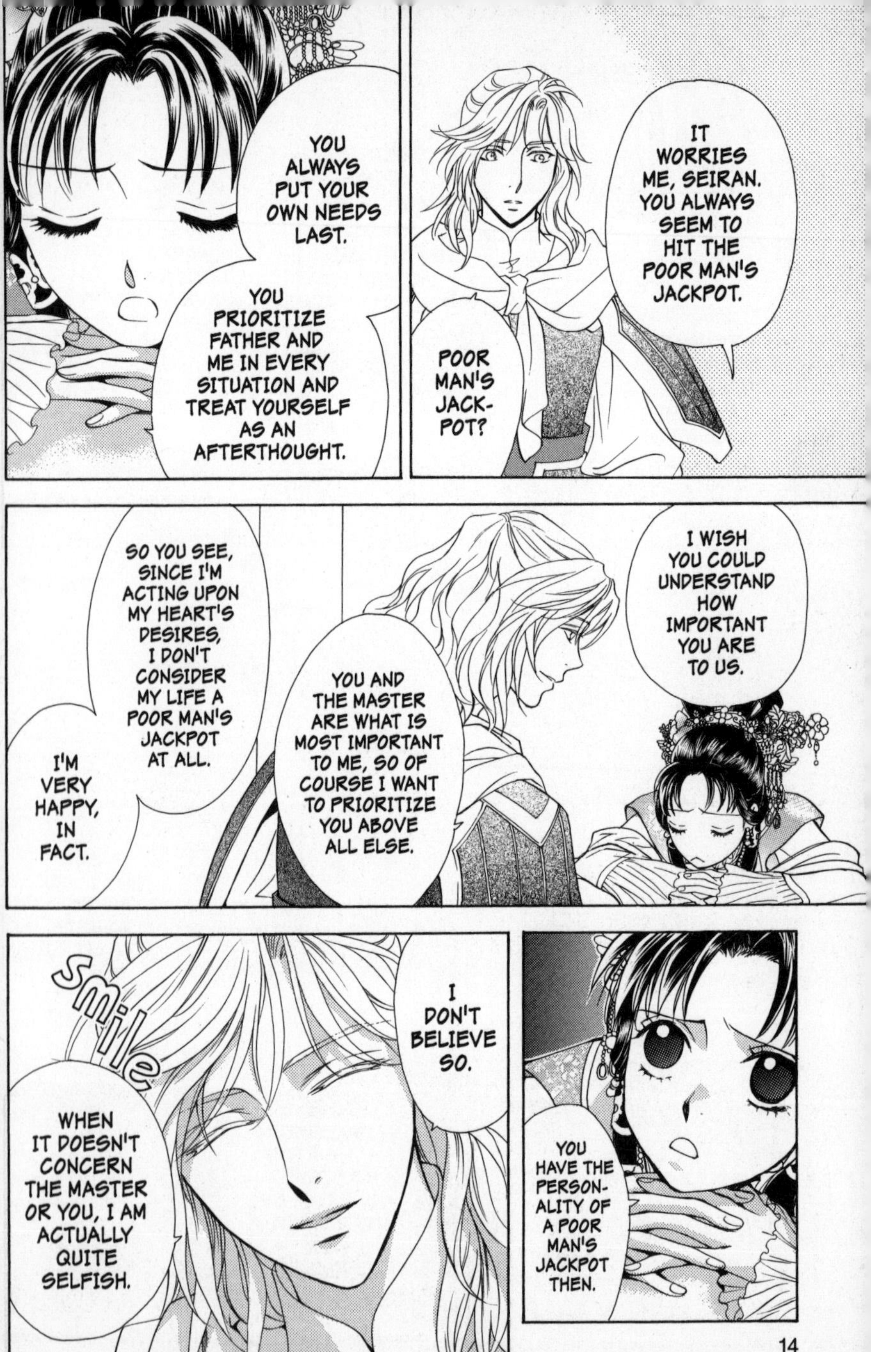
IT WORRIES ME, SEIRAN. YOU ALWAYS SEEM TO HIT THE POOR MAN'S JACKPOT.
POOR MAN'S JACK-POT?
YOU ALWAYS PUT YOUR OWN NEEDS LAST.
YOU PRIORITIZE FATHER AND ME IN EVERY SITUATION AND TREAT YOURSELF AS AN AFTERTHOUGHT.
I WISH YOU COULD UNDERSTAND HOW IMPORTANT YOU ARE TO US.
YOU AND THE MASTER ARE WHAT IS MOST IMPORTANT TO ME, SO OF COURSE I WANT TO PRIORITIZE YOU ABOVE ALL ELSE.
SO YOU SEE, SINCE I'M ACTING UPON MY HEART'S DESIRES, I DON'T CONSIDER MY LIFE A POOR MAN'S JACKPOT AT ALL.
I'M VERY HAPPY, IN FACT.
YOU HAVE THE PERSON-ALITY OF A POOR MAN'S JACKPOT THEN.
I DON'T BELIEVE SO.
Smile
WHEN IT DOESN'T CONCERN THE MASTER OR YOU, I AM ACTUALLY QUITE SELFISH.

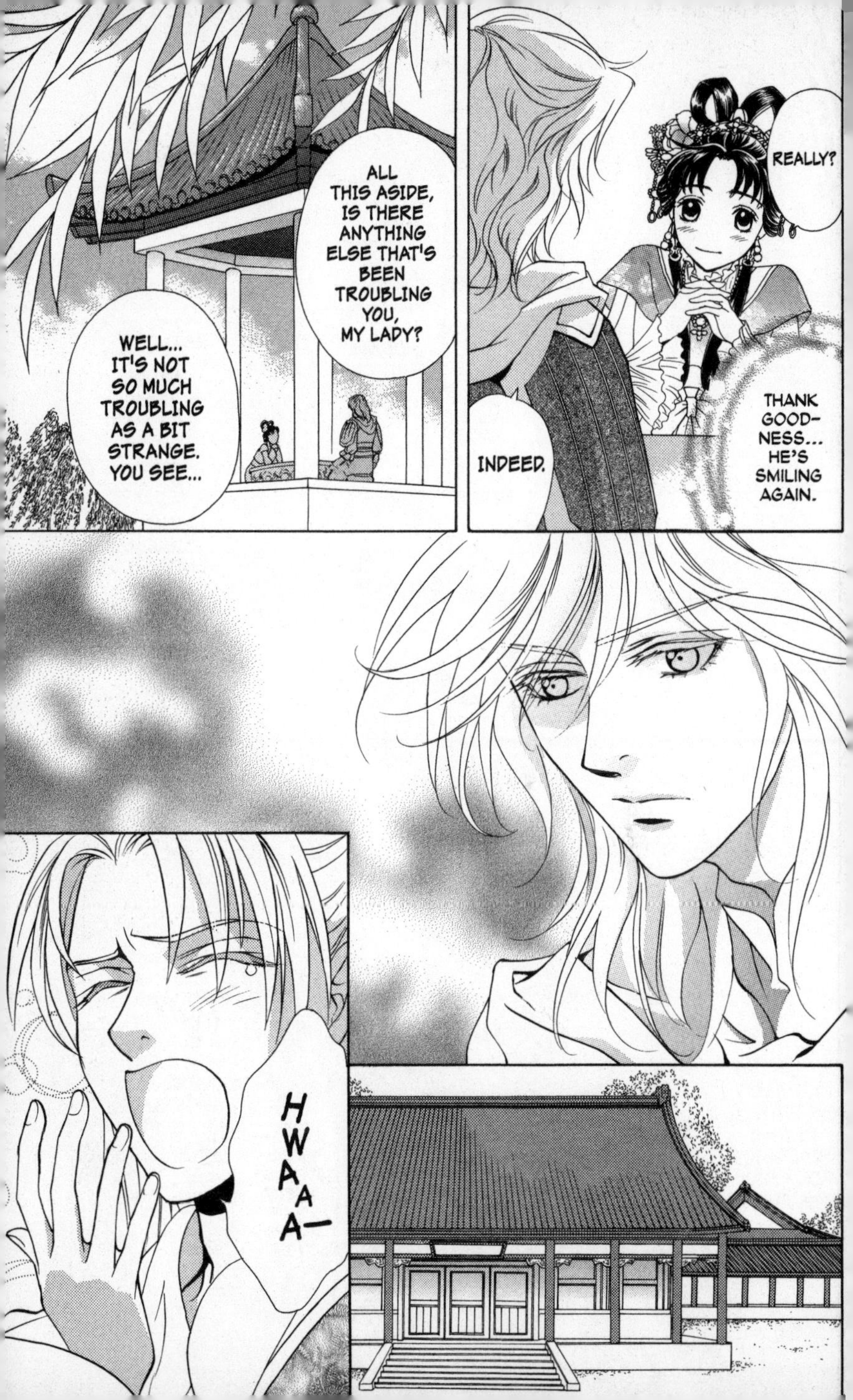
REALLY?
INDEED.
THANK GOODNESS... HE'S SMILING AGAIN.
ALL THIS ASIDE, IS THERE ANYTHING ELSE THAT'S BEEN TROUBLING YOU, MY LADY?
WELL... IT'S NOT SO MUCH TROUBLING AS A BIT STRANGE. YOU SEE...
HWAAAA—

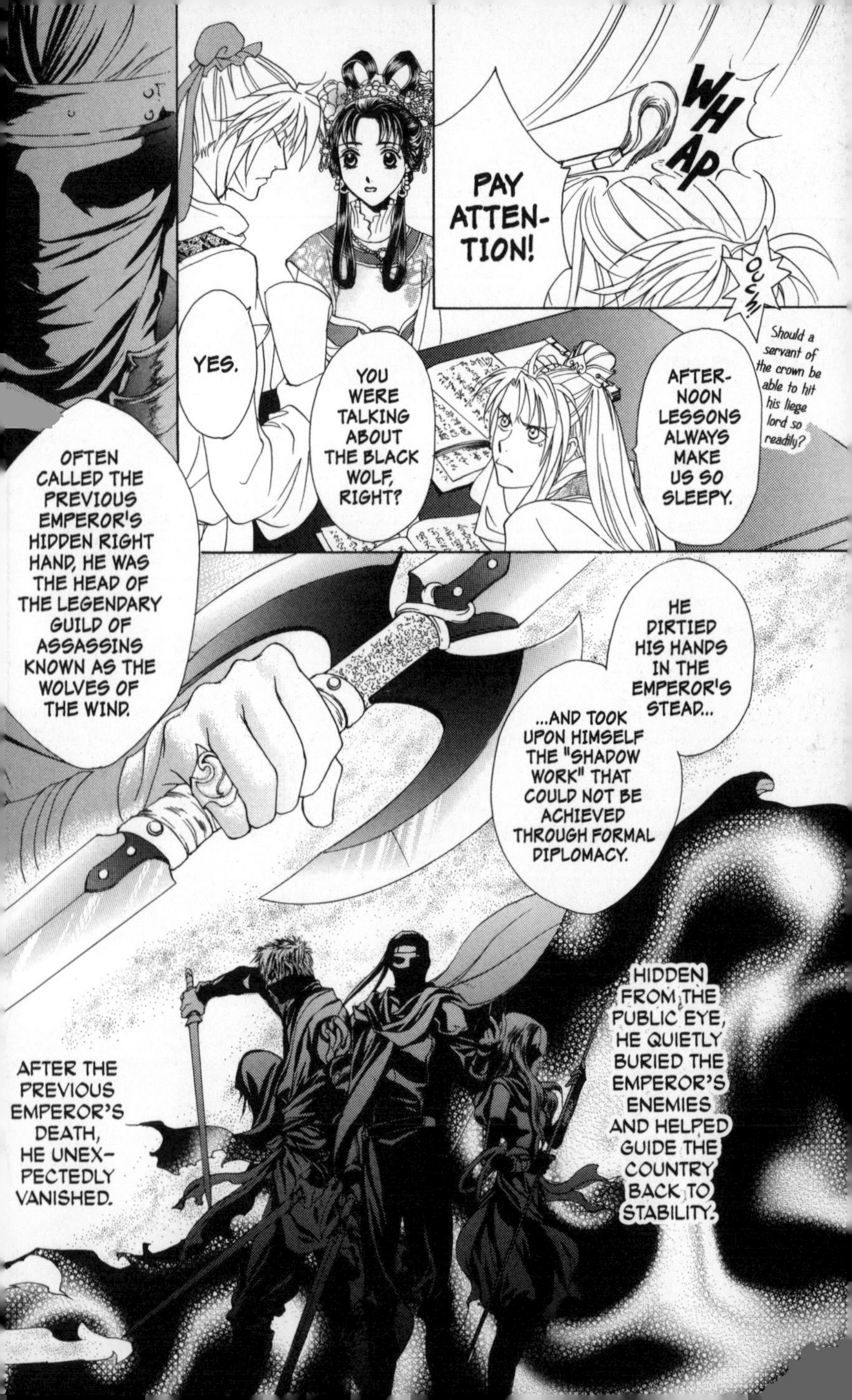
WHAP
PAY ATTENTION!
OUCH!
Should a servant of the crown be able to hit his liege lord so readily?
AFTERNOON LESSONS ALWAYS MAKE US SO SLEEPY.
YOU WERE TALKING ABOUT THE BLACK WOLF, RIGHT?
YES.
OFTEN CALLED THE PREVIOUS EMPEROR'S HIDDEN RIGHT HAND, HE WAS THE HEAD OF THE LEGENDARY GUILD OF ASSASSINS KNOWN AS THE WOLVES OF THE WIND.
HE DIRTIED HIS HANDS IN THE EMPEROR'S STEAD...
...AND TOOK UPON HIMSELF THE "SHADOW WORK" THAT COULD NOT BE ACHIEVED THROUGH FORMAL DIPLOMACY.
HIDDEN FROM THE PUBLIC EYE, HE QUIETLY BURIED THE EMPEROR'S ENEMIES AND HELPED GUIDE THE COUNTRY BACK TO STABILITY.
AFTER THE PREVIOUS EMPEROR'S DEATH, HE UNEXPECTEDLY VANISHED.

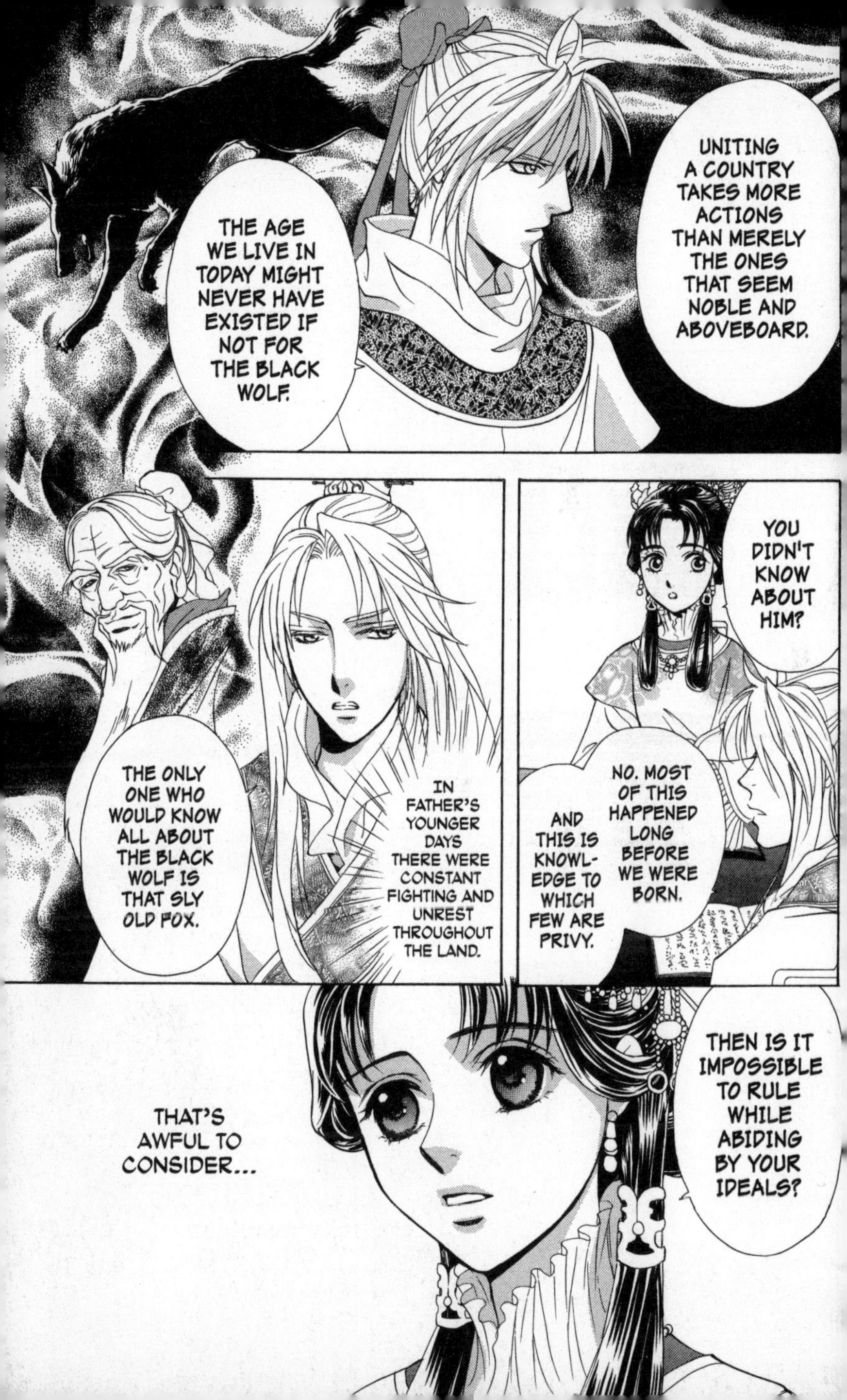
UNITING A COUNTRY TAKES MORE ACTIONS THAN MERELY THE ONES THAT SEEM NOBLE AND ABOVEBOARD.
THE AGE WE LIVE IN TODAY MIGHT NEVER HAVE EXISTED IF NOT FOR THE BLACK WOLF.
YOU DIDN'T KNOW ABOUT HIM?
NO. MOST OF THIS HAPPENED LONG BEFORE WE WERE BORN.
AND THIS IS KNOWL-EDGE TO WHICH FEW ARE PRIVY.
IN FATHER'S YOUNGER DAYS THERE WERE CONSTANT FIGHTING AND UNREST THROUGHOUT THE LAND.
THE ONLY ONE WHO WOULD KNOW ALL ABOUT THE BLACK WOLF IS THAT SLY OLD FOX.
THEN IS IT IMPOSSIBLE TO RULE WHILE ABIDING BY YOUR IDEALS?
THAT'S AWFUL TO CONSIDER...

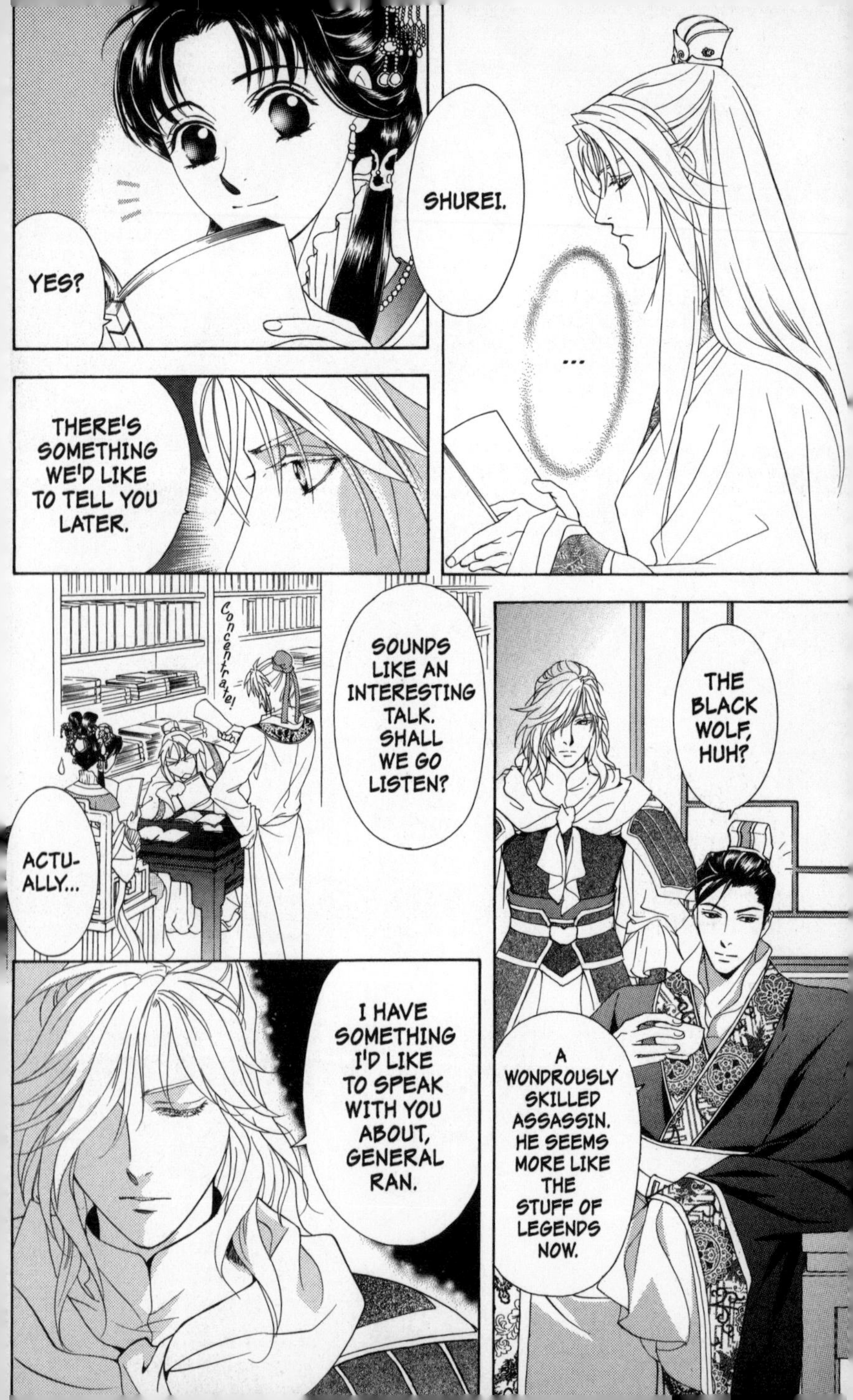
SHUREI.
...
YES?
THERE'S SOMETHING WE'D LIKE TO TELL YOU LATER.
THE BLACK WOLF, HUH?
A WONDROUSLY SKILLED ASSASSIN. HE SEEMS MORE LIKE THE STUFF OF LEGENDS NOW.
SOUNDS LIKE AN INTERESTING TALK. SHALL WE GO LISTEN?
Concentrate!
ACTU-ALLY...
I HAVE SOMETHING I'D LIKE TO SPEAK WITH YOU ABOUT, GENERAL RAN.

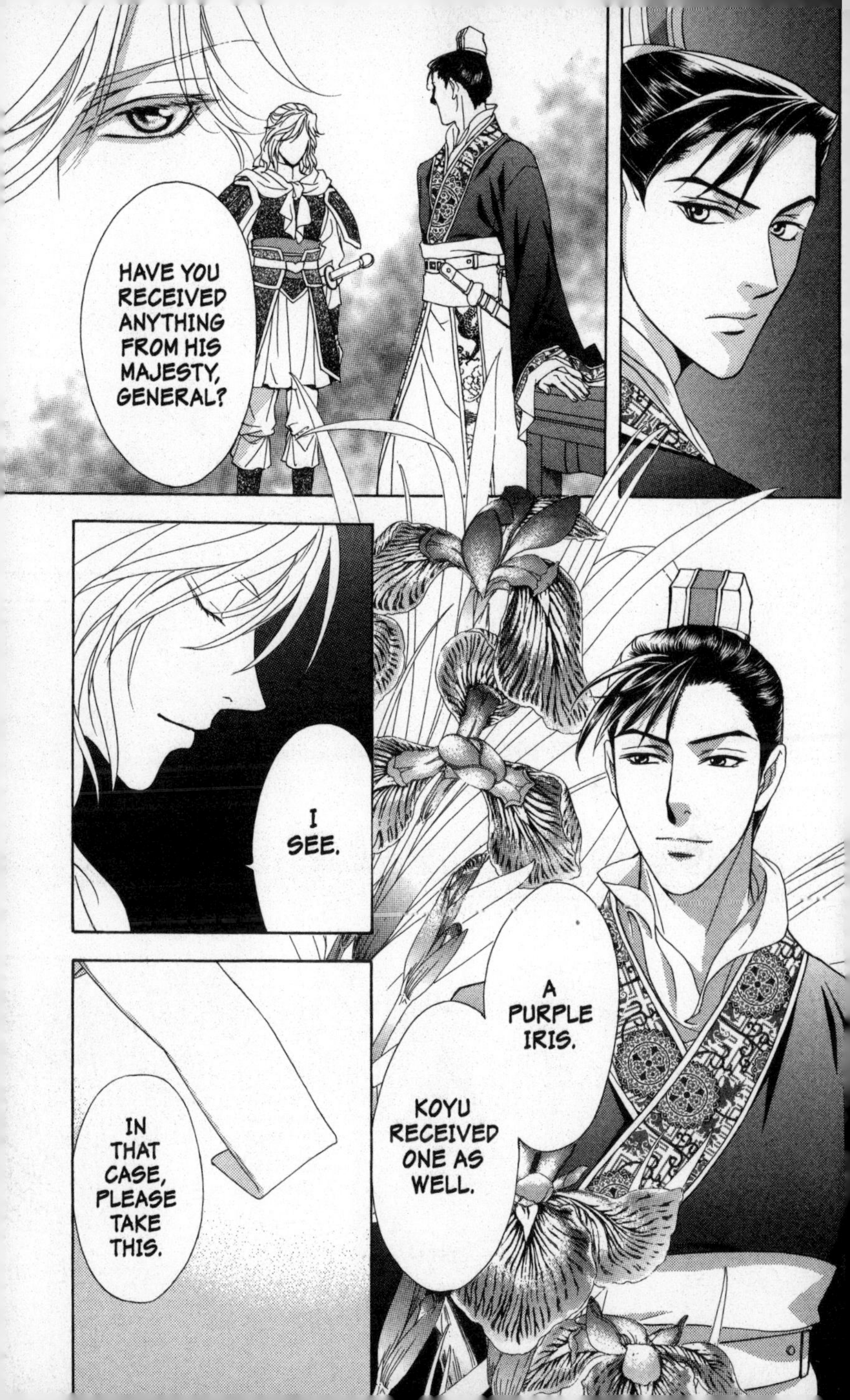
HAVE YOU RECEIVED ANYTHING FROM HIS MAJESTY, GENERAL?
A PURPLE IRIS.
KOYU RECEIVED ONE AS WELL.
I SEE.
IN THAT CASE, PLEASE TAKE THIS.

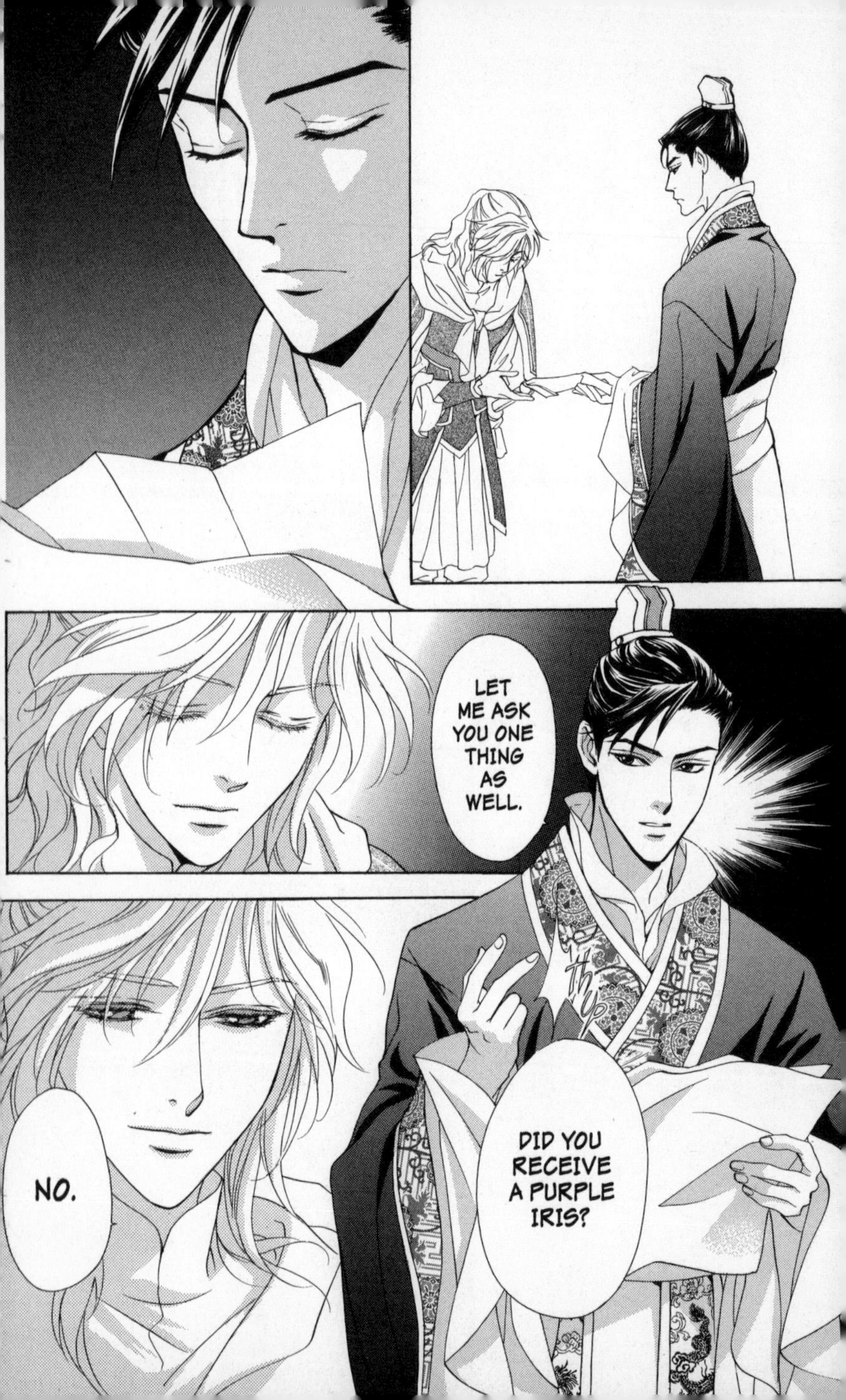
LET ME ASK YOU ONE THING AS WELL.
THUP
DID YOU RECEIVE A PURPLE IRIS?
NO.

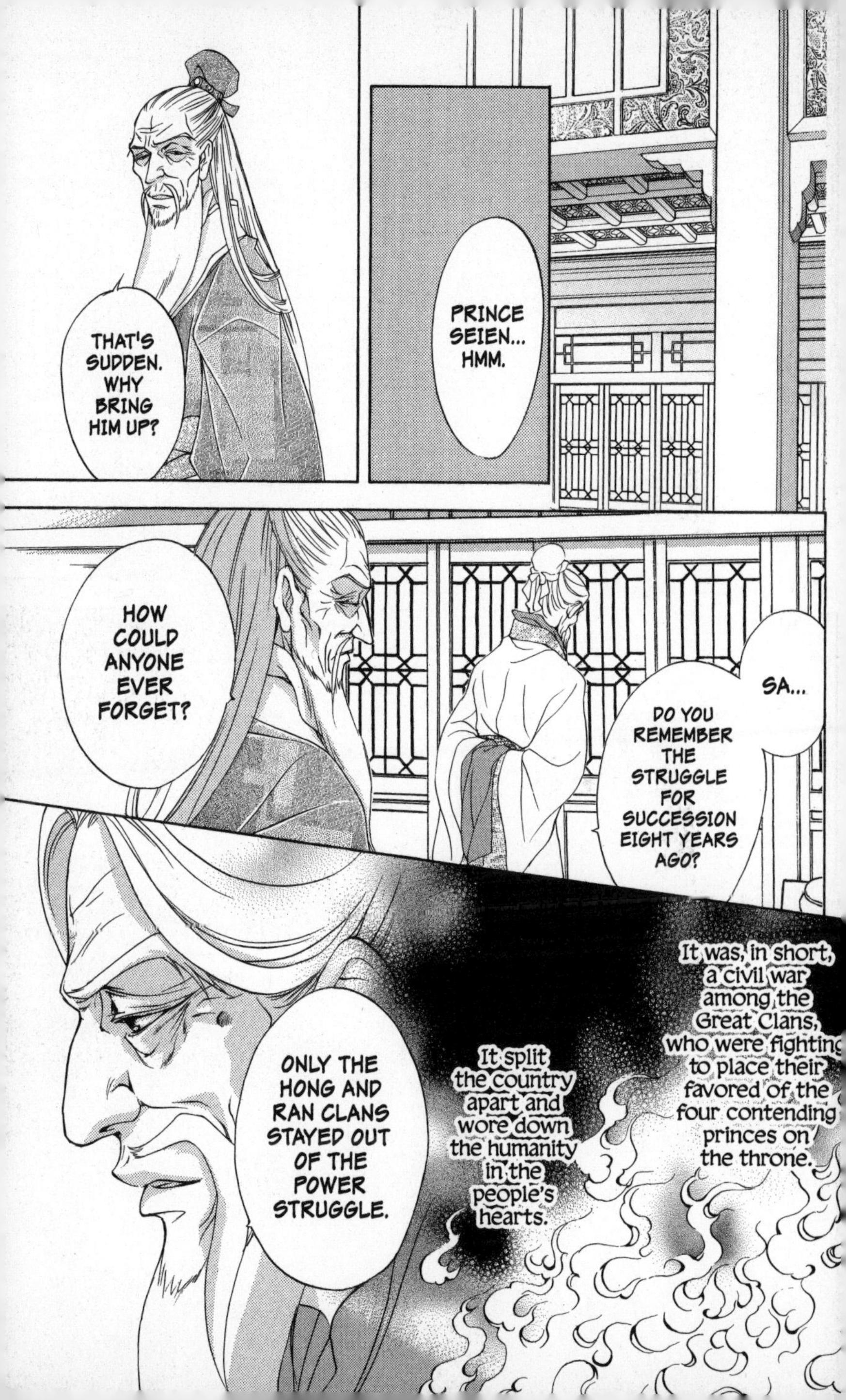
PRINCE SEIEN... HMM.
THAT'S SUDDEN. WHY BRING HIM UP?
SA...
DO YOU REMEMBER THE STRUGGLE FOR SUCCESSION EIGHT YEARS AGO?
HOW COULD ANYONE EVER FORGET?
It was, in short, a civil war among the Great Clans, who were fighting to place their favored of the four contending princes on the throne.
It split the country apart and wore down the humanity in the people's hearts.
ONLY THE HONG AND RAN CLANS STAYED OUT OF THE POWER STRUGGLE.

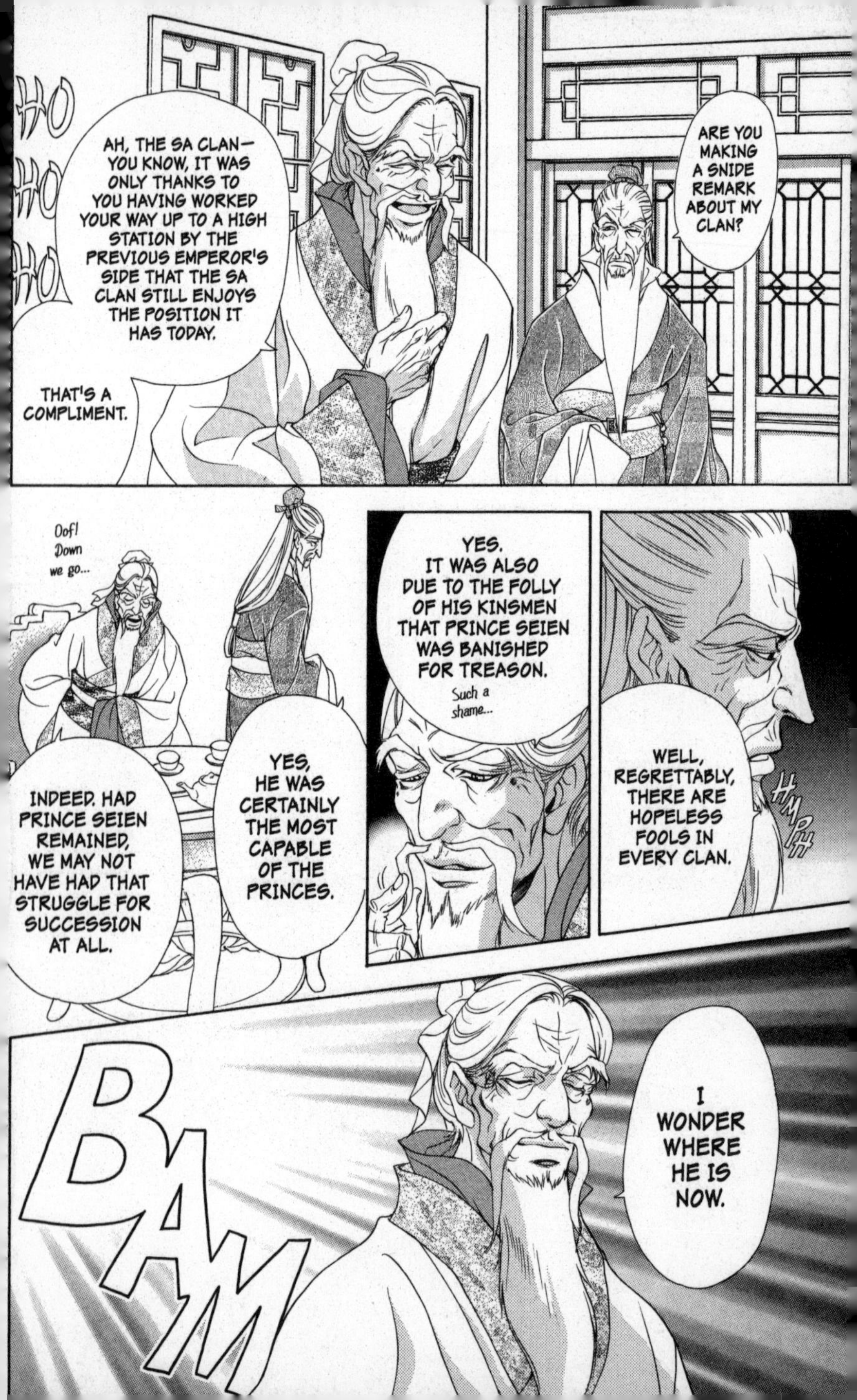
ARE YOU MAKING A SNIDE REMARK ABOUT MY CLAN?
AH, THE SA CLAN—YOU KNOW, IT WAS ONLY THANKS TO YOU HAVING WORKED YOUR WAY UP TO A HIGH STATION BY THE PREVIOUS EMPEROR'S SIDE THAT THE SA CLAN STILL ENJOYS THE POSITION IT HAS TODAY.
HO HO HO
THAT'S A COMPLIMENT.
HMPH
WELL, REGRETTABLY, THERE ARE HOPELESS FOOLS IN EVERY CLAN.
YES. IT WAS ALSO DUE TO THE FOLLY OF HIS KINSMEN THAT PRINCE SEIEN WAS BANISHED FOR TREASON.
Such a shame...
Oof! Down we go...
YES, HE WAS CERTAINLY THE MOST CAPABLE OF THE PRINCES.
INDEED. HAD PRINCE SEIEN REMAINED, WE MAY NOT HAVE HAD THAT STRUGGLE FOR SUCCESSION AT ALL.
I WONDER WHERE HE IS NOW.
BAM

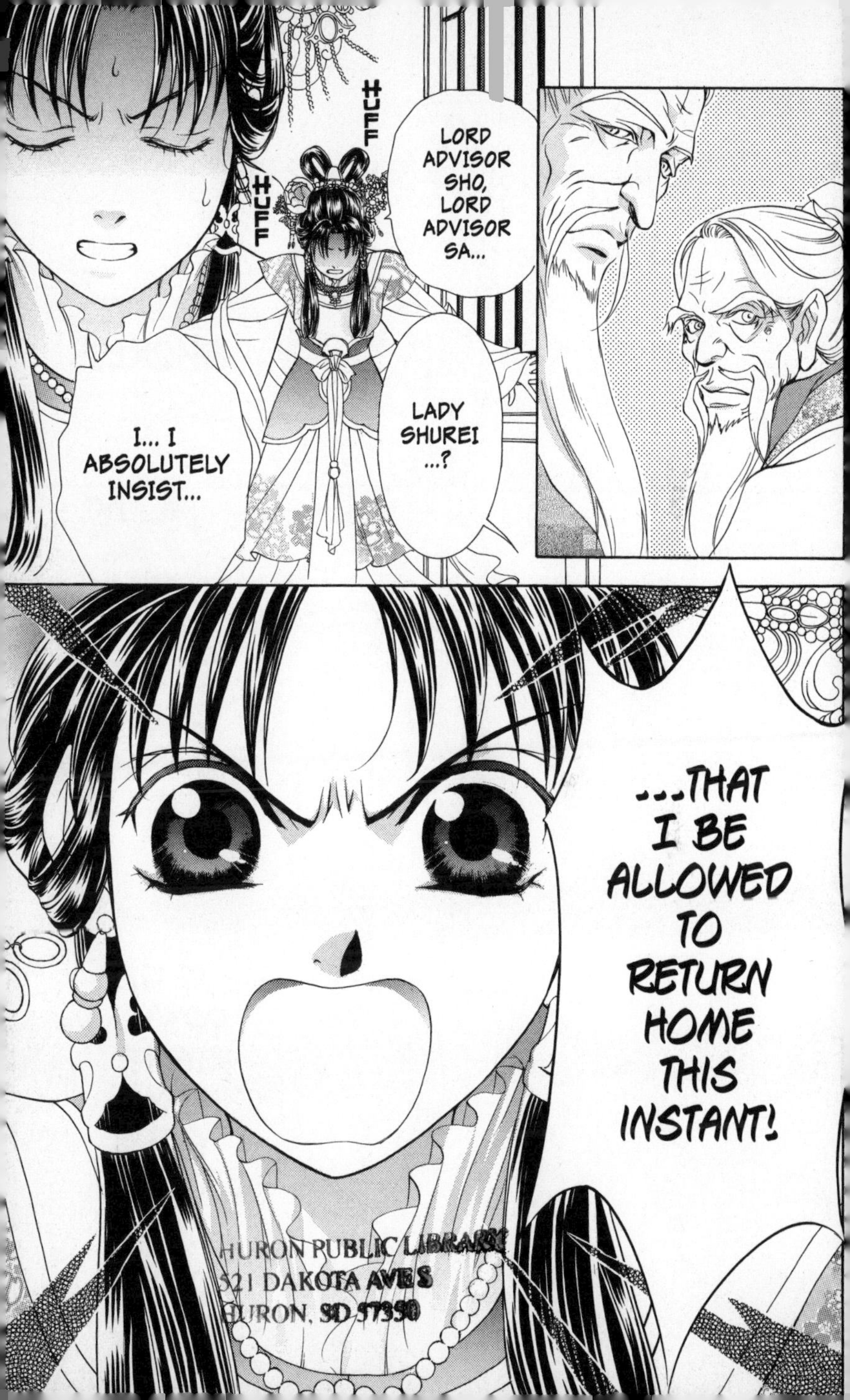
LORD ADVISOR SHO, LORD ADVISOR SA...
HUFF
HUFF
LADY SHUREI ...?
I... I ABSOLUTELY INSIST...
...THAT I BE ALLOWED TO RETURN HOME THIS INSTANT!

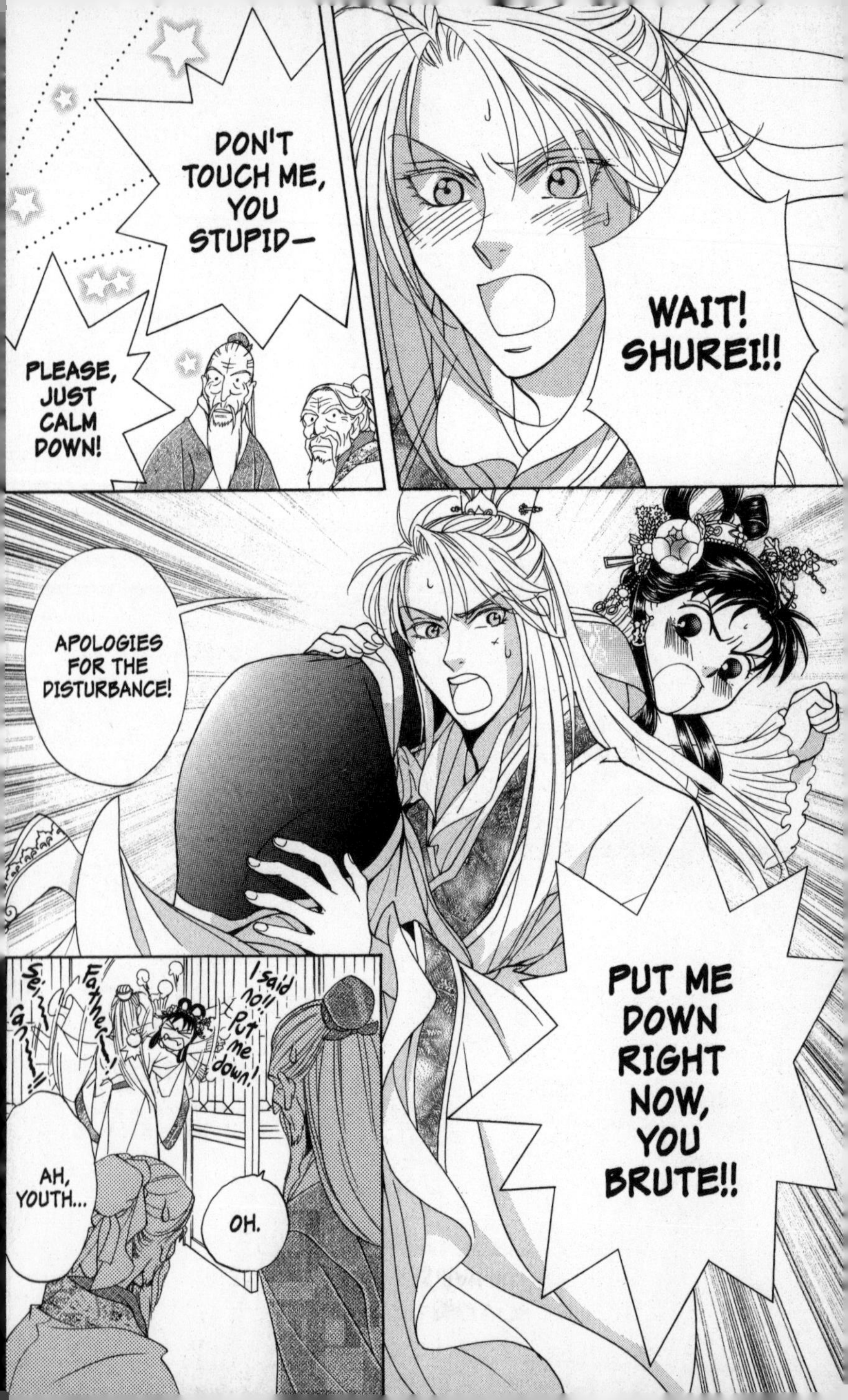
WAIT! SHUREI!!
DON'T TOUCH ME, YOU STUPID—
PLEASE, JUST CALM DOWN!
PUT ME DOWN RIGHT NOW, YOU BRUTE!!
APOLOGIES FOR THE DISTURBANCE!
I said no!! Put me down!
Father~!
Sei~ran~!!
OH.
AH, YOUTH...

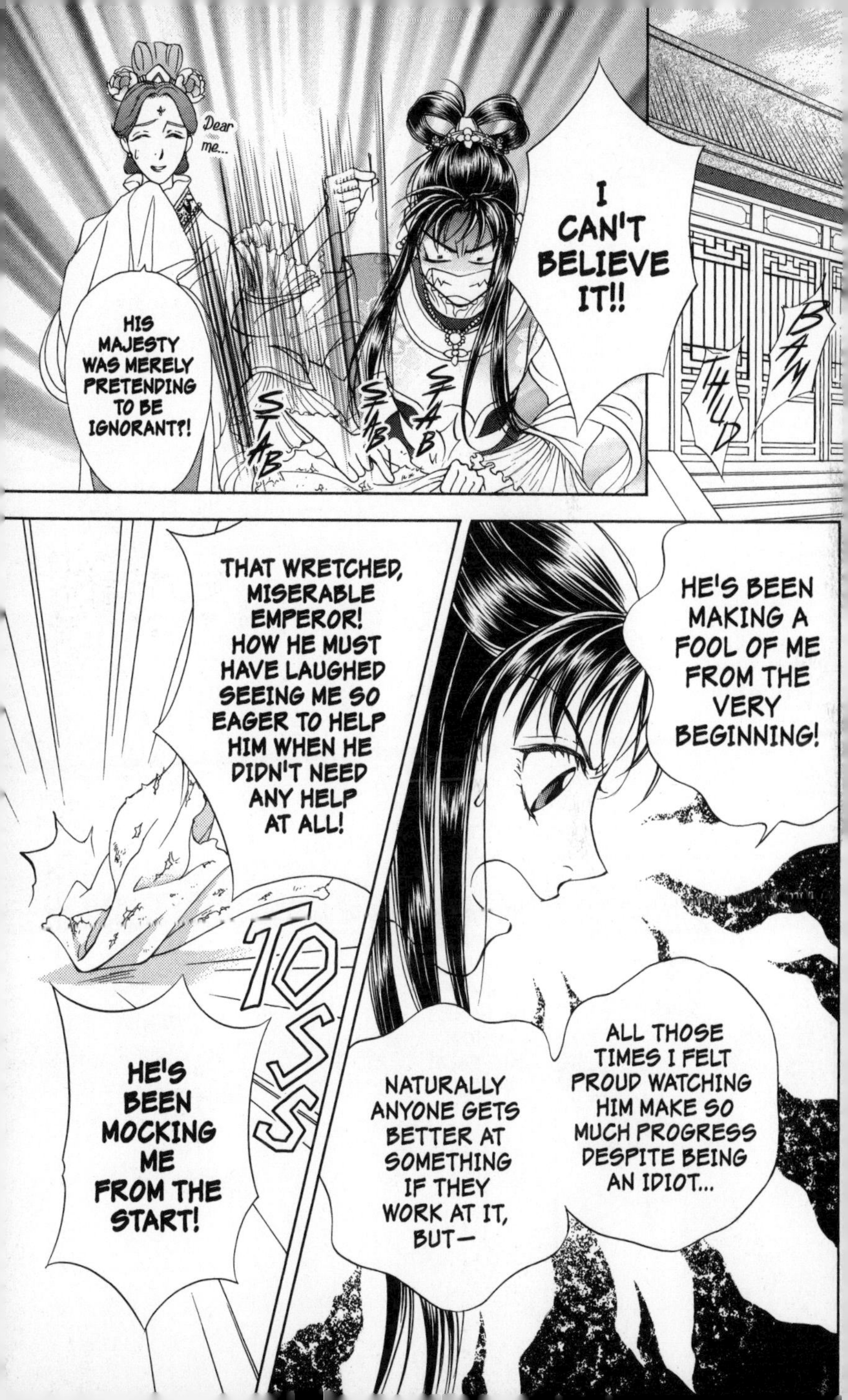
BAM
THUD
I CAN'T BELIEVE IT!!
STAB
STAB
STAB
Dear me...
HIS MAJESTY WAS MERELY PRETENDING TO BE IGNORANT?!
HE'S BEEN MAKING A FOOL OF ME FROM THE VERY BEGINNING!
ALL THOSE TIMES I FELT PROUD WATCHING HIM MAKE SO MUCH PROGRESS DESPITE BEING AN IDIOT...
NATURALLY ANYONE GETS BETTER AT SOMETHING IF THEY WORK AT IT, BUT—
THAT WRETCHED, MISERABLE EMPEROR! HOW HE MUST HAVE LAUGHED SEEING ME SO EAGER TO HELP HIM WHEN HE DIDN'T NEED ANY HELP AT ALL!
TOSS
HE'S BEEN MOCKING ME FROM THE START!

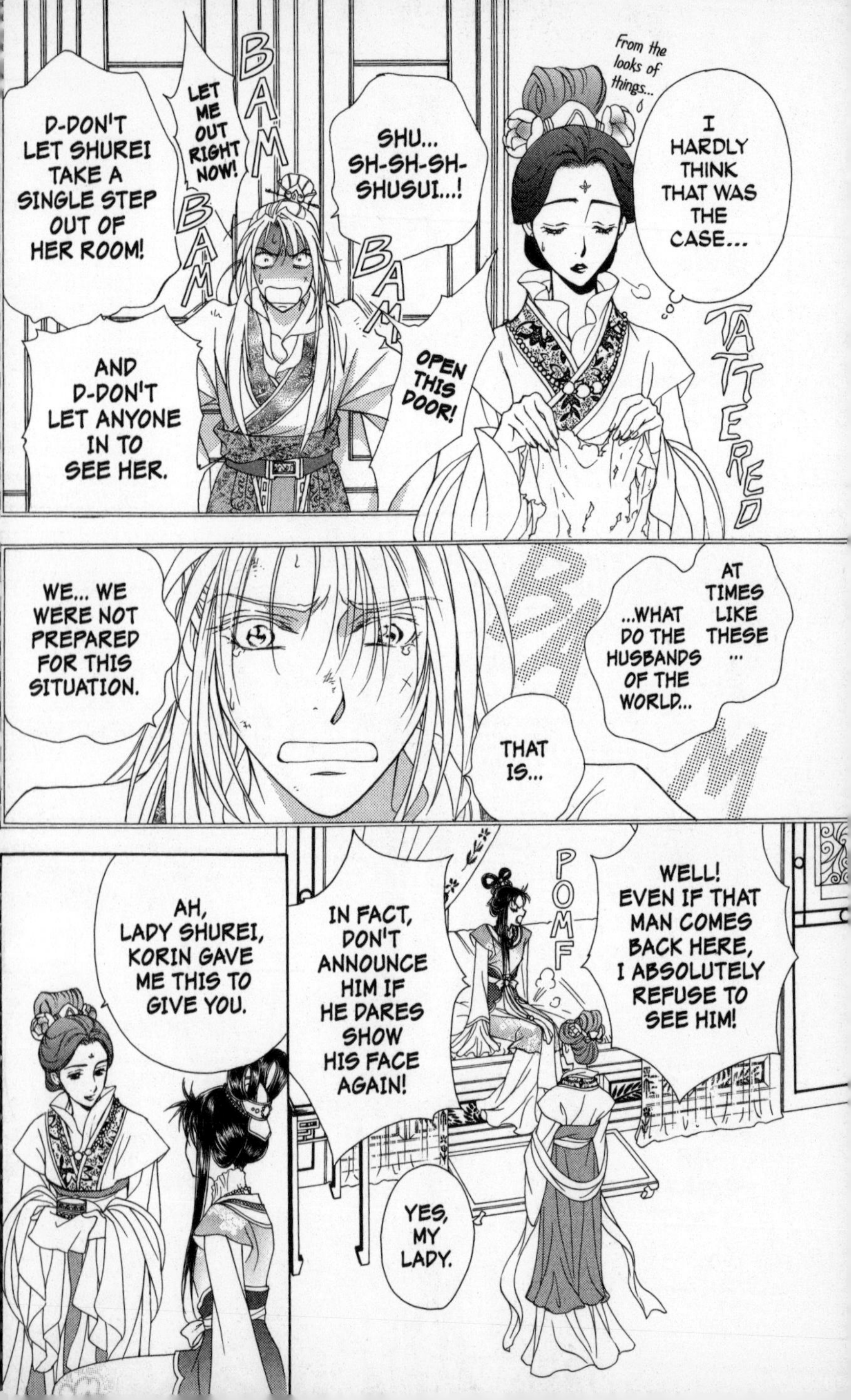
From the looks of things...
I HARDLY THINK THAT WAS THE CASE...
TATTERED
SHU... SH-SH-SH-SHUSUI...!
BAM
BAM
BAM
LET ME OUT RIGHT NOW!
OPEN THIS DOOR!
D-DON'T LET SHUREI TAKE A SINGLE STEP OUT OF HER ROOM!
AND D-DON'T LET ANYONE IN TO SEE HER.
AT TIMES LIKE THESE ...
...WHAT DO THE HUSBANDS OF THE WORLD...
BAM
THAT IS...
WE... WE WERE NOT PREPARED FOR THIS SITUATION.
WELL! EVEN IF THAT MAN COMES BACK HERE, I ABSOLUTELY REFUSE TO SEE HIM!
POMF
IN FACT, DON'T ANNOUNCE HIM IF HE DARES SHOW HIS FACE AGAIN!
YES, MY LADY.
AH, LADY SHUREI, KORIN GAVE ME THIS TO GIVE YOU.

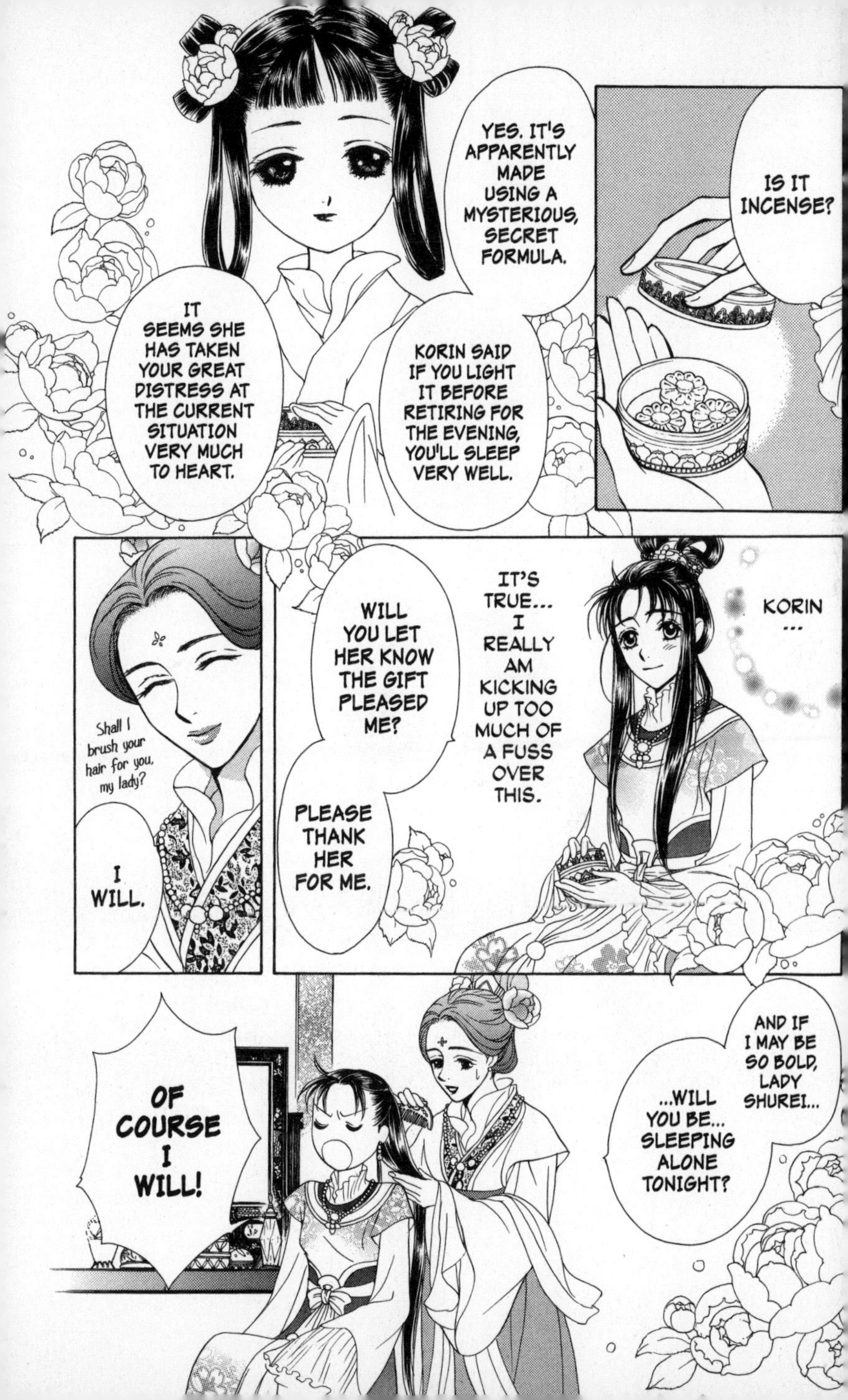
IS IT INCENSE?
YES. IT'S APPARENTLY MADE USING A MYSTERIOUS, SECRET FORMULA.
KORIN SAID IF YOU LIGHT IT BEFORE RETIRING FOR THE EVENING, YOU'LL SLEEP VERY WELL.
IT SEEMS SHE HAS TAKEN YOUR GREAT DISTRESS AT THE CURRENT SITUATION VERY MUCH TO HEART.
KORIN ...
IT'S TRUE... I REALLY AM KICKING UP TOO MUCH OF A FUSS OVER THIS.
WILL YOU LET HER KNOW THE GIFT PLEASED ME?
PLEASE THANK HER FOR ME.
Shall I brush your hair for you, my lady?
I WILL.
AND IF I MAY BE SO BOLD, LADY SHUREI...
...WILL YOU BE... SLEEPING ALONE TONIGHT?
OF COURSE I WILL!

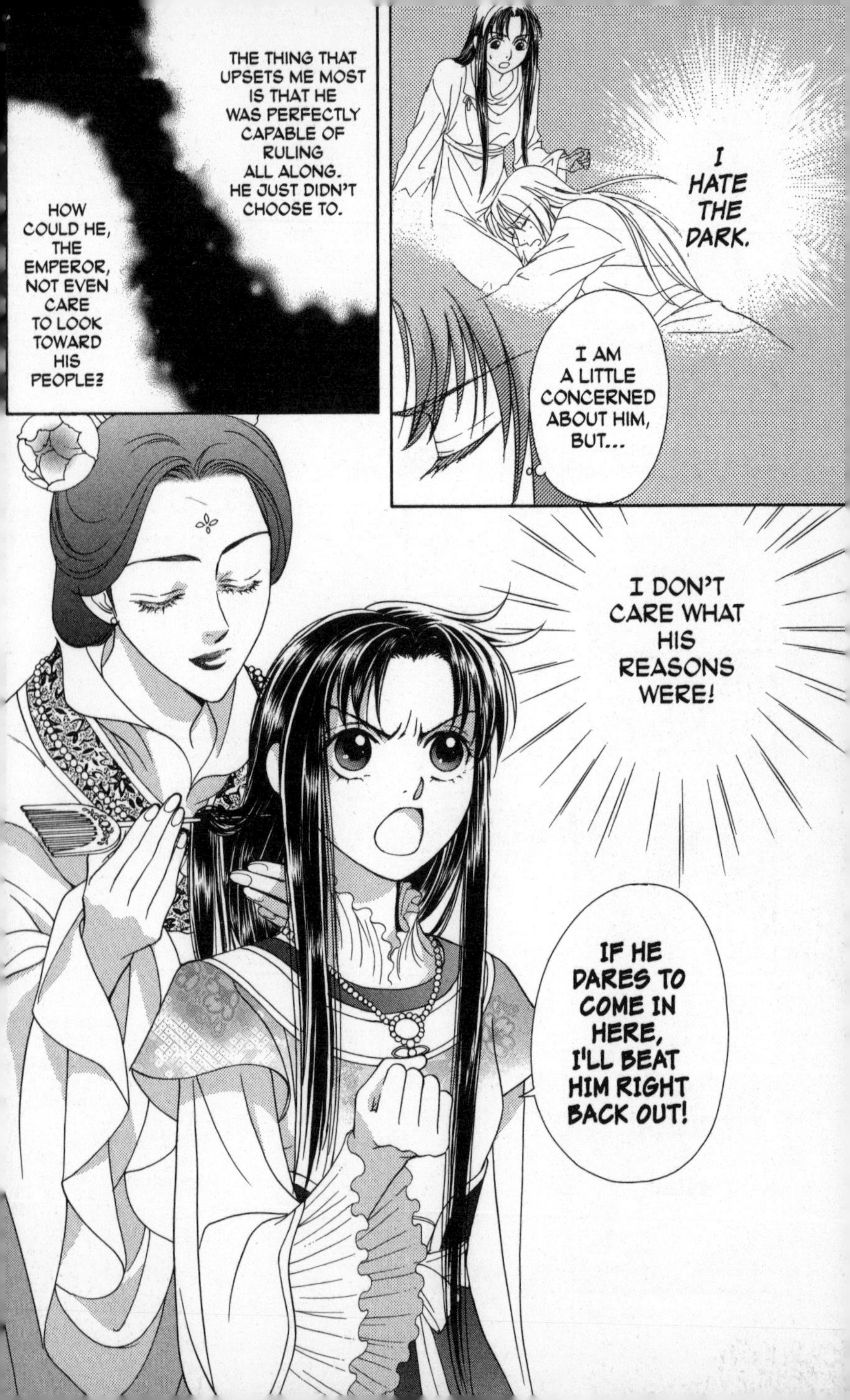
I HATE THE DARK.
I AM A LITTLE CONCERNED ABOUT HIM, BUT...
THE THING THAT UPSETS ME MOST IS THAT HE WAS PERFECTLY CAPABLE OF RULING ALL ALONG. HE JUST DIDN'T CHOOSE TO.
HOW COULD HE, THE EMPEROR, NOT EVEN CARE TO LOOK TOWARD HIS PEOPLE?
I DON'T CARE WHAT HIS REASONS WERE!
IF HE DARES TO COME IN HERE, I'LL BEAT HIM RIGHT BACK OUT!

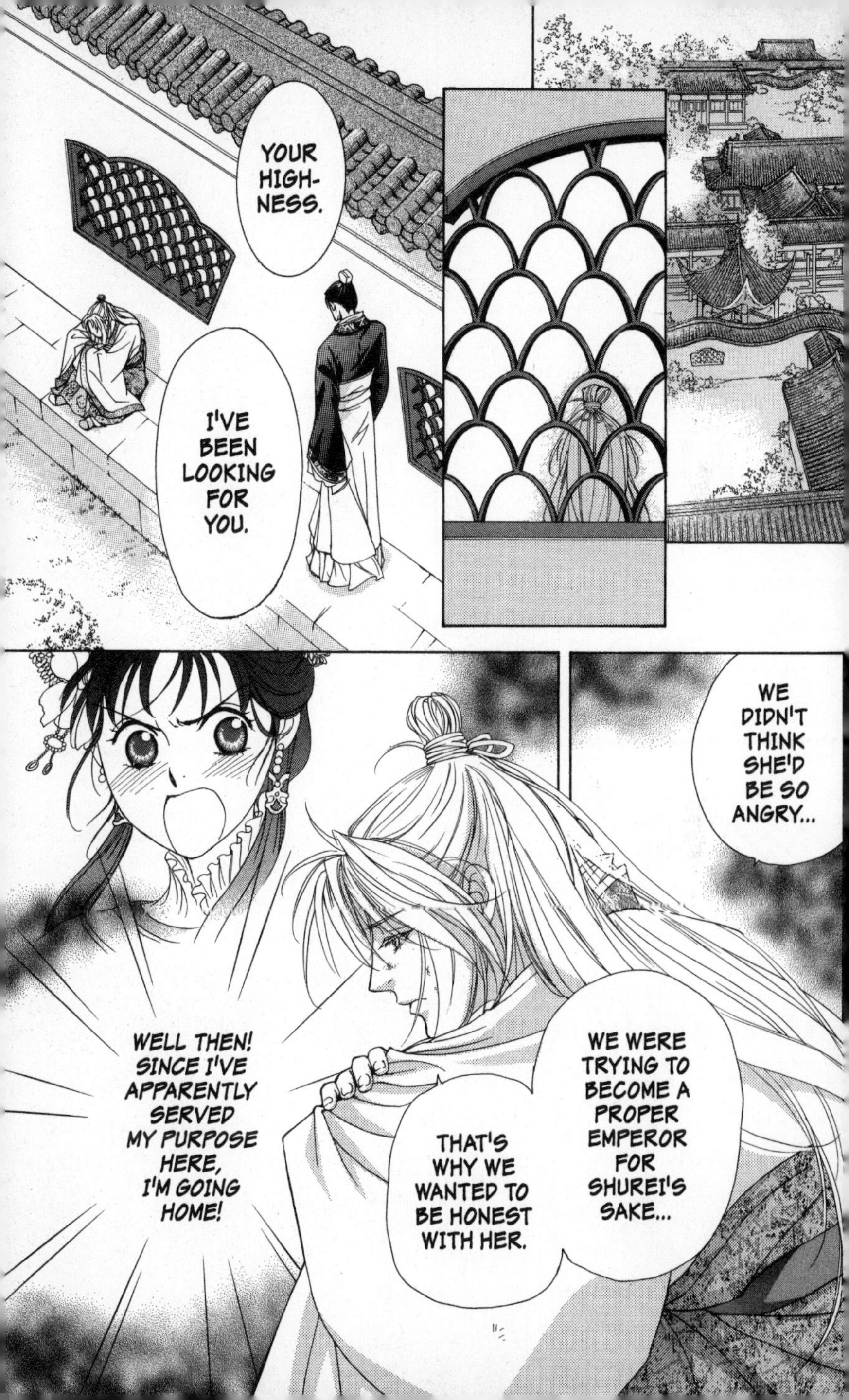
YOUR HIGH-NESS.
I'VE BEEN LOOKING FOR YOU.
WE DIDN'T THINK SHE'D BE SO ANGRY...
WE WERE TRYING TO BECOME A PROPER EMPEROR FOR SHUREI'S SAKE...
THAT'S WHY WE WANTED TO BE HONEST WITH HER.
WELL THEN! SINCE I'VE APPARENTLY SERVED MY PURPOSE HERE, I'M GOING HOME!

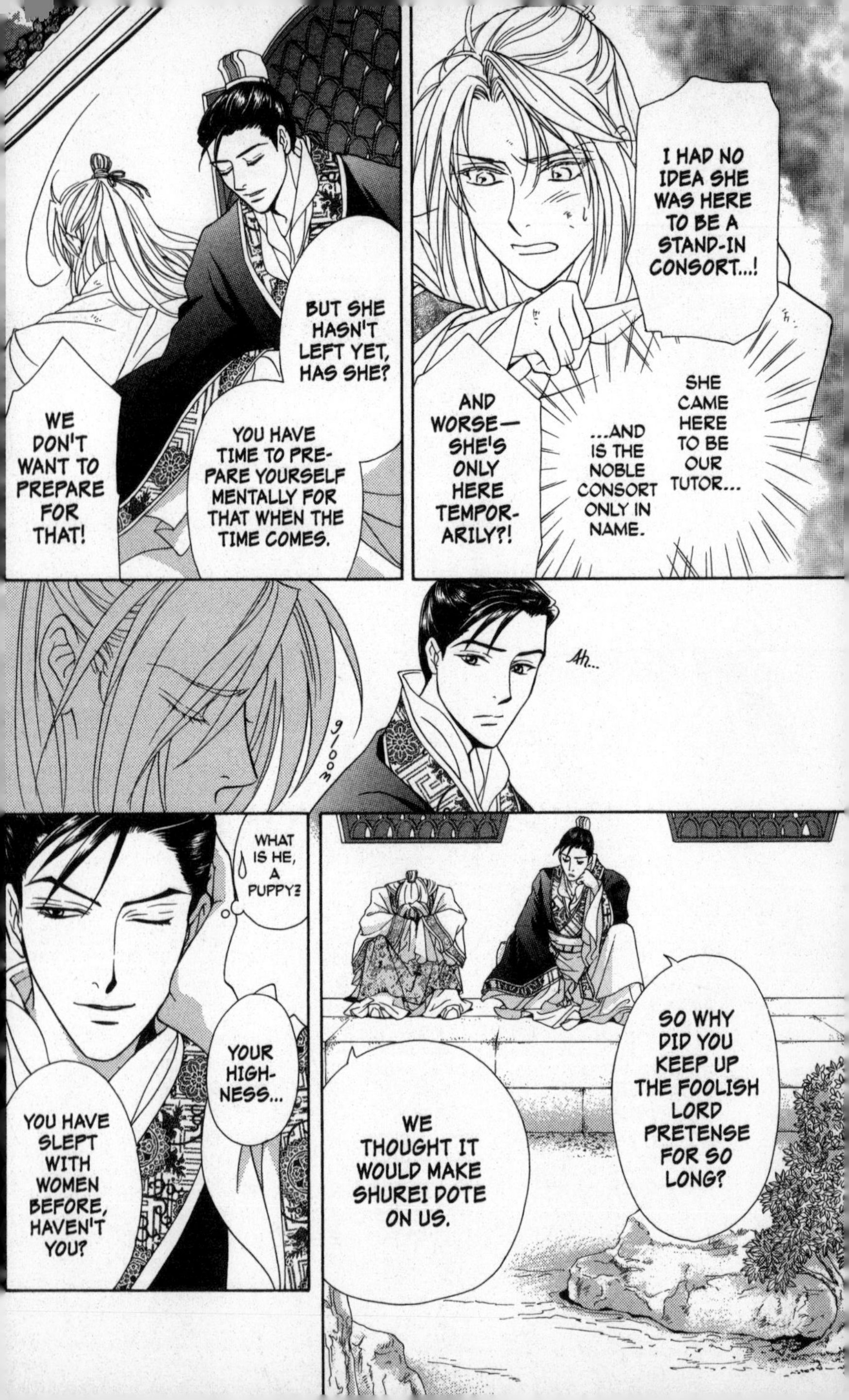
I HAD NO IDEA SHE WAS HERE TO BE A STAND-IN CONSORT...!
SHE CAME HERE TO BE OUR TUTOR...
...AND IS THE NOBLE CONSORT ONLY IN NAME.
AND WORSE—SHE'S ONLY HERE TEMPORARILY?!
BUT SHE HASN'T LEFT YET, HAS SHE?
YOU HAVE TIME TO PREPARE YOURSELF MENTALLY FOR THAT WHEN THE TIME COMES.
WE DON'T WANT TO PREPARE FOR THAT!
Ah...
gloom
SO WHY DID YOU KEEP UP THE FOOLISH LORD PRETENSE FOR SO LONG?
WE THOUGHT IT WOULD MAKE SHUREI DOTE ON US.
WHAT IS HE, A PUPPY?
YOUR HIGHNESS...
YOU HAVE SLEPT WITH WOMEN BEFORE, HAVEN'T YOU?

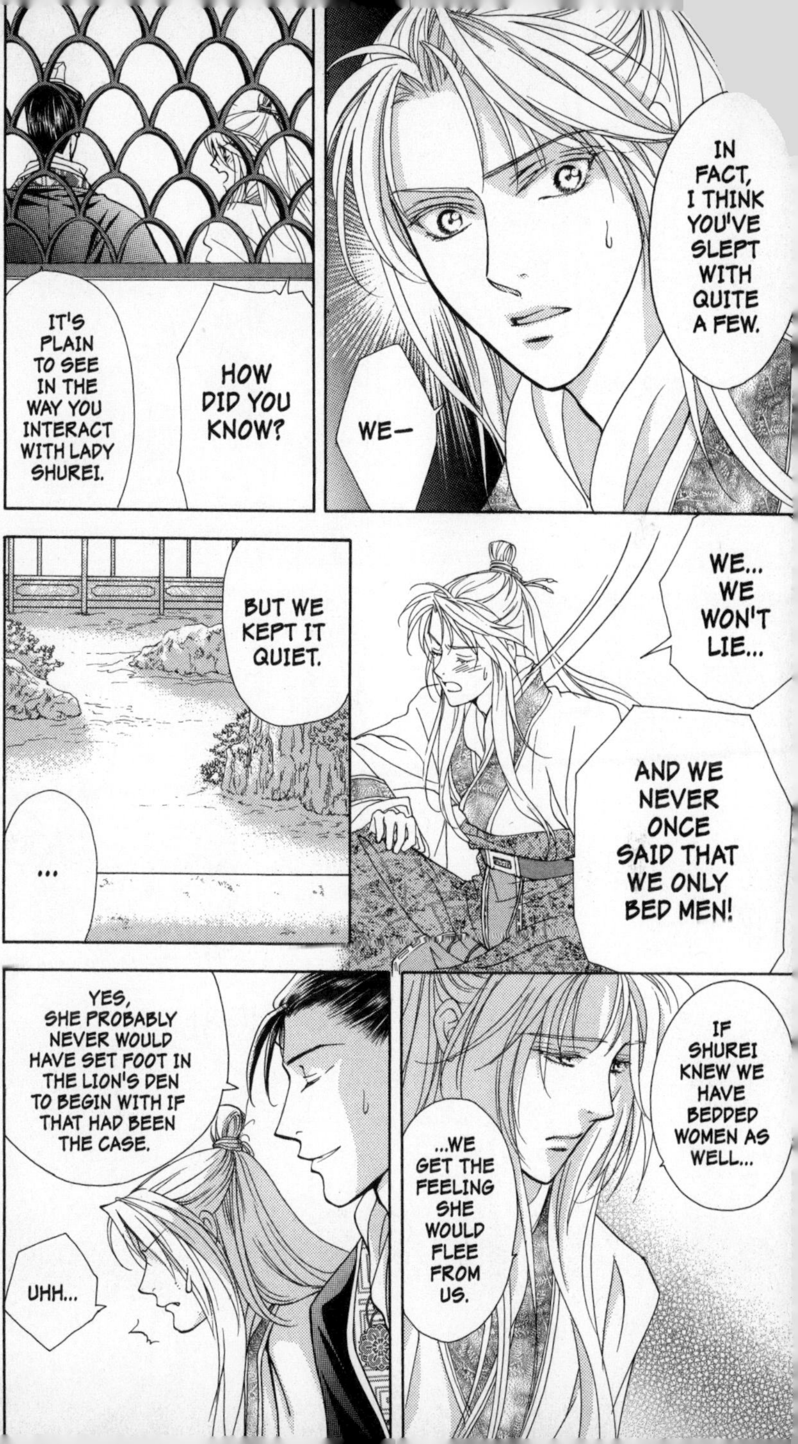
IN FACT, I THINK YOU'VE SLEPT WITH QUITE A FEW.
WE—
HOW DID YOU KNOW?
IT'S PLAIN TO SEE IN THE WAY YOU INTERACT WITH LADY SHUREI.
WE... WE WON'T LIE...
AND WE NEVER ONCE SAID THAT WE ONLY BED MEN!
BUT WE KEPT IT QUIET.
...
IF SHUREI KNEW WE HAVE BEDDED WOMEN AS WELL...
...WE GET THE FEELING SHE WOULD FLEE FROM US.
YES, SHE PROBABLY NEVER WOULD HAVE SET FOOT IN THE LION'S DEN TO BEGIN WITH IF THAT HAD BEEN THE CASE.
UHH...

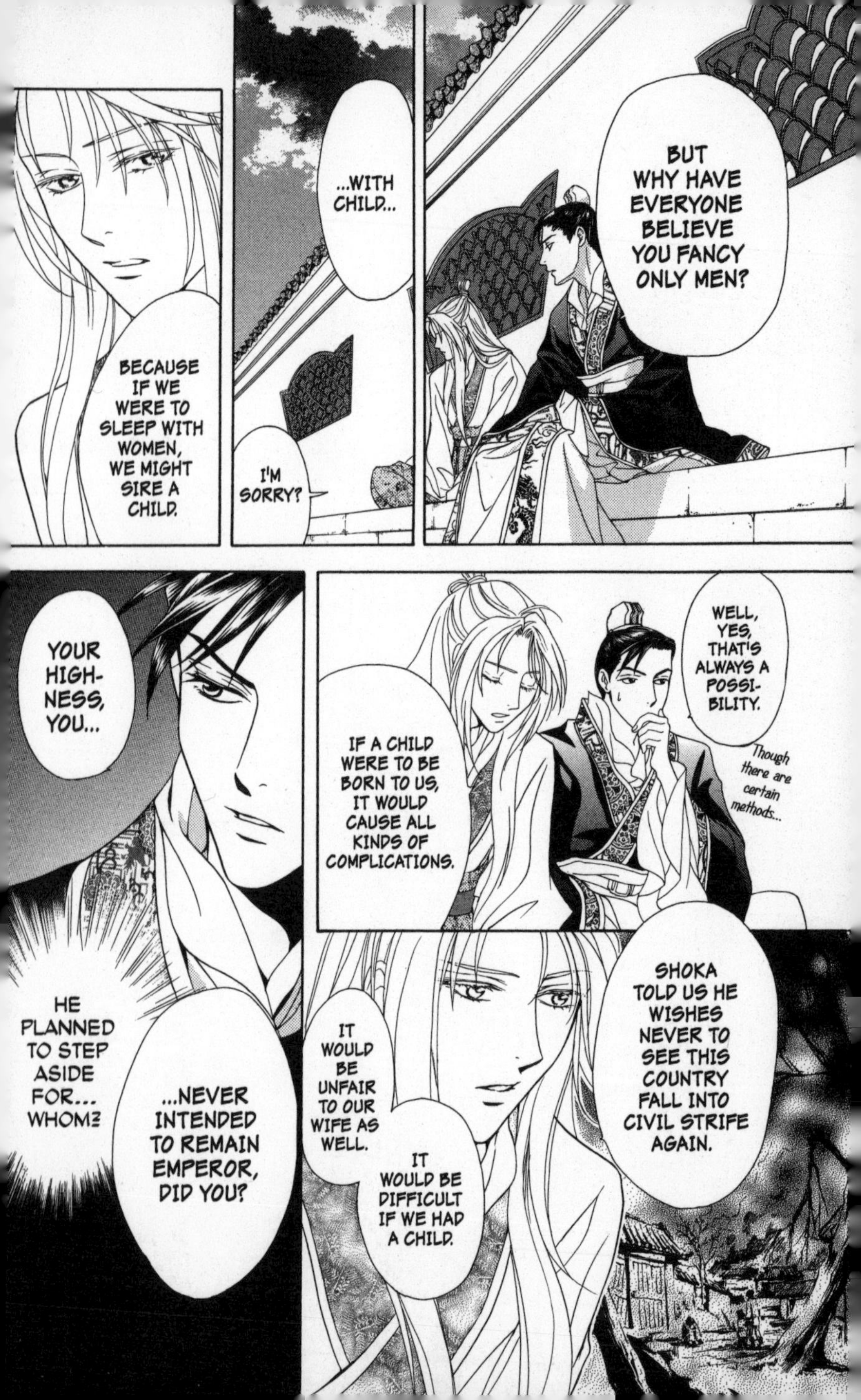
BUT WHY HAVE EVERYONE BELIEVE YOU FANCY ONLY MEN?
...WITH CHILD...
I'M SORRY?
BECAUSE IF WE WERE TO SLEEP WITH WOMEN, WE MIGHT SIRE A CHILD.
WELL, YES, THAT'S ALWAYS A POSSIBILITY.
Though there are certain methods...
IF A CHILD WERE TO BE BORN TO US, IT WOULD CAUSE ALL KINDS OF COMPLICATIONS.
SHOKA TOLD US HE WISHES NEVER TO SEE THIS COUNTRY FALL INTO CIVIL STRIFE AGAIN.
IT WOULD BE UNFAIR TO OUR WIFE AS WELL.
IT WOULD BE DIFFICULT IF WE HAD A CHILD.
YOUR HIGHNESS, YOU...
...NEVER INTENDED TO REMAIN EMPEROR, DID YOU?
HE PLANNED TO STEP ASIDE FOR... WHOM?

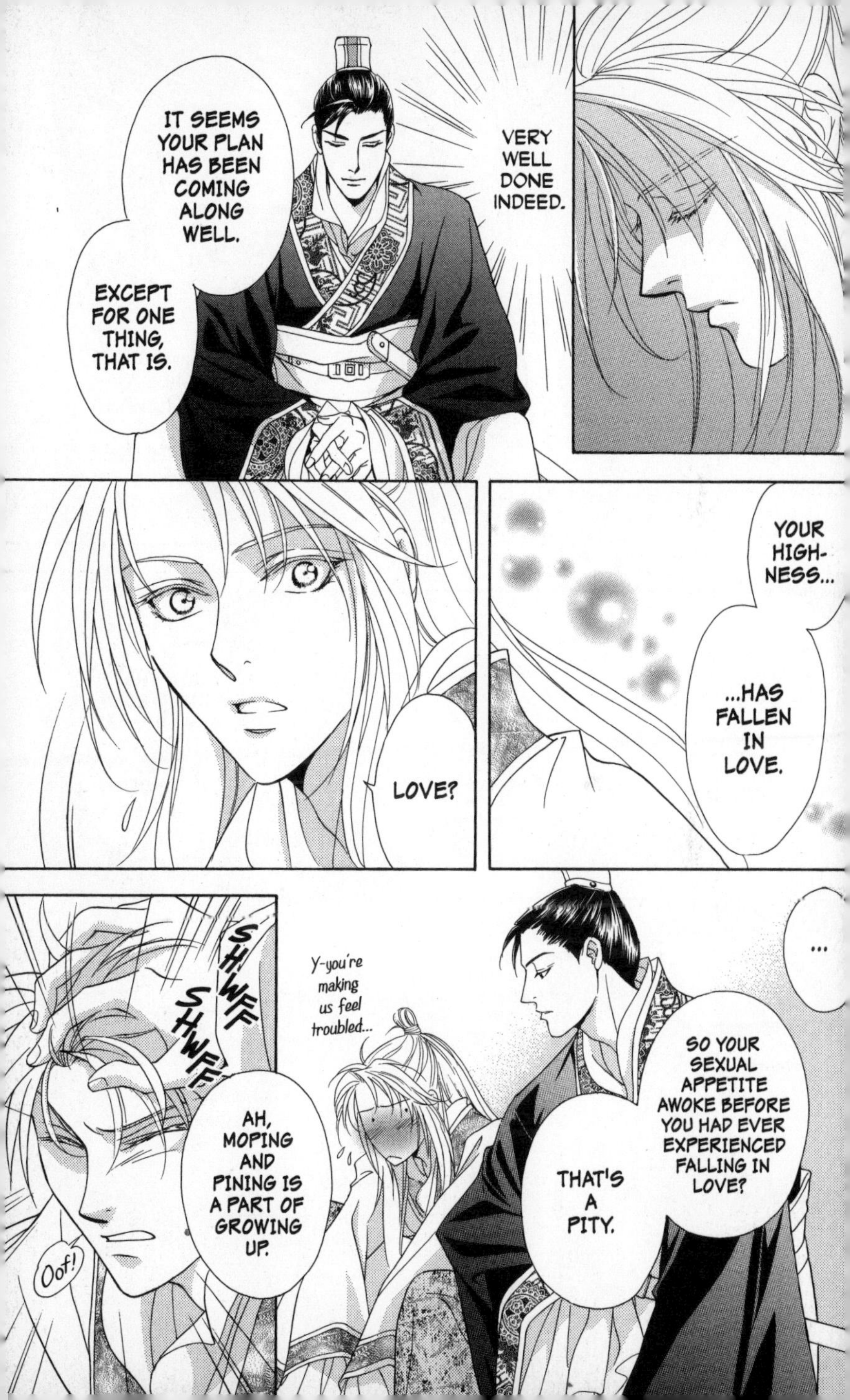
IT SEEMS YOUR PLAN HAS BEEN COMING ALONG WELL.
VERY WELL DONE INDEED.
EXCEPT FOR ONE THING, THAT IS.
YOUR HIGHNESS...
...HAS FALLEN IN LOVE.
LOVE?
...
SO YOUR SEXUAL APPETITE AWOKE BEFORE YOU HAD EVER EXPERIENCED FALLING IN LOVE?
THAT'S A PITY.
Y-you're making us feel troubled...
AH, MOPING AND PINING IS A PART OF GROWING UP.
SHWFF
SHWFF
Oof!

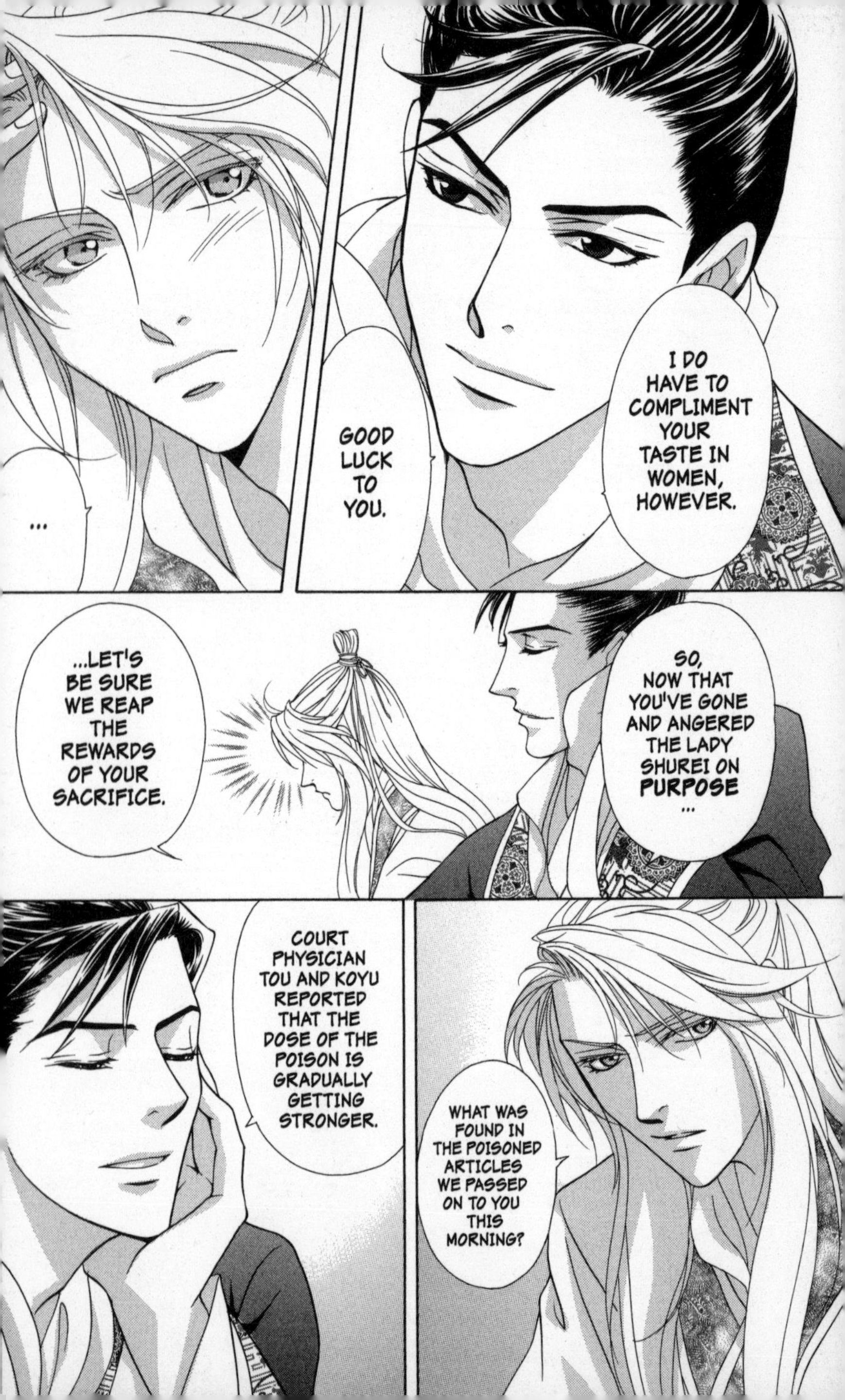
I DO HAVE TO COMPLIMENT YOUR TASTE IN WOMEN, HOWEVER.
GOOD LUCK TO YOU.
...
SO, NOW THAT YOU'VE GONE AND ANGERED THE LADY SHUREI ON PURPOSE ...
...LET'S BE SURE WE REAP THE REWARDS OF YOUR SACRIFICE.
WHAT WAS FOUND IN THE POISONED ARTICLES WE PASSED ON TO YOU THIS MORNING?
COURT PHYSICIAN TOU AND KOYU REPORTED THAT THE DOSE OF THE POISON IS GRADUALLY GETTING STRONGER.

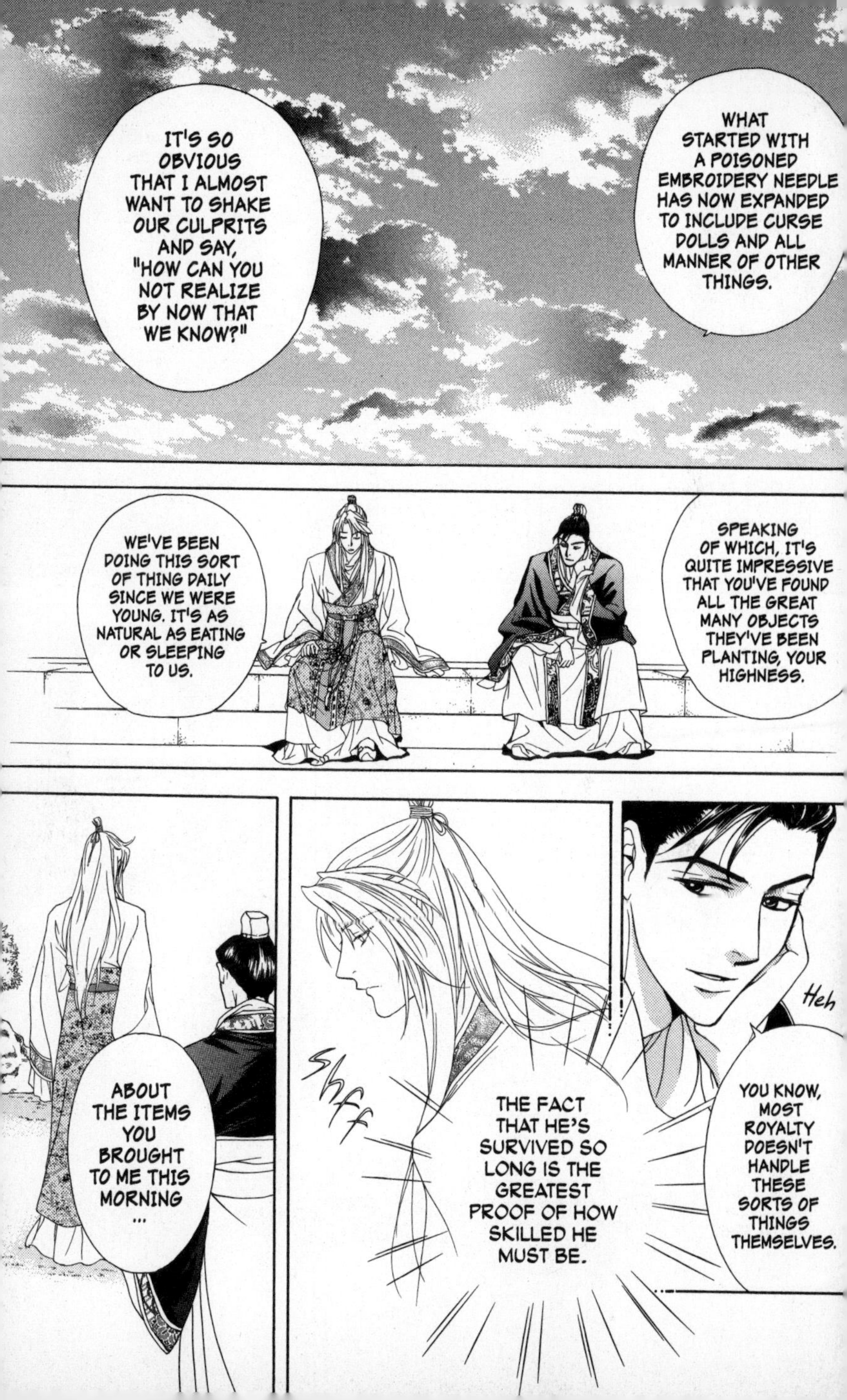
WHAT STARTED WITH A POISONED EMBROIDERY NEEDLE HAS NOW EXPANDED TO INCLUDE CURSE DOLLS AND ALL MANNER OF OTHER THINGS.
IT'S SO OBVIOUS THAT I ALMOST WANT TO SHAKE OUR CULPRITS AND SAY, "HOW CAN YOU NOT REALIZE BY NOW THAT WE KNOW?"
SPEAKING OF WHICH, IT'S QUITE IMPRESSIVE THAT YOU'VE FOUND ALL THE GREAT MANY OBJECTS THEY'VE BEEN PLANTING, YOUR HIGHNESS.
WE'VE BEEN DOING THIS SORT OF THING DAILY SINCE WE WERE YOUNG. IT'S AS NATURAL AS EATING OR SLEEPING TO US.
Heh
YOU KNOW, MOST ROYALTY DOESN'T HANDLE THESE SORTS OF THINGS THEMSELVES.
Shff
THE FACT THAT HE'S SURVIVED SO LONG IS THE GREATEST PROOF OF HOW SKILLED HE MUST BE.
ABOUT THE ITEMS YOU BROUGHT TO ME THIS MORNING ...

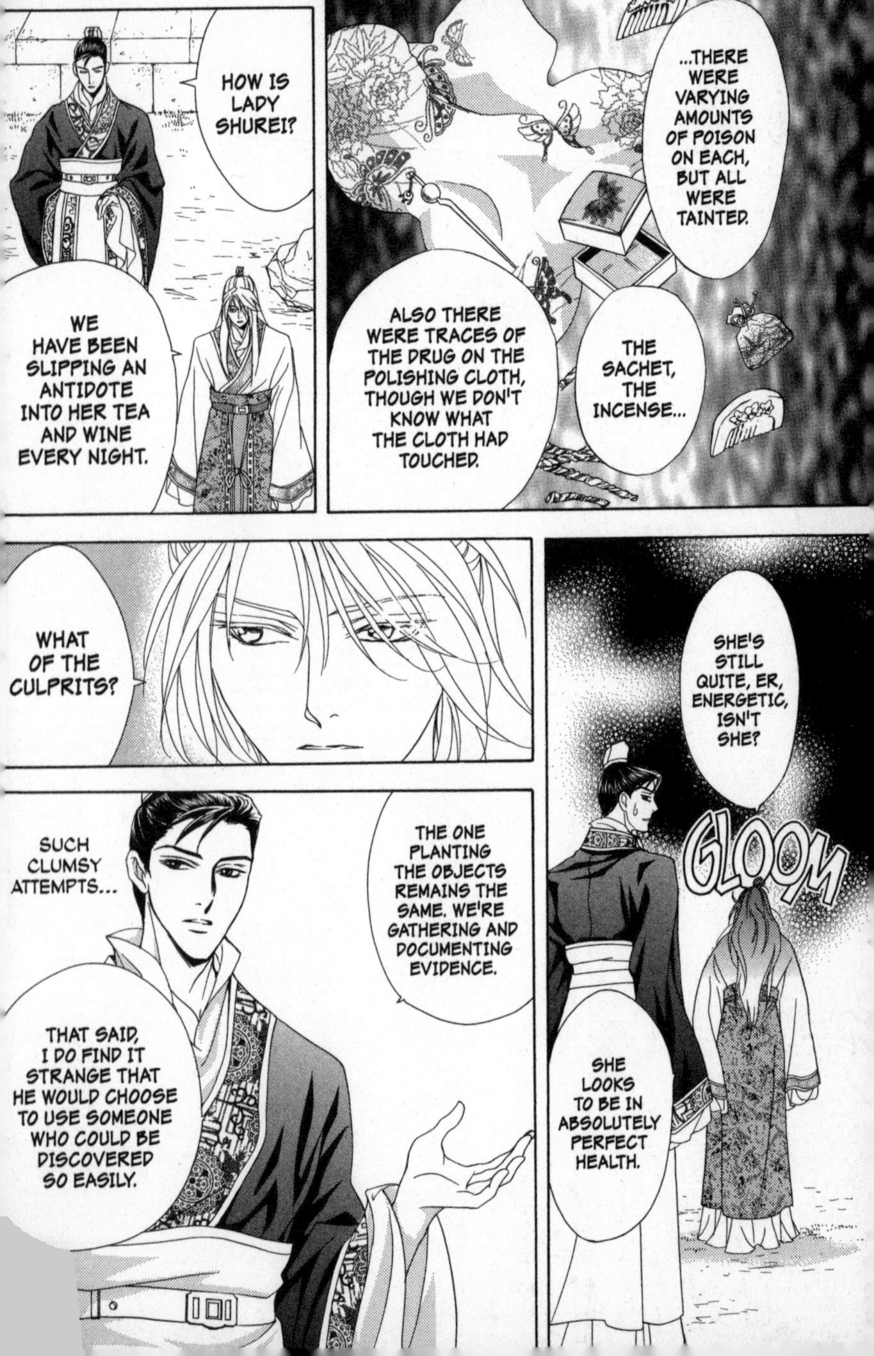
...THERE WERE VARYING AMOUNTS OF POISON ON EACH, BUT ALL WERE TAINTED.
THE SACHET, THE INCENSE...
ALSO THERE WERE TRACES OF THE DRUG ON THE POLISHING CLOTH, THOUGH WE DON'T KNOW WHAT THE CLOTH HAD TOUCHED.
HOW IS LADY SHUREI?
WE HAVE BEEN SLIPPING AN ANTIDOTE INTO HER TEA AND WINE EVERY NIGHT.
SHE'S STILL QUITE, ER, ENERGETIC, ISN'T SHE?
GLOOM
SHE LOOKS TO BE IN ABSOLUTELY PERFECT HEALTH.
WHAT OF THE CULPRITS?
THE ONE PLANTING THE OBJECTS REMAINS THE SAME. WE'RE GATHERING AND DOCUMENTING EVIDENCE.
SUCH CLUMSY ATTEMPTS...
THAT SAID, I DO FIND IT STRANGE THAT HE WOULD CHOOSE TO USE SOMEONE WHO COULD BE DISCOVERED SO EASILY.

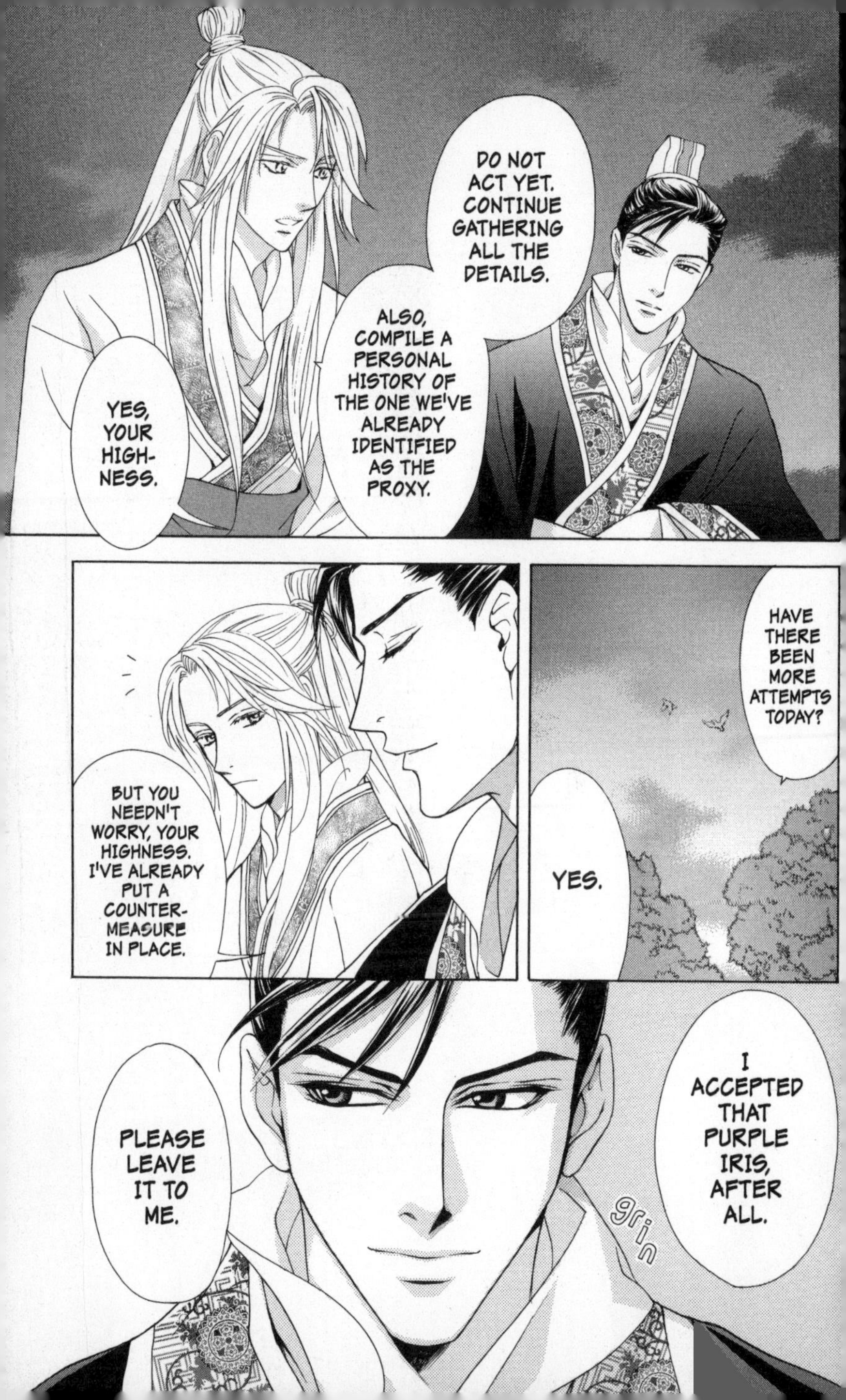
DO NOT ACT YET. CONTINUE GATHERING ALL THE DETAILS.
ALSO, COMPILE A PERSONAL HISTORY OF THE ONE WE'VE ALREADY IDENTIFIED AS THE PROXY.
YES, YOUR HIGH-NESS.
HAVE THERE BEEN MORE ATTEMPTS TODAY?
YES.
BUT YOU NEEDN'T WORRY, YOUR HIGHNESS. I'VE ALREADY PUT A COUNTER-MEASURE IN PLACE.
I ACCEPTED THAT PURPLE IRIS, AFTER ALL.
grin
PLEASE LEAVE IT TO ME.

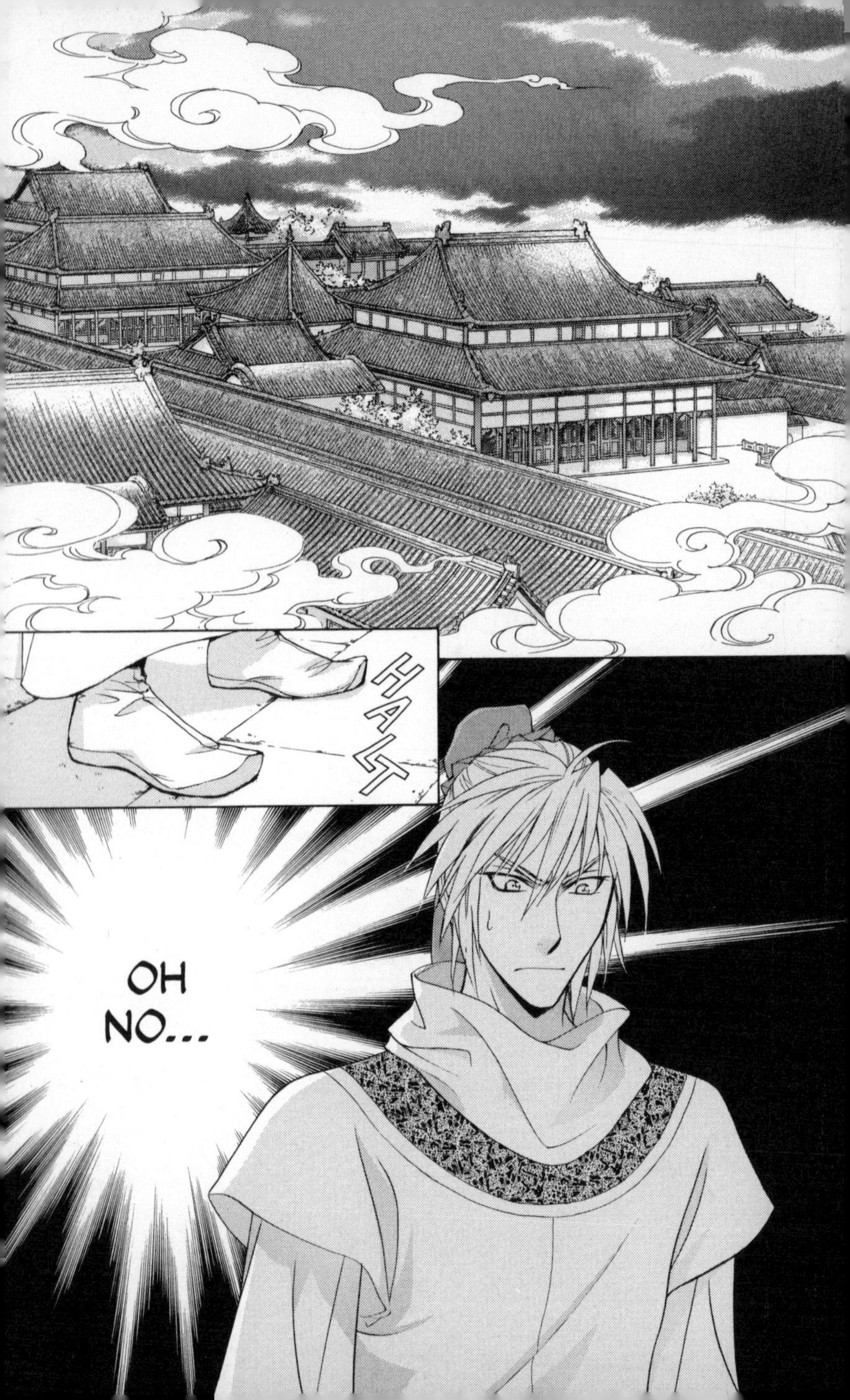
HALT
OH NO...

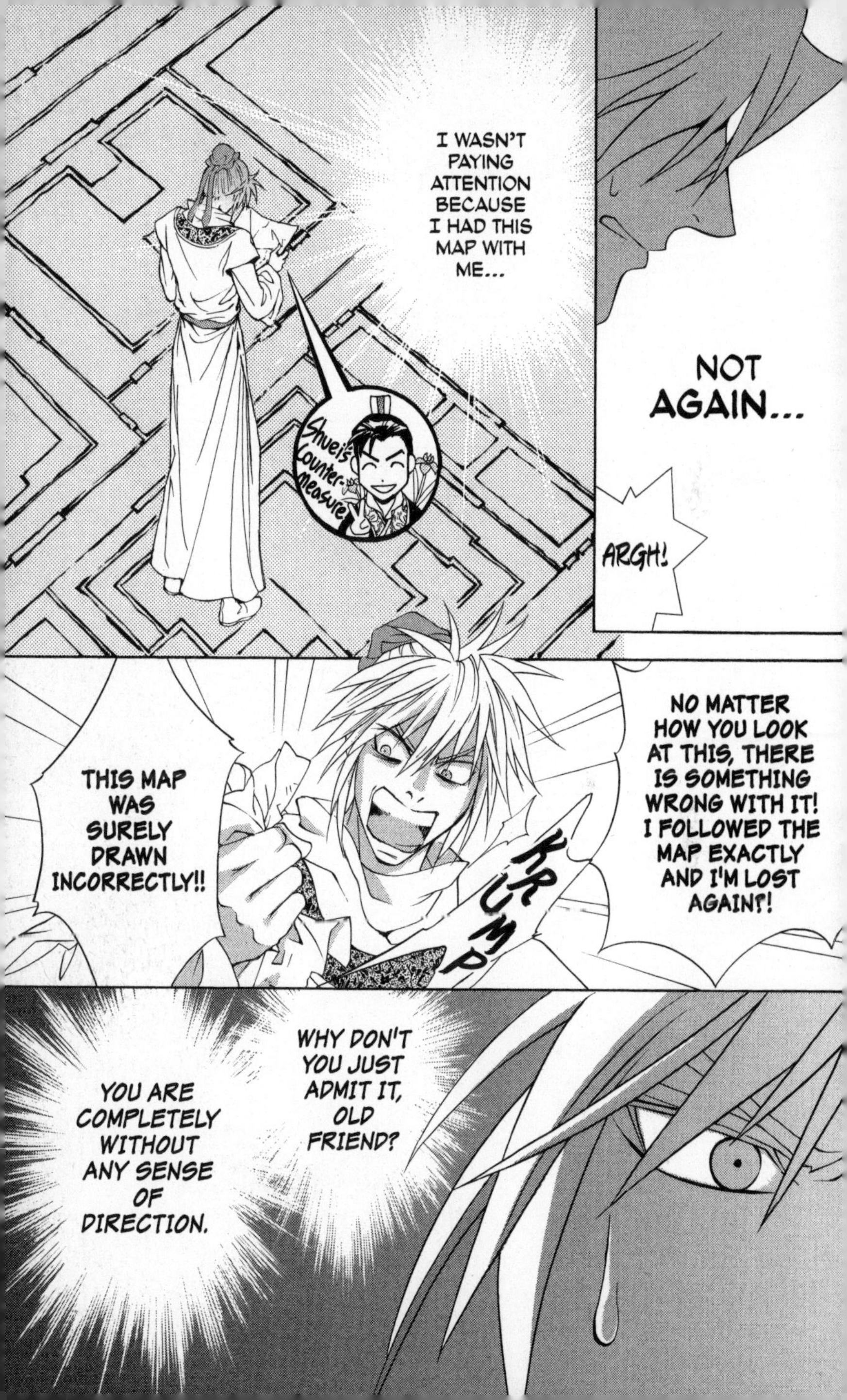
NOT AGAIN...
ARGH!
I WASN'T PAYING ATTENTION BECAUSE I HAD THIS MAP WITH ME...
Shuei's Counter-measure
NO MATTER HOW YOU LOOK AT THIS, THERE IS SOMETHING WRONG WITH IT! I FOLLOWED THE MAP EXACTLY AND I'M LOST AGAIN?!
KRUMP
THIS MAP WAS SURELY DRAWN INCORRECTLY!!
WHY DON'T YOU JUST ADMIT IT, OLD FRIEND?
YOU ARE COMPLETELY WITHOUT ANY SENSE OF DIRECTION.

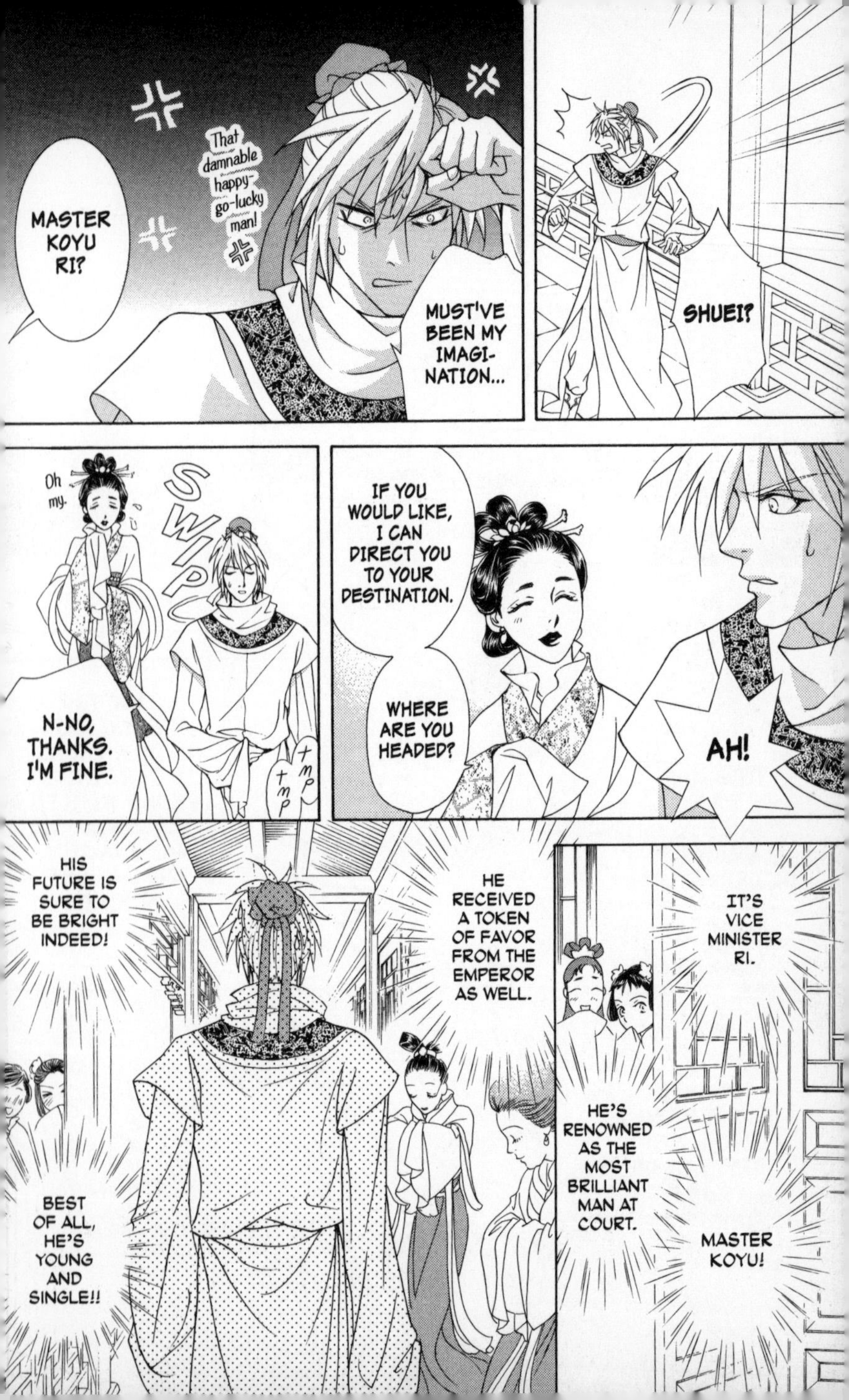

SHUEI?
MUST'VE BEEN MY IMAGINATION...
That damnable happy-go-lucky man!
MASTER KOYU RI?
AH!
IF YOU WOULD LIKE, I CAN DIRECT YOU TO YOUR DESTINATION.
WHERE ARE YOU HEADED?
Oh my.
SWIP
N-NO, THANKS. I'M FINE.
tmp tmp
IT'S VICE MINISTER RI.
MASTER KOYU!
HE'S RENOWNED AS THE MOST BRILLIANT MAN AT COURT.
HE RECEIVED A TOKEN OF FAVOR FROM THE EMPEROR AS WELL.
HIS FUTURE IS SURE TO BE BRIGHT INDEED!
BEST OF ALL, HE'S YOUNG AND SINGLE!!

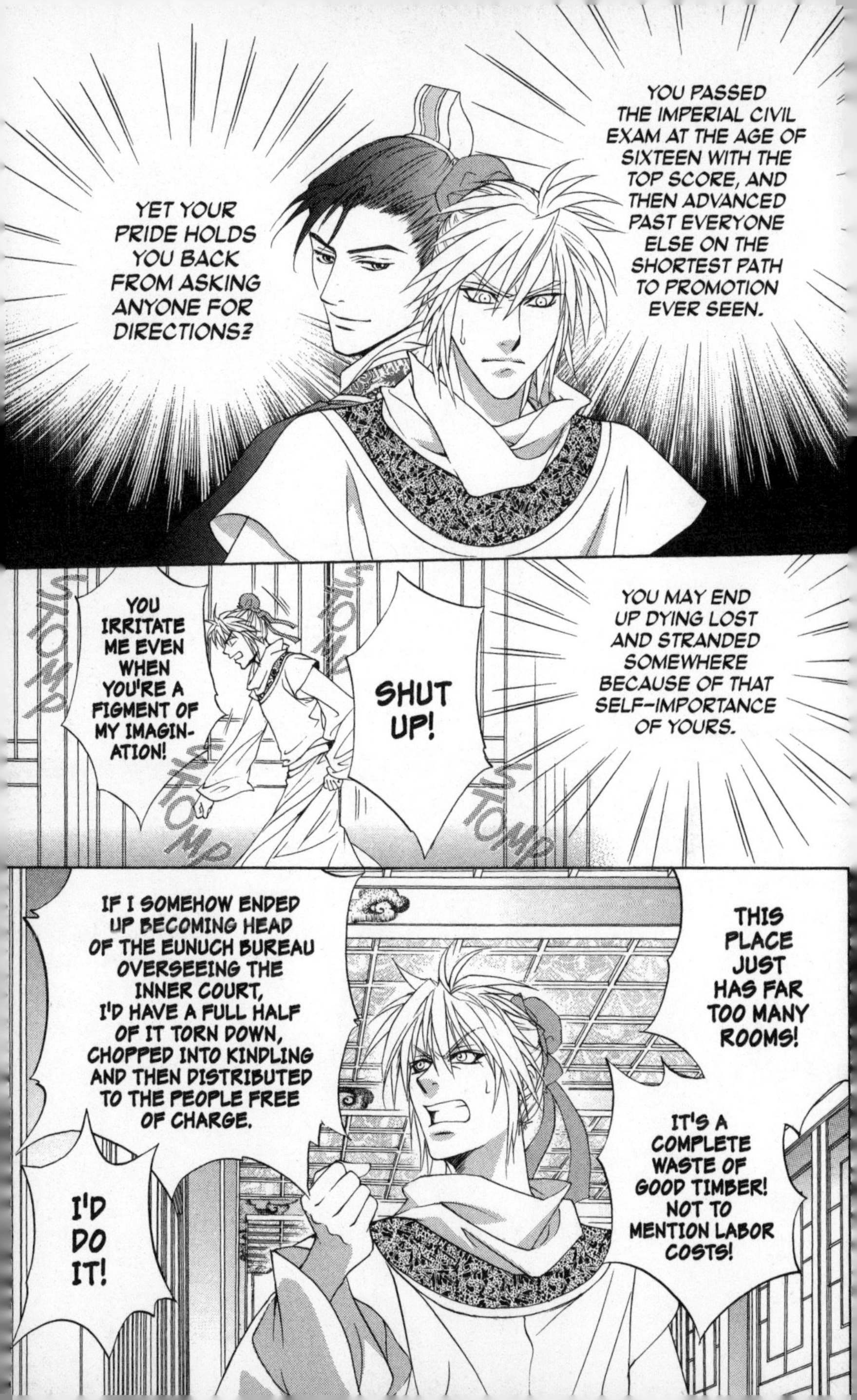
YOU PASSED THE IMPERIAL CIVIL EXAM AT THE AGE OF SIXTEEN WITH THE TOP SCORE, AND THEN ADVANCED PAST EVERYONE ELSE ON THE SHORTEST PATH TO PROMOTION EVER SEEN.
YET YOUR PRIDE HOLDS YOU BACK FROM ASKING ANYONE FOR DIRECTIONS?
YOU MAY END UP DYING LOST AND STRANDED SOMEWHERE BECAUSE OF THAT SELF-IMPORTANCE OF YOURS.
STOMP
SHUT UP!
STOMP
YOU IRRITATE ME EVEN WHEN YOU'RE A FIGMENT OF MY IMAGINATION!
STOMP
STOMP
THIS PLACE JUST HAS FAR TOO MANY ROOMS!
IT'S A COMPLETE WASTE OF GOOD TIMBER! NOT TO MENTION LABOR COSTS!
IF I SOMEHOW ENDED UP BECOMING HEAD OF THE EUNUCH BUREAU OVERSEEING THE INNER COURT, I'D HAVE A FULL HALF OF IT TORN DOWN, CHOPPED INTO KINDLING AND THEN DISTRIBUTED TO THE PEOPLE FREE OF CHARGE.
I'D DO IT!

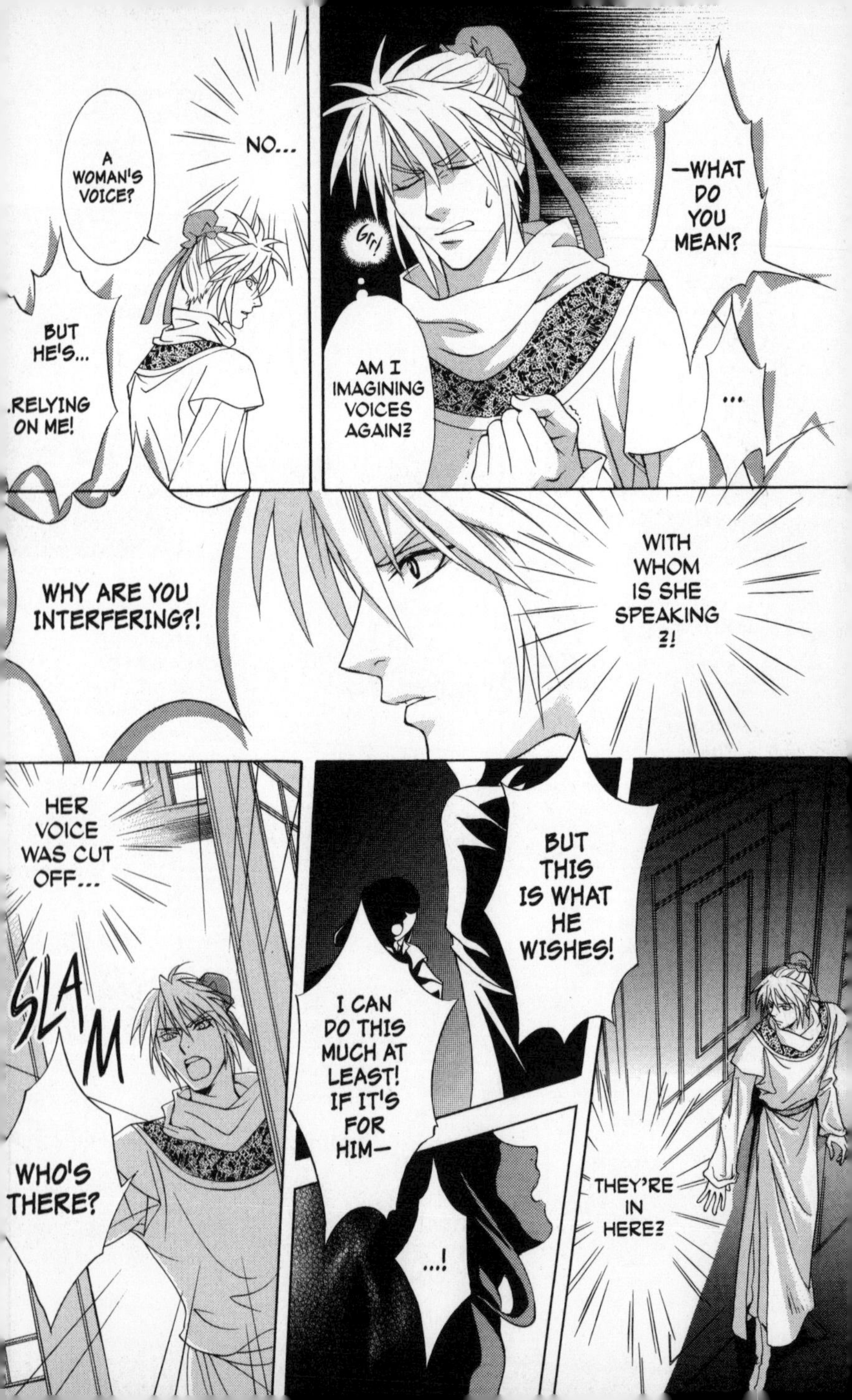

—WHAT DO YOU MEAN?
...
Grr!
AM I IMAGINING VOICES AGAIN?
NO...
A WOMAN'S VOICE?
BUT HE'S...
...RELYING ON ME!
WITH WHOM IS SHE SPEAKING?!
WHY ARE YOU INTERFERING?!
BUT THIS IS WHAT HE WISHES!
I CAN DO THIS MUCH AT LEAST! IF IT'S FOR HIM—
THEY'RE IN HERE?
...!
HER VOICE WAS CUT OFF...
SLAM
WHO'S THERE?

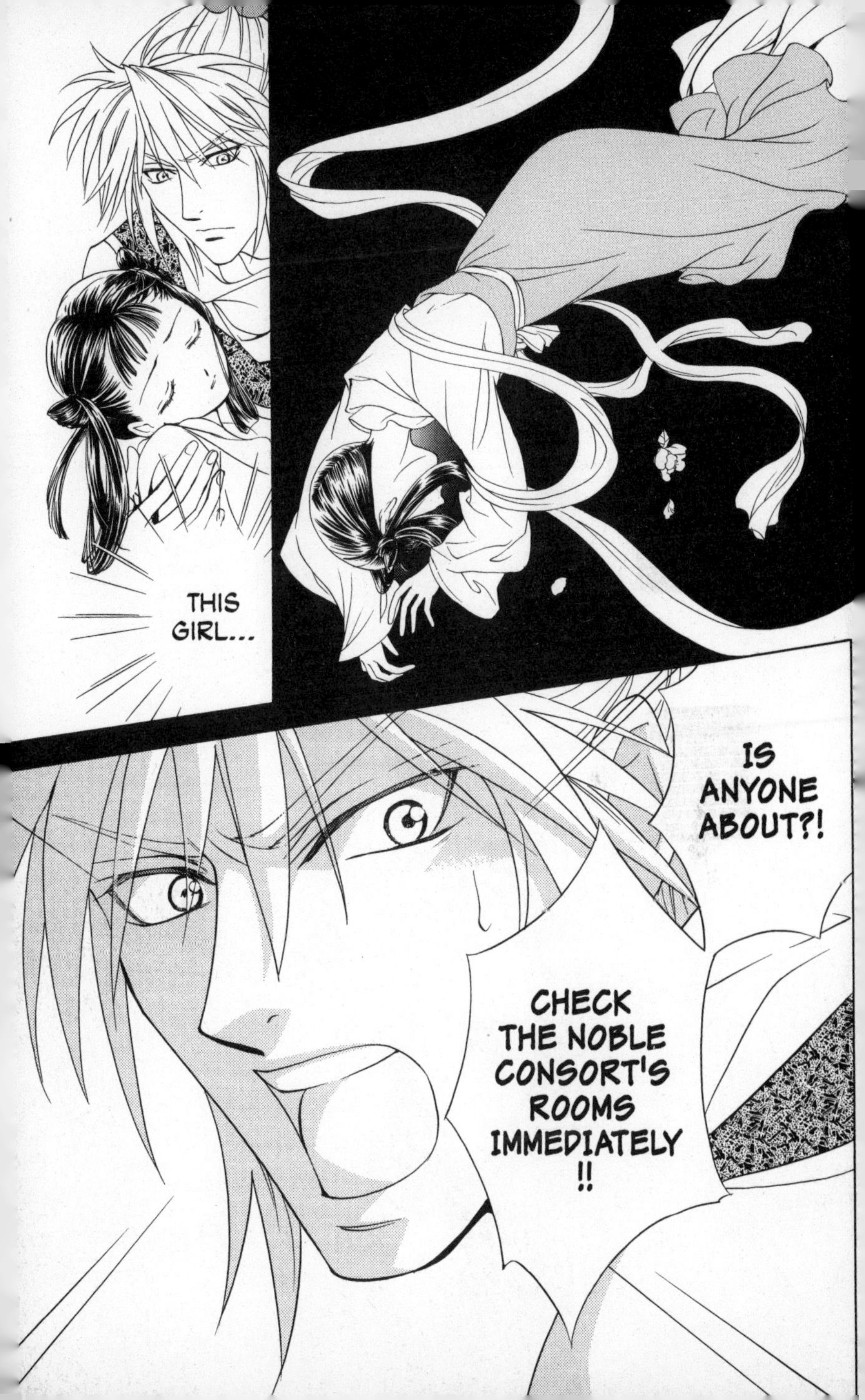
THIS GIRL...
IS ANYONE ABOUT?!
CHECK THE NOBLE CONSORT'S ROOMS IMMEDIATELY!!

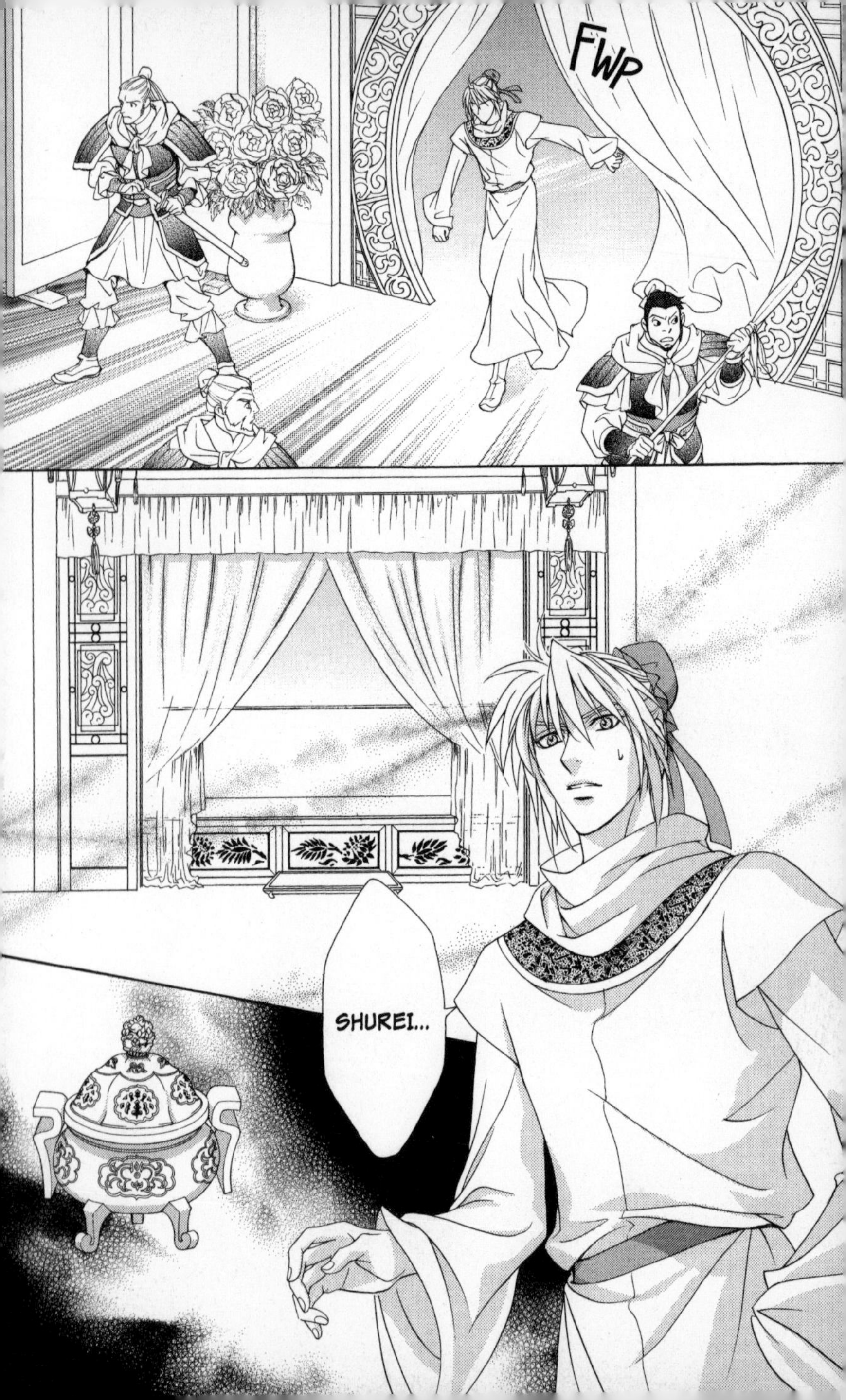
FWP
SHUREI...

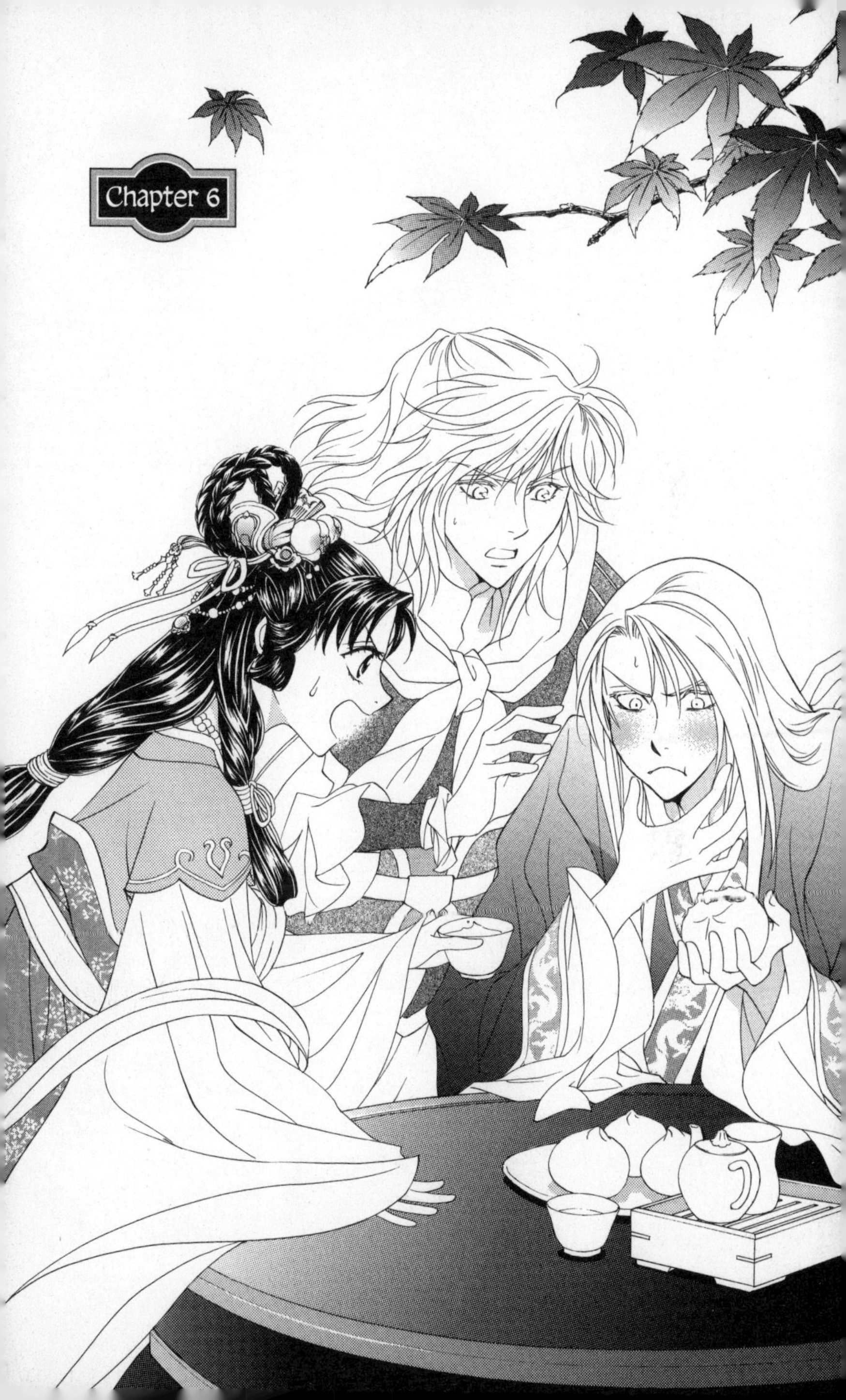
Chapter 6

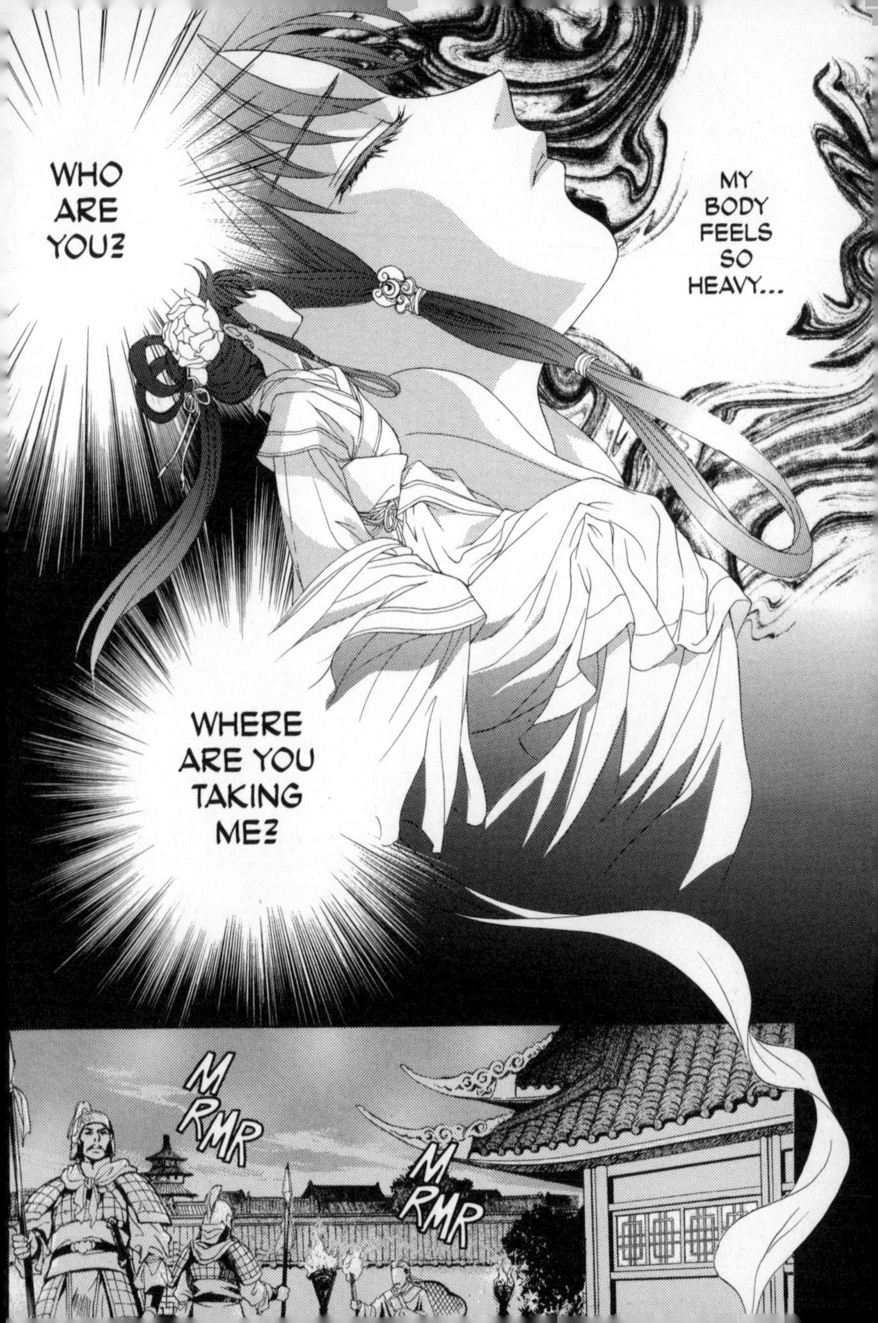
MY BODY FEELS SO HEAVY...
WHO ARE YOU?
WHERE ARE YOU TAKING ME?
MRMR
MRMR

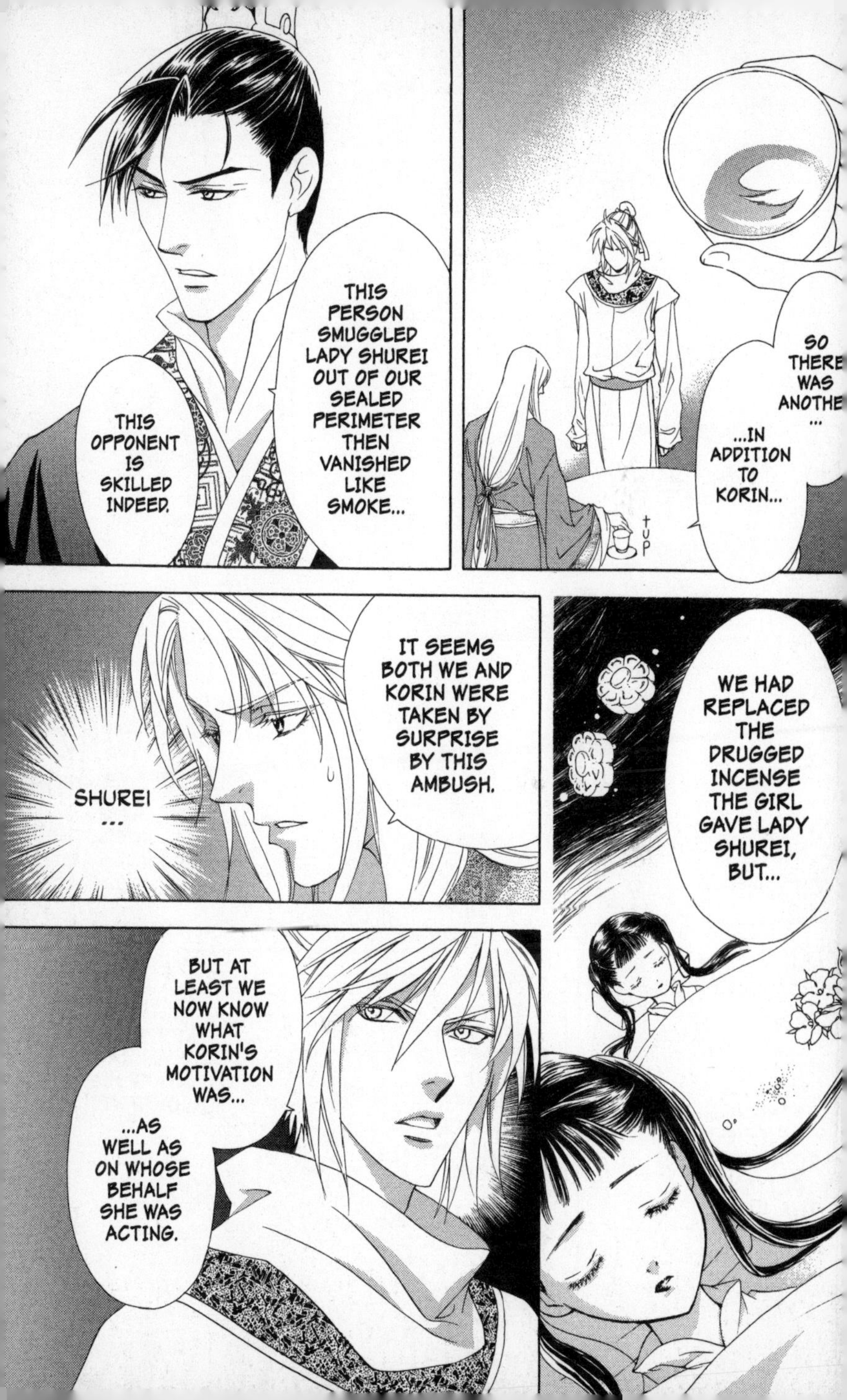
SO THERE WAS ANOTHE...
...IN ADDITION TO KORIN...
TUP
THIS PERSON SMUGGLED LADY SHUREI OUT OF OUR SEALED PERIMETER THEN VANISHED LIKE SMOKE...
THIS OPPONENT IS SKILLED INDEED.
WE HAD REPLACED THE DRUGGED INCENSE THE GIRL GAVE LADY SHUREI, BUT...
IT SEEMS BOTH WE AND KORIN WERE TAKEN BY SURPRISE BY THIS AMBUSH.
SHUREI...
BUT AT LEAST WE NOW KNOW WHAT KORIN'S MOTIVATION WAS...
...AS WELL AS ON WHOSE BEHALF SHE WAS ACTING.

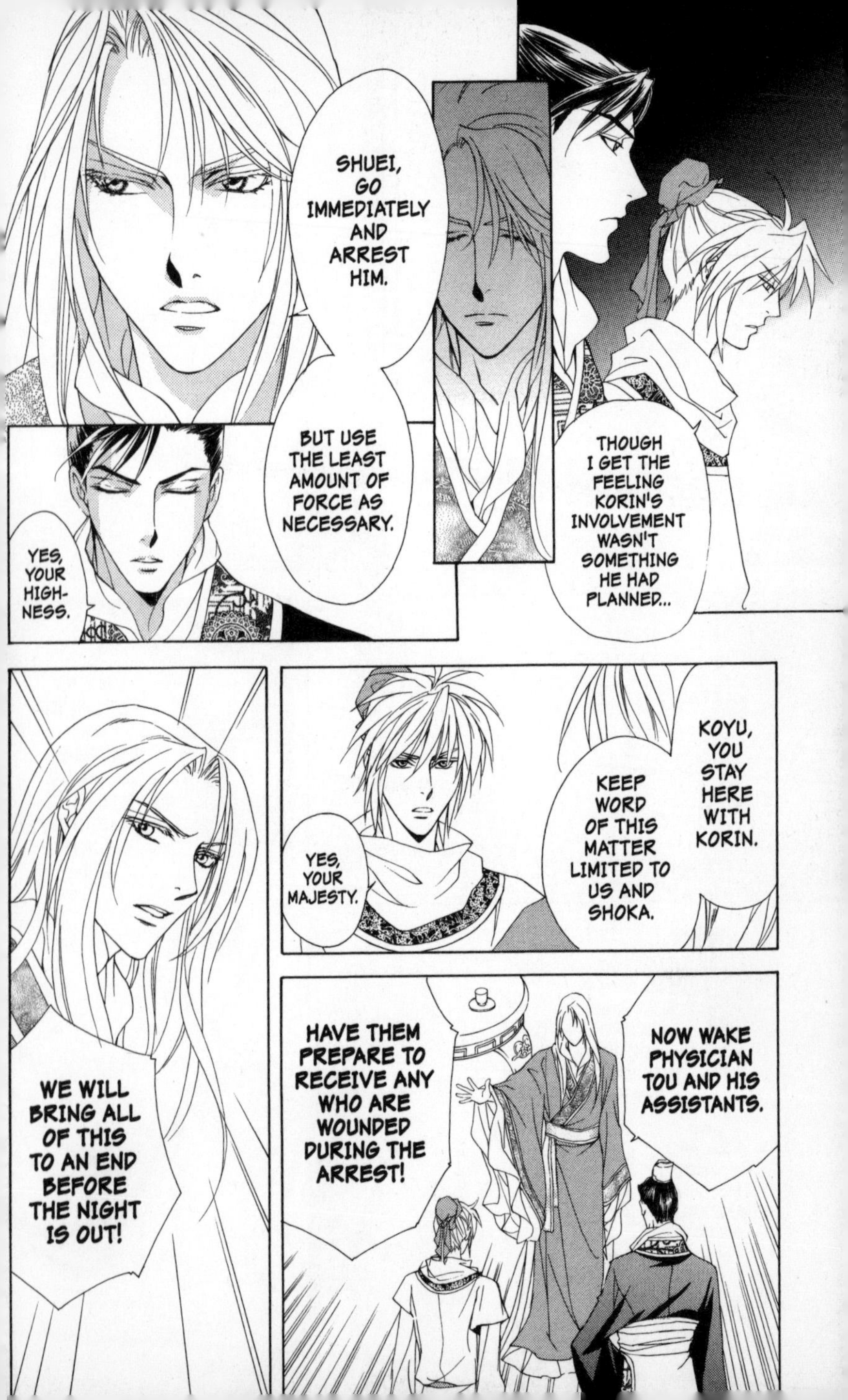

THOUGH I GET THE FEELING KORIN'S INVOLVEMENT WASN'T SOMETHING HE HAD PLANNED...
SHUEI, GO IMMEDIATELY AND ARREST HIM.
BUT USE THE LEAST AMOUNT OF FORCE AS NECESSARY.
YES, YOUR HIGH-NESS.
KOYU, YOU STAY HERE WITH KORIN.
KEEP WORD OF THIS MATTER LIMITED TO US AND SHOKA.
YES, YOUR MAJESTY.
NOW WAKE PHYSICIAN TOU AND HIS ASSISTANTS.
HAVE THEM PREPARE TO RECEIVE ANY WHO ARE WOUNDED DURING THE ARREST!
WE WILL BRING ALL OF THIS TO AN END BEFORE THE NIGHT IS OUT!

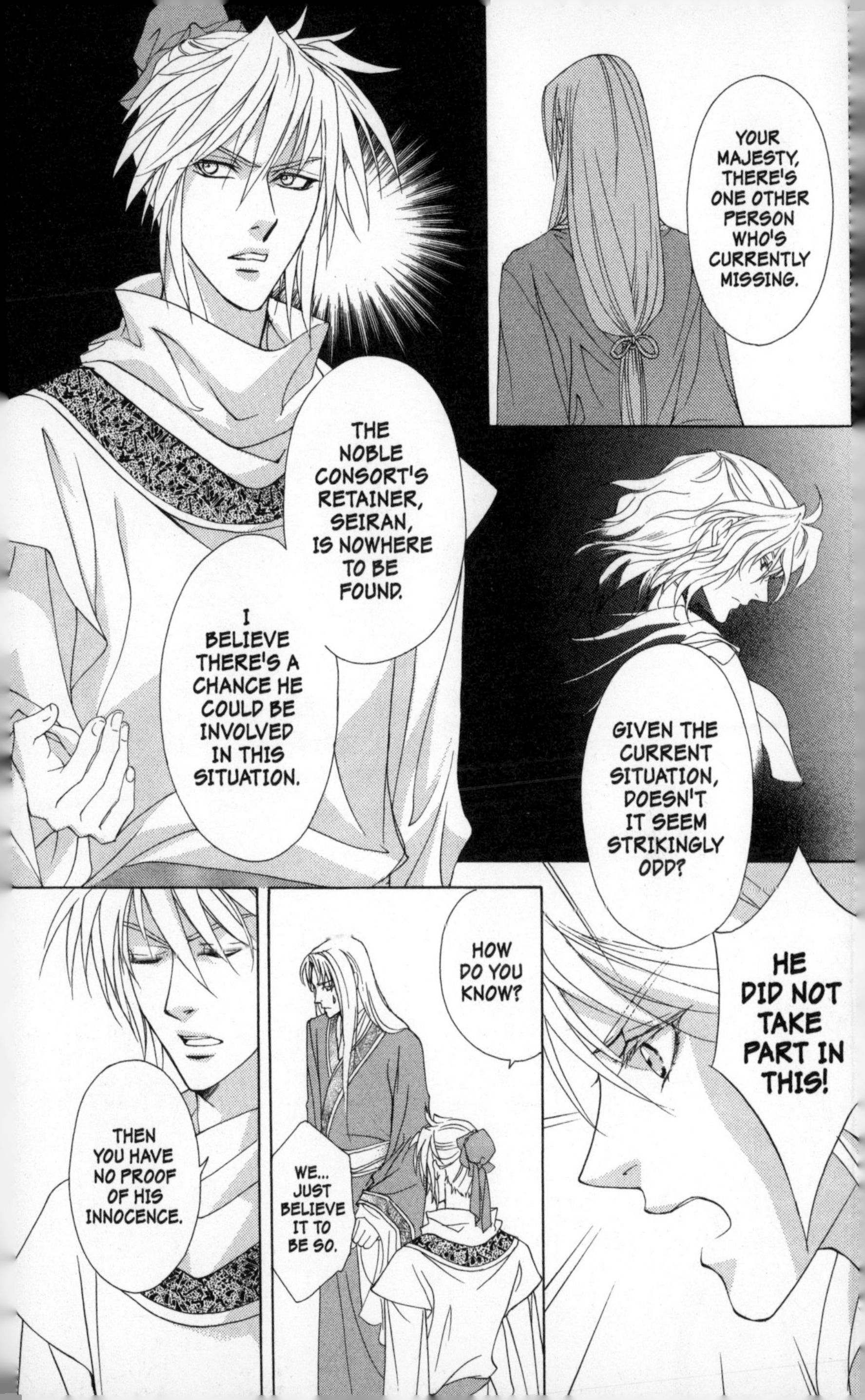
YOUR MAJESTY, THERE'S ONE OTHER PERSON WHO'S CURRENTLY MISSING.
GIVEN THE CURRENT SITUATION, DOESN'T IT SEEM STRIKINGLY ODD?
THE NOBLE CONSORT'S RETAINER, SEIRAN, IS NOWHERE TO BE FOUND.
I BELIEVE THERE'S A CHANCE HE COULD BE INVOLVED IN THIS SITUATION.
HE DID NOT TAKE PART IN THIS!
HOW DO YOU KNOW?
WE... JUST BELIEVE IT TO BE SO.
THEN YOU HAVE NO PROOF OF HIS INNOCENCE.

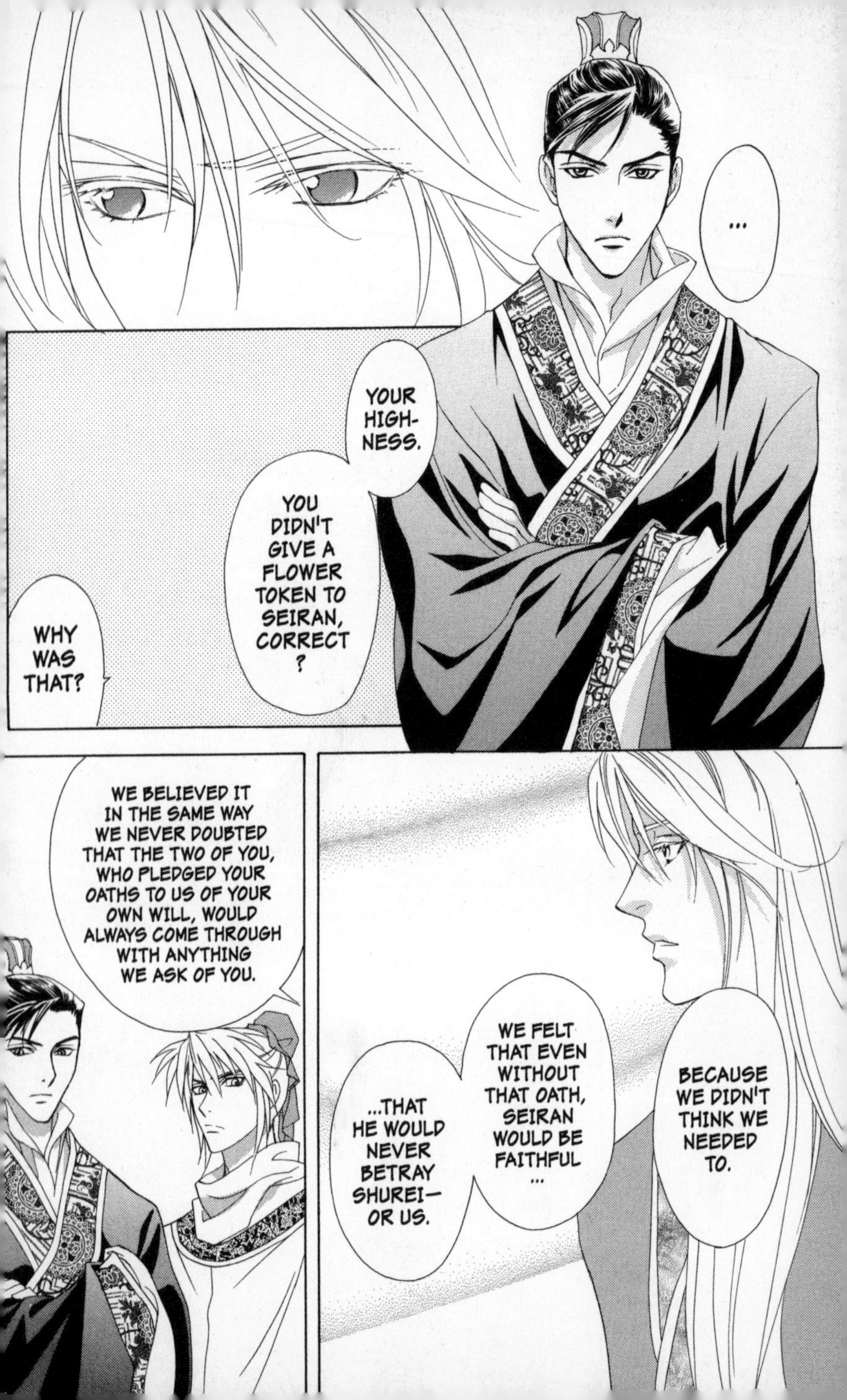
...
YOUR HIGHNESS.
YOU DIDN'T GIVE A FLOWER TOKEN TO SEIRAN, CORRECT?
WHY WAS THAT?
BECAUSE WE DIDN'T THINK WE NEEDED TO.
WE FELT THAT EVEN WITHOUT THAT OATH, SEIRAN WOULD BE FAITHFUL...
...THAT HE WOULD NEVER BETRAY SHUREI— OR US.
WE BELIEVED IT IN THE SAME WAY WE NEVER DOUBTED THAT THE TWO OF YOU, WHO PLEDGED YOUR OATHS TO US OF YOUR OWN WILL, WOULD ALWAYS COME THROUGH WITH ANYTHING WE ASK OF YOU.

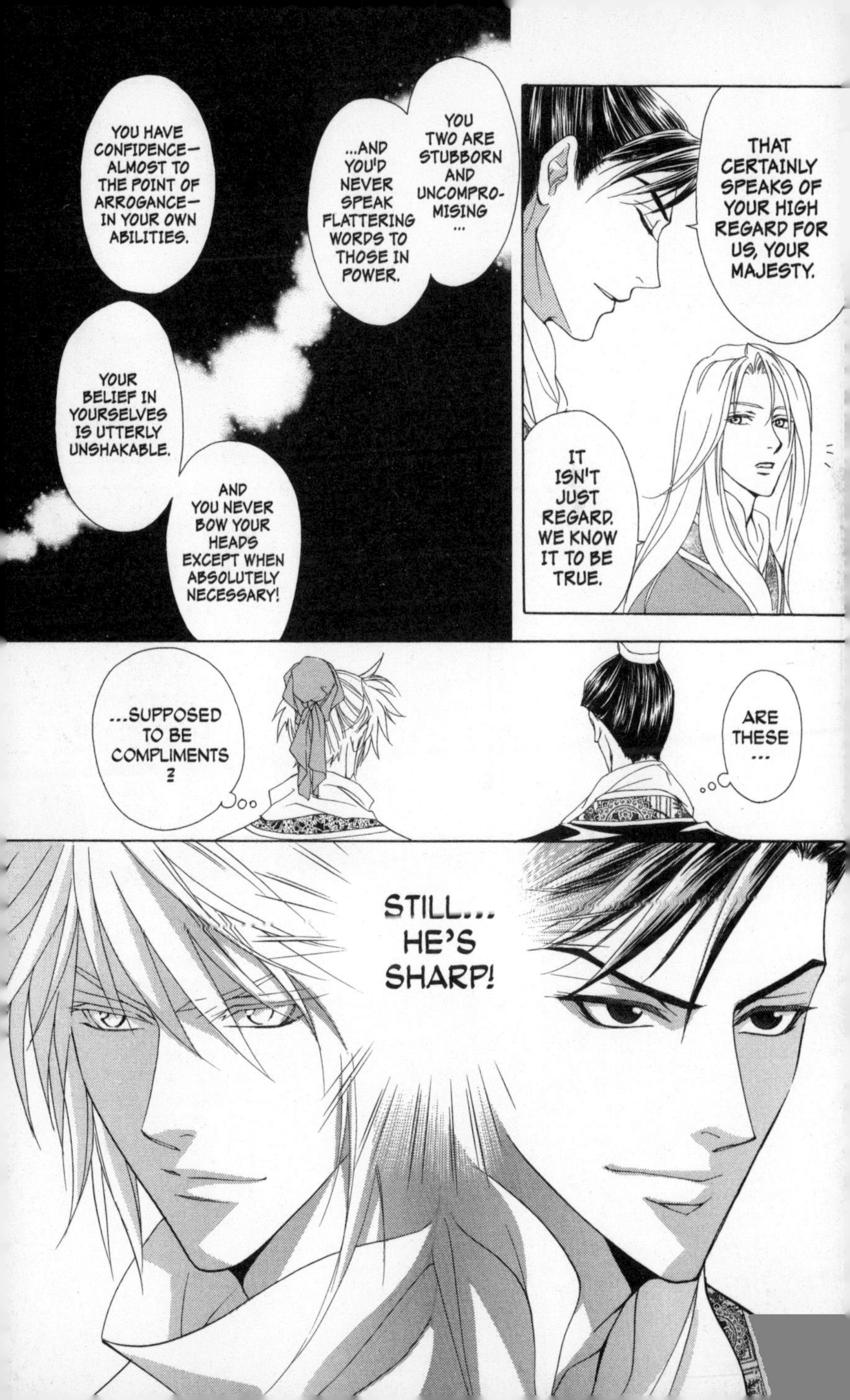
THAT CERTAINLY SPEAKS OF YOUR HIGH REGARD FOR US, YOUR MAJESTY.
IT ISN'T JUST REGARD. WE KNOW IT TO BE TRUE.
YOU TWO ARE STUBBORN AND UNCOMPRO-MISING...
...AND YOU'D NEVER SPEAK FLATTERING WORDS TO THOSE IN POWER.
YOU HAVE CONFIDENCE—ALMOST TO THE POINT OF ARROGANCE—IN YOUR OWN ABILITIES.
YOUR BELIEF IN YOURSELVES IS UTTERLY UNSHAKABLE.
AND YOU NEVER BOW YOUR HEADS EXCEPT WHEN ABSOLUTELY NECESSARY!
ARE THESE...
...SUPPOSED TO BE COMPLIMENTS?
STILL... HE'S SHARP!

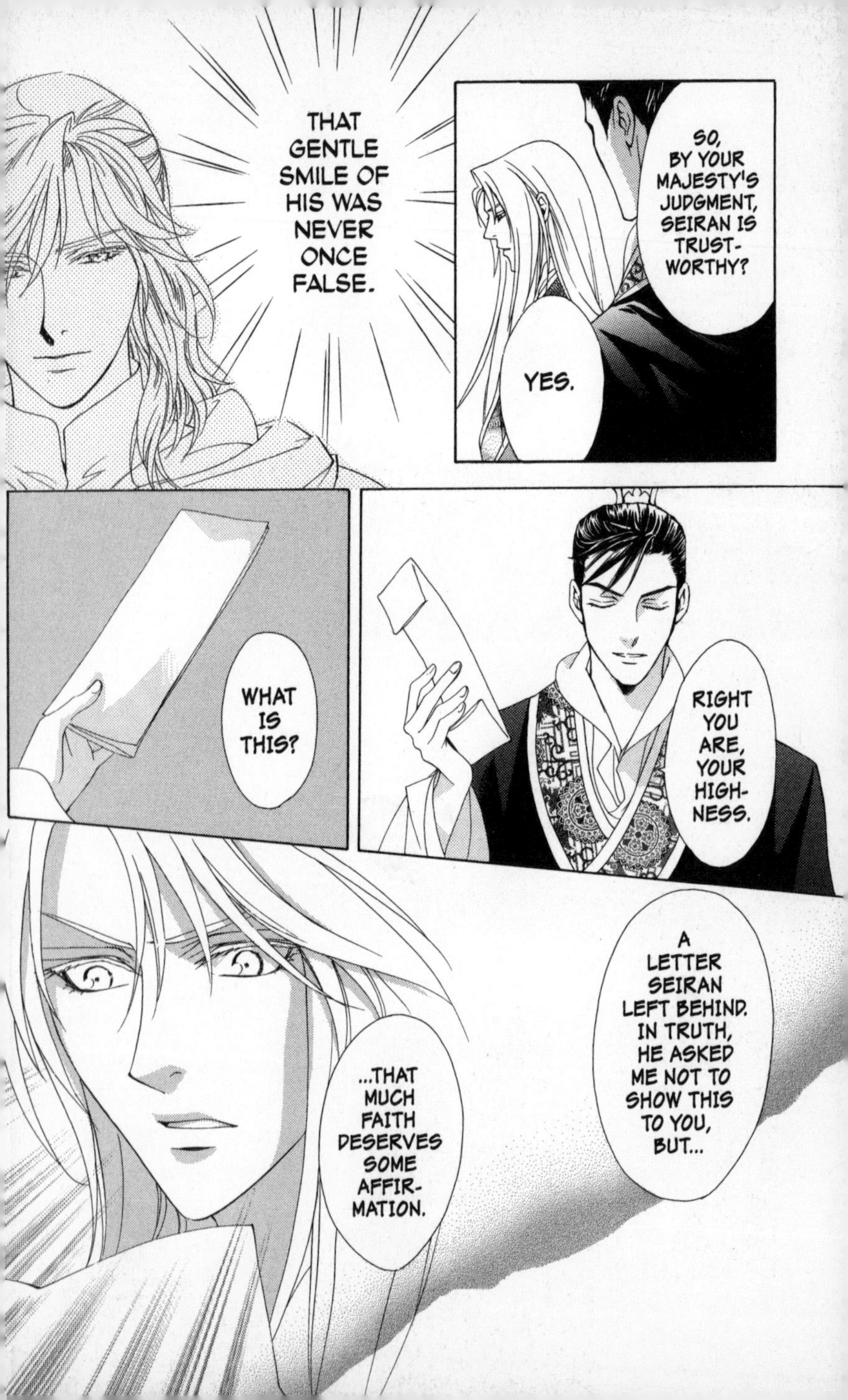
SO, BY YOUR MAJESTY'S JUDGMENT, SEIRAN IS TRUST-WORTHY?
YES.
THAT GENTLE SMILE OF HIS WAS NEVER ONCE FALSE.
RIGHT YOU ARE, YOUR HIGH-NESS.
WHAT IS THIS?
A LETTER SEIRAN LEFT BEHIND. IN TRUTH, HE ASKED ME NOT TO SHOW THIS TO YOU, BUT...
...THAT MUCH FAITH DESERVES SOME AFFIR-MATION.

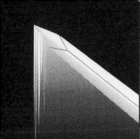

HOW GOOD TO SEE YOU AGAIN AFTER SO LONG... THAT'S HOW I SHOULD GREET YOU, RIGHT...

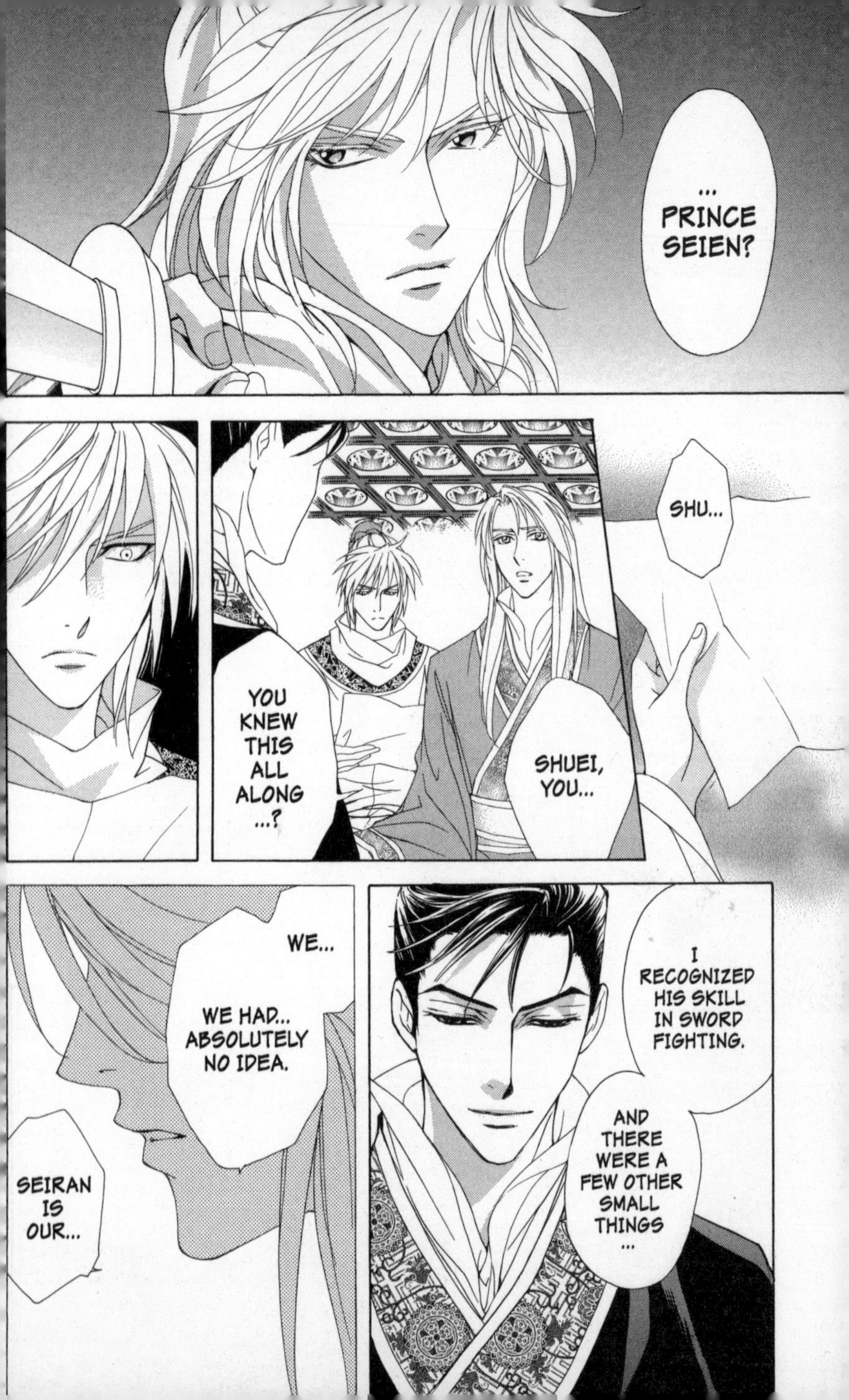
... PRINCE SEIEN?
SHU...
SHUEI, YOU...
YOU KNEW THIS ALL ALONG ...?
I RECOGNIZED HIS SKILL IN SWORD FIGHTING.
AND THERE WERE A FEW OTHER SMALL THINGS ...
WE...
WE HAD... ABSOLUTELY NO IDEA.
SEIRAN IS OUR...

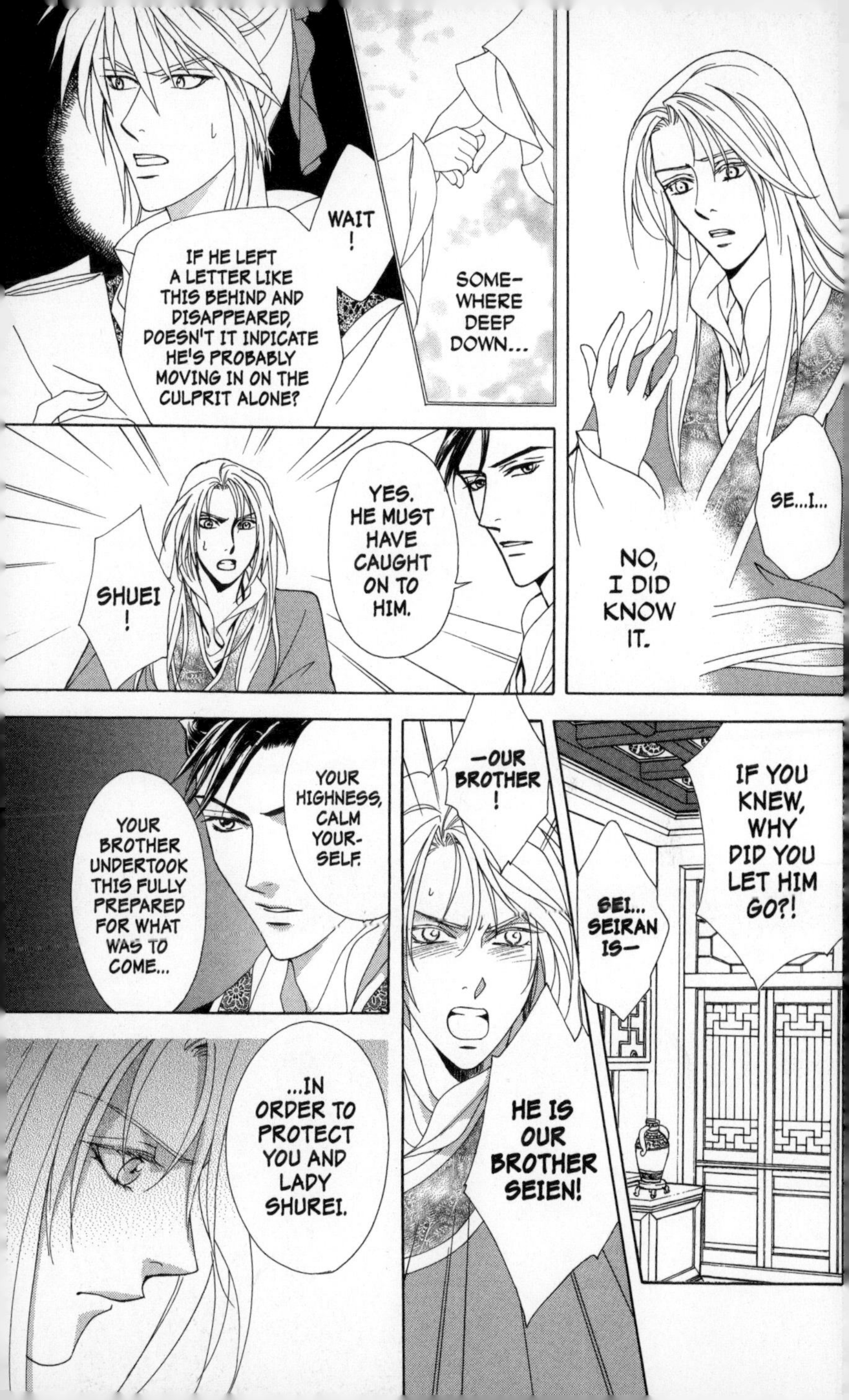
SE...I...
NO, I DID KNOW IT.
WAIT!
SOMEWHERE DEEP DOWN...
IF HE LEFT A LETTER LIKE THIS BEHIND AND DISAPPEARED, DOESN'T IT INDICATE HE'S PROBABLY MOVING IN ON THE CULPRIT ALONE?
YES. HE MUST HAVE CAUGHT ON TO HIM.
SHUEI!
IF YOU KNEW, WHY DID YOU LET HIM GO?!
SEI... SEIRAN IS—
—OUR BROTHER!
HE IS OUR BROTHER SEIEN!
YOUR HIGHNESS, CALM YOURSELF.
YOUR BROTHER UNDERTOOK THIS FULLY PREPARED FOR WHAT WAS TO COME...
...IN ORDER TO PROTECT YOU AND LADY SHUREI.

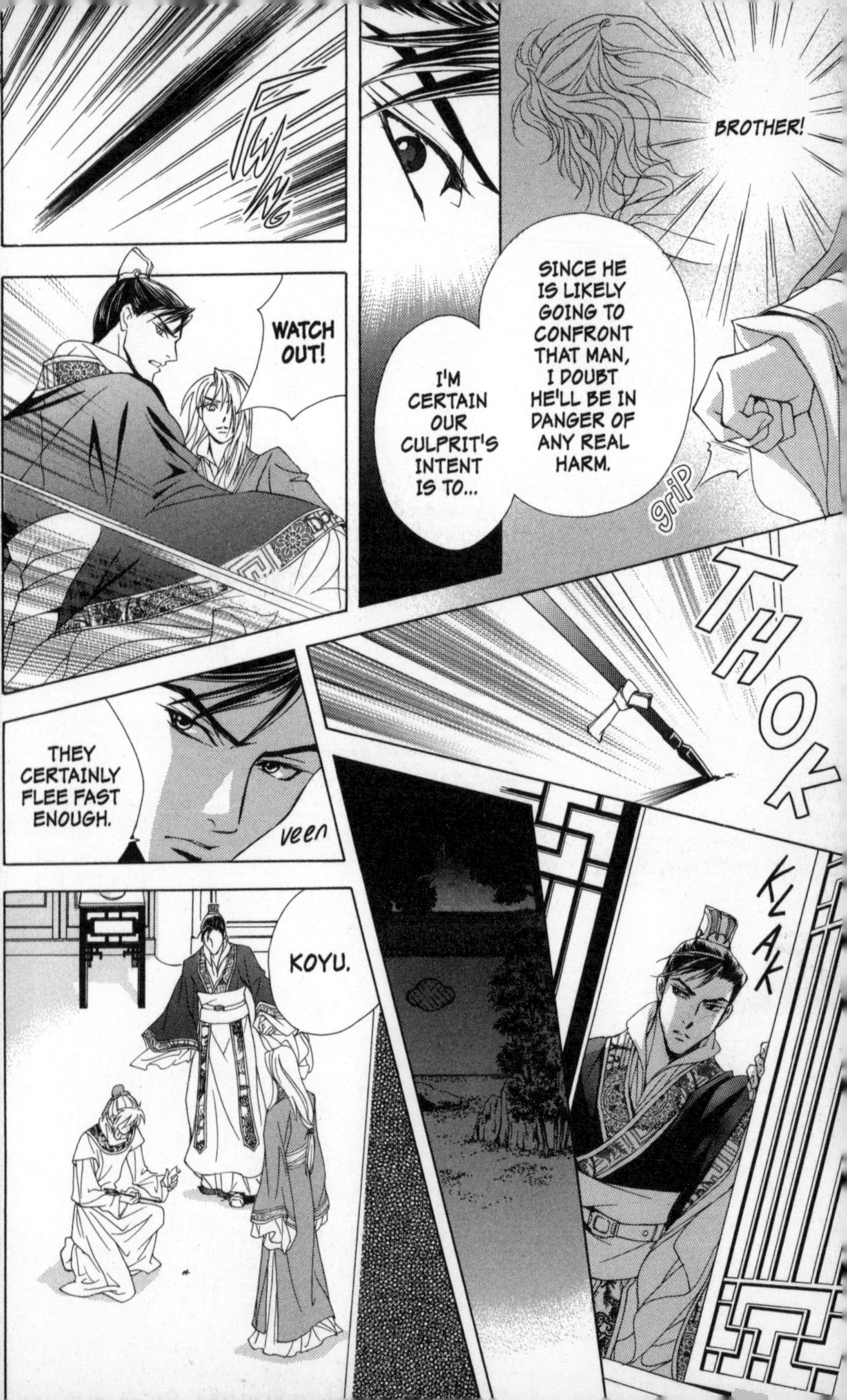
BROTHER!
SINCE HE IS LIKELY GOING TO CONFRONT THAT MAN, I DOUBT HE'LL BE IN DANGER OF ANY REAL HARM.
I'M CERTAIN OUR CULPRIT'S INTENT IS TO...
griP
FWING
WATCH OUT!
THOK
THEY CERTAINLY FLEE FAST ENOUGH.
veen
KLAK
KOYU.

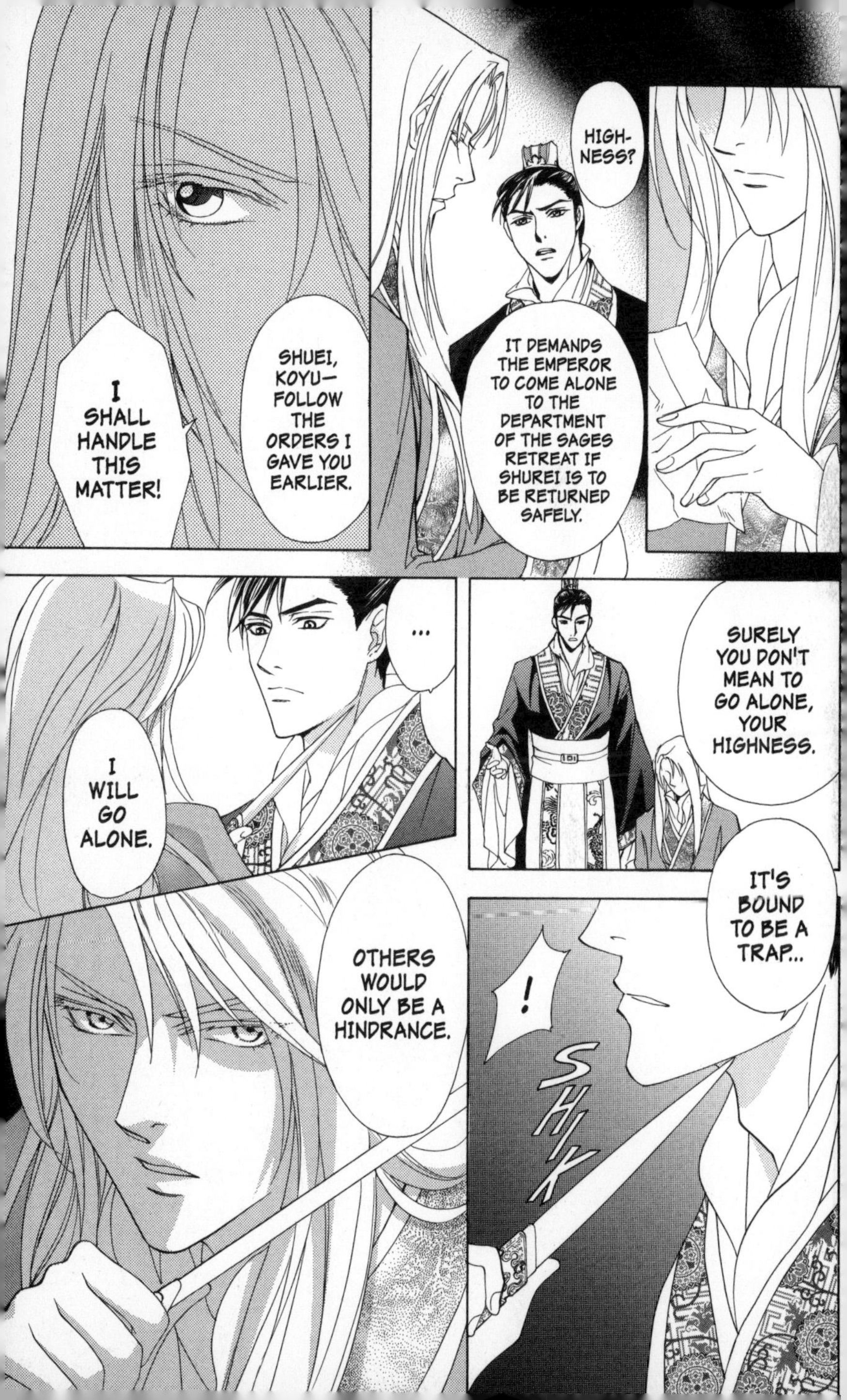
HIGH-NESS?
IT DEMANDS THE EMPEROR TO COME ALONE TO THE DEPARTMENT OF THE SAGES RETREAT IF SHUREI IS TO BE RETURNED SAFELY.
SHUEI, KOYU— FOLLOW THE ORDERS I GAVE YOU EARLIER.
I SHALL HANDLE THIS MATTER!
SURELY YOU DON'T MEAN TO GO ALONE, YOUR HIGHNESS.
...
I WILL GO ALONE.
IT'S SURELY BOUND TO BE A TRAP...
!
SHIK
OTHERS WOULD ONLY BE A HINDRANCE.

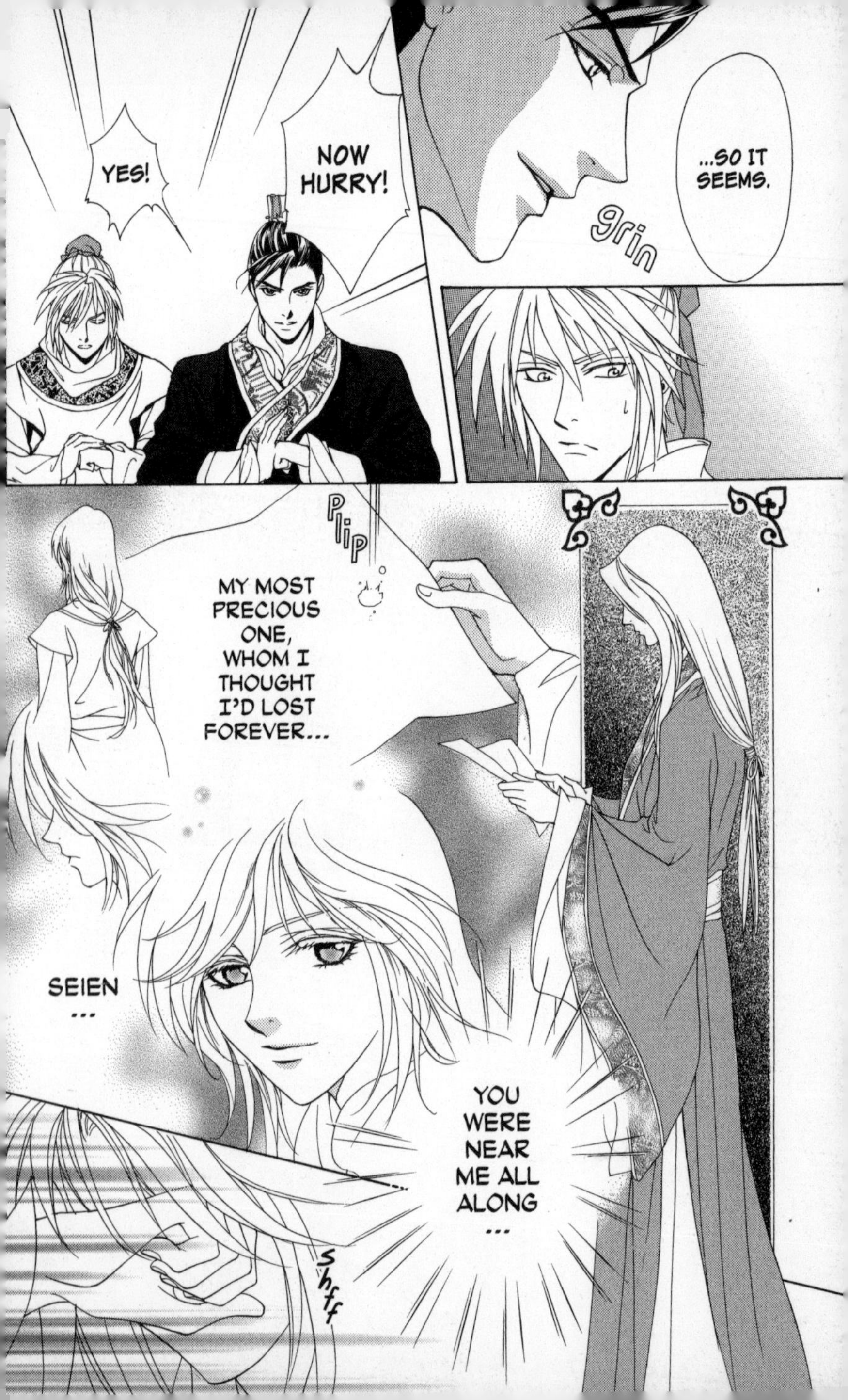
...SO IT SEEMS.
grin
NOW HURRY!
YES!
Plip
MY MOST PRECIOUS ONE, WHOM I THOUGHT I'D LOST FOREVER...
YOU WERE NEAR ME ALL ALONG...
SEIEN...
shff

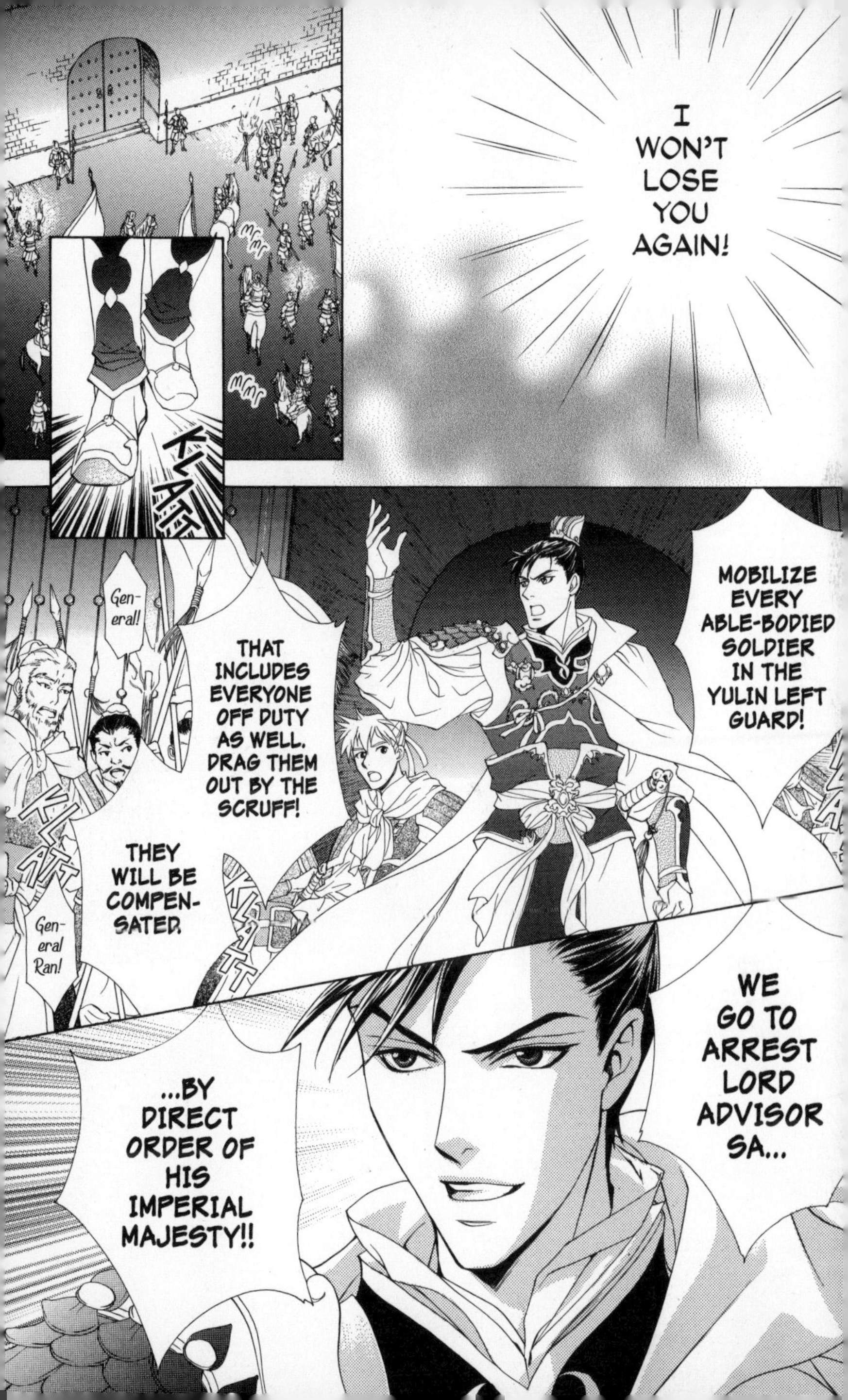
I WON'T LOSE YOU AGAIN!
KLATT
MOBILIZE EVERY ABLE-BODIED SOLDIER IN THE YULIN LEFT GUARD!
THAT INCLUDES EVERYONE OFF DUTY AS WELL. DRAG THEM OUT BY THE SCRUFF!
Gen-eral!
KLATT
THEY WILL BE COMPEN-SATED.
KLATT
Gen-eral Ran!
WE GO TO ARREST LORD ADVISOR SA...
...BY DIRECT ORDER OF HIS IMPERIAL MAJESTY!!

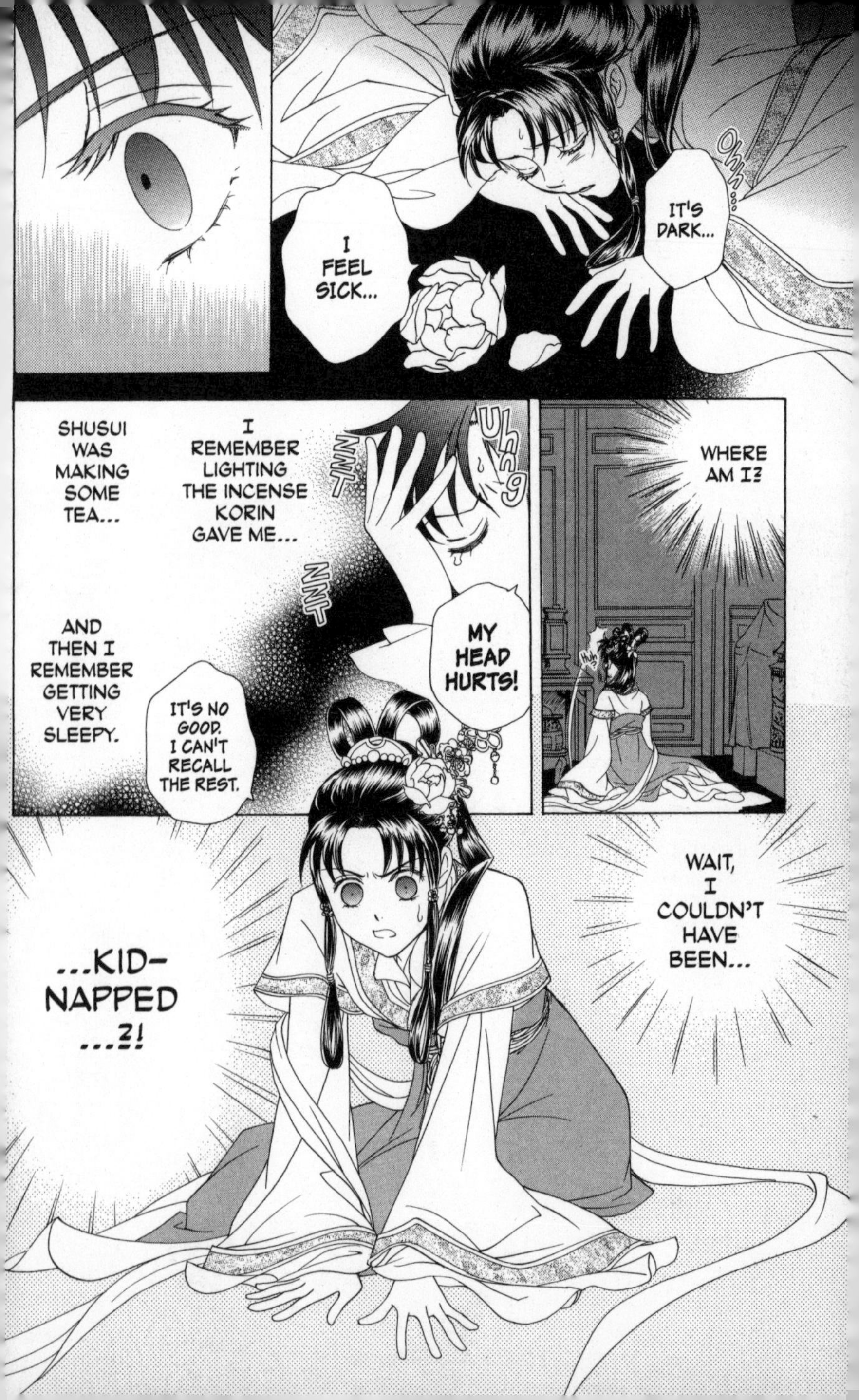
Ohh...
IT'S DARK...
I FEEL SICK...
WHERE AM I?
Huh
Uhng
NNT
NNT
MY HEAD HURTS!
I REMEMBER LIGHTING THE INCENSE KORIN GAVE ME...
SHUSUI WAS MAKING SOME TEA...
AND THEN I REMEMBER GETTING VERY SLEEPY.
IT'S NO GOOD. I CAN'T RECALL THE REST.
WAIT, I COULDN'T HAVE BEEN...
...KID-NAPPED ...?!

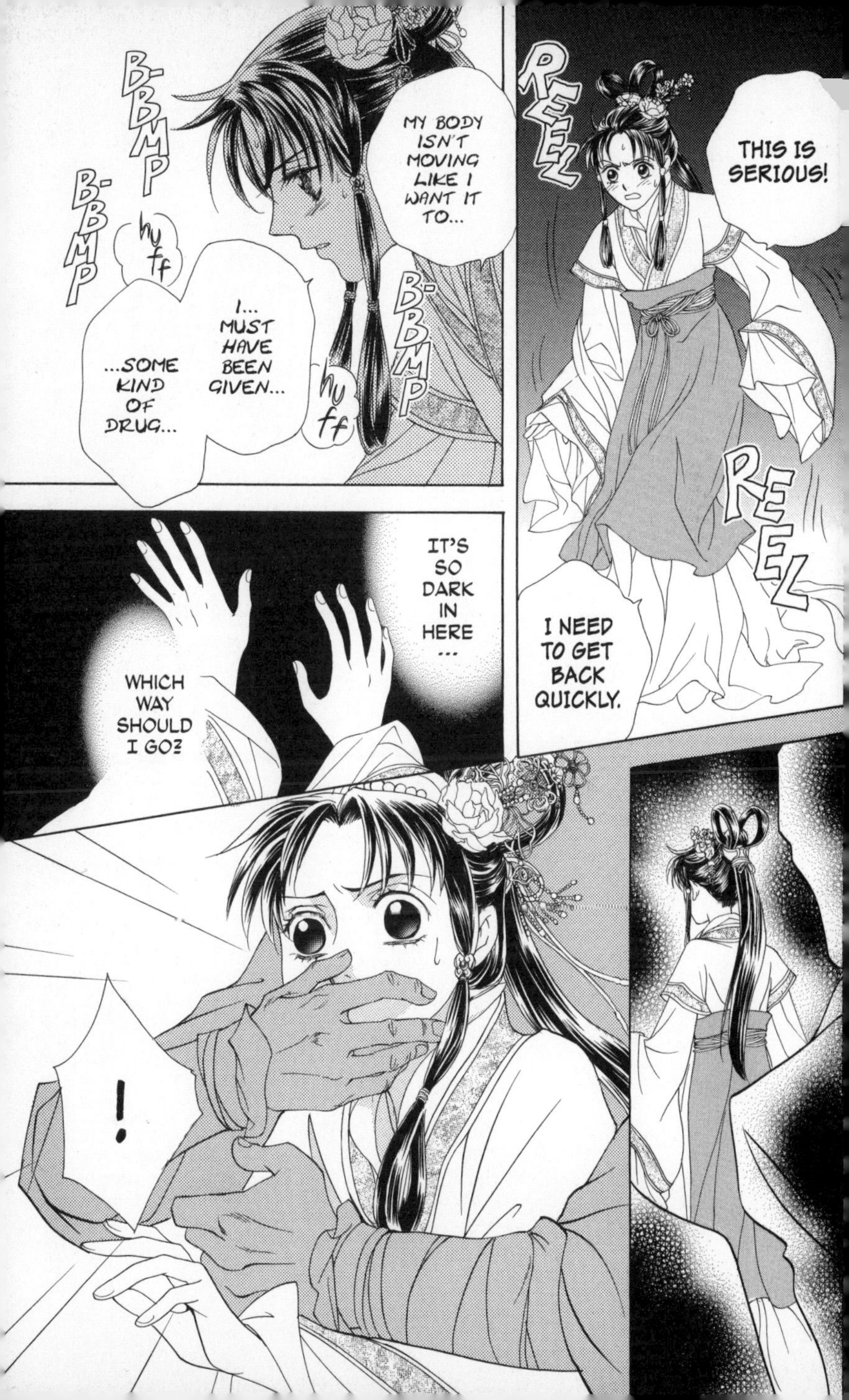

REEL
THIS IS SERIOUS!
REEL
I NEED TO GET BACK QUICKLY.
B-BMP
B-BMP
MY BODY ISN'T MOVING LIKE I WANT IT TO...
huff
I... MUST HAVE BEEN GIVEN...
...SOME KIND OF DRUG...
B-BMP
huff
IT'S SO DARK IN HERE ...
WHICH WAY SHOULD I GO?
!

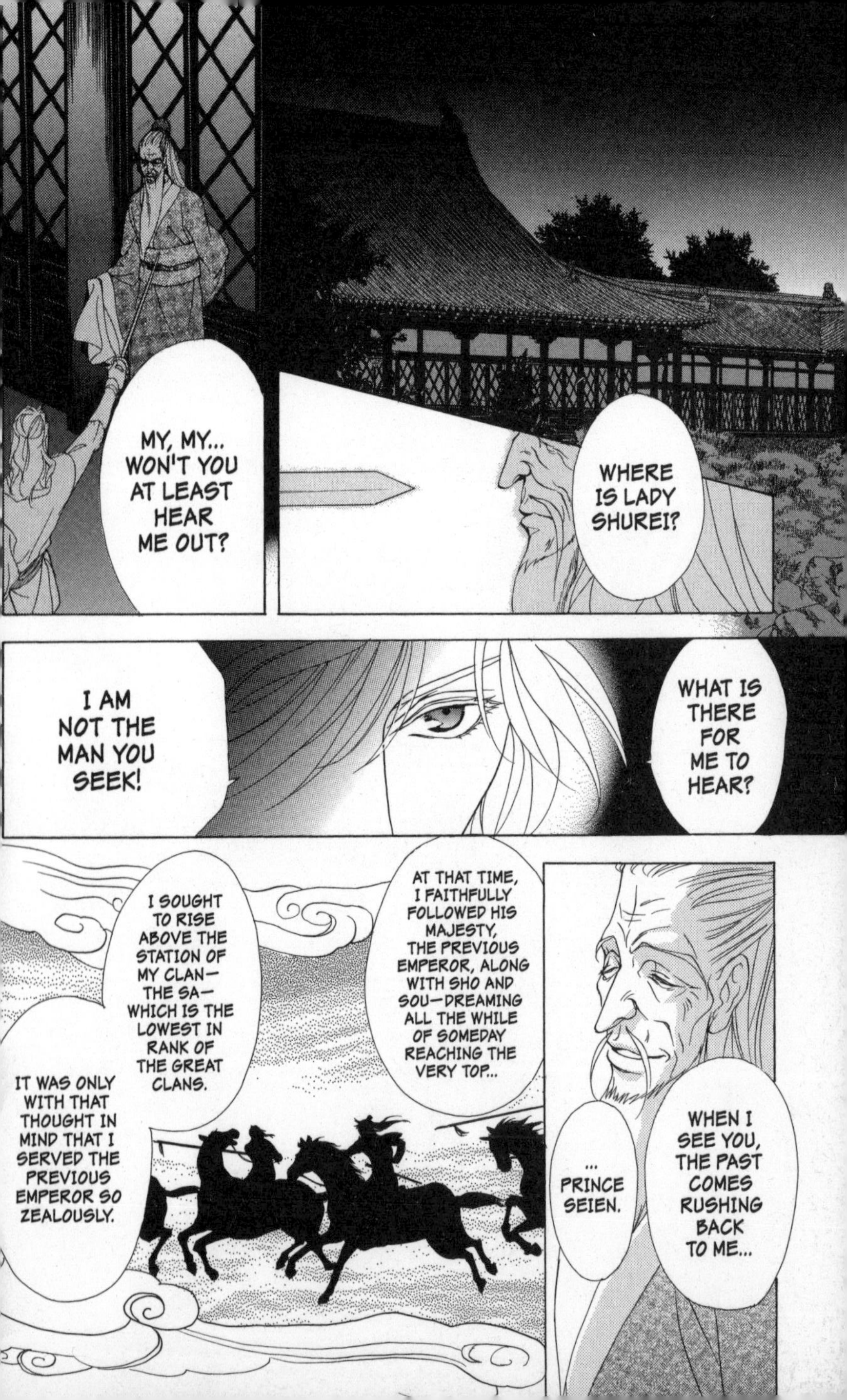
WHERE IS LADY SHUREI?
MY, MY... WON'T YOU AT LEAST HEAR ME OUT?
WHAT IS THERE FOR ME TO HEAR?
I AM NOT THE MAN YOU SEEK!
WHEN I SEE YOU, THE PAST COMES RUSHING BACK TO ME...
... PRINCE SEIEN.
AT THAT TIME, I FAITHFULLY FOLLOWED HIS MAJESTY, THE PREVIOUS EMPEROR, ALONG WITH SHO AND SOU—DREAMING ALL THE WHILE OF SOMEDAY REACHING THE VERY TOP...
I SOUGHT TO RISE ABOVE THE STATION OF MY CLAN—THE SA—WHICH IS THE LOWEST IN RANK OF THE GREAT CLANS.
IT WAS ONLY WITH THAT THOUGHT IN MIND THAT I SERVED THE PREVIOUS EMPEROR SO ZEALOUSLY.

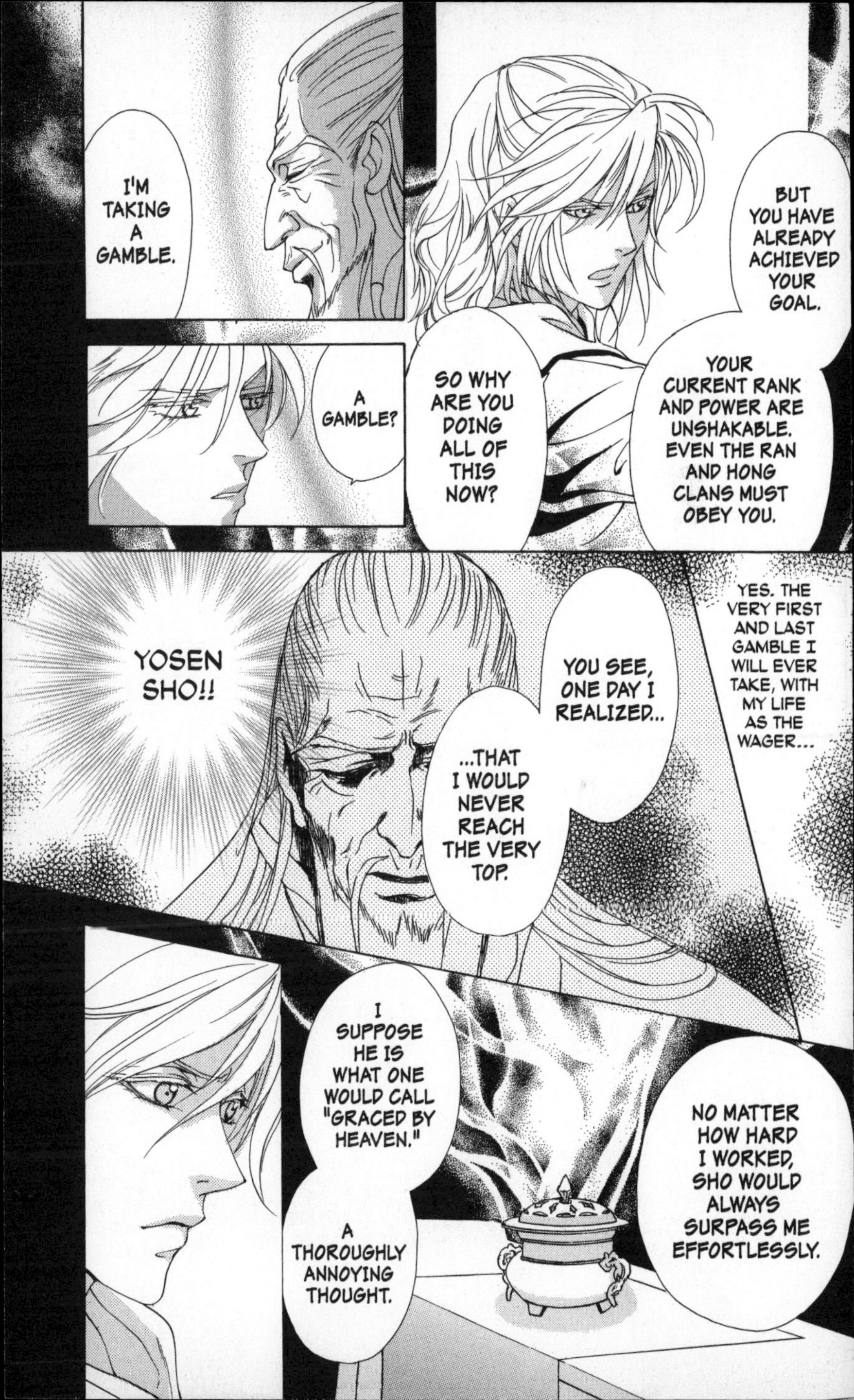
BUT YOU HAVE ALREADY ACHIEVED YOUR GOAL.
YOUR CURRENT RANK AND POWER ARE UNSHAKABLE. EVEN THE RAN AND HONG CLANS MUST OBEY YOU.
SO WHY ARE YOU DOING ALL OF THIS NOW?
I'M TAKING A GAMBLE.
A GAMBLE?
YES. THE VERY FIRST AND LAST GAMBLE I WILL EVER TAKE, WITH MY LIFE AS THE WAGER...
YOU SEE, ONE DAY I REALIZED...
...THAT I WOULD NEVER REACH THE VERY TOP.
YOSEN SHO!!
NO MATTER HOW HARD I WORKED, SHO WOULD ALWAYS SURPASS ME EFFORTLESSLY.
I SUPPOSE HE IS WHAT ONE WOULD CALL "GRACED BY HEAVEN."
A THOROUGHLY ANNOYING THOUGHT.

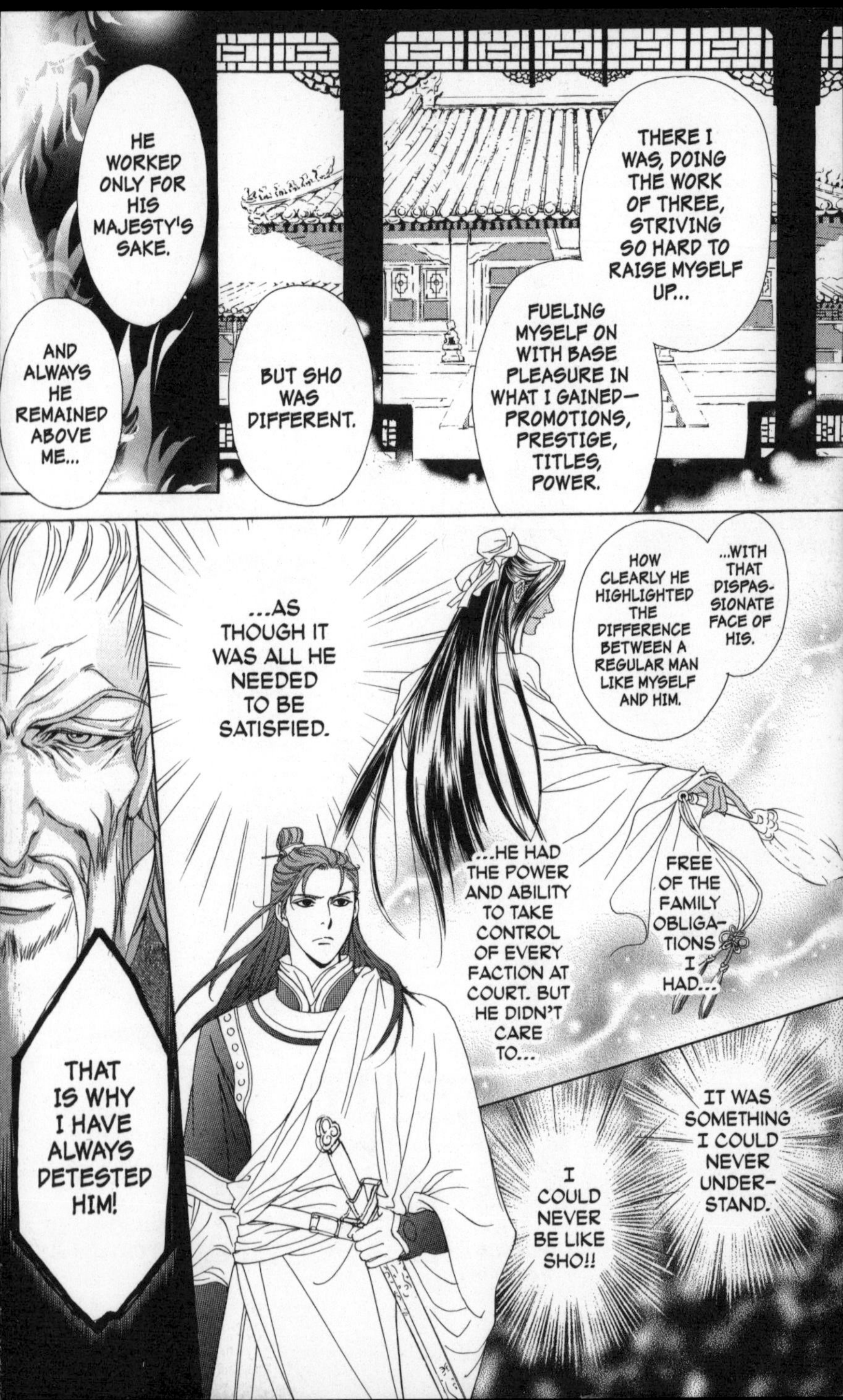

THERE I WAS, DOING THE WORK OF THREE, STRIVING SO HARD TO RAISE MYSELF UP...
FUELING MYSELF ON WITH BASE PLEASURE IN WHAT I GAINED—PROMOTIONS, PRESTIGE, TITLES, POWER.
BUT SHO WAS DIFFERENT.
HE WORKED ONLY FOR HIS MAJESTY'S SAKE.
AND ALWAYS HE REMAINED ABOVE ME...
HOW CLEARLY HE HIGHLIGHTED THE DIFFERENCE BETWEEN A REGULAR MAN LIKE MYSELF AND HIM.
...WITH THAT DISPASSIONATE FACE OF HIS.
FREE OF THE FAMILY OBLIGATIONS I HAD...
...HE HAD THE POWER AND ABILITY TO TAKE CONTROL OF EVERY FACTION AT COURT. BUT HE DIDN'T CARE TO...
...AS THOUGH IT WAS ALL HE NEEDED TO BE SATISFIED.
IT WAS SOMETHING I COULD NEVER UNDERSTAND.
I COULD NEVER BE LIKE SHO!!
THAT IS WHY I HAVE ALWAYS DETESTED HIM!

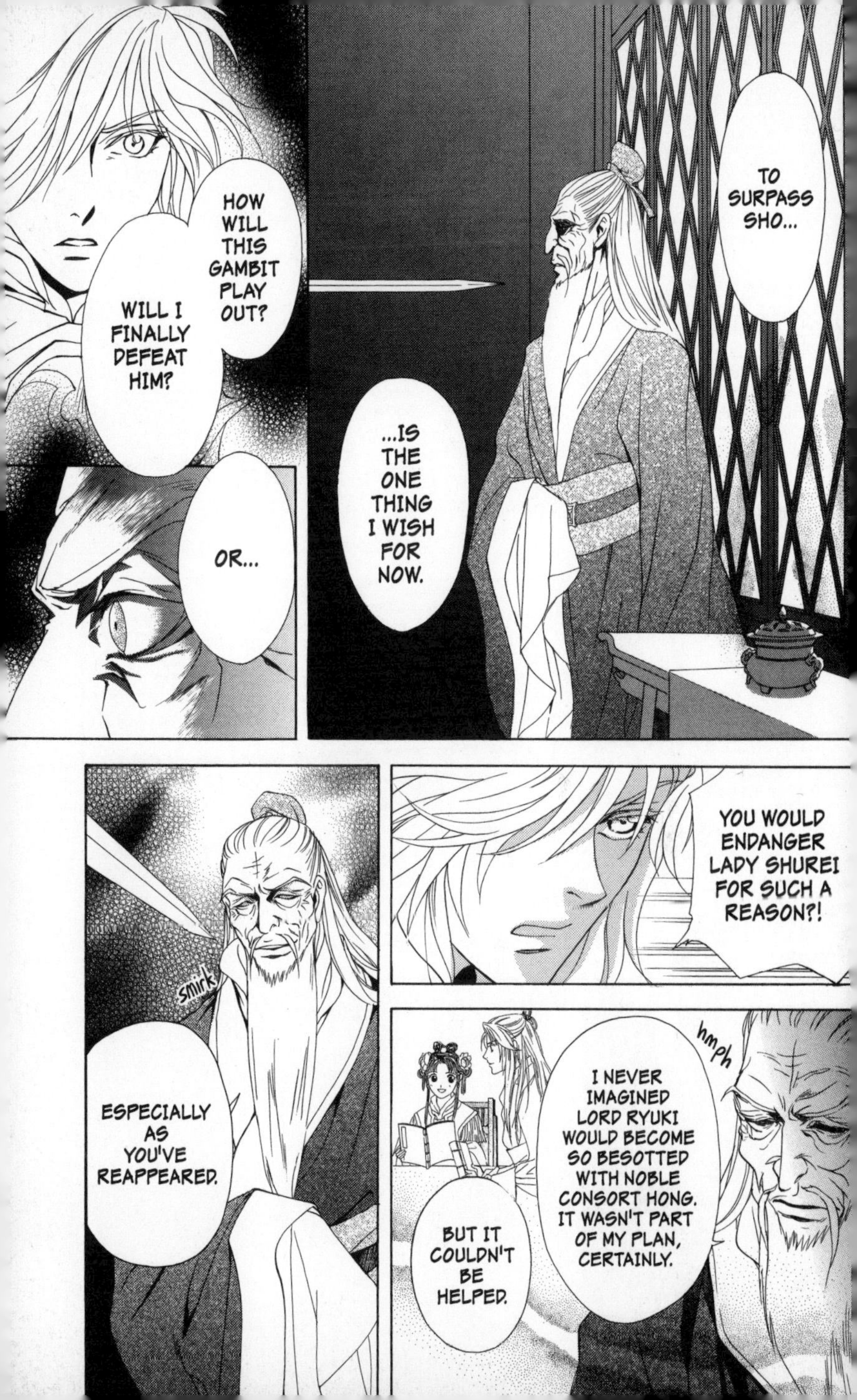
TO SURPASS SHO...
...IS THE ONE THING I WISH FOR NOW.
HOW WILL THIS GAMBIT PLAY OUT?
WILL I FINALLY DEFEAT HIM?
OR...
YOU WOULD ENDANGER LADY SHUREI FOR SUCH A REASON?!
hmph
I NEVER IMAGINED LORD RYUKI WOULD BECOME SO BESOTTED WITH NOBLE CONSORT HONG. IT WASN'T PART OF MY PLAN, CERTAINLY.
BUT IT COULDN'T BE HELPED.
smirk
ESPECIALLY AS YOU'VE REAPPEARED.

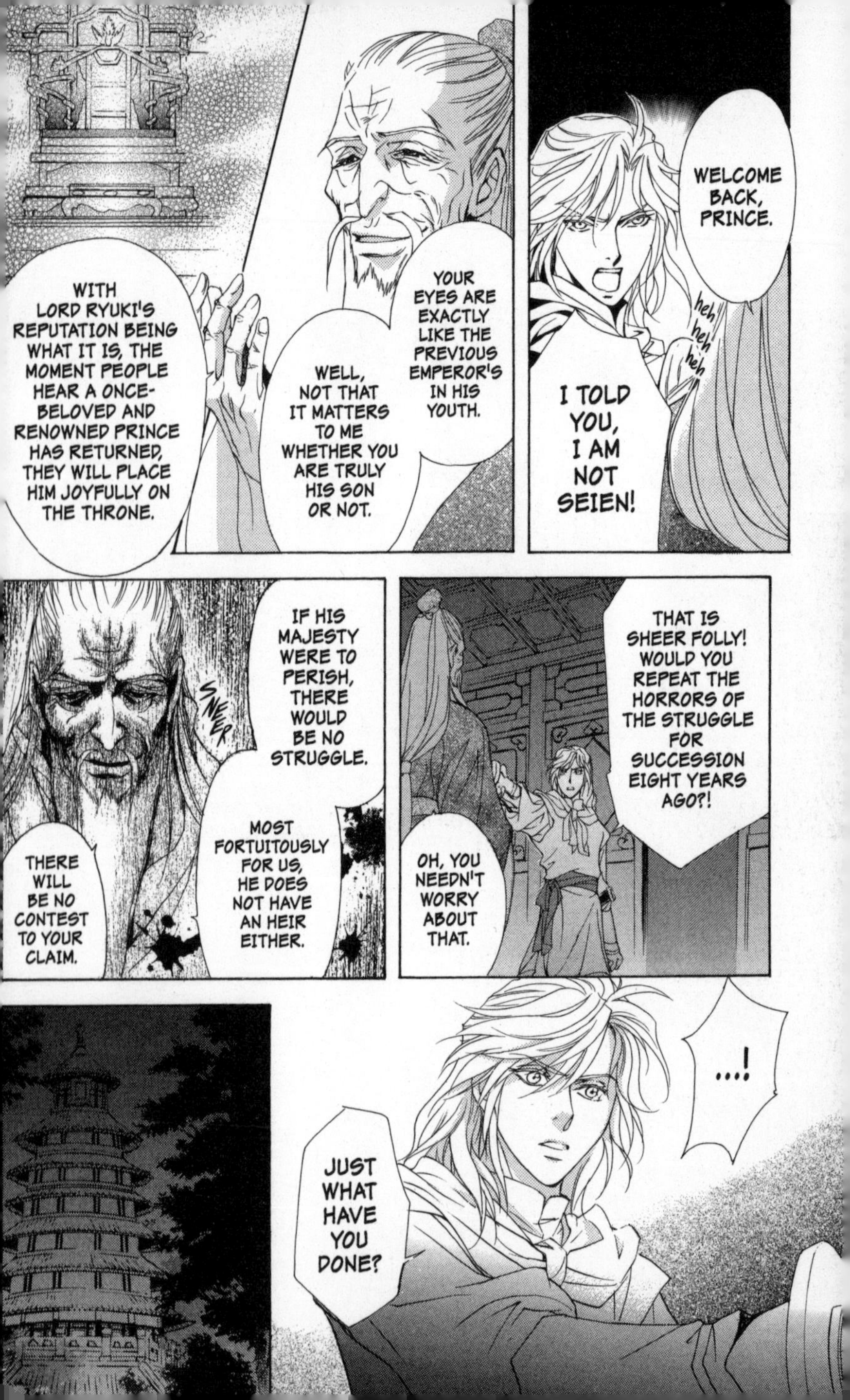
WELCOME BACK, PRINCE.
heh heh heh
I TOLD YOU, I AM NOT SEIEN!
YOUR EYES ARE EXACTLY LIKE THE PREVIOUS EMPEROR'S IN HIS YOUTH.
WELL, NOT THAT IT MATTERS TO ME WHETHER YOU ARE TRULY HIS SON OR NOT.
WITH LORD RYUKI'S REPUTATION BEING WHAT IT IS, THE MOMENT PEOPLE HEAR A ONCE-BELOVED AND RENOWNED PRINCE HAS RETURNED, THEY WILL PLACE HIM JOYFULLY ON THE THRONE.
THAT IS SHEER FOLLY! WOULD YOU REPEAT THE HORRORS OF THE STRUGGLE FOR SUCCESSION EIGHT YEARS AGO?!
OH, YOU NEEDN'T WORRY ABOUT THAT.
IF HIS MAJESTY WERE TO PERISH, THERE WOULD BE NO STRUGGLE.
SNEER
MOST FORTUITOUSLY FOR US, HE DOES NOT HAVE AN HEIR EITHER.
THERE WILL BE NO CONTEST TO YOUR CLAIM.
...!
JUST WHAT HAVE YOU DONE?

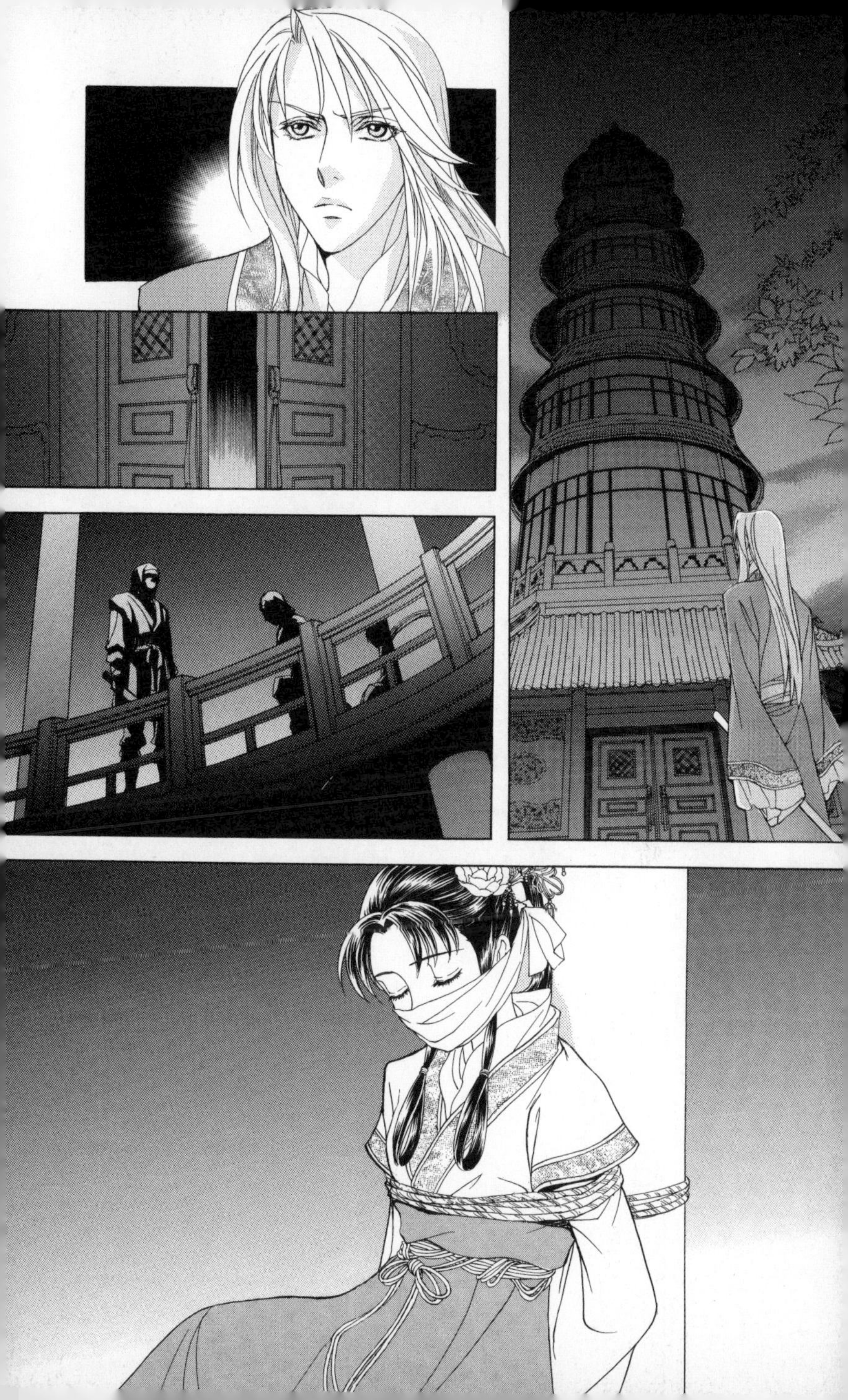

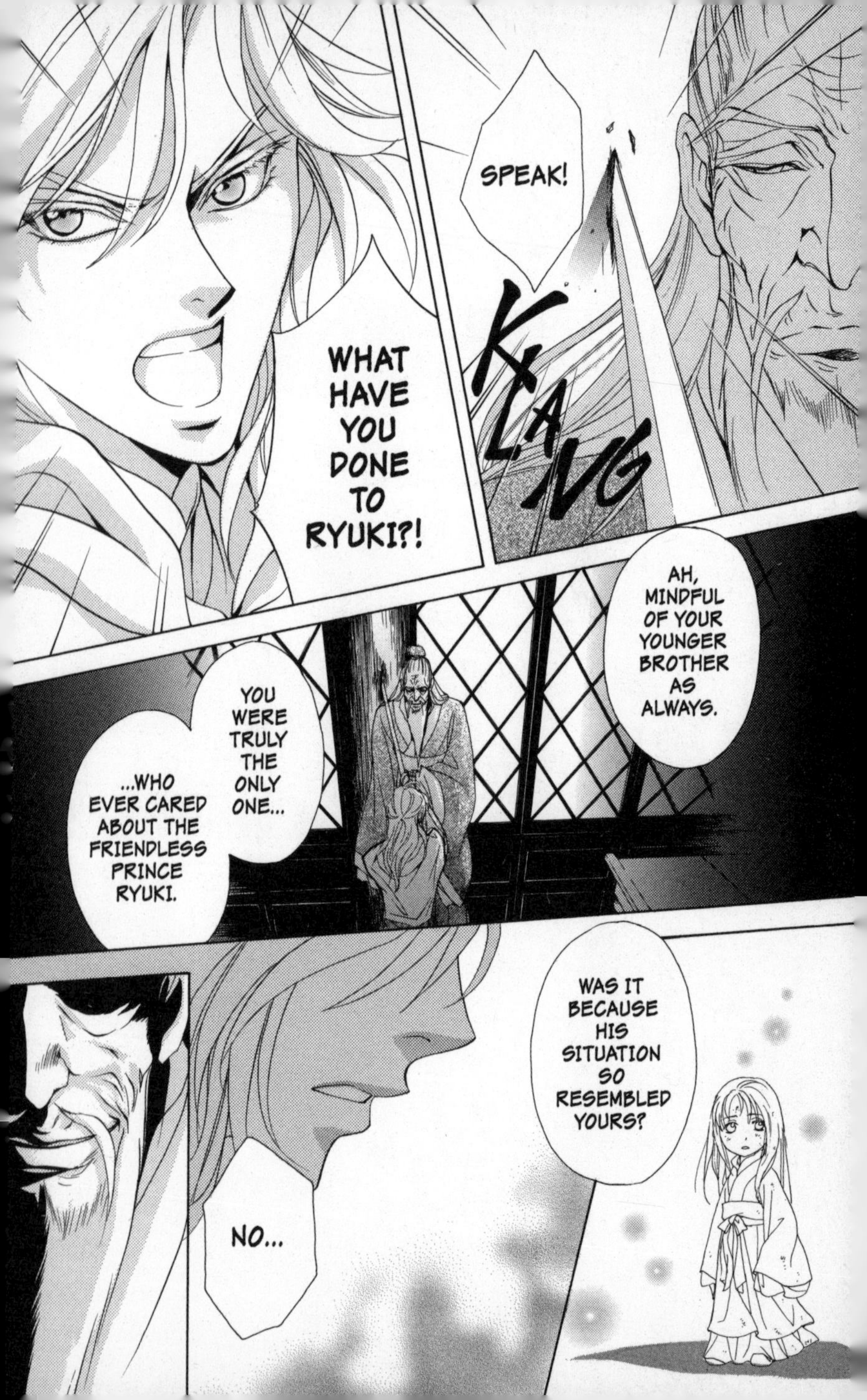
SPEAK!
KLANG
WHAT HAVE YOU DONE TO RYUKI?!
AH, MINDFUL OF YOUR YOUNGER BROTHER AS ALWAYS.
YOU WERE TRULY THE ONLY ONE...
...WHO EVER CARED ABOUT THE FRIENDLESS PRINCE RYUKI.
WAS IT BECAUSE HIS SITUATION SO RESEMBLED YOURS?
NO...

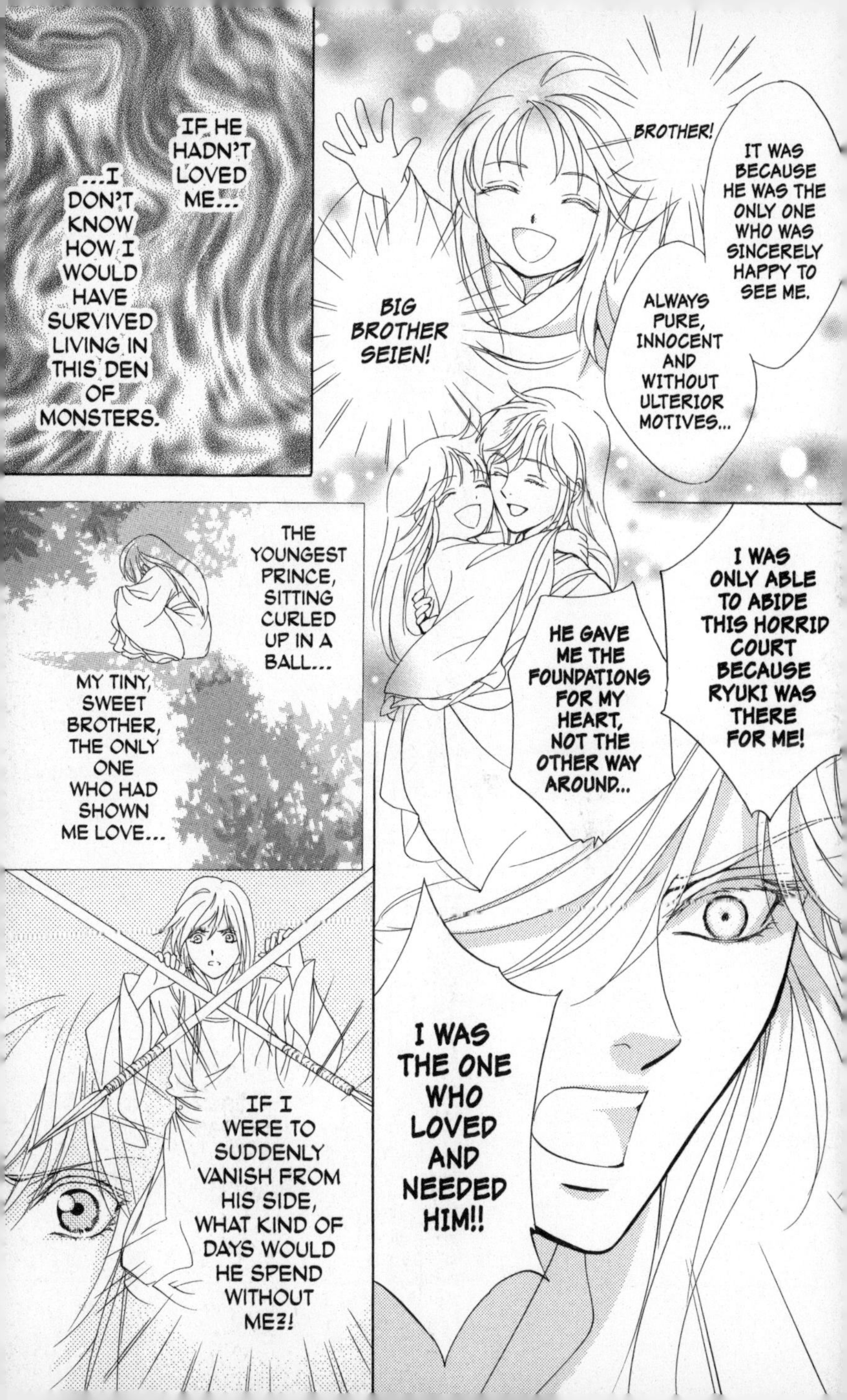
BROTHER!
IT WAS BECAUSE HE WAS THE ONLY ONE WHO WAS SINCERELY HAPPY TO SEE ME.
ALWAYS PURE, INNOCENT AND WITHOUT ULTERIOR MOTIVES...
BIG BROTHER SEIEN!
IF HE HADN'T LOVED ME...
...I DON'T KNOW HOW I WOULD HAVE SURVIVED LIVING IN THIS DEN OF MONSTERS.
I WAS ONLY ABLE TO ABIDE THIS HORRID COURT BECAUSE RYUKI WAS THERE FOR ME!
HE GAVE ME THE FOUNDATIONS FOR MY HEART, NOT THE OTHER WAY AROUND...
THE YOUNGEST PRINCE, SITTING CURLED UP IN A BALL...
MY TINY, SWEET BROTHER, THE ONLY ONE WHO HAD SHOWN ME LOVE...
I WAS THE ONE WHO LOVED AND NEEDED HIM!!
IF I WERE TO SUDDENLY VANISH FROM HIS SIDE, WHAT KIND OF DAYS WOULD HE SPEND WITHOUT ME?!

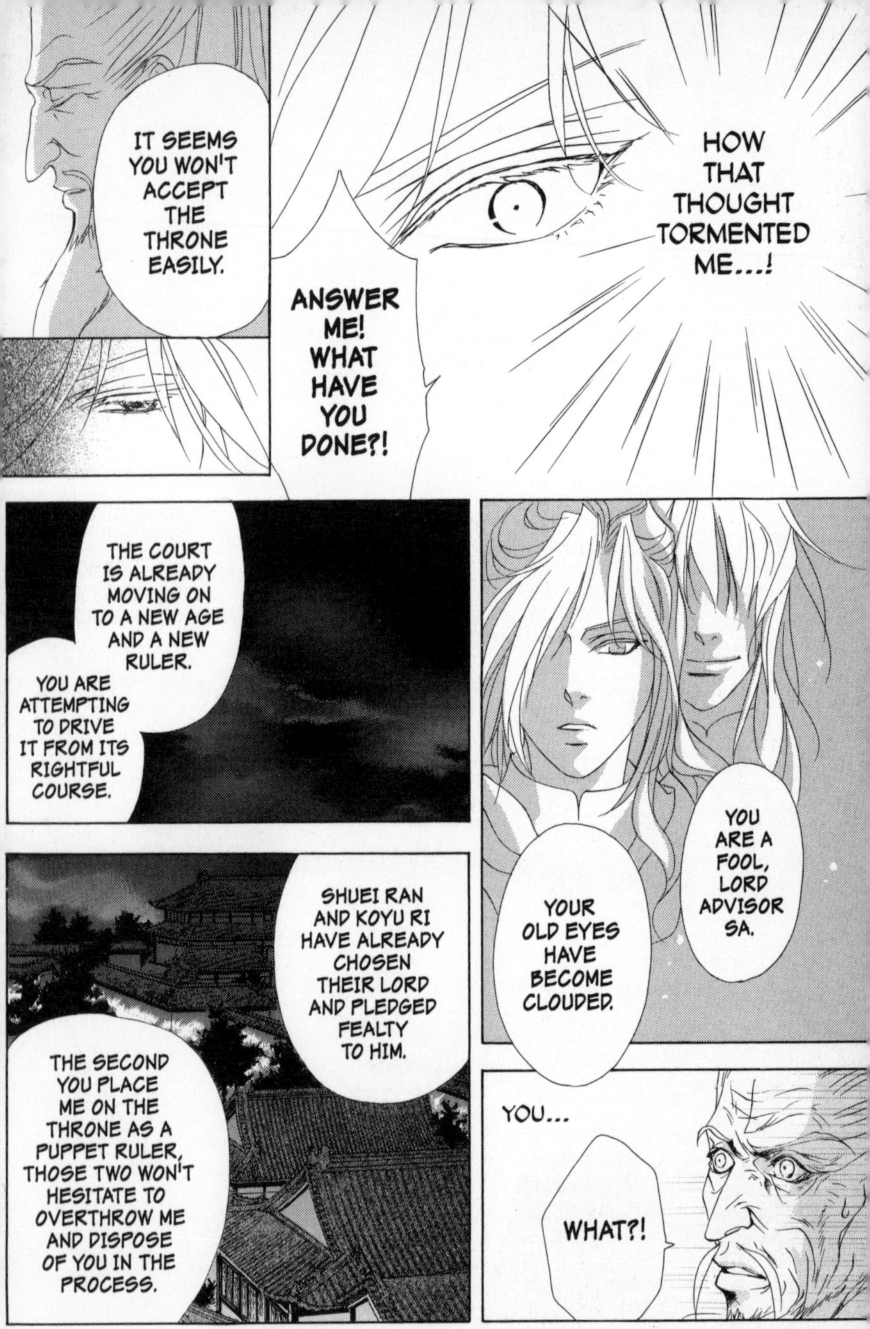
HOW THAT THOUGHT TORMENTED ME...!
ANSWER ME! WHAT HAVE YOU DONE?!
IT SEEMS YOU WON'T ACCEPT THE THRONE EASILY.
YOU ARE A FOOL, LORD ADVISOR SA.
YOUR OLD EYES HAVE BECOME CLOUDED.
THE COURT IS ALREADY MOVING ON TO A NEW AGE AND A NEW RULER.
YOU ARE ATTEMPTING TO DRIVE IT FROM ITS RIGHTFUL COURSE.
SHUEI RAN AND KOYU RI HAVE ALREADY CHOSEN THEIR LORD AND PLEDGED FEALTY TO HIM.
THE SECOND YOU PLACE ME ON THE THRONE AS A PUPPET RULER, THOSE TWO WON'T HESITATE TO OVERTHROW ME AND DISPOSE OF YOU IN THE PROCESS.
YOU...
WHAT?!

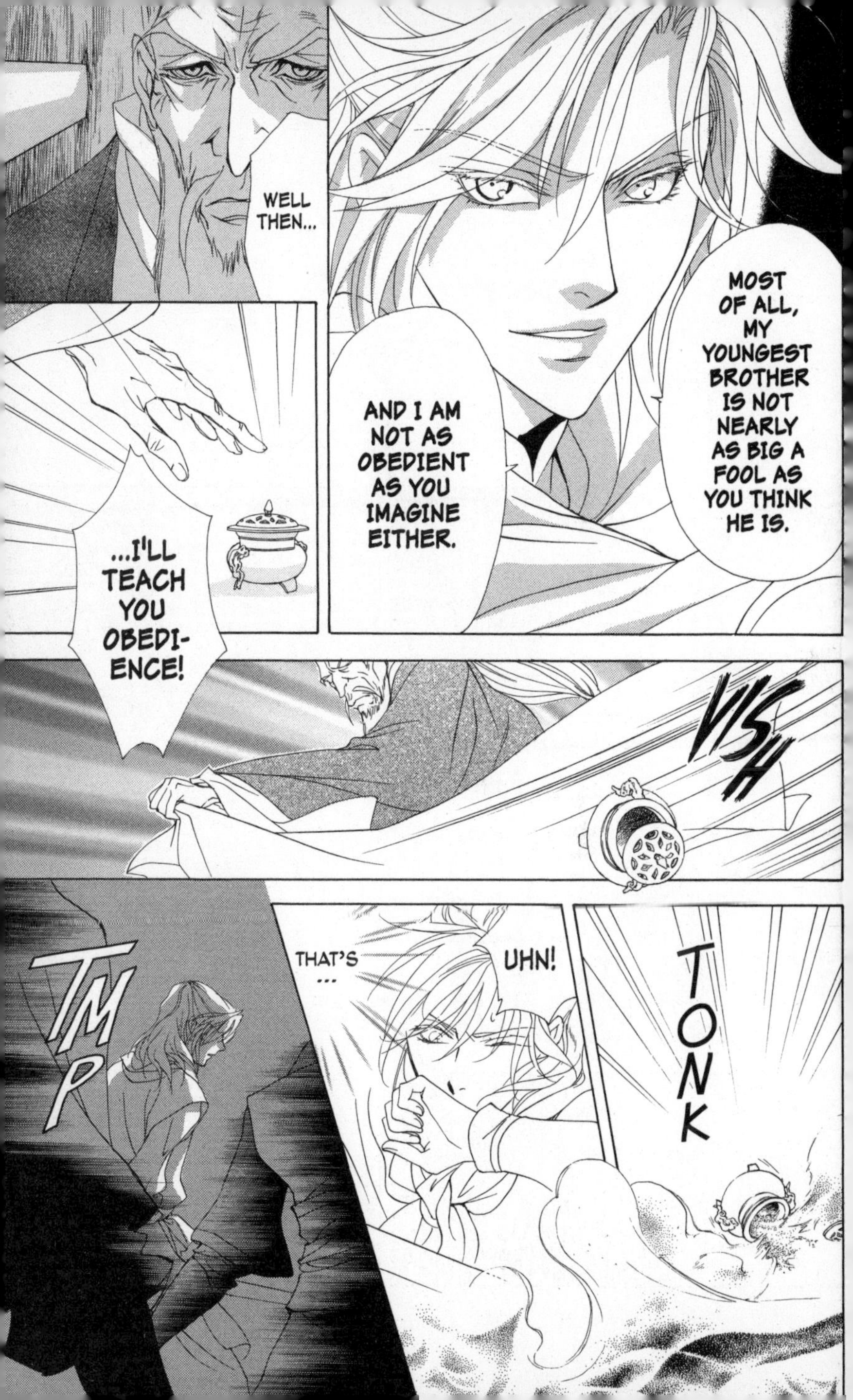
MOST OF ALL, MY YOUNGEST BROTHER IS NOT NEARLY AS BIG A FOOL AS YOU THINK HE IS.
AND I AM NOT AS OBEDIENT AS YOU IMAGINE EITHER.
WELL THEN...
...I'LL TEACH YOU OBEDI-ENCE!
VISH
TONK
UHN!
THAT'S ...
TMP

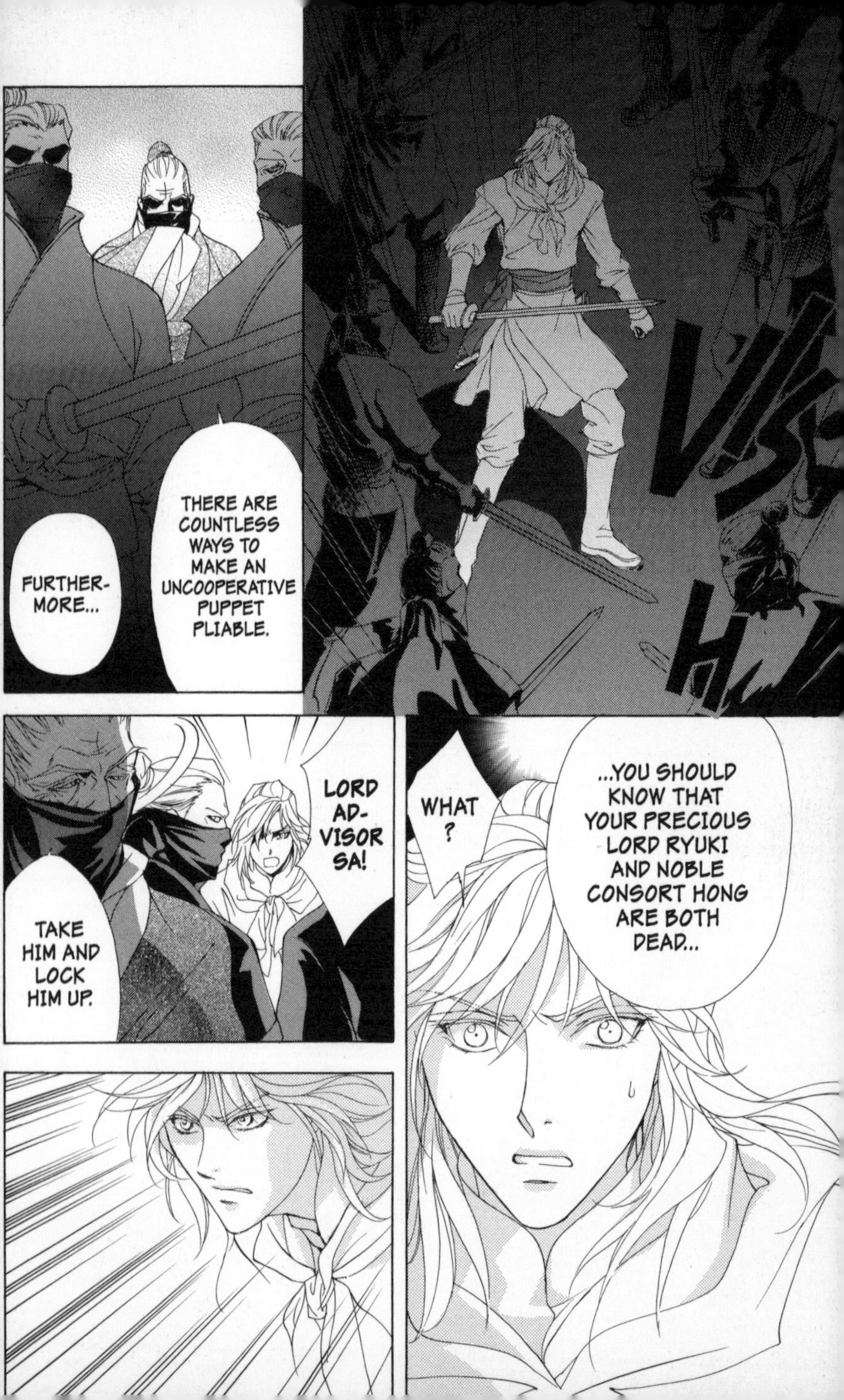
THERE ARE COUNTLESS WAYS TO MAKE AN UNCOOPERATIVE PUPPET PLIABLE.
FURTHER-MORE...
...YOU SHOULD KNOW THAT YOUR PRECIOUS LORD RYUKI AND NOBLE CONSORT HONG ARE BOTH DEAD...
WHAT?
LORD AD-VISOR SA!
TAKE HIM AND LOCK HIM UP.

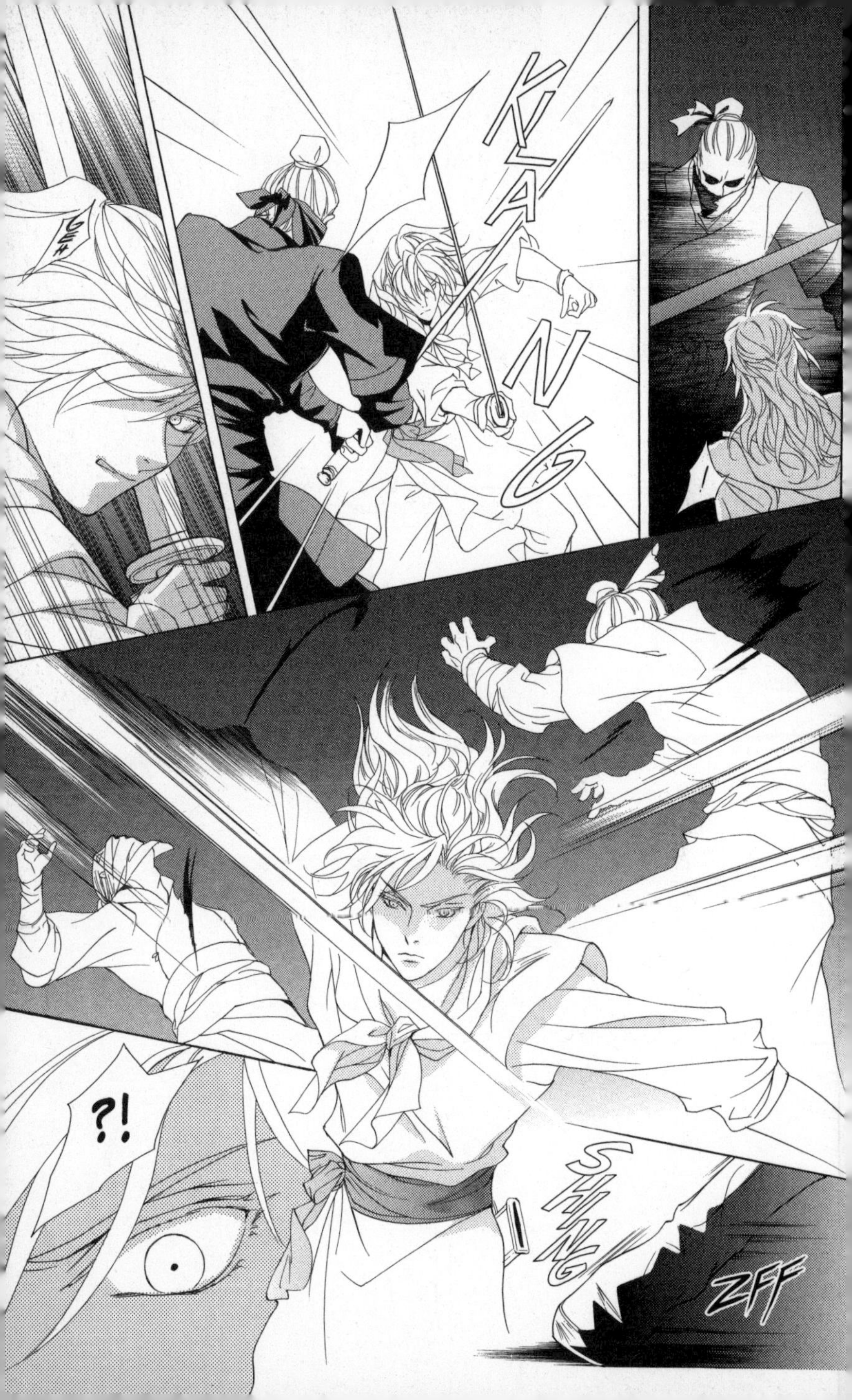
KLANG
GEH
SHING
ZFF
?!

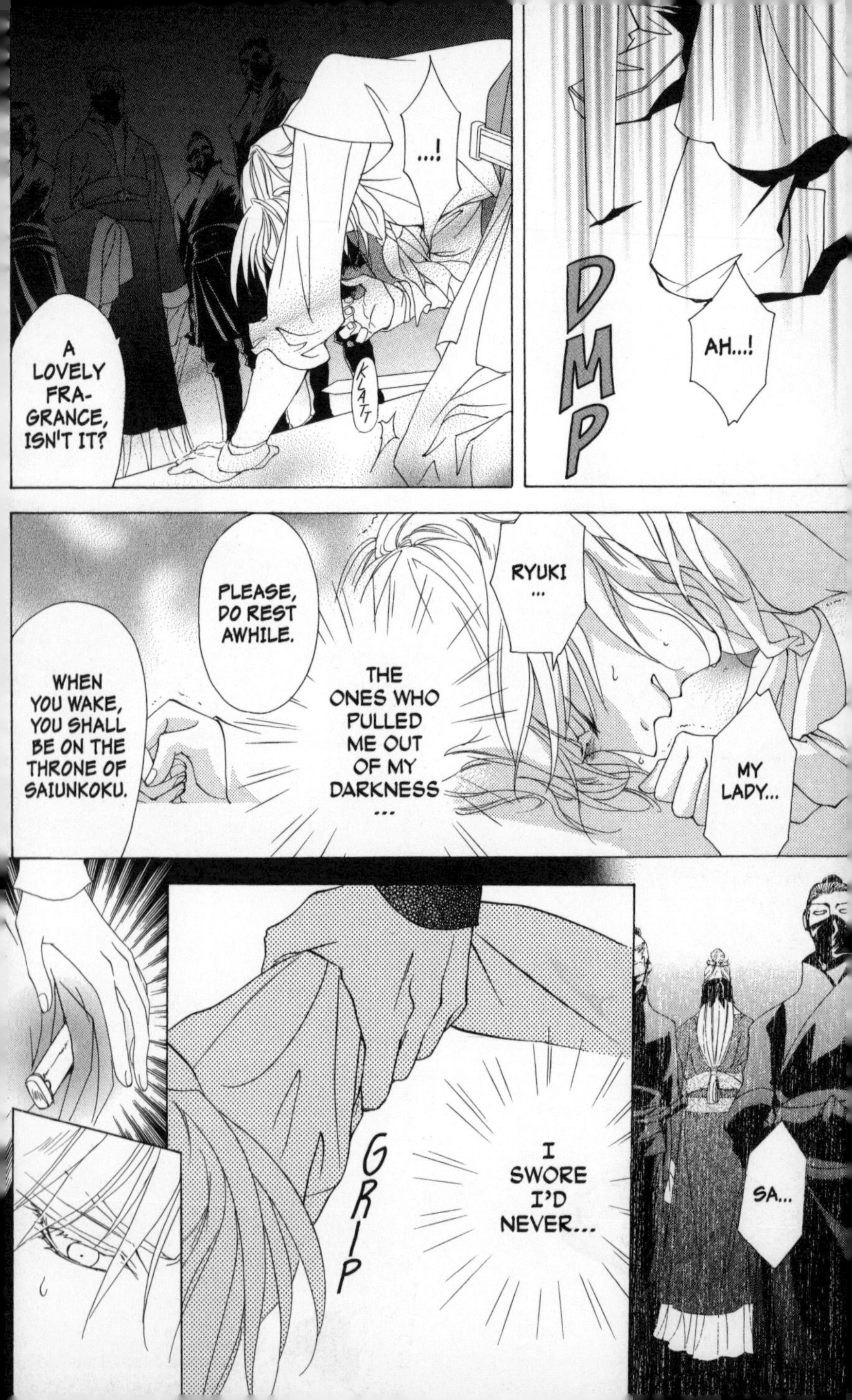
DMP
AH...!
...!
KLATT
A LOVELY FRAGRANCE, ISN'T IT?
RYUKI ...
MY LADY...
THE ONES WHO PULLED ME OUT OF MY DARKNESS ...
PLEASE, DO REST AWHILE.
WHEN YOU WAKE, YOU SHALL BE ON THE THRONE OF SAIUNKOKU.
SA...
I SWORE I'D NEVER...
GRIP

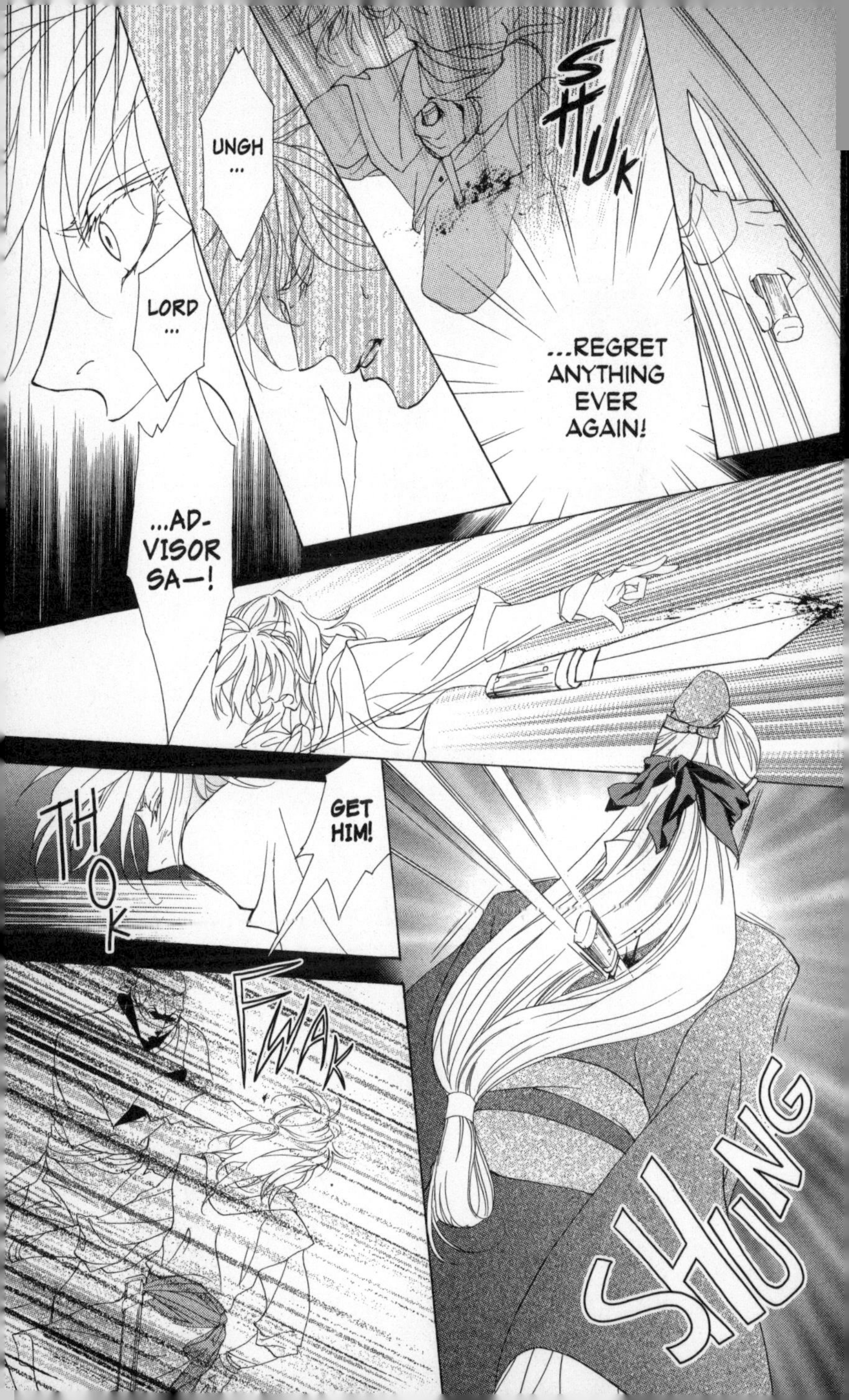
SHUK
...REGRET ANYTHING EVER AGAIN!
UNGH ...
LORD ...
...AD-VISOR SA—!
SHUNG
GET HIM!
THOK
FWAK

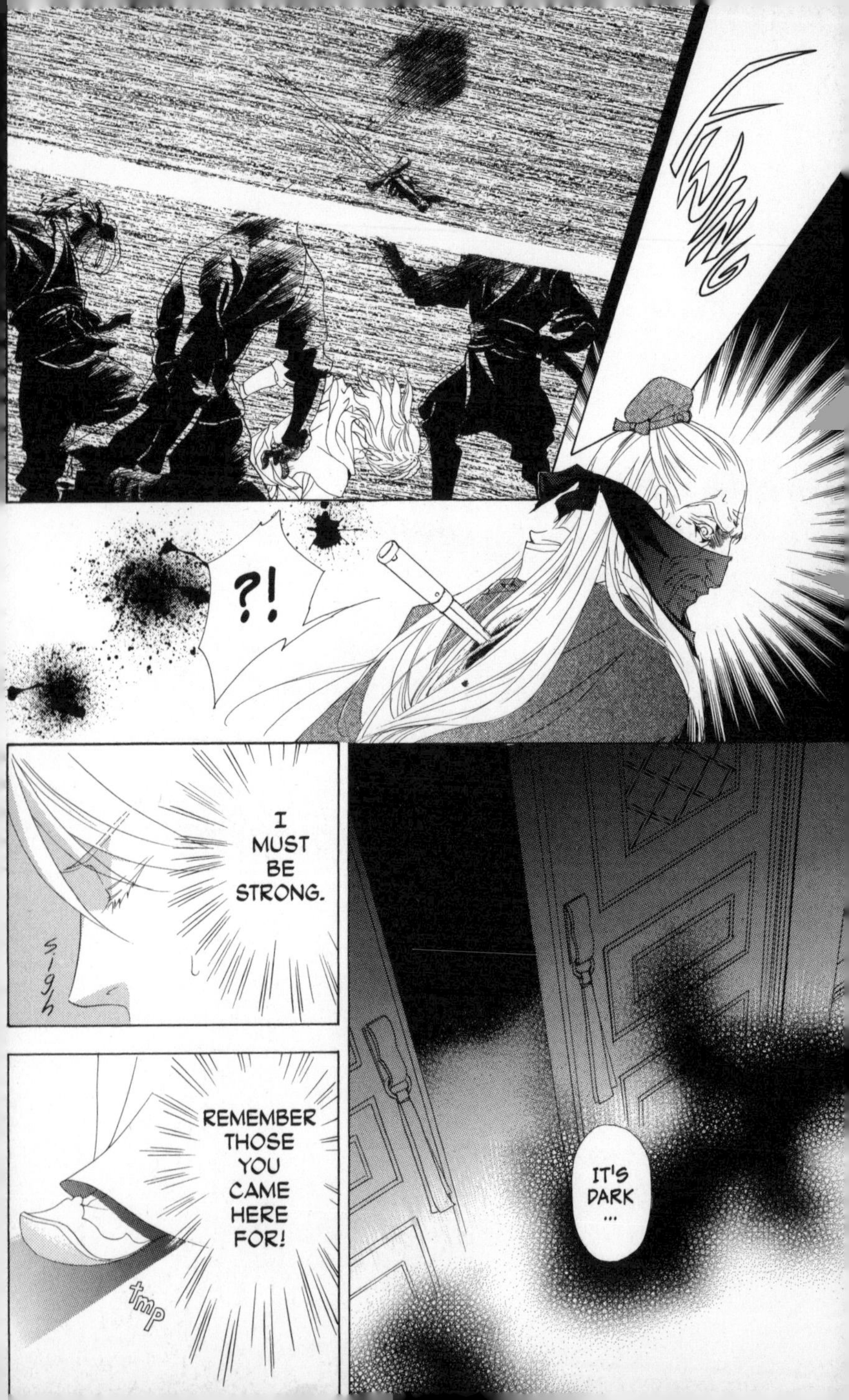
KWING
?!
IT'S DARK ...
I MUST BE STRONG.
sigh
REMEMBER THOSE YOU CAME HERE FOR!
tmp

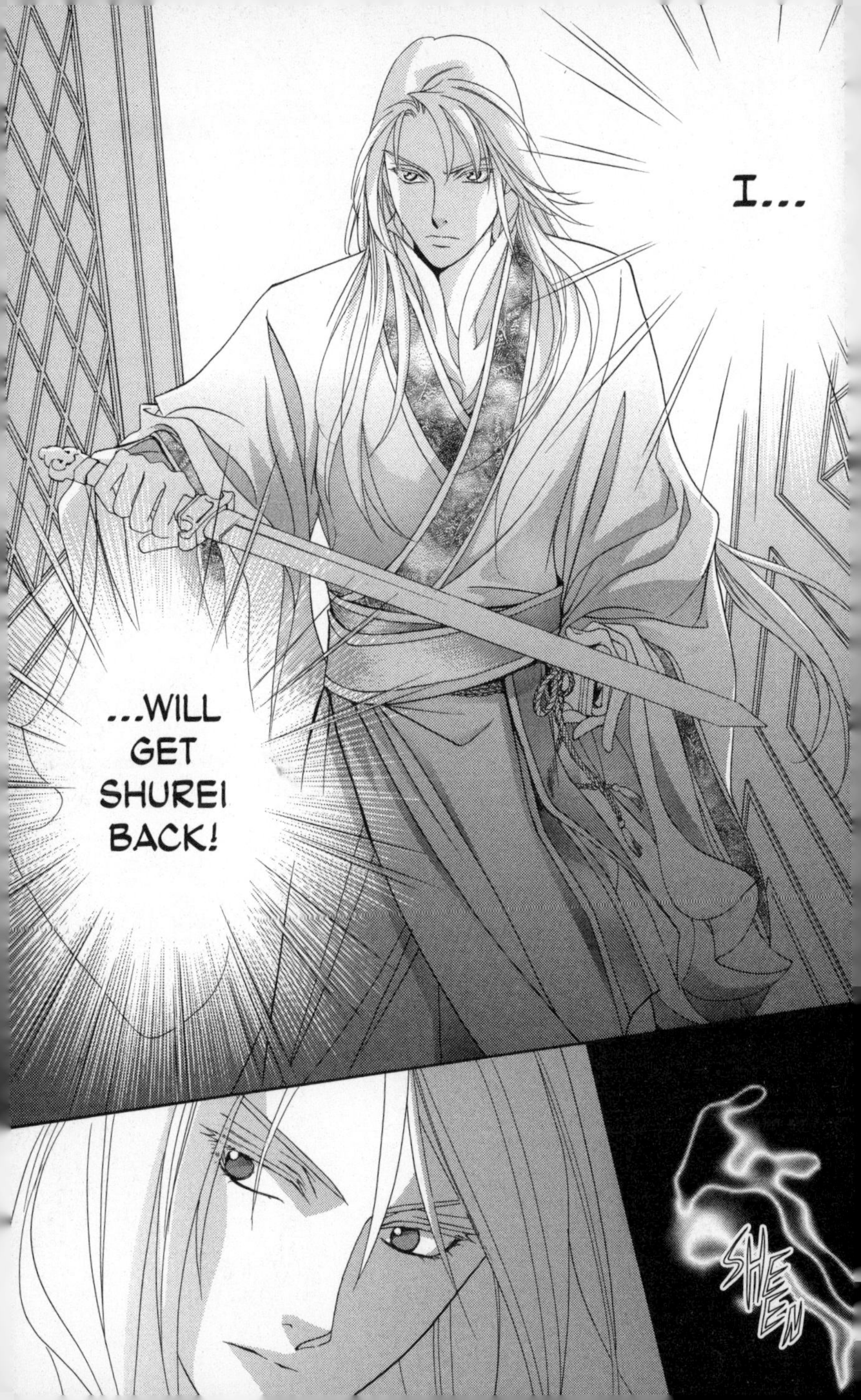
I...
...WILL GET SHUREI BACK!
SHEEN

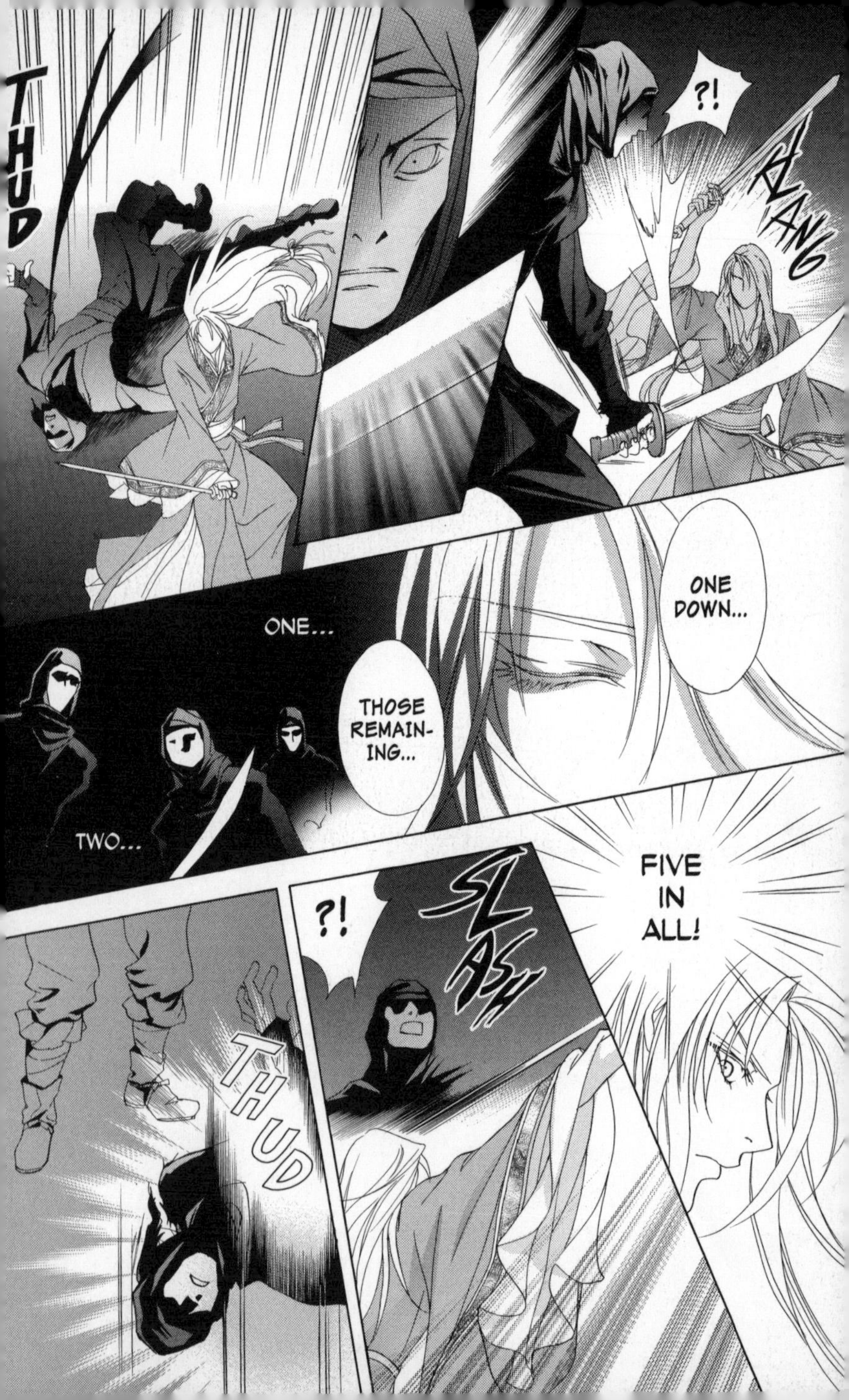
?!
KLANG
THUD
ONE DOWN...
THOSE REMAIN-ING...
ONE...
TWO...
FIVE IN ALL!
?!
SLASH
THUD

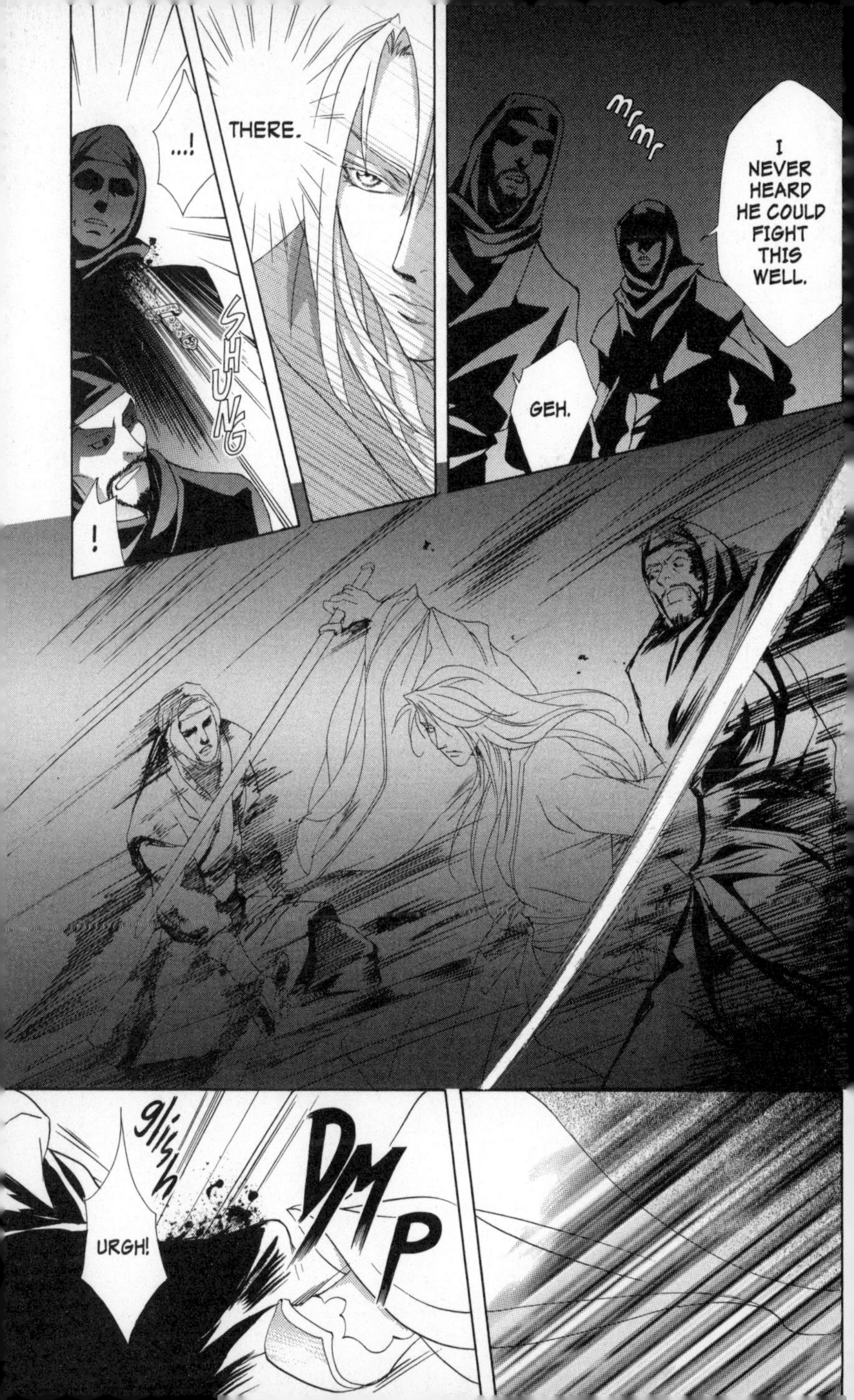

mrmr
I NEVER HEARD HE COULD FIGHT THIS WELL.
GEH.
THERE.
...!
SHUNG
!
DMP
glish
URGH!

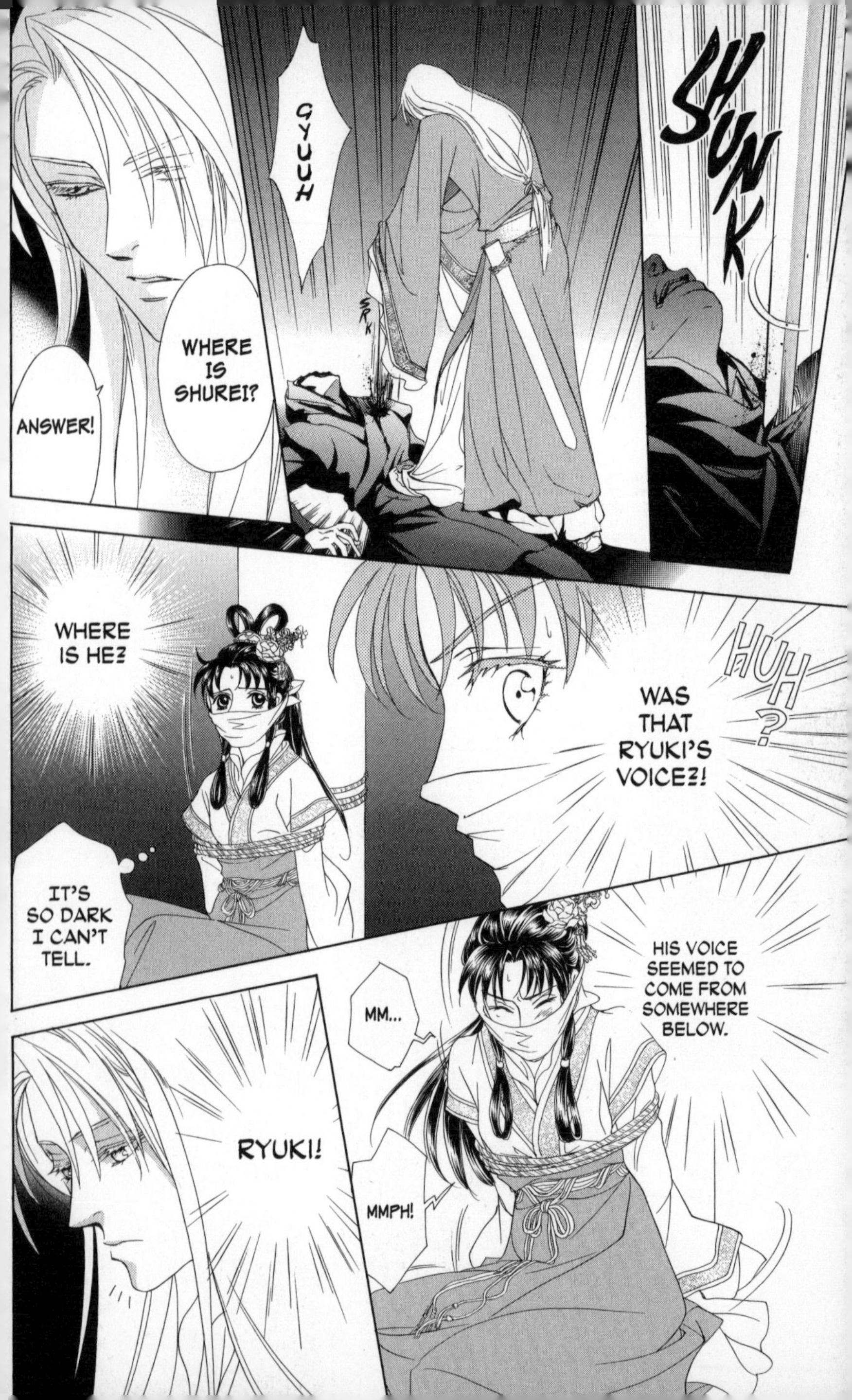
SHUNK
GYUUH
SRK
WHERE IS SHUREI?
ANSWER!
HUH?
WAS THAT RYUKI'S VOICE?!
WHERE IS HE?
IT'S SO DARK I CAN'T TELL.
HIS VOICE SEEMED TO COME FROM SOMEWHERE BELOW.
MM...
MMPH!
RYUKI!

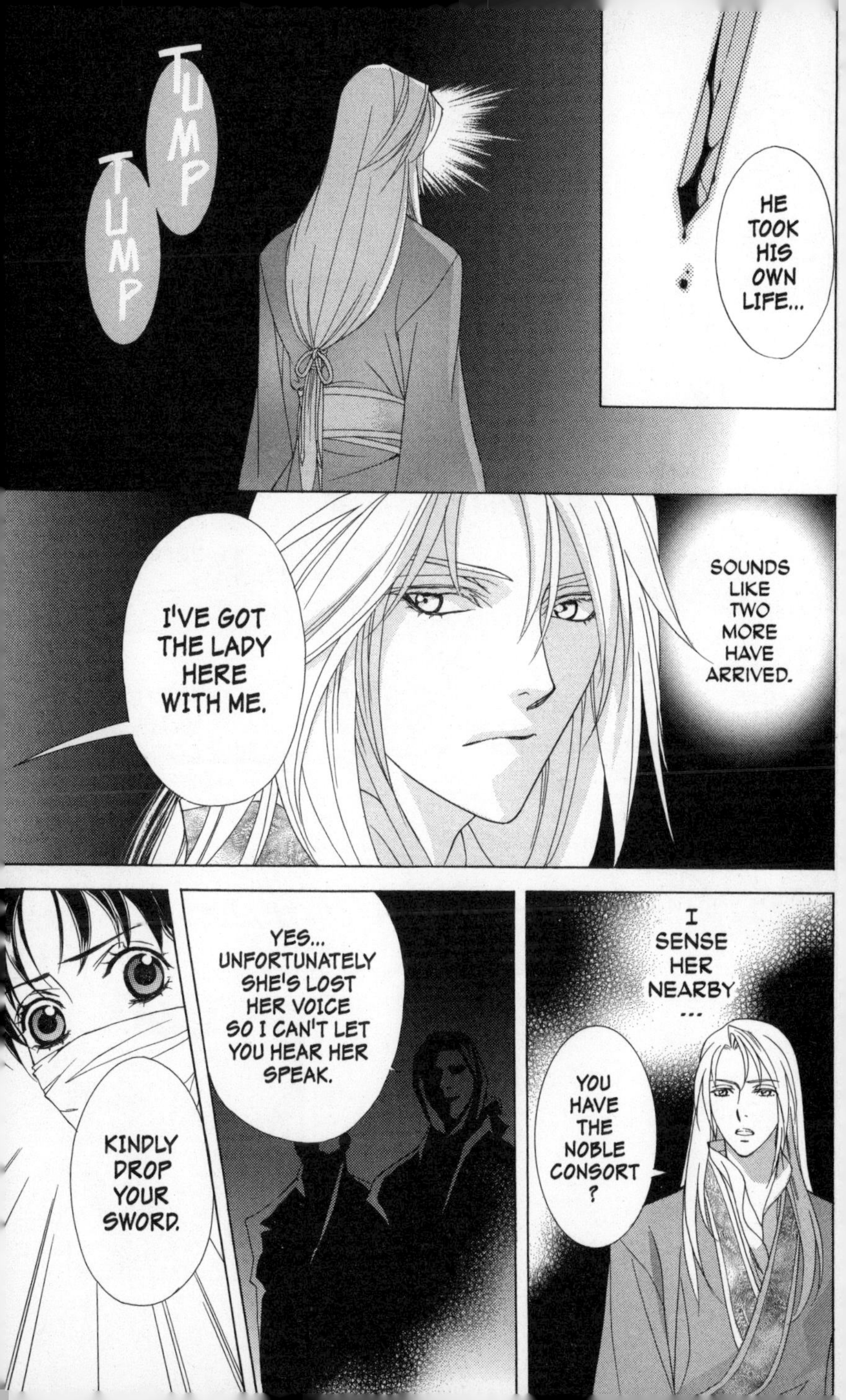
HE TOOK HIS OWN LIFE...
TUMP
TUMP
SOUNDS LIKE TWO MORE HAVE ARRIVED.
I'VE GOT THE LADY HERE WITH ME.
I SENSE HER NEARBY...
YOU HAVE THE NOBLE CONSORT?
YES... UNFORTUNATELY SHE'S LOST HER VOICE SO I CAN'T LET YOU HEAR HER SPEAK.
KINDLY DROP YOUR SWORD.

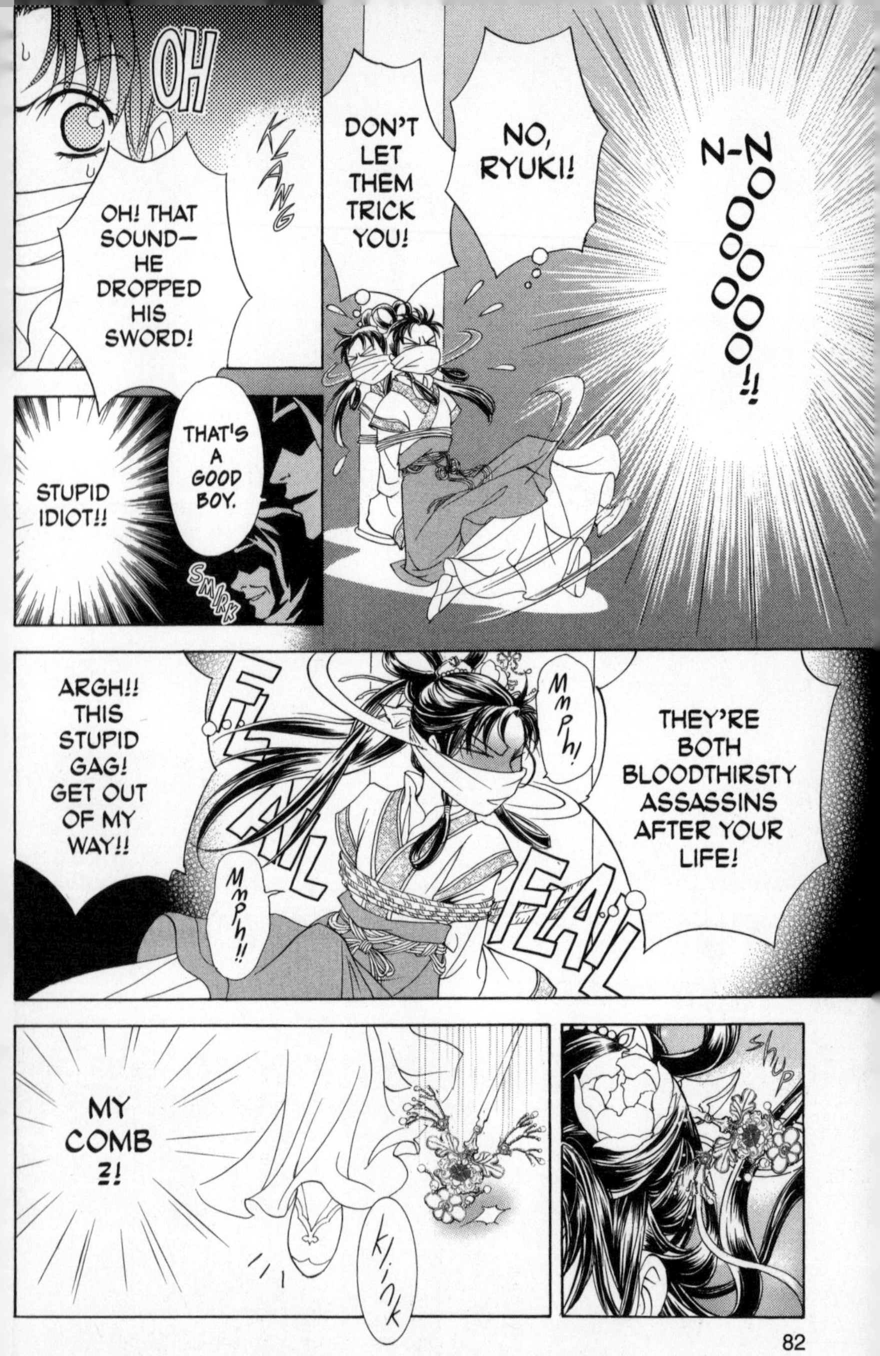
N-NOOOOOO!!
NO, RYUKI!
DON'T LET THEM TRICK YOU!
OH
KLANG
OH! THAT SOUND— HE DROPPED HIS SWORD!
THAT'S A GOOD BOY.
SMIRK
STUPID IDIOT!!
THEY'RE BOTH BLOODTHIRSTY ASSASSINS AFTER YOUR LIFE!
Mmph!
FLAIL
FLAIL
Mmph!!
ARGH!! THIS STUPID GAG! GET OUT OF MY WAY!!
shup
klink
MY COMB?!

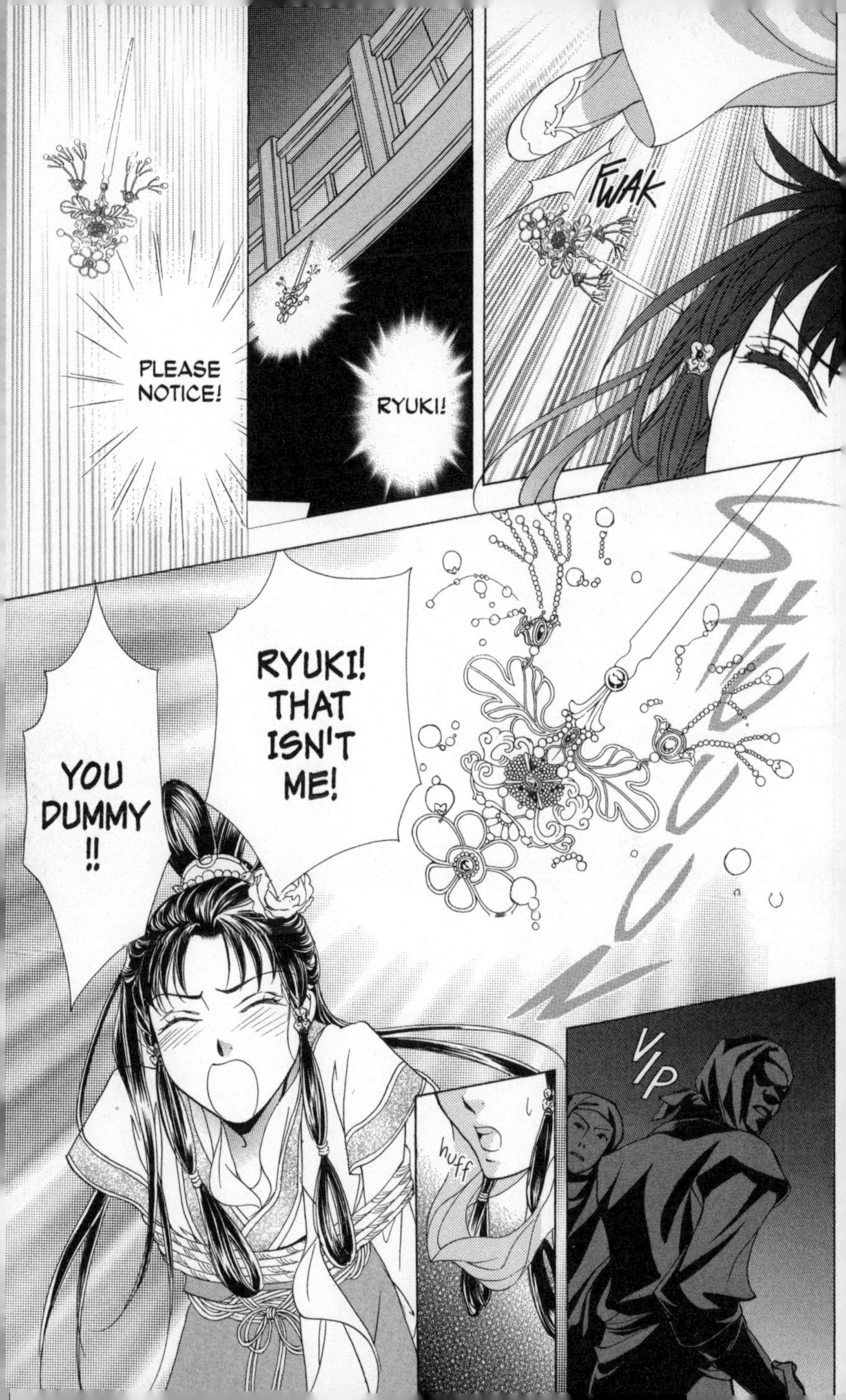
FWAK
RYUKI!
PLEASE NOTICE!
SHUUUN
RYUKI! THAT ISN'T ME!
YOU DUMMY !!
VIP
huff

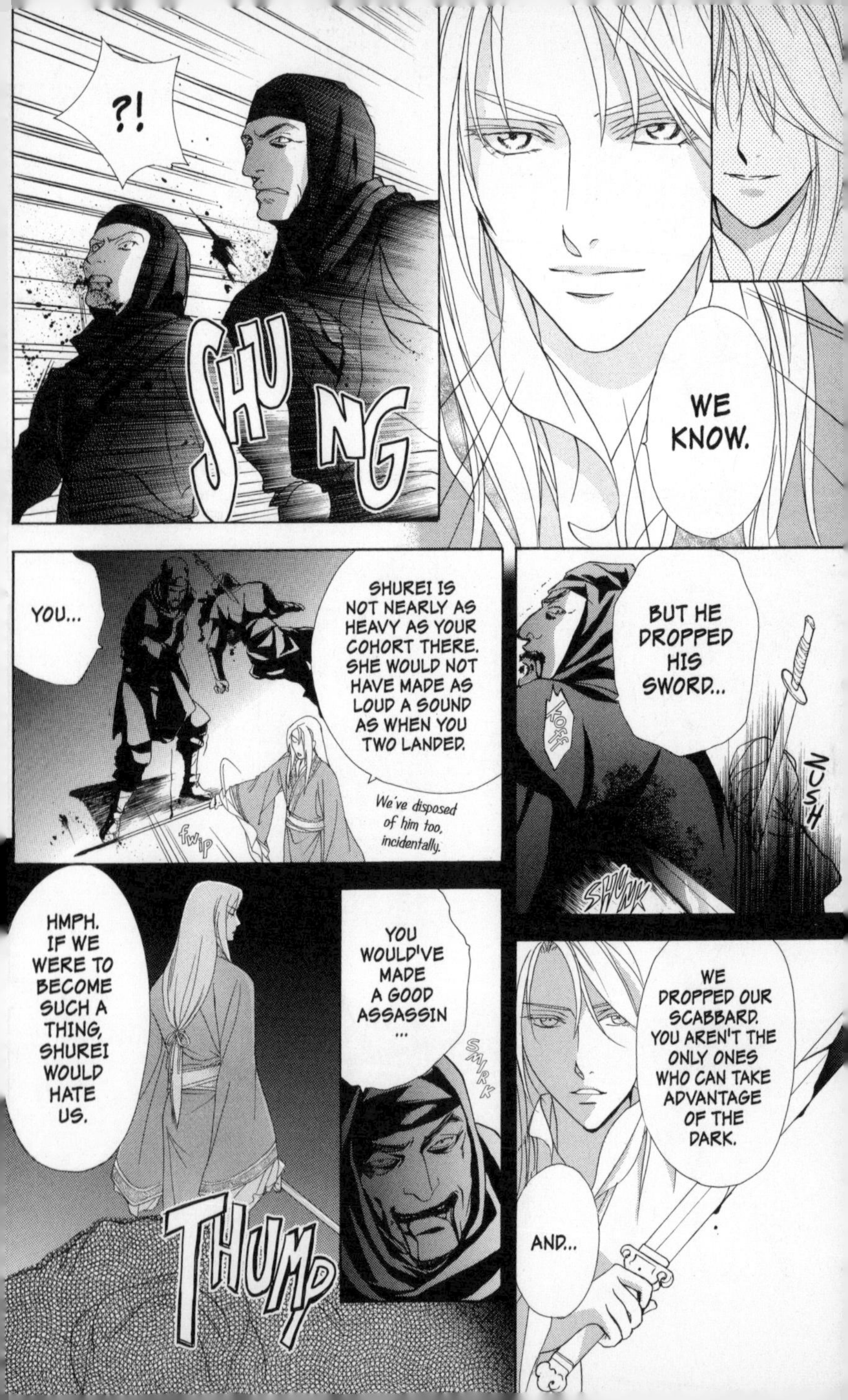
WE KNOW.
?!
SHUNG
BUT HE DROPPED HIS SWORD...
koff
ZUSH
SHUNK
SHUREI IS NOT NEARLY AS HEAVY AS YOUR COHORT THERE. SHE WOULD NOT HAVE MADE AS LOUD A SOUND AS WHEN YOU TWO LANDED.
YOU...
We've disposed of him too, incidentally.
fwip
WE DROPPED OUR SCABBARD. YOU AREN'T THE ONLY ONES WHO CAN TAKE ADVANTAGE OF THE DARK.
AND...
YOU WOULD'VE MADE A GOOD ASSASSIN ...
SMIRK
HMPH. IF WE WERE TO BECOME SUCH A THING, SHUREI WOULD HATE US.
THUMP

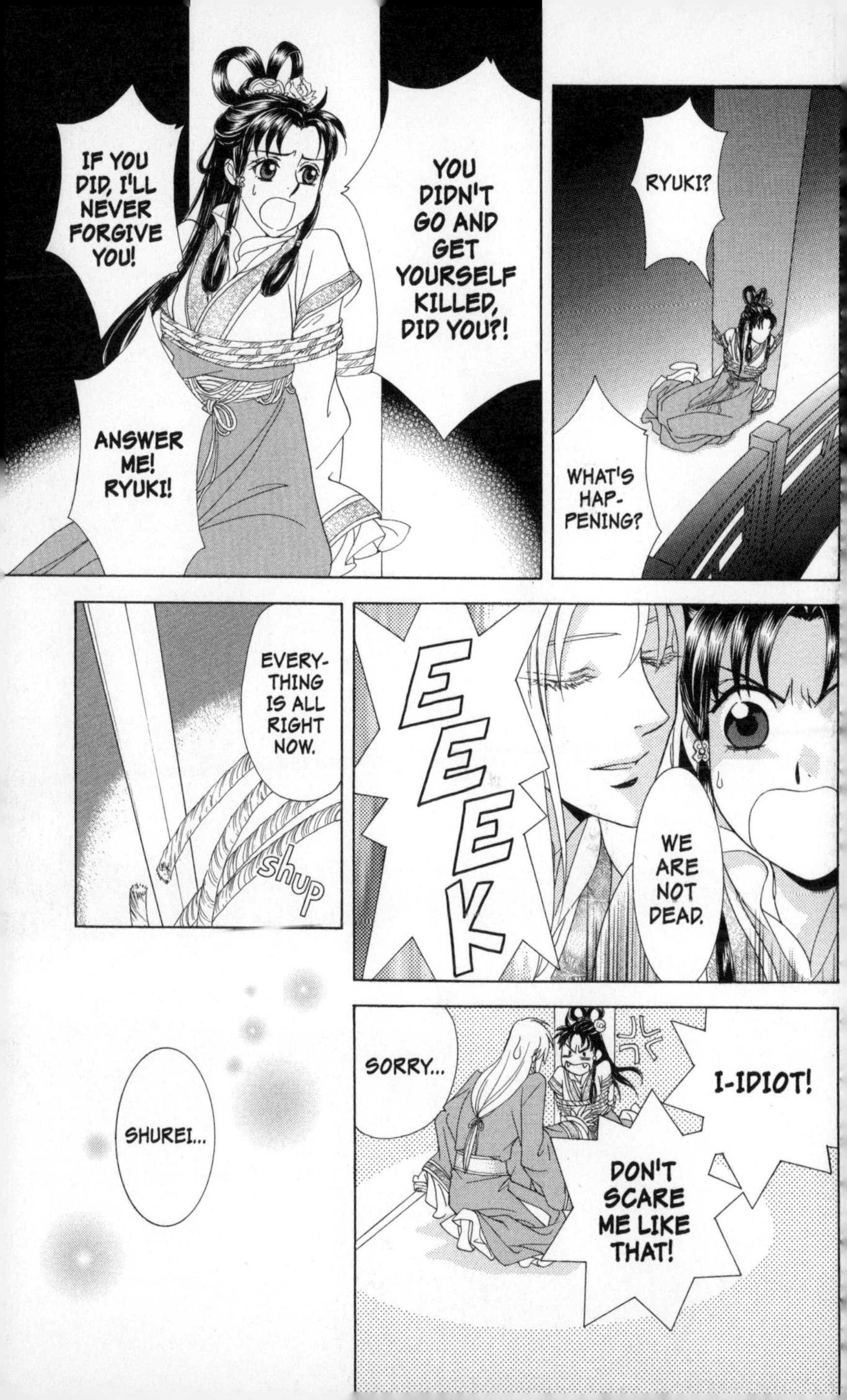
RYUKI?
WHAT'S HAP-PENING?
YOU DIDN'T GO AND GET YOURSELF KILLED, DID YOU?!
IF YOU DID, I'LL NEVER FORGIVE YOU!
ANSWER ME! RYUKI!
EEEEK
WE ARE NOT DEAD.
EVERY-THING IS ALL RIGHT NOW.
shup
I-IDIOT!
DON'T SCARE ME LIKE THAT!
SORRY...
SHUREI...

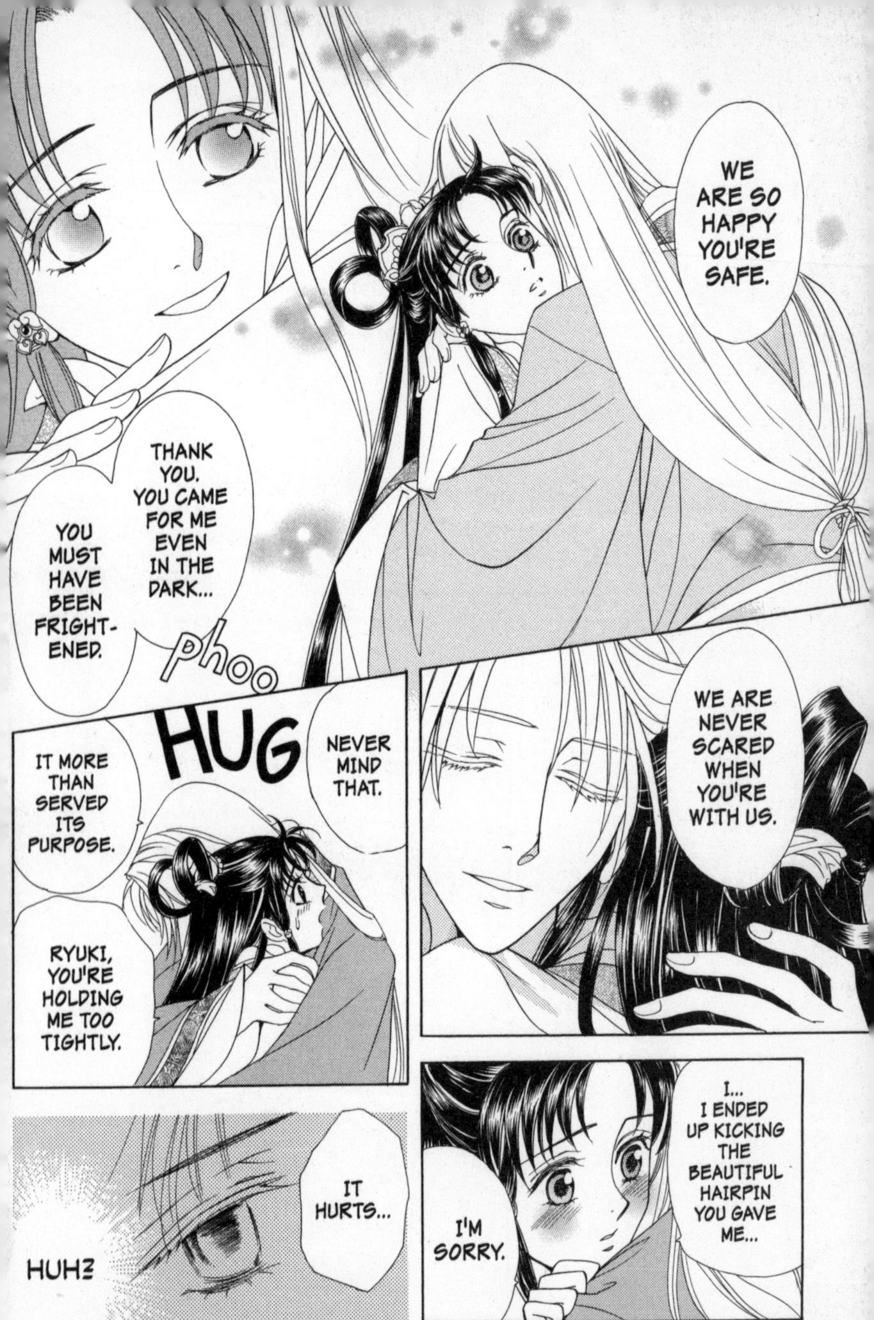
WE ARE SO HAPPY YOU'RE SAFE.
THANK YOU. YOU CAME FOR ME EVEN IN THE DARK...
YOU MUST HAVE BEEN FRIGHT-ENED.
phoo
WE ARE NEVER SCARED WHEN YOU'RE WITH US.
HUG
NEVER MIND THAT.
IT MORE THAN SERVED ITS PURPOSE.
RYUKI, YOU'RE HOLDING ME TOO TIGHTLY.
I... I ENDED UP KICKING THE BEAUTIFUL HAIRPIN YOU GAVE ME...
I'M SORRY.
IT HURTS...
HUH?

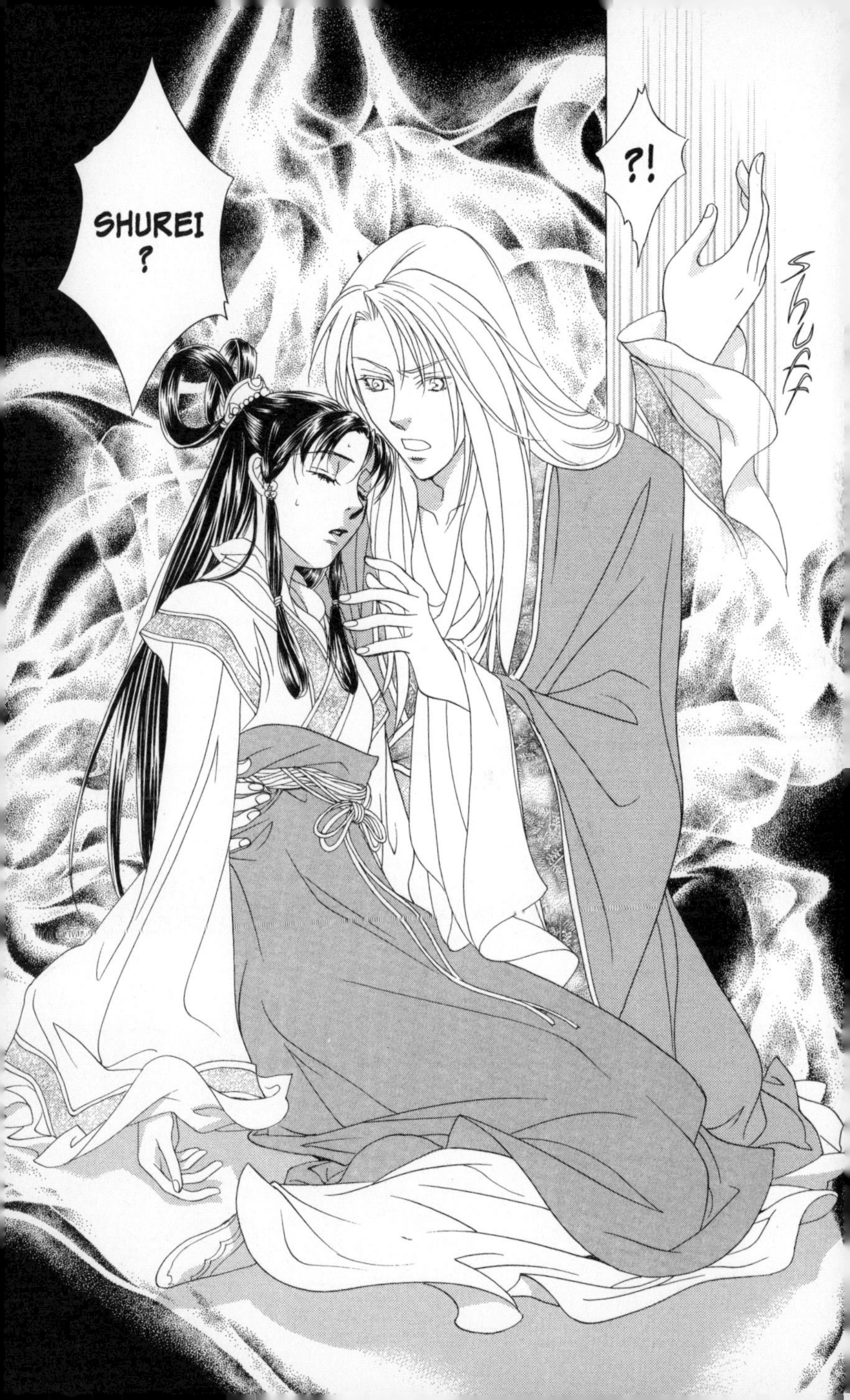
?!
SHUFFF
SHUREI ?

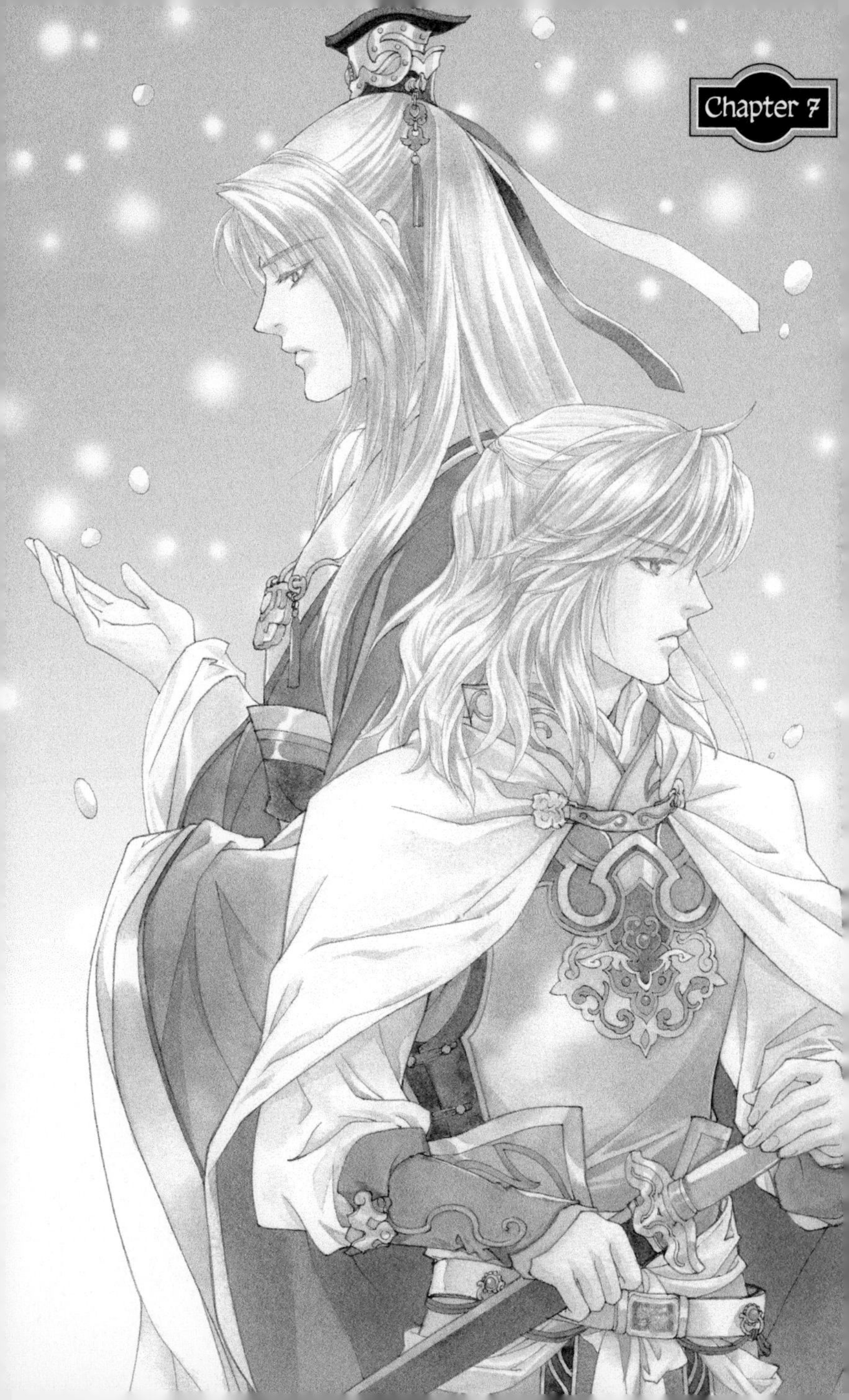
Chapter 7

The Story of
SAIUNKOKU

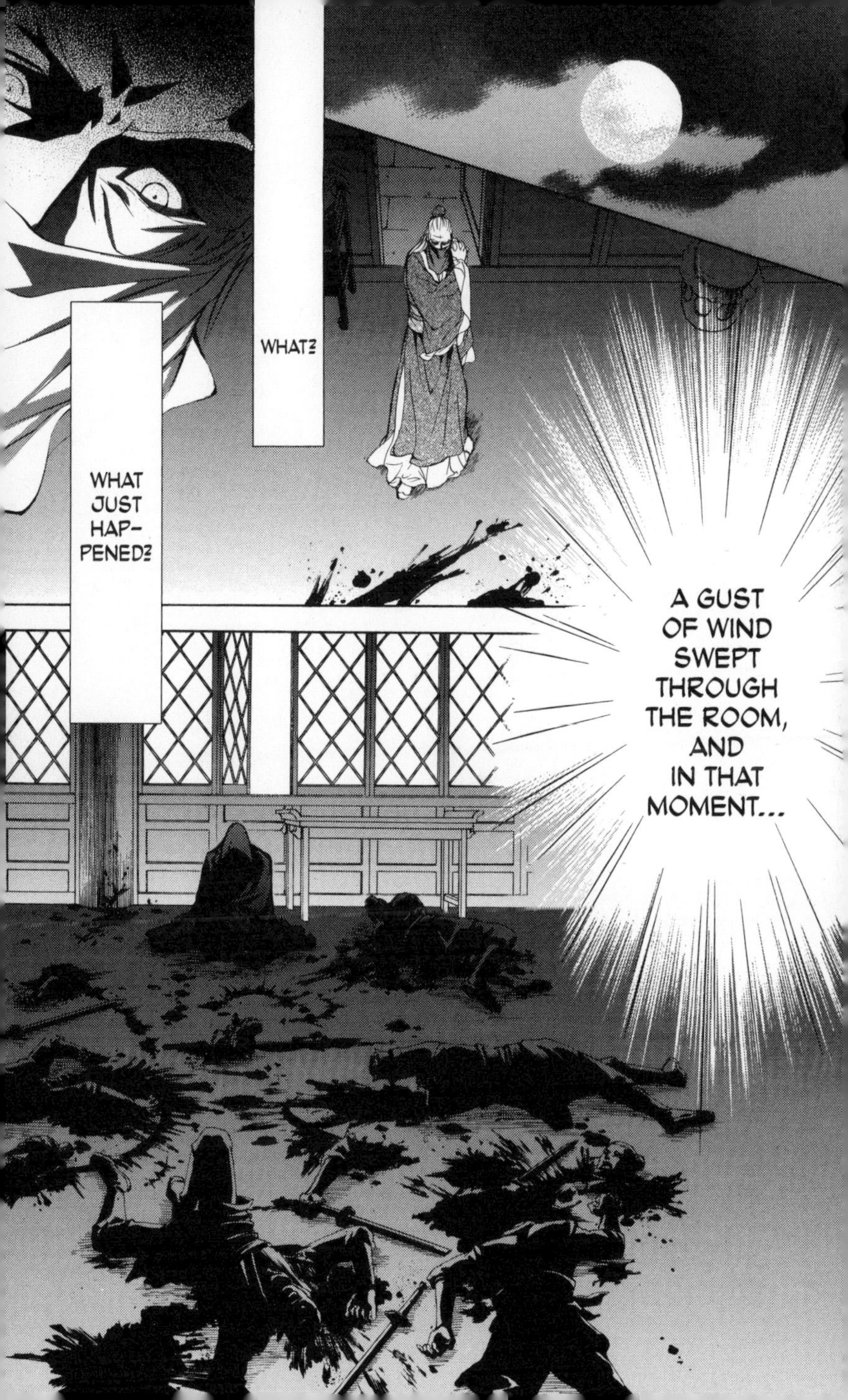
A GUST OF WIND SWEPT THROUGH THE ROOM, AND IN THAT MOMENT...
WHAT?
WHAT JUST HAP-PENED?

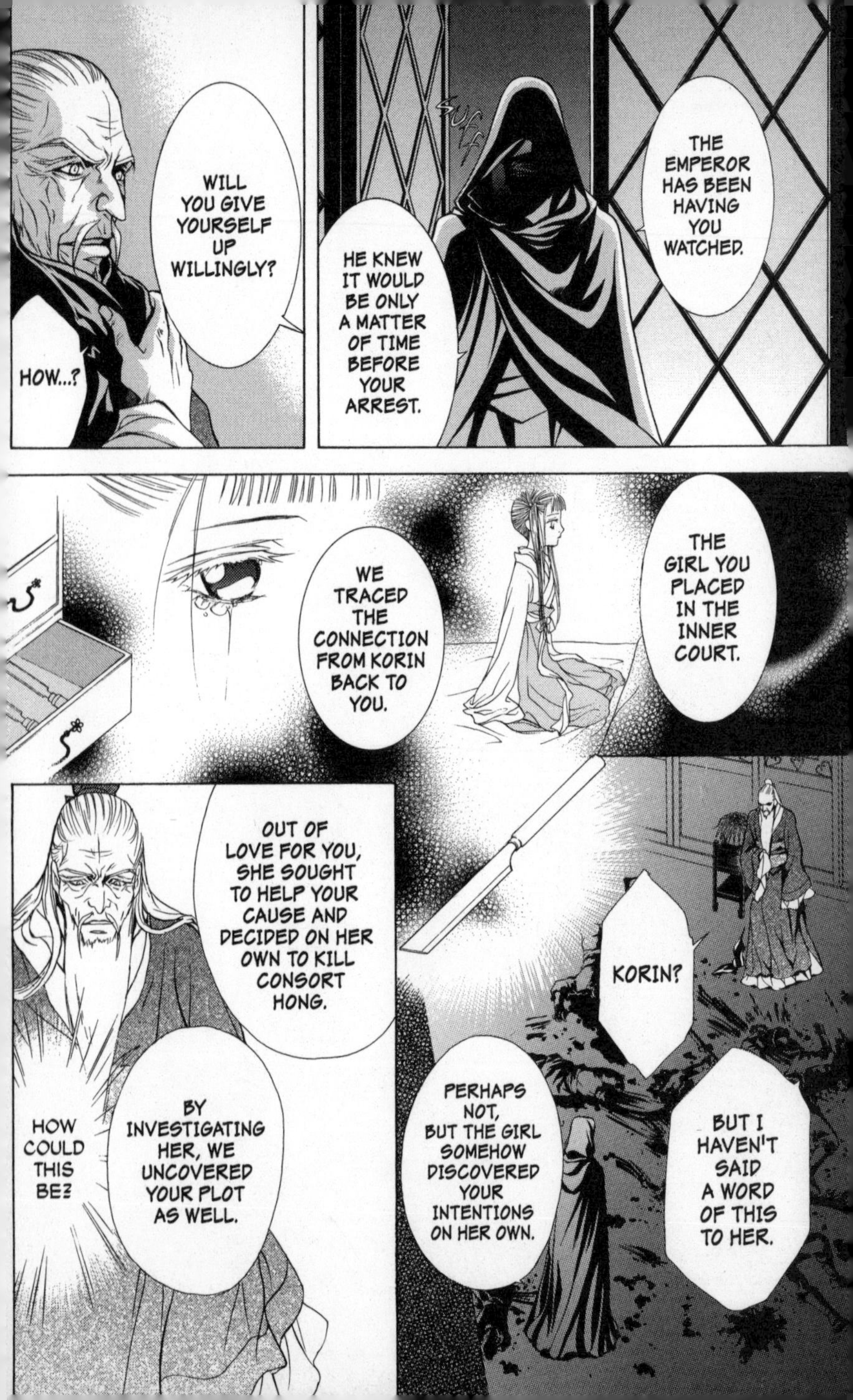
THE EMPEROR HAS BEEN HAVING YOU WATCHED.
HE KNEW IT WOULD BE ONLY A MATTER OF TIME BEFORE YOUR ARREST.
WILL YOU GIVE YOURSELF UP WILLINGLY?
HOW...?
THE GIRL YOU PLACED IN THE INNER COURT.
WE TRACED THE CONNECTION FROM KORIN BACK TO YOU.
KORIN?
BUT I HAVEN'T SAID A WORD OF THIS TO HER.
PERHAPS NOT, BUT THE GIRL SOMEHOW DISCOVERED YOUR INTENTIONS ON HER OWN.
OUT OF LOVE FOR YOU, SHE SOUGHT TO HELP YOUR CAUSE AND DECIDED ON HER OWN TO KILL CONSORT HONG.
BY INVESTIGATING HER, WE UNCOVERED YOUR PLOT AS WELL.
HOW COULD THIS BE?

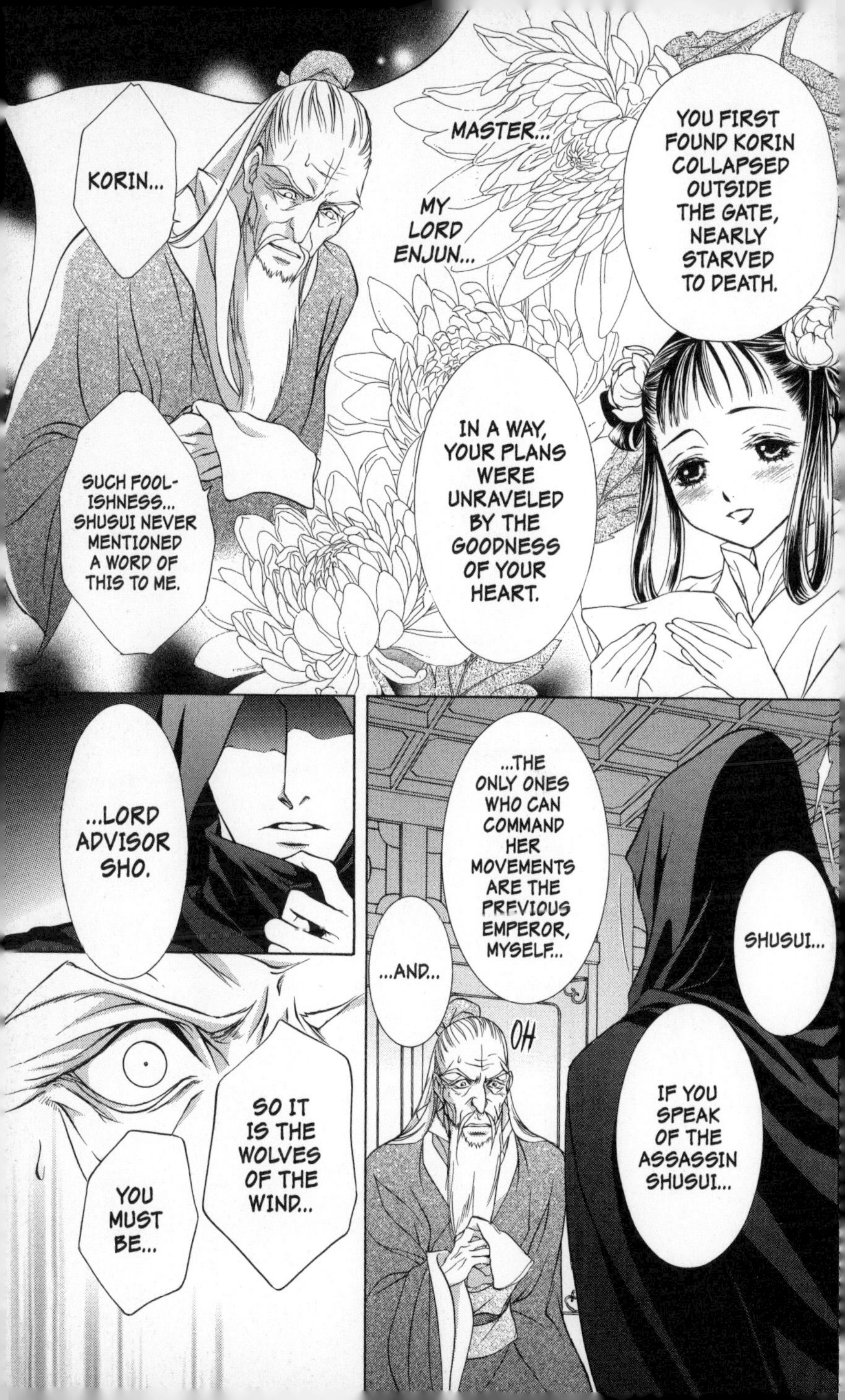
YOU FIRST FOUND KORIN COLLAPSED OUTSIDE THE GATE, NEARLY STARVED TO DEATH.
MASTER...
MY LORD ENJUN...
IN A WAY, YOUR PLANS WERE UNRAVELED BY THE GOODNESS OF YOUR HEART.
KORIN...
SUCH FOOL-ISHNESS... SHUSUI NEVER MENTIONED A WORD OF THIS TO ME.
SHUSUI...
IF YOU SPEAK OF THE ASSASSIN SHUSUI...
...THE ONLY ONES WHO CAN COMMAND HER MOVEMENTS ARE THE PREVIOUS EMPEROR, MYSELF...
...AND...
OH
...LORD ADVISOR SHO.
SO IT IS THE WOLVES OF THE WIND...
YOU MUST BE...

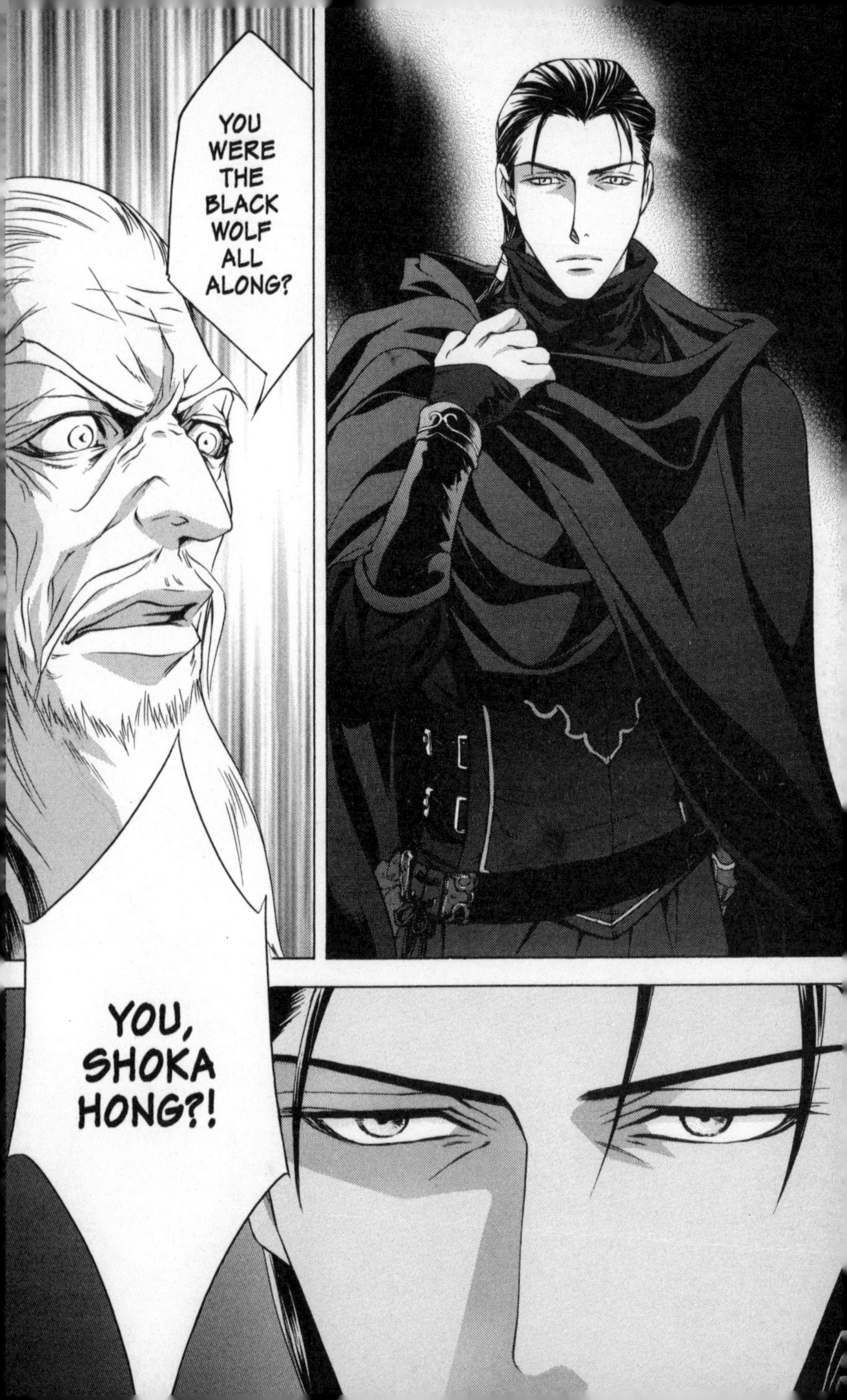
YOU WERE THE BLACK WOLF ALL ALONG?
YOU, SHOKA HONG?!

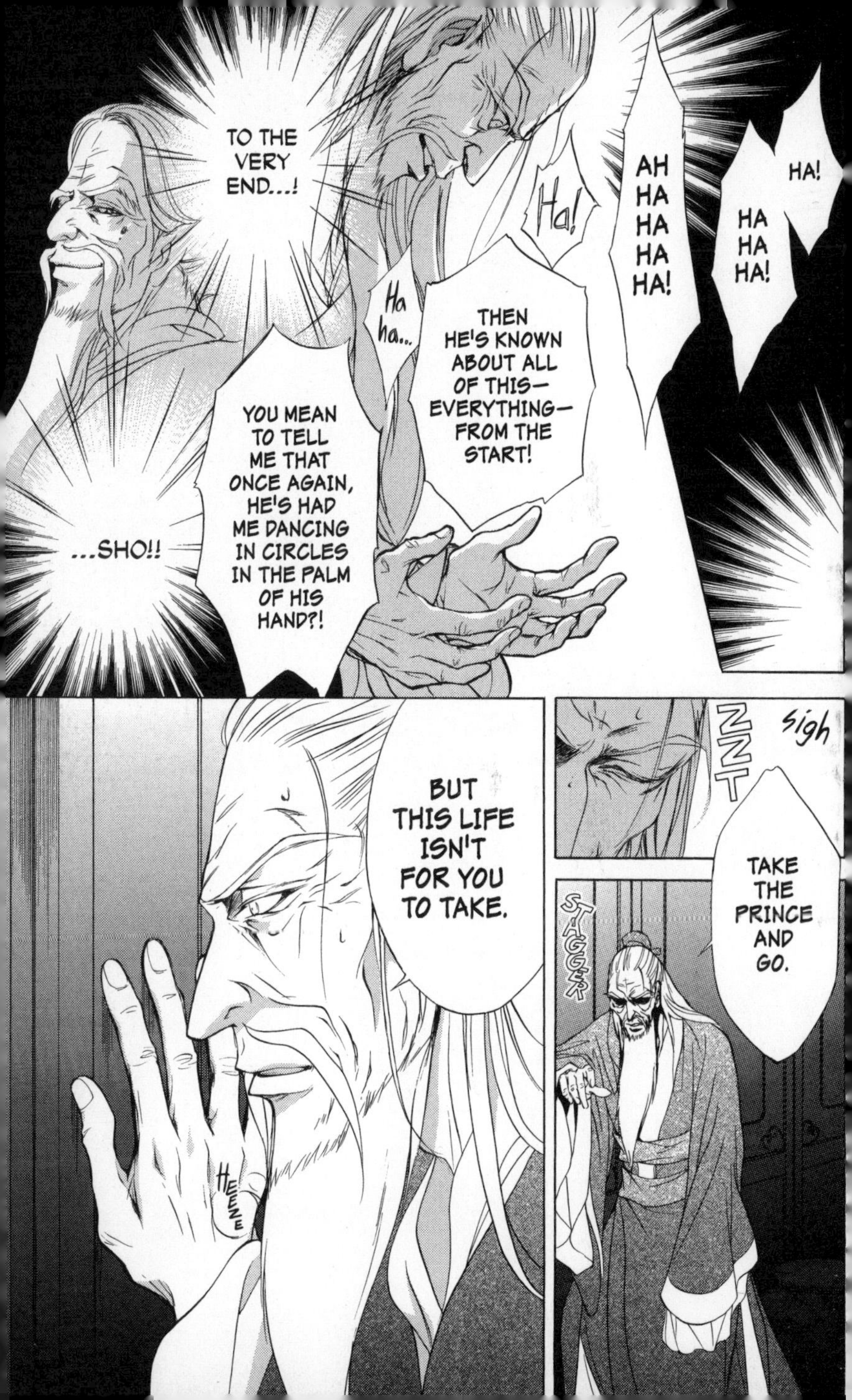
HA! HA HA HA!
AH HA HA HA HA!
Ha!
THEN HE'S KNOWN ABOUT ALL OF THIS— EVERYTHING— FROM THE START!
Ha ha...
TO THE VERY END...!
YOU MEAN TO TELL ME THAT ONCE AGAIN, HE'S HAD ME DANCING IN CIRCLES IN THE PALM OF HIS HAND?!
...SHO!!
sigh
ZZT
TAKE THE PRINCE AND GO.
STAGGER
BUT THIS LIFE ISN'T FOR YOU TO TAKE.
HEEZE

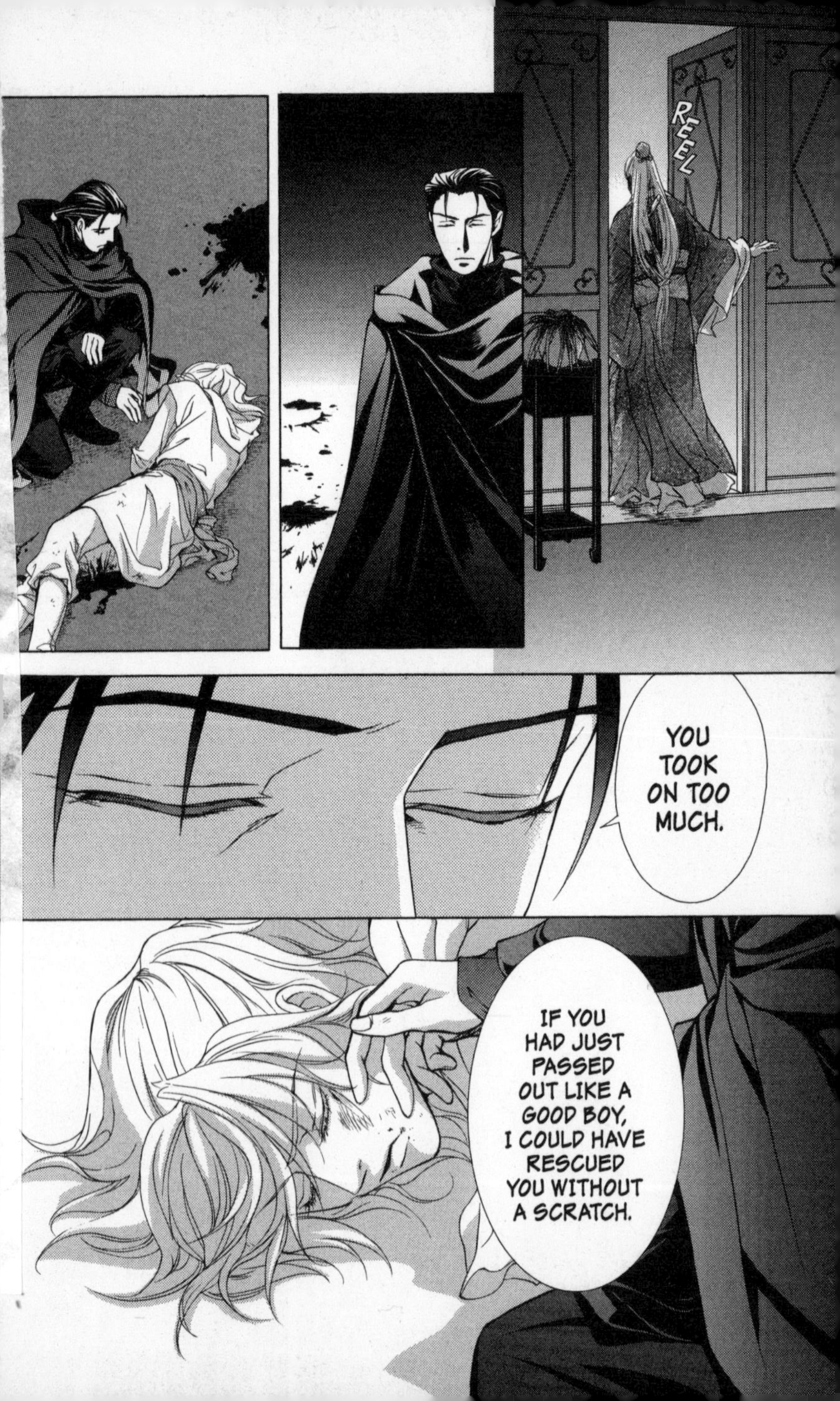
REEL
YOU TOOK ON TOO MUCH.
IF YOU HAD JUST PASSED OUT LIKE A GOOD BOY, I COULD HAVE RESCUED YOU WITHOUT A SCRATCH.

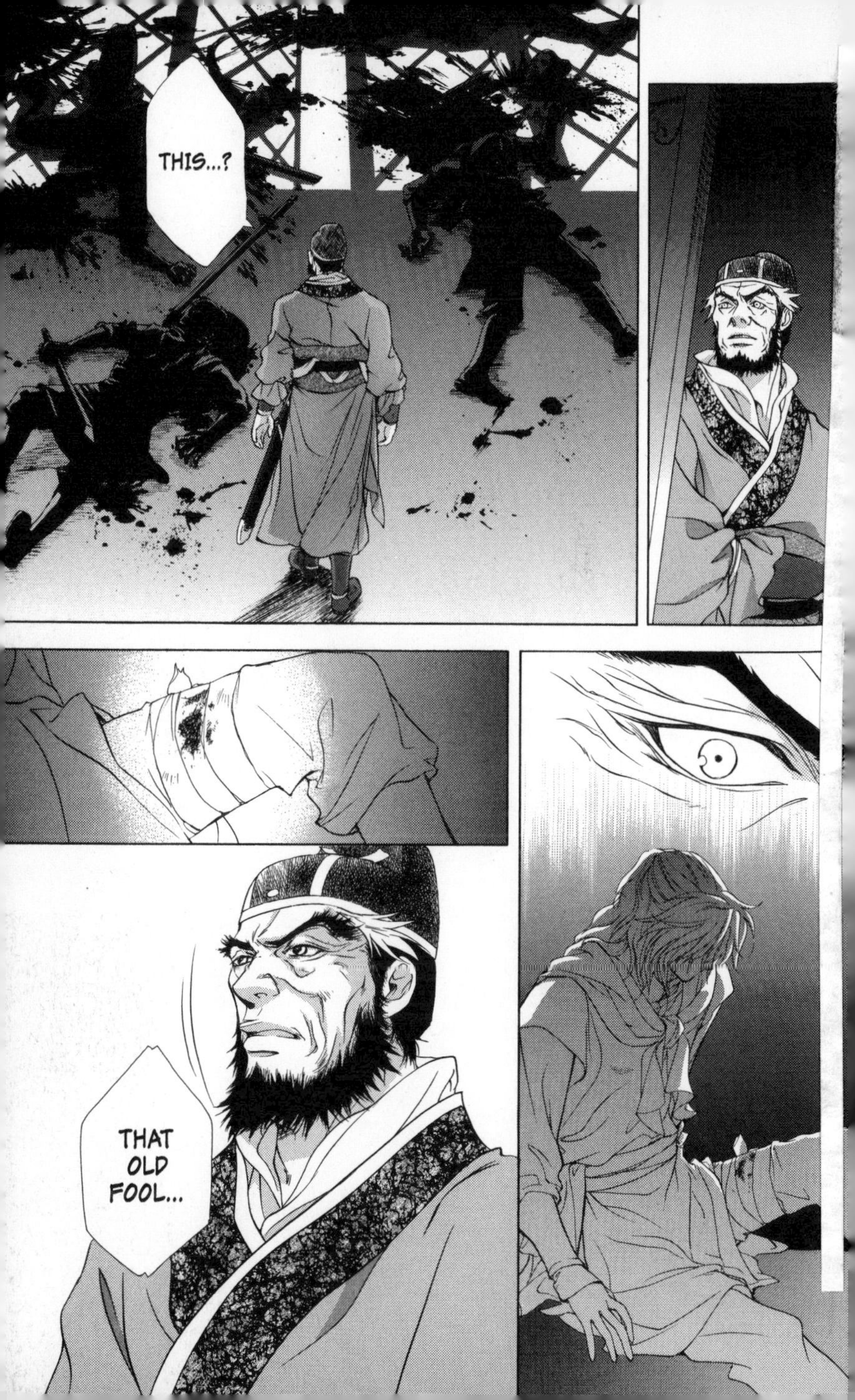
THIS...?
THAT OLD FOOL...

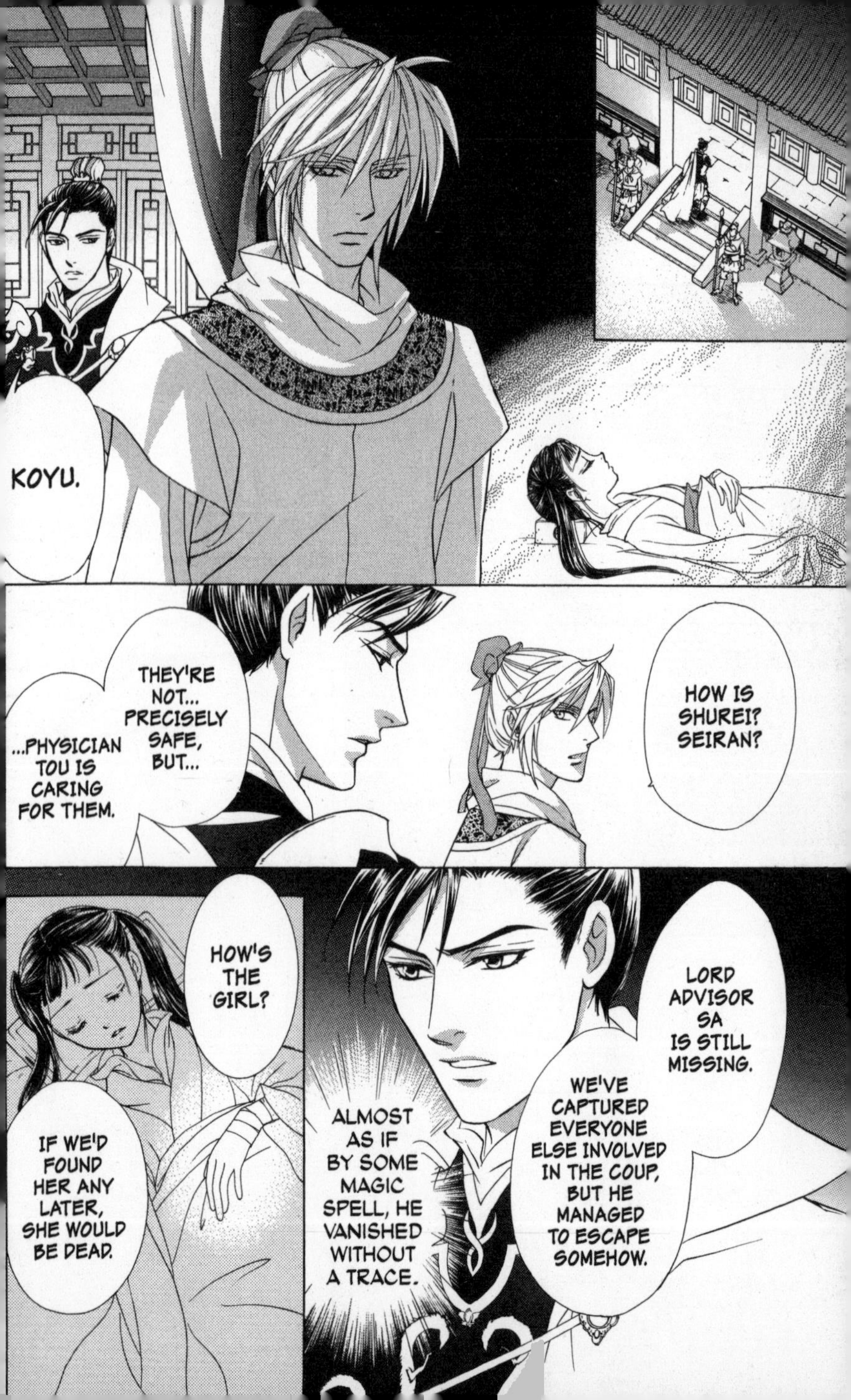
KOYU.
HOW IS SHUREI? SEIRAN?
THEY'RE NOT... PRECISELY SAFE, BUT...
...PHYSICIAN TOU IS CARING FOR THEM.
LORD ADVISOR SA IS STILL MISSING.
WE'VE CAPTURED EVERYONE ELSE INVOLVED IN THE COUP, BUT HE MANAGED TO ESCAPE SOMEHOW.
ALMOST AS IF BY SOME MAGIC SPELL, HE VANISHED WITHOUT A TRACE.
HOW'S THE GIRL?
IF WE'D FOUND HER ANY LATER, SHE WOULD BE DEAD.

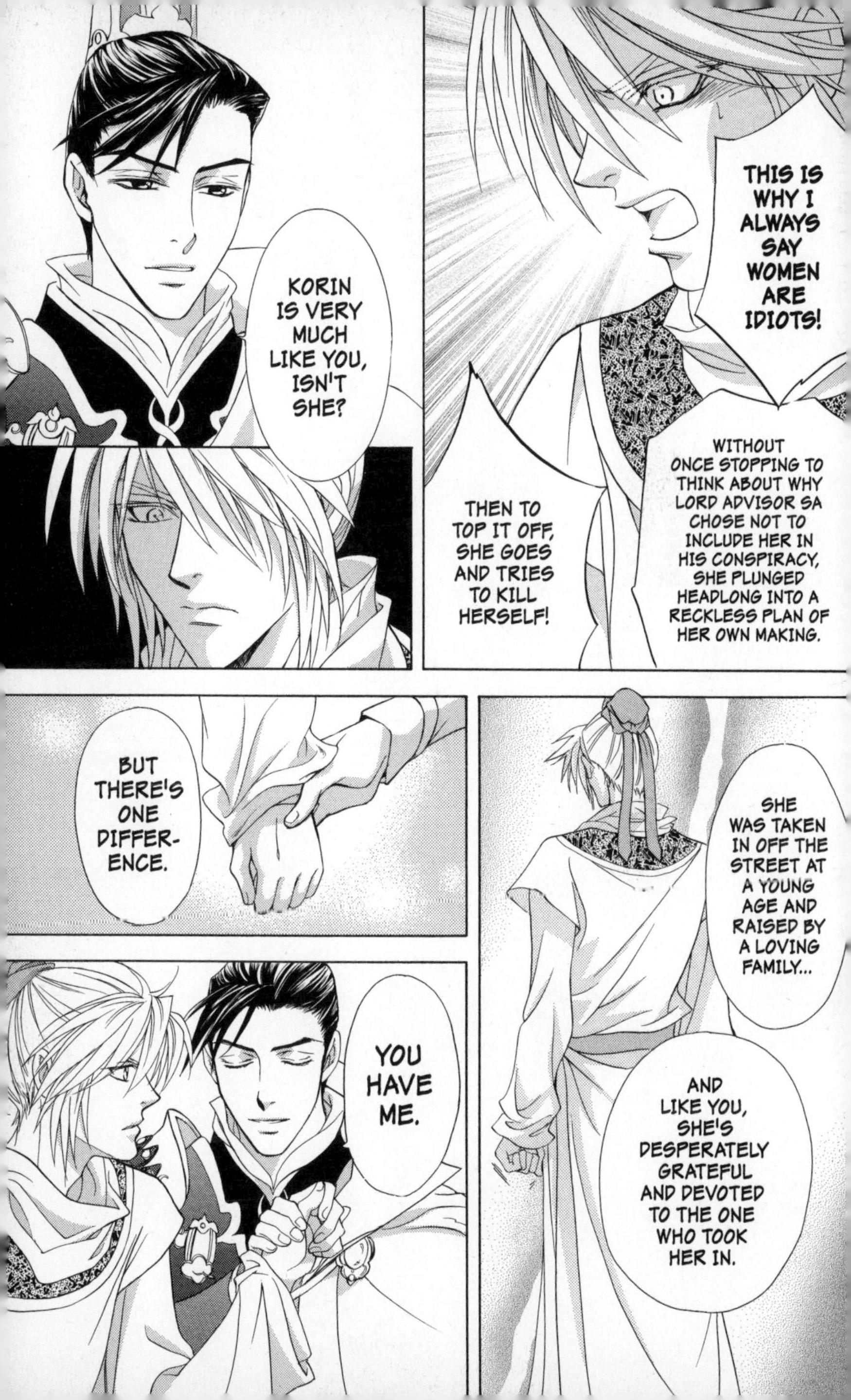
THIS IS WHY I ALWAYS SAY WOMEN ARE IDIOTS!
WITHOUT ONCE STOPPING TO THINK ABOUT WHY LORD ADVISOR SA CHOSE NOT TO INCLUDE HER IN HIS CONSPIRACY, SHE PLUNGED HEADLONG INTO A RECKLESS PLAN OF HER OWN MAKING.
THEN TO TOP IT OFF, SHE GOES AND TRIES TO KILL HERSELF!
KORIN IS VERY MUCH LIKE YOU, ISN'T SHE?
SHE WAS TAKEN IN OFF THE STREET AT A YOUNG AGE AND RAISED BY A LOVING FAMILY...
AND LIKE YOU, SHE'S DESPERATELY GRATEFUL AND DEVOTED TO THE ONE WHO TOOK HER IN.
BUT THERE'S ONE DIFFER-ENCE.
YOU HAVE ME.

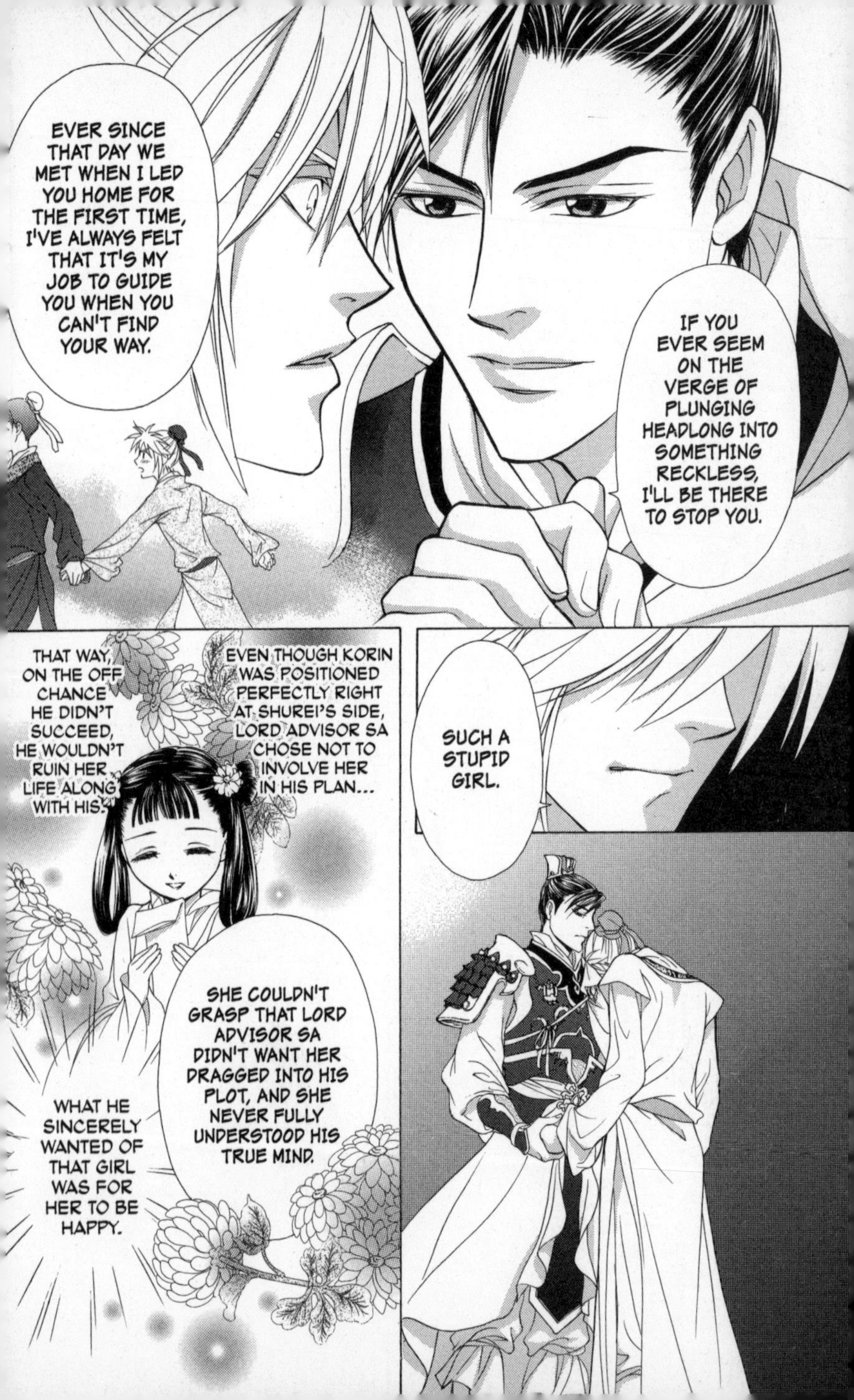
EVER SINCE THAT DAY WE MET WHEN I LED YOU HOME FOR THE FIRST TIME, I'VE ALWAYS FELT THAT IT'S MY JOB TO GUIDE YOU WHEN YOU CAN'T FIND YOUR WAY.
IF YOU EVER SEEM ON THE VERGE OF PLUNGING HEADLONG INTO SOMETHING RECKLESS, I'LL BE THERE TO STOP YOU.
SUCH A STUPID GIRL.
EVEN THOUGH KORIN WAS POSITIONED PERFECTLY RIGHT AT SHUREI'S SIDE, LORD ADVISOR SA CHOSE NOT TO INVOLVE HER IN HIS PLAN...
THAT WAY, ON THE OFF CHANCE HE DIDN'T SUCCEED, HE WOULDN'T RUIN HER LIFE ALONG WITH HIS.
SHE COULDN'T GRASP THAT LORD ADVISOR SA DIDN'T WANT HER DRAGGED INTO HIS PLOT, AND SHE NEVER FULLY UNDERSTOOD HIS TRUE MIND.
WHAT HE SINCERELY WANTED OF THAT GIRL WAS FOR HER TO BE HAPPY.

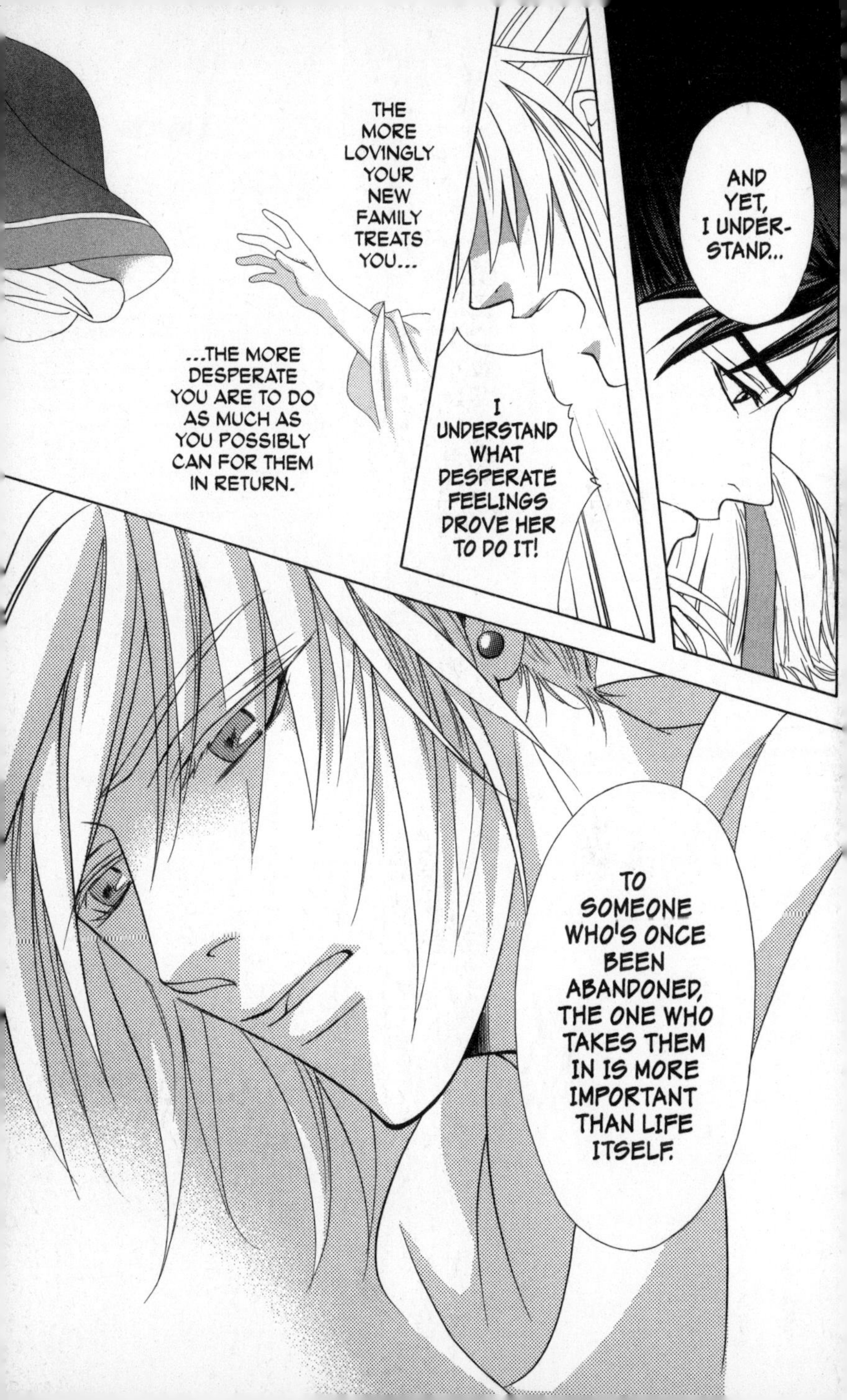
AND YET, I UNDER-STAND...
I UNDERSTAND WHAT DESPERATE FEELINGS DROVE HER TO DO IT!
THE MORE LOVINGLY YOUR NEW FAMILY TREATS YOU...
...THE MORE DESPERATE YOU ARE TO DO AS MUCH AS YOU POSSIBLY CAN FOR THEM IN RETURN.
TO SOMEONE WHO'S ONCE BEEN ABANDONED, THE ONE WHO TAKES THEM IN IS MORE IMPORTANT THAN LIFE ITSELF.

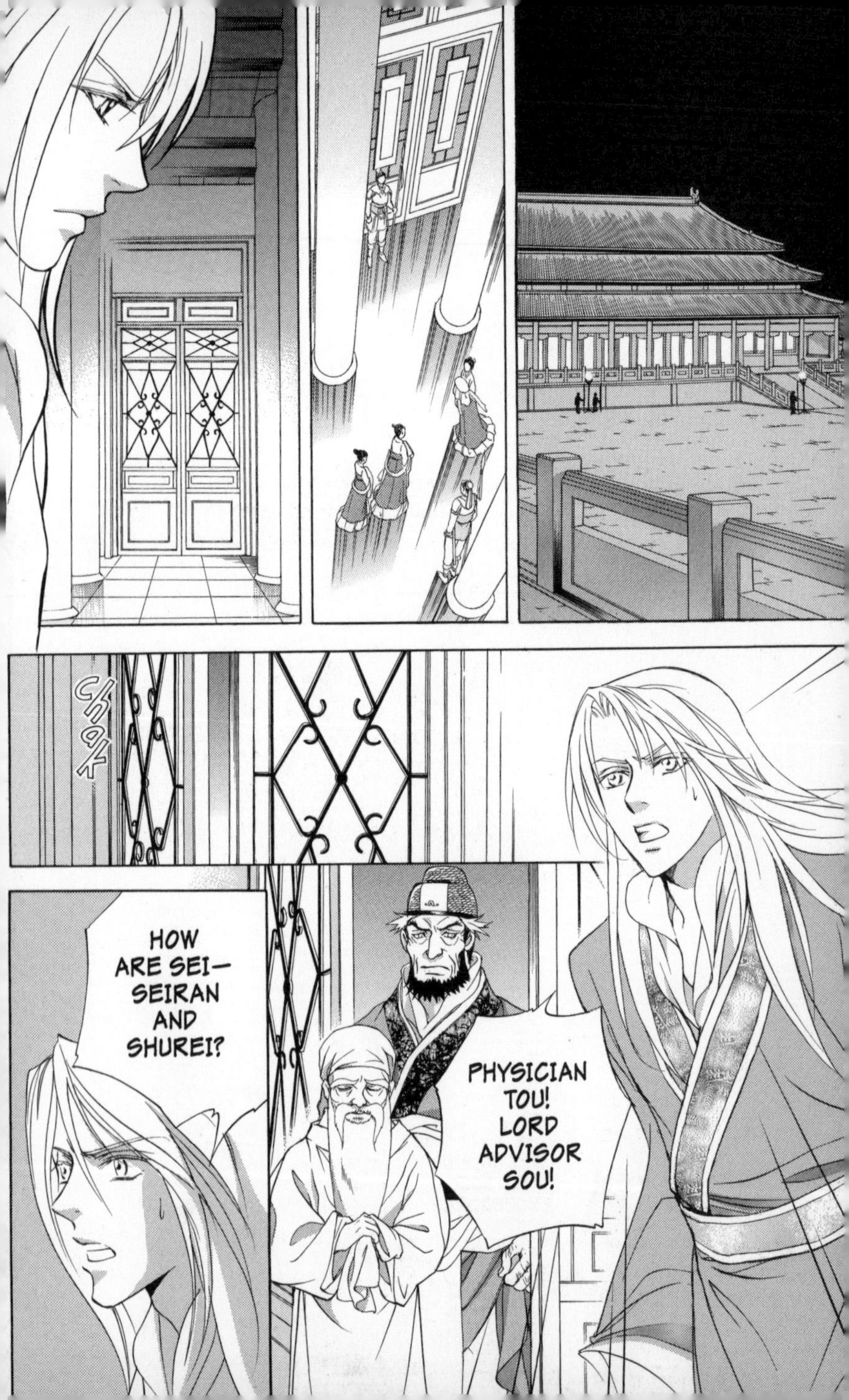
Chak
PHYSICIAN TOU! LORD ADVISOR SOU!
HOW ARE SEI-SEIRAN AND SHUREI?

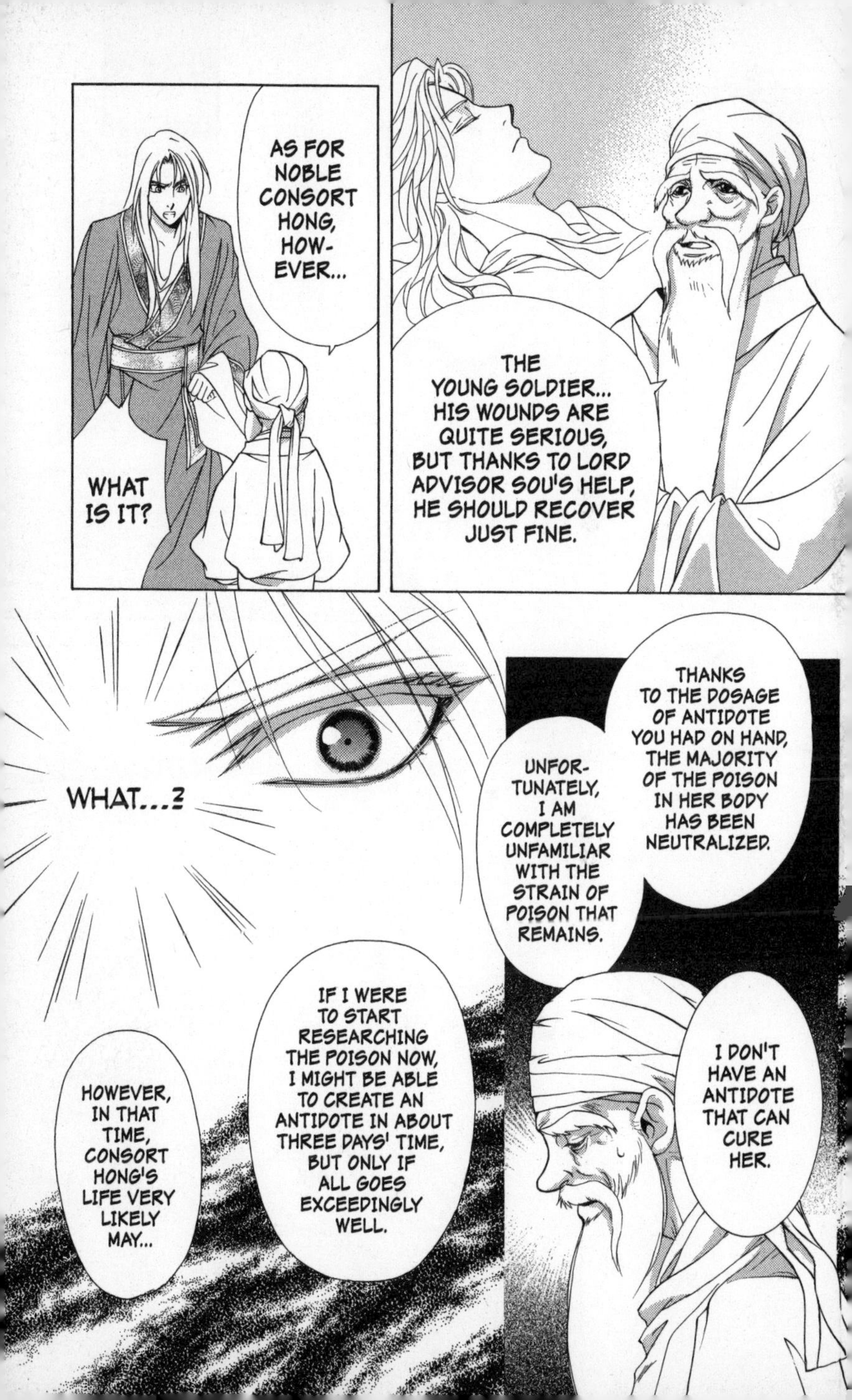
THE YOUNG SOLDIER... HIS WOUNDS ARE QUITE SERIOUS, BUT THANKS TO LORD ADVISOR SOU'S HELP, HE SHOULD RECOVER JUST FINE.
AS FOR NOBLE CONSORT HONG, HOW-EVER...
WHAT IS IT?
THANKS TO THE DOSAGE OF ANTIDOTE YOU HAD ON HAND, THE MAJORITY OF THE POISON IN HER BODY HAS BEEN NEUTRALIZED.
UNFOR-TUNATELY, I AM COMPLETELY UNFAMILIAR WITH THE STRAIN OF POISON THAT REMAINS.
WHAT...?
I DON'T HAVE AN ANTIDOTE THAT CAN CURE HER.
IF I WERE TO START RESEARCHING THE POISON NOW, I MIGHT BE ABLE TO CREATE AN ANTIDOTE IN ABOUT THREE DAYS' TIME, BUT ONLY IF ALL GOES EXCEEDINGLY WELL.
HOWEVER, IN THAT TIME, CONSORT HONG'S LIFE VERY LIKELY MAY...

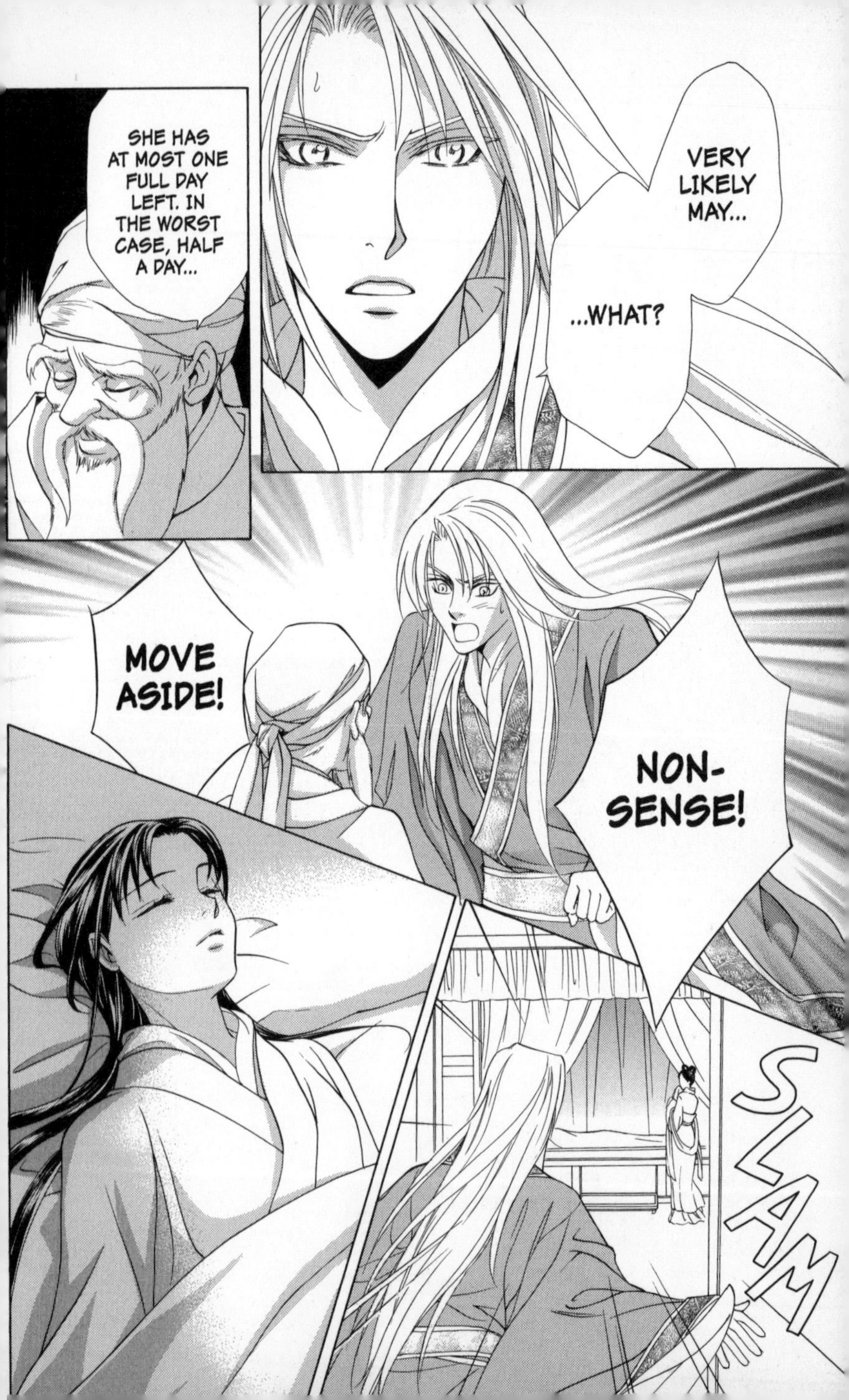
VERY LIKELY MAY...
...WHAT?
SHE HAS AT MOST ONE FULL DAY LEFT. IN THE WORST CASE, HALF A DAY...
NON-SENSE!
MOVE ASIDE!
SLAM

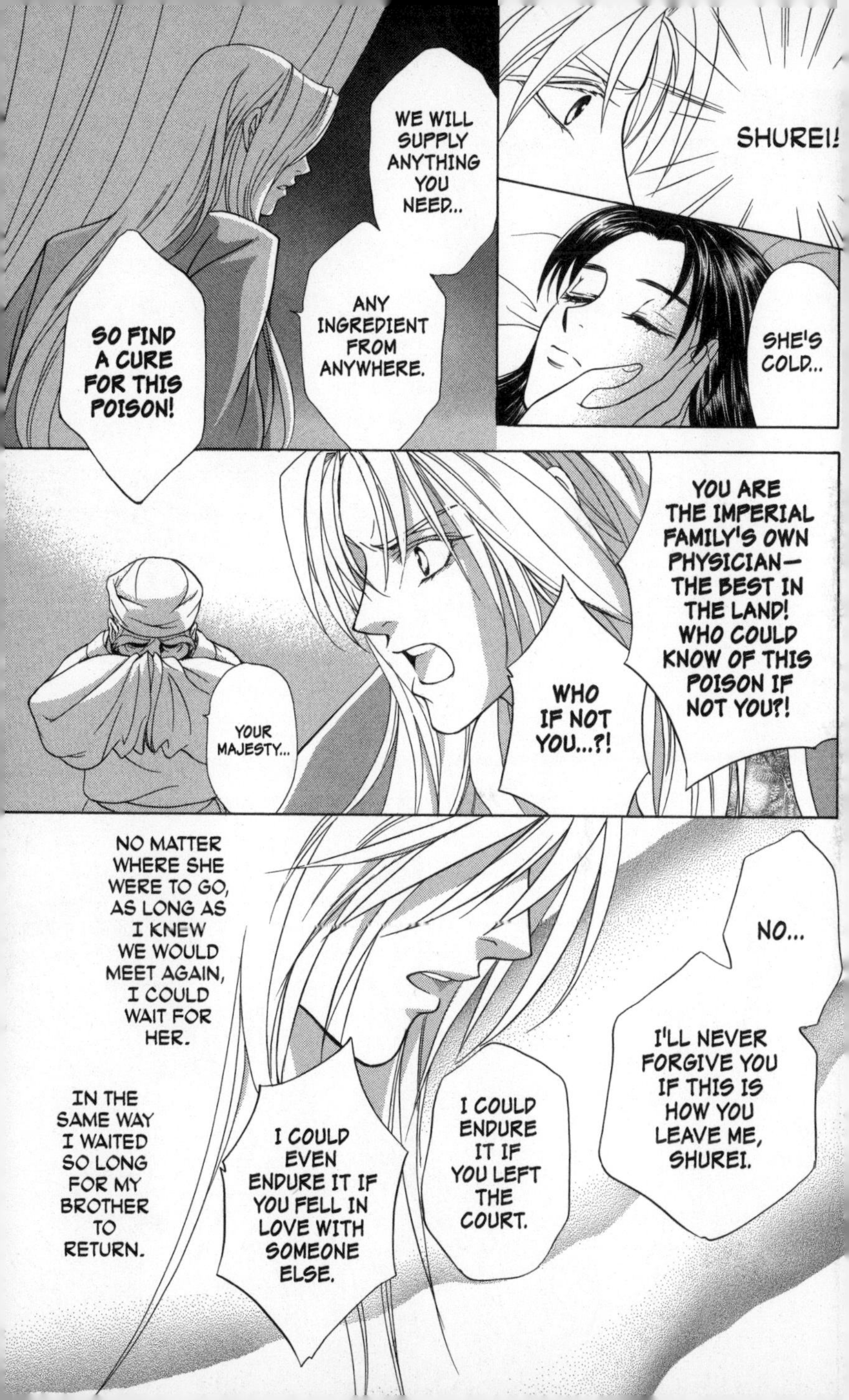
SHUREI!
SHE'S COLD...
WE WILL SUPPLY ANYTHING YOU NEED...
ANY INGREDIENT FROM ANYWHERE.
SO FIND A CURE FOR THIS POISON!
YOU ARE THE IMPERIAL FAMILY'S OWN PHYSICIAN—THE BEST IN THE LAND! WHO COULD KNOW OF THIS POISON IF NOT YOU?!
WHO IF NOT YOU...?!
YOUR MAJESTY...
NO...
I'LL NEVER FORGIVE YOU IF THIS IS HOW YOU LEAVE ME, SHUREI.
NO MATTER WHERE SHE WERE TO GO, AS LONG AS I KNEW WE WOULD MEET AGAIN, I COULD WAIT FOR HER.
I COULD ENDURE IT IF YOU LEFT THE COURT.
I COULD EVEN ENDURE IT IF YOU FELL IN LOVE WITH SOMEONE ELSE.
IN THE SAME WAY I WAITED SO LONG FOR MY BROTHER TO RETURN.

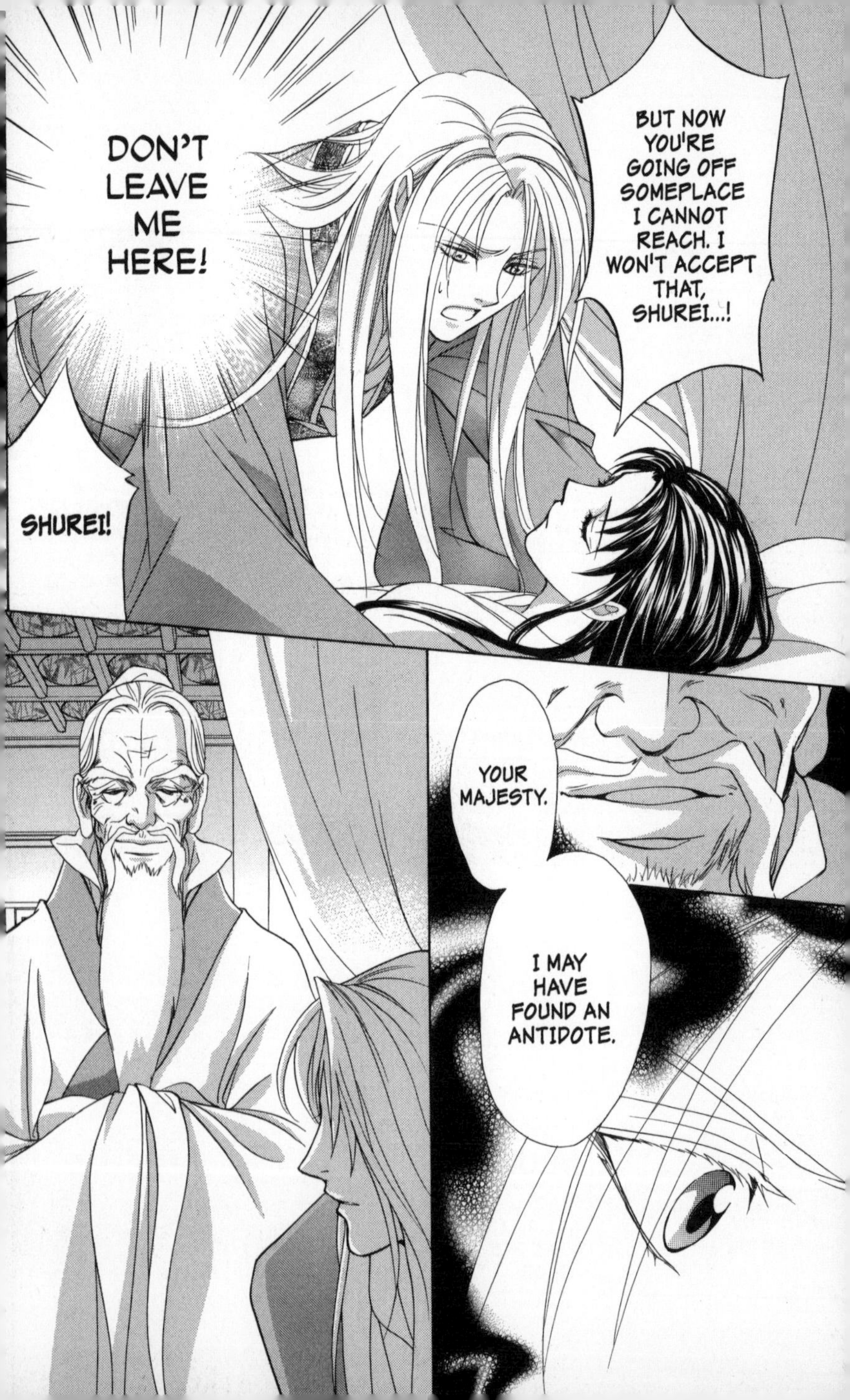
BUT NOW YOU'RE GOING OFF SOMEPLACE I CANNOT REACH. I WON'T ACCEPT THAT, SHUREI...!
DON'T LEAVE ME HERE!
SHUREI!
YOUR MAJESTY.
I MAY HAVE FOUND AN ANTIDOTE.

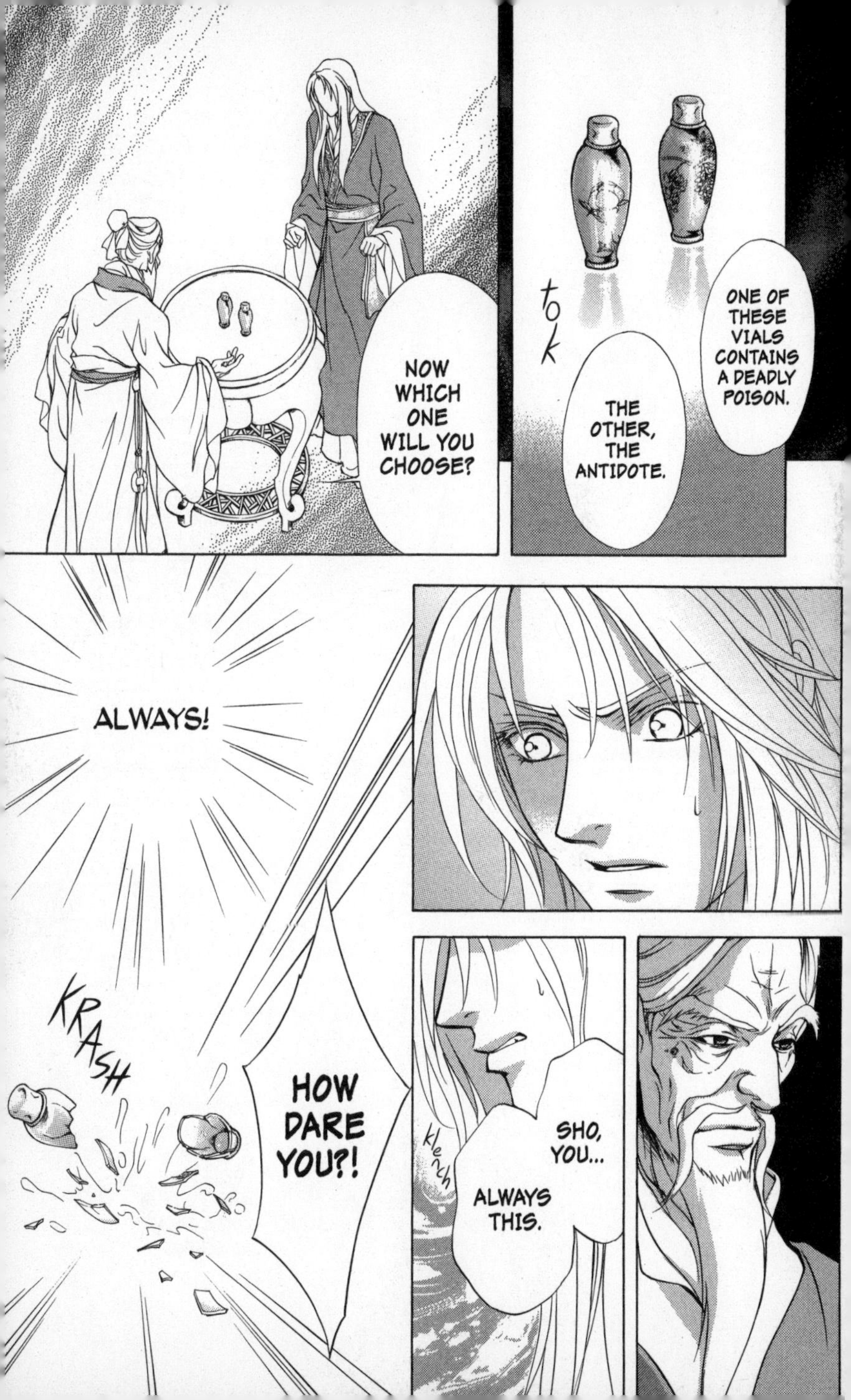
ONE OF THESE VIALS CONTAINS A DEADLY POISON.
THE OTHER, THE ANTIDOTE.
tok
NOW WHICH ONE WILL YOU CHOOSE?
SHO, YOU...
ALWAYS THIS.
klench
ALWAYS!
KRASH
HOW DARE YOU?!

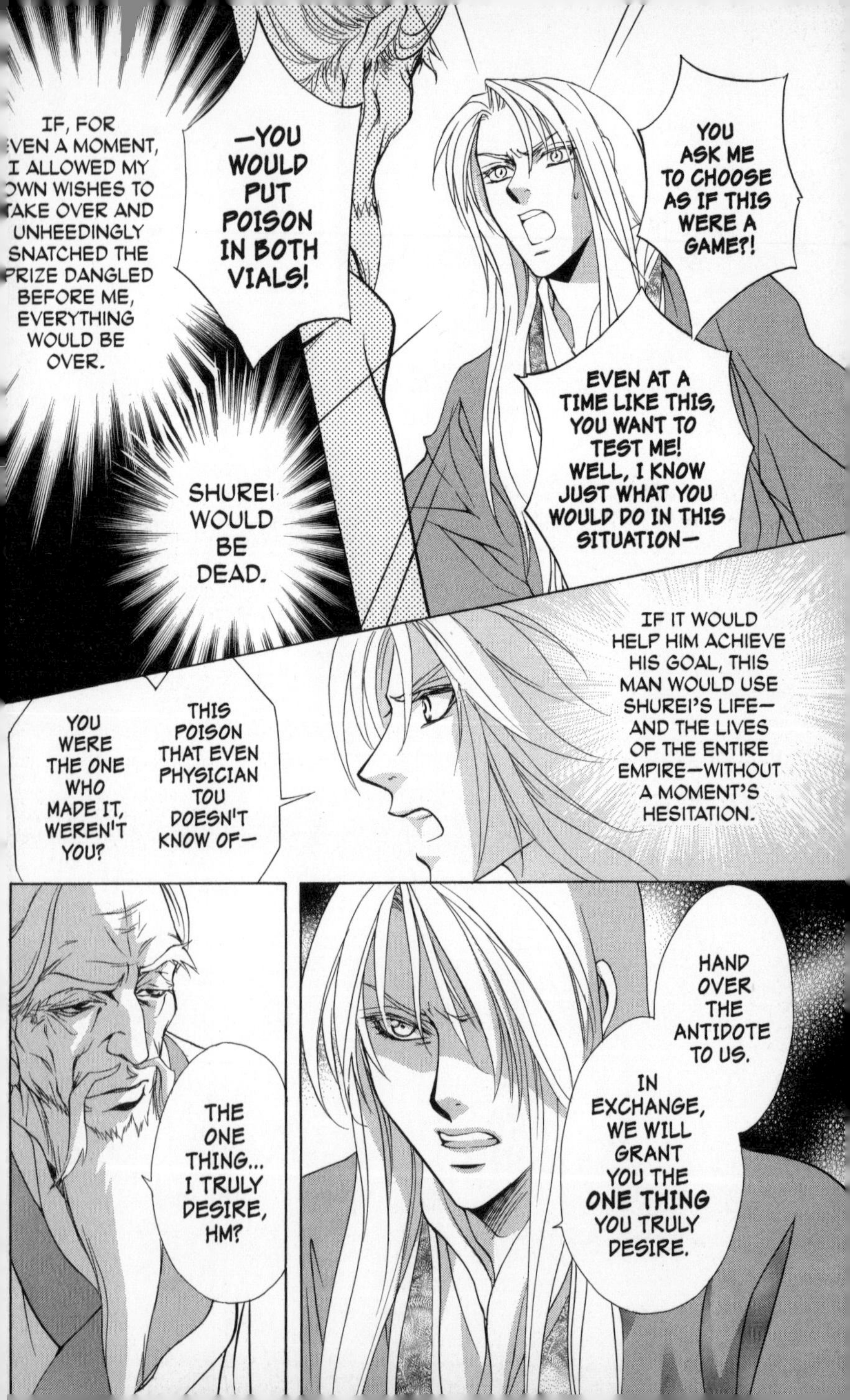

YOU ASK ME TO CHOOSE AS IF THIS WERE A GAME?!
EVEN AT A TIME LIKE THIS, YOU WANT TO TEST ME! WELL, I KNOW JUST WHAT YOU WOULD DO IN THIS SITUATION—
—YOU WOULD PUT POISON IN BOTH VIALS!
IF, FOR EVEN A MOMENT, I ALLOWED MY OWN WISHES TO TAKE OVER AND UNHEEDINGLY SNATCHED THE PRIZE DANGLED BEFORE ME, EVERYTHING WOULD BE OVER.
SHUREI WOULD BE DEAD.
IF IT WOULD HELP HIM ACHIEVE HIS GOAL, THIS MAN WOULD USE SHUREI'S LIFE—AND THE LIVES OF THE ENTIRE EMPIRE—WITHOUT A MOMENT'S HESITATION.
THIS POISON THAT EVEN PHYSICIAN TOU DOESN'T KNOW OF—
YOU WERE THE ONE WHO MADE IT, WEREN'T YOU?
HAND OVER THE ANTIDOTE TO US.
IN EXCHANGE, WE WILL GRANT YOU THE ONE THING YOU TRULY DESIRE.
THE ONE THING... I TRULY DESIRE, HM?

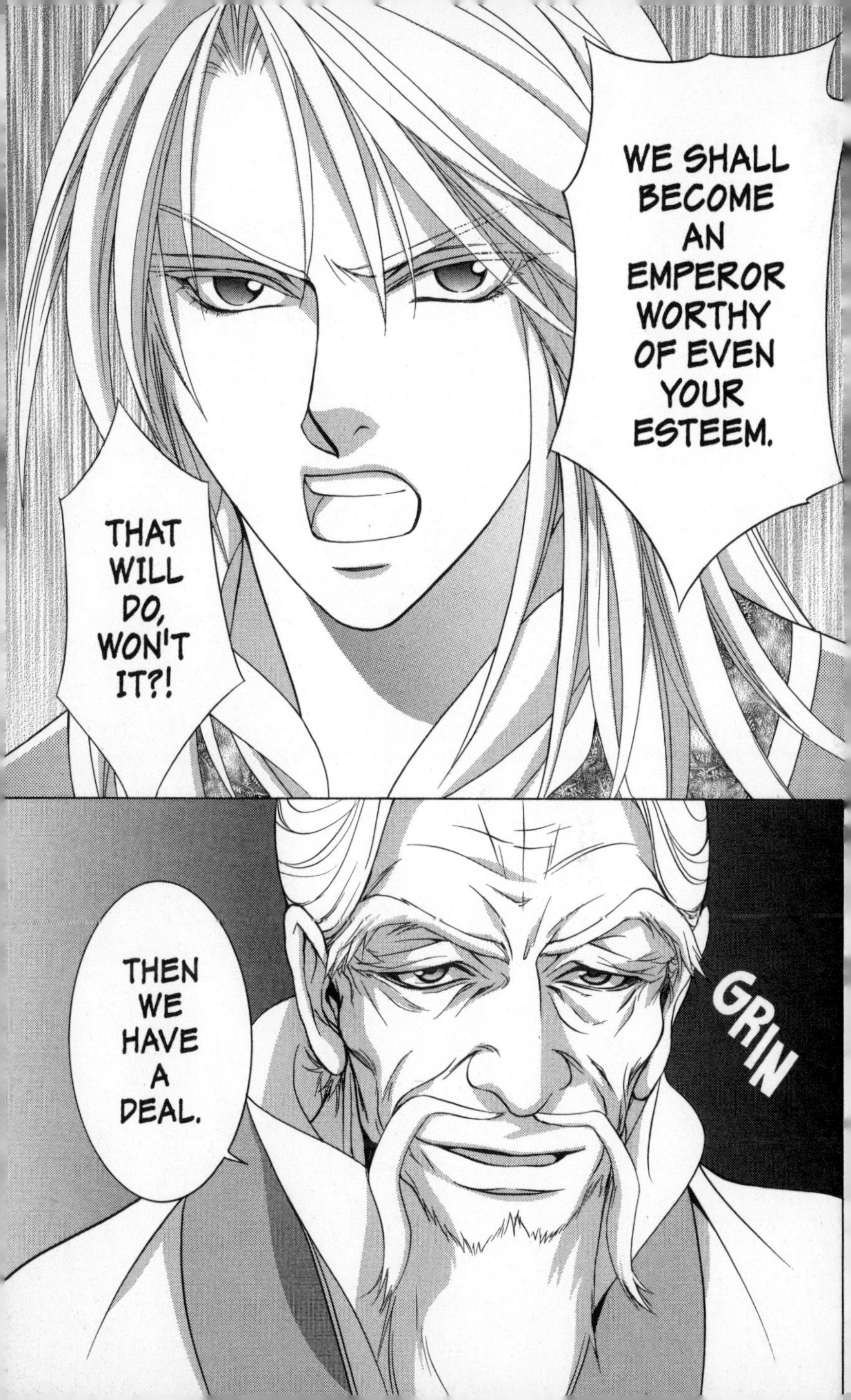
WE SHALL BECOME AN EMPEROR WORTHY OF EVEN YOUR ESTEEM.
THAT WILL DO, WON'T IT?!
THEN WE HAVE A DEAL.
GRIN

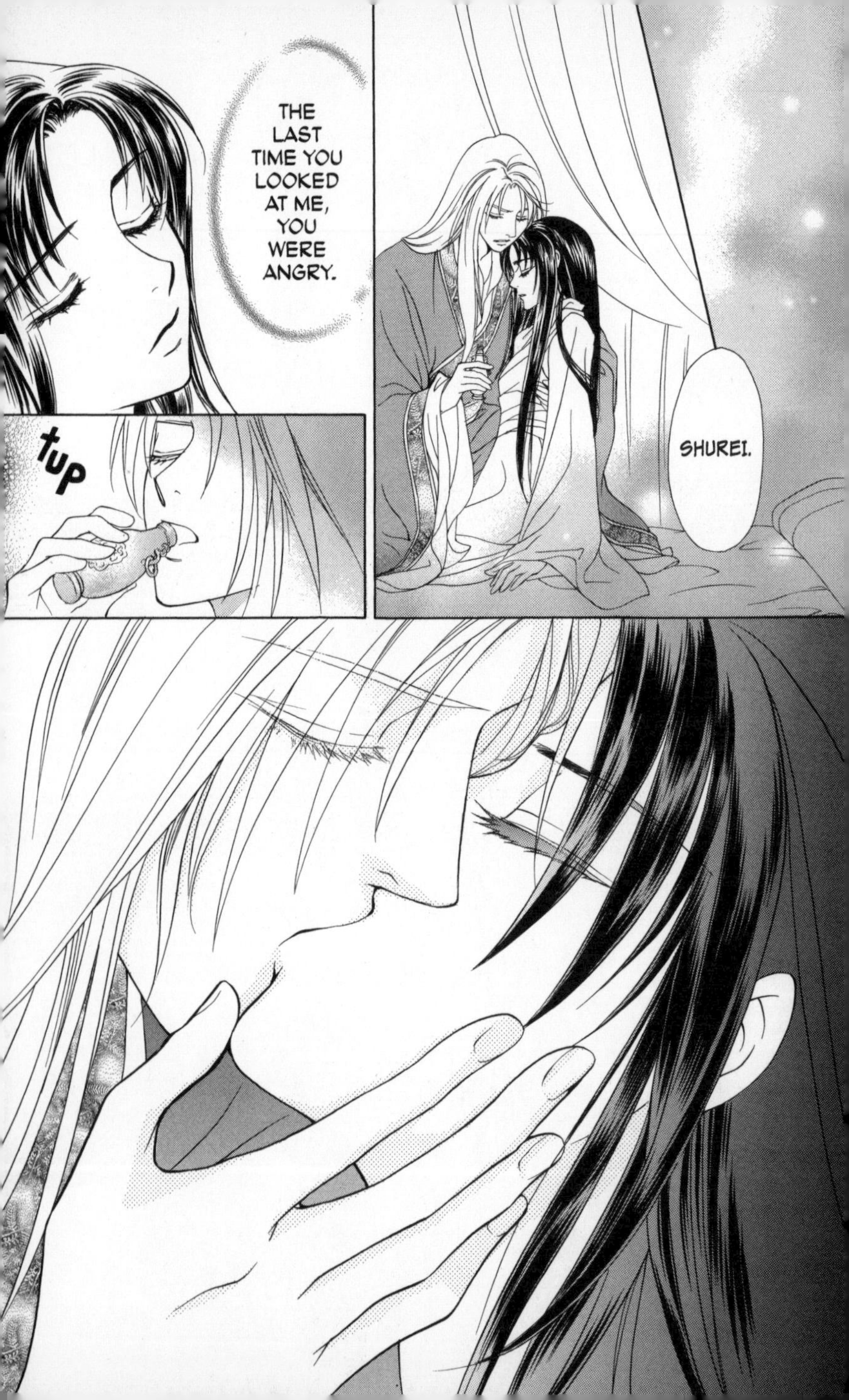
SHUREI.
THE LAST TIME YOU LOOKED AT ME, YOU WERE ANGRY.
tup

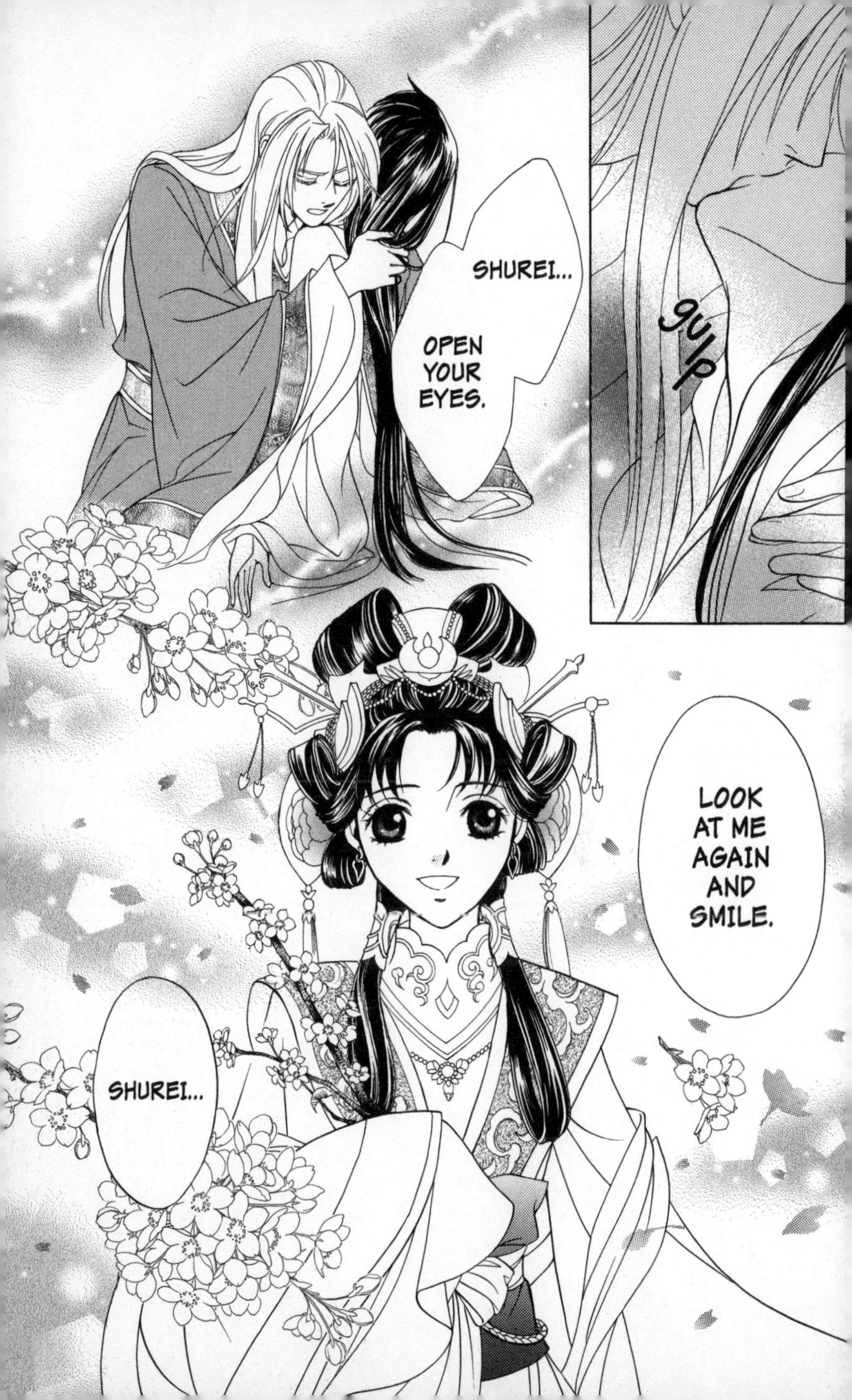
gulp
SHUREI...
OPEN YOUR EYES.
LOOK AT ME AGAIN AND SMILE.
SHUREI...

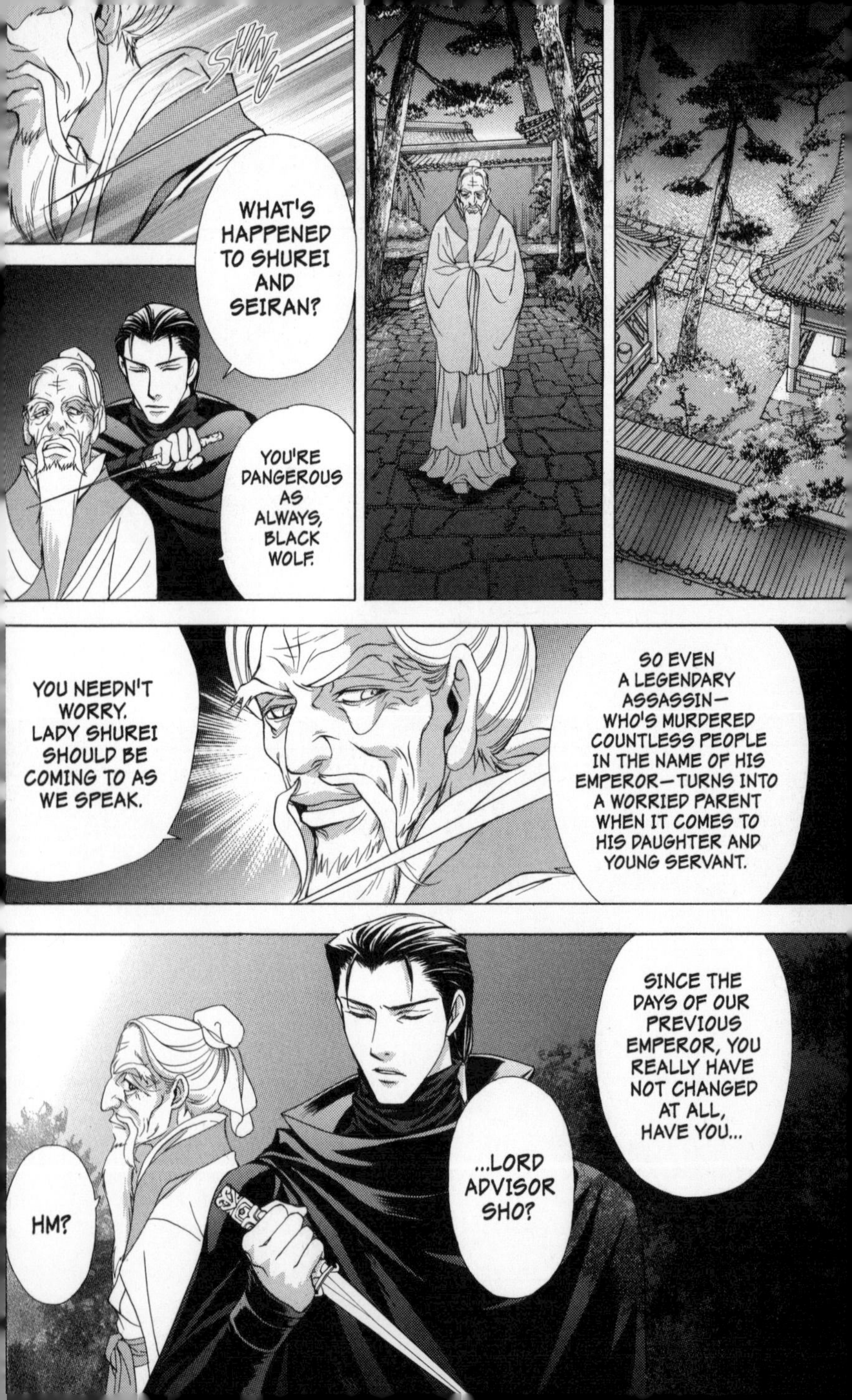
SHING
WHAT'S HAPPENED TO SHUREI AND SEIRAN?
YOU'RE DANGEROUS AS ALWAYS, BLACK WOLF.
SO EVEN A LEGENDARY ASSASSIN—WHO'S MURDERED COUNTLESS PEOPLE IN THE NAME OF HIS EMPEROR—TURNS INTO A WORRIED PARENT WHEN IT COMES TO HIS DAUGHTER AND YOUNG SERVANT.
YOU NEEDN'T WORRY. LADY SHUREI SHOULD BE COMING TO AS WE SPEAK.
SINCE THE DAYS OF OUR PREVIOUS EMPEROR, YOU REALLY HAVE NOT CHANGED AT ALL, HAVE YOU...
...LORD ADVISOR SHO?
HM?

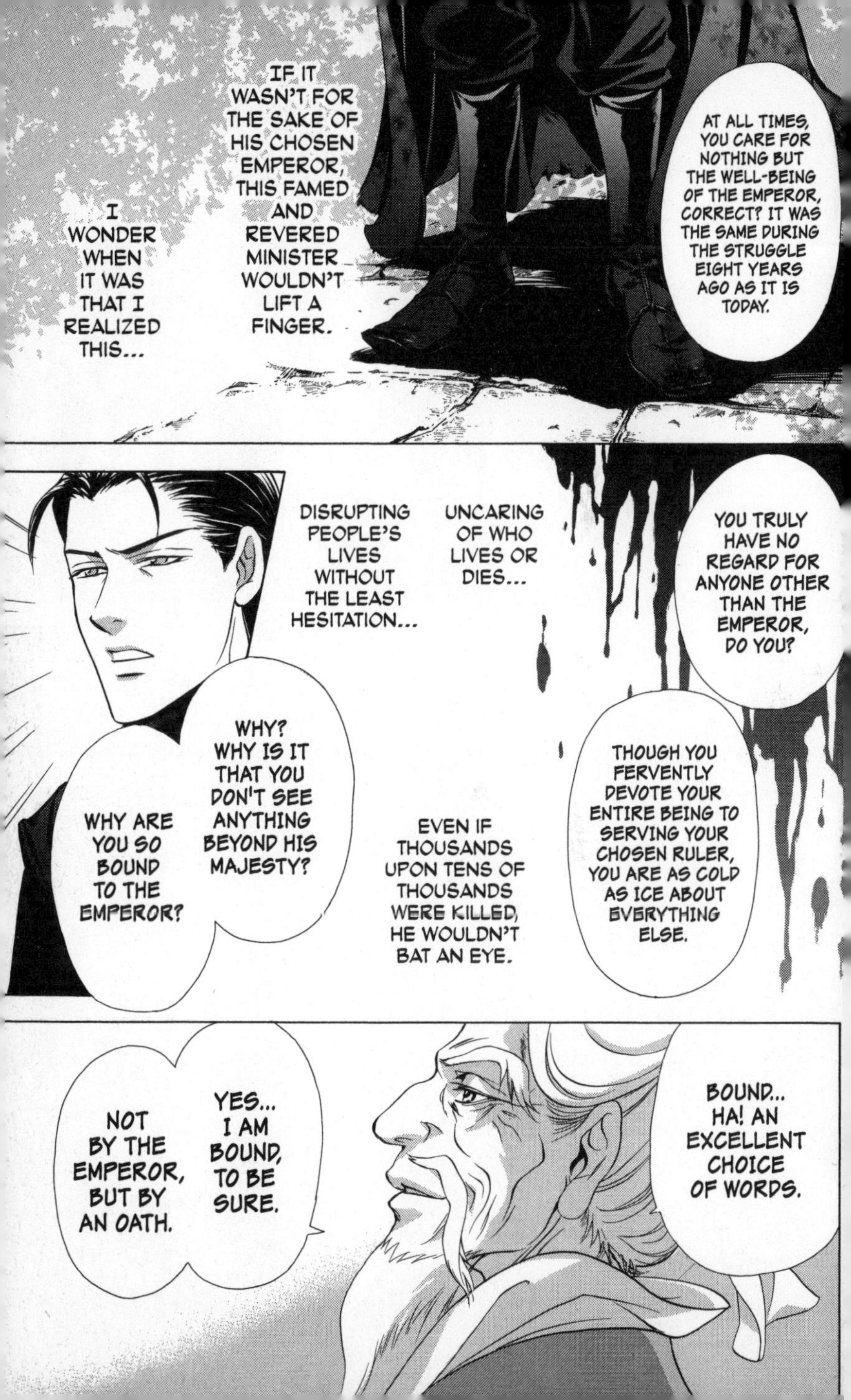
AT ALL TIMES, YOU CARE FOR NOTHING BUT THE WELL-BEING OF THE EMPEROR, CORRECT? IT WAS THE SAME DURING THE STRUGGLE EIGHT YEARS AGO AS IT IS TODAY.
IF IT WASN'T FOR THE SAKE OF HIS CHOSEN EMPEROR, THIS FAMED AND REVERED MINISTER WOULDN'T LIFT A FINGER.
I WONDER WHEN IT WAS THAT I REALIZED THIS...
YOU TRULY HAVE NO REGARD FOR ANYONE OTHER THAN THE EMPEROR, DO YOU?
UNCARING OF WHO LIVES OR DIES...
DISRUPTING PEOPLE'S LIVES WITHOUT THE LEAST HESITATION...
THOUGH YOU FERVENTLY DEVOTE YOUR ENTIRE BEING TO SERVING YOUR CHOSEN RULER, YOU ARE AS COLD AS ICE ABOUT EVERYTHING ELSE.
EVEN IF THOUSANDS UPON TENS OF THOUSANDS WERE KILLED, HE WOULDN'T BAT AN EYE.
WHY? WHY IS IT THAT YOU DON'T SEE ANYTHING BEYOND HIS MAJESTY?
WHY ARE YOU SO BOUND TO THE EMPEROR?
BOUND... HA! AN EXCELLENT CHOICE OF WORDS.
YES... I AM BOUND, TO BE SURE.
NOT BY THE EMPEROR, BUT BY AN OATH.

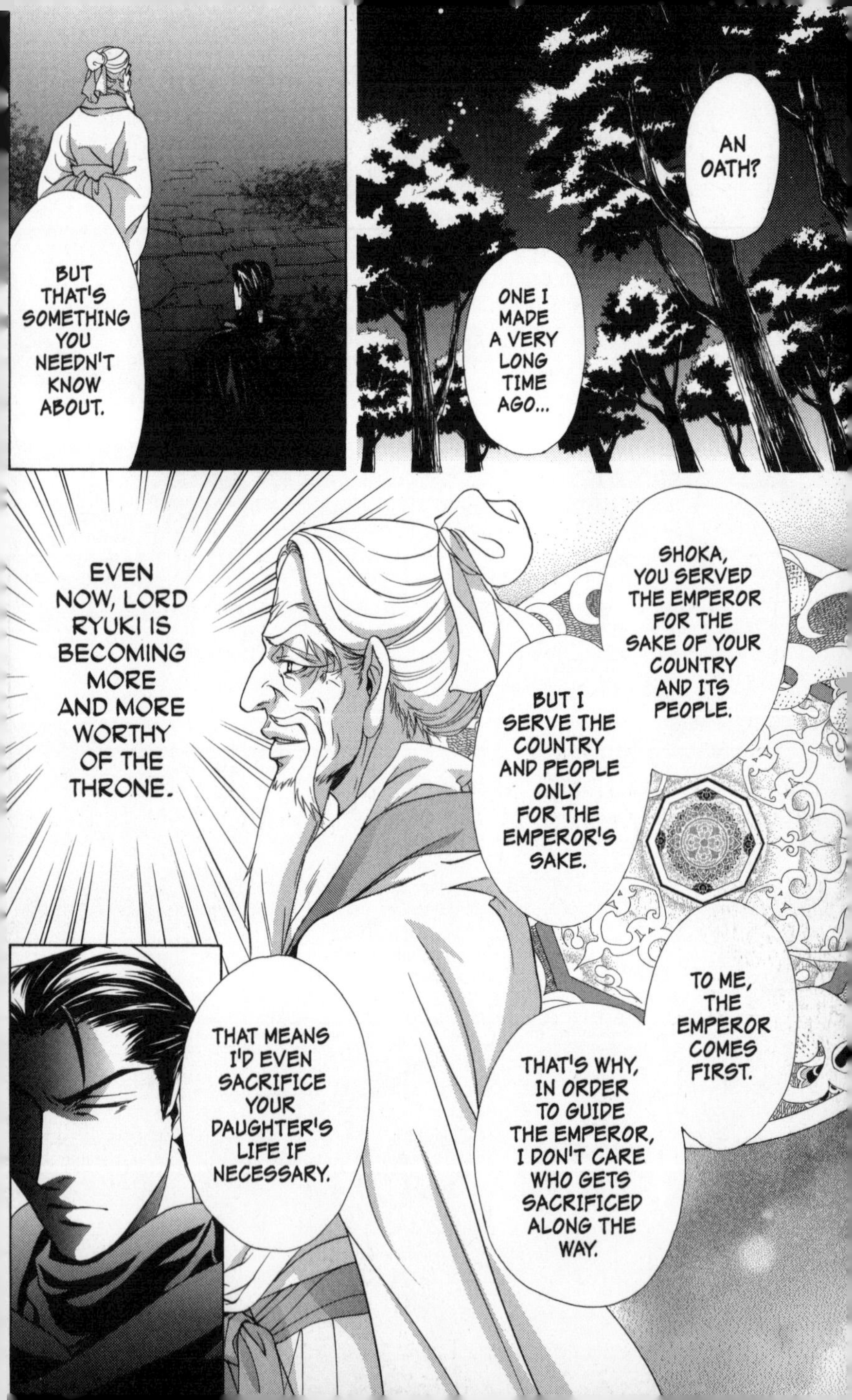
AN OATH?
ONE I MADE A VERY LONG TIME AGO...
BUT THAT'S SOMETHING YOU NEEDN'T KNOW ABOUT.
SHOKA, YOU SERVED THE EMPEROR FOR THE SAKE OF YOUR COUNTRY AND ITS PEOPLE.
BUT I SERVE THE COUNTRY AND PEOPLE ONLY FOR THE EMPEROR'S SAKE.
EVEN NOW, LORD RYUKI IS BECOMING MORE AND MORE WORTHY OF THE THRONE.
TO ME, THE EMPEROR COMES FIRST.
THAT'S WHY, IN ORDER TO GUIDE THE EMPEROR, I DON'T CARE WHO GETS SACRIFICED ALONG THE WAY.
THAT MEANS I'D EVEN SACRIFICE YOUR DAUGHTER'S LIFE IF NECESSARY.

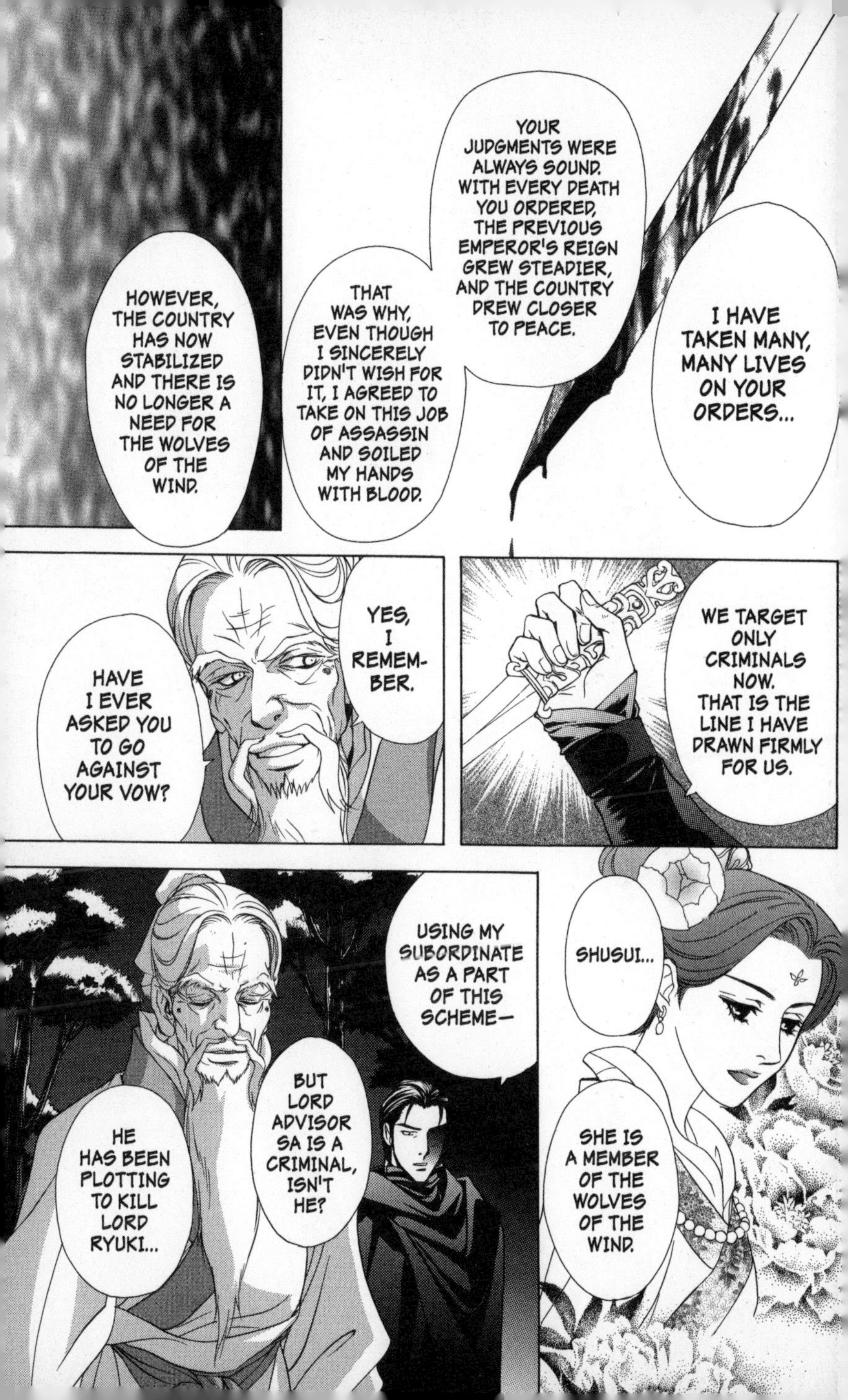
I HAVE TAKEN MANY, MANY LIVES ON YOUR ORDERS...
YOUR JUDGMENTS WERE ALWAYS SOUND. WITH EVERY DEATH YOU ORDERED, THE PREVIOUS EMPEROR'S REIGN GREW STEADIER, AND THE COUNTRY DREW CLOSER TO PEACE.
THAT WAS WHY, EVEN THOUGH I SINCERELY DIDN'T WISH FOR IT, I AGREED TO TAKE ON THIS JOB OF ASSASSIN AND SOILED MY HANDS WITH BLOOD.
HOWEVER, THE COUNTRY HAS NOW STABILIZED AND THERE IS NO LONGER A NEED FOR THE WOLVES OF THE WIND.
WE TARGET ONLY CRIMINALS NOW. THAT IS THE LINE I HAVE DRAWN FIRMLY FOR US.
YES, I REMEMBER.
HAVE I EVER ASKED YOU TO GO AGAINST YOUR VOW?
SHUSUI...
SHE IS A MEMBER OF THE WOLVES OF THE WIND.
USING MY SUBORDINATE AS A PART OF THIS SCHEME—
BUT LORD ADVISOR SA IS A CRIMINAL, ISN'T HE?
HE HAS BEEN PLOTTING TO KILL LORD RYUKI...

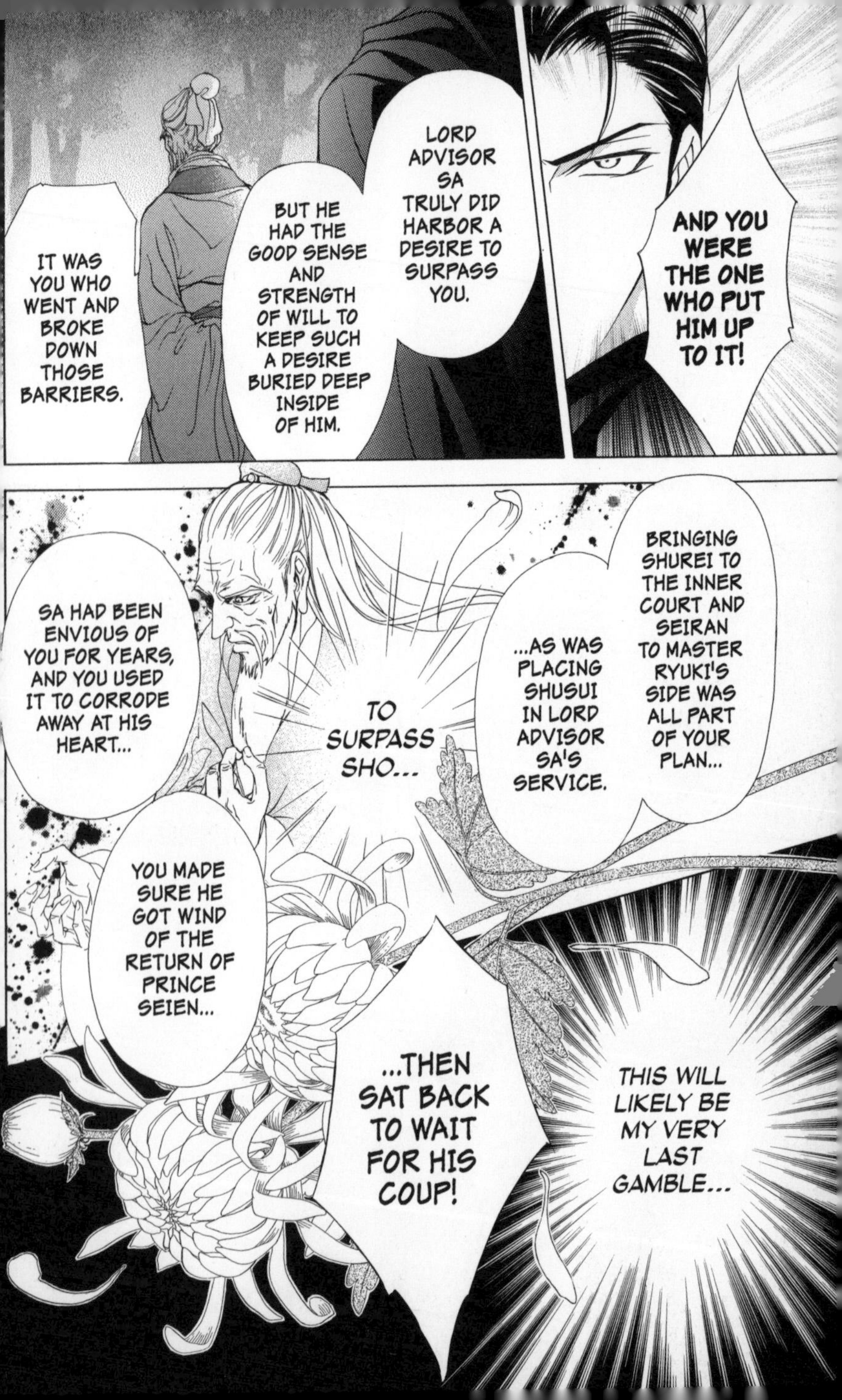
AND YOU WERE THE ONE WHO PUT HIM UP TO IT!
LORD ADVISOR SA TRULY DID HARBOR A DESIRE TO SURPASS YOU.
BUT HE HAD THE GOOD SENSE AND STRENGTH OF WILL TO KEEP SUCH A DESIRE BURIED DEEP INSIDE OF HIM.
IT WAS YOU WHO WENT AND BROKE DOWN THOSE BARRIERS.
BRINGING SHUREI TO THE INNER COURT AND SEIRAN TO MASTER RYUKI'S SIDE WAS ALL PART OF YOUR PLAN...
...AS WAS PLACING SHUSUI IN LORD ADVISOR SA'S SERVICE.
TO SURPASS SHO...
SA HAD BEEN ENVIOUS OF YOU FOR YEARS, AND YOU USED IT TO CORRODE AWAY AT HIS HEART...
YOU MADE SURE HE GOT WIND OF THE RETURN OF PRINCE SEIEN...
...THEN SAT BACK TO WAIT FOR HIS COUP!
THIS WILL LIKELY BE MY VERY LAST GAMBLE...

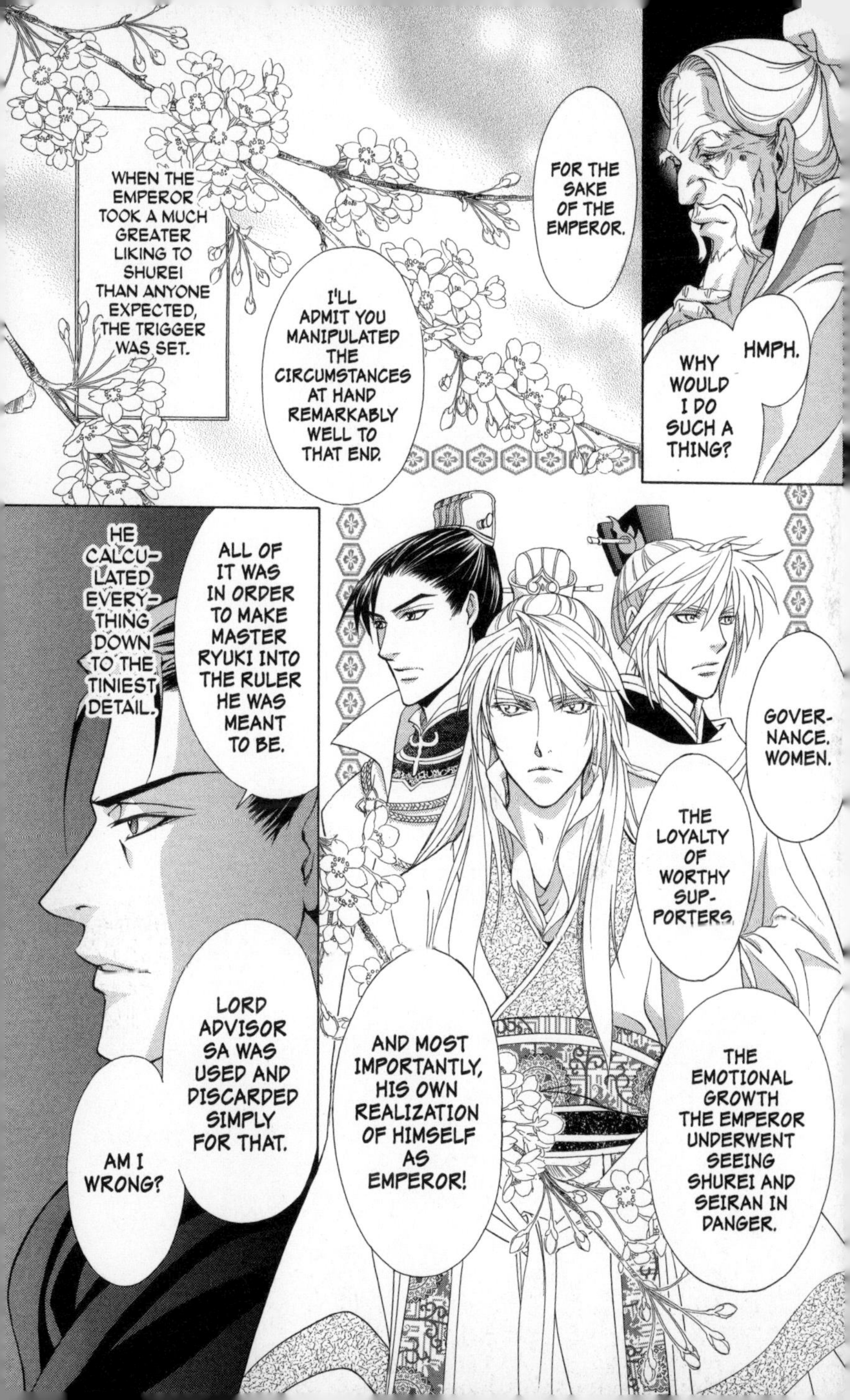
HMPH.
WHY WOULD I DO SUCH A THING?
FOR THE SAKE OF THE EMPEROR.
I'LL ADMIT YOU MANIPULATED THE CIRCUMSTANCES AT HAND REMARKABLY WELL TO THAT END.
WHEN THE EMPEROR TOOK A MUCH GREATER LIKING TO SHUREI THAN ANYONE EXPECTED, THE TRIGGER WAS SET.
GOVERNANCE. WOMEN.
THE LOYALTY OF WORTHY SUPPORTERS.
THE EMOTIONAL GROWTH THE EMPEROR UNDERWENT SEEING SHUREI AND SEIRAN IN DANGER.
AND MOST IMPORTANTLY, HIS OWN REALIZATION OF HIMSELF AS EMPEROR!
ALL OF IT WAS IN ORDER TO MAKE MASTER RYUKI INTO THE RULER HE WAS MEANT TO BE.
HE CALCULATED EVERYTHING DOWN TO THE TINIEST DETAIL.
LORD ADVISOR SA WAS USED AND DISCARDED SIMPLY FOR THAT.
AM I WRONG?

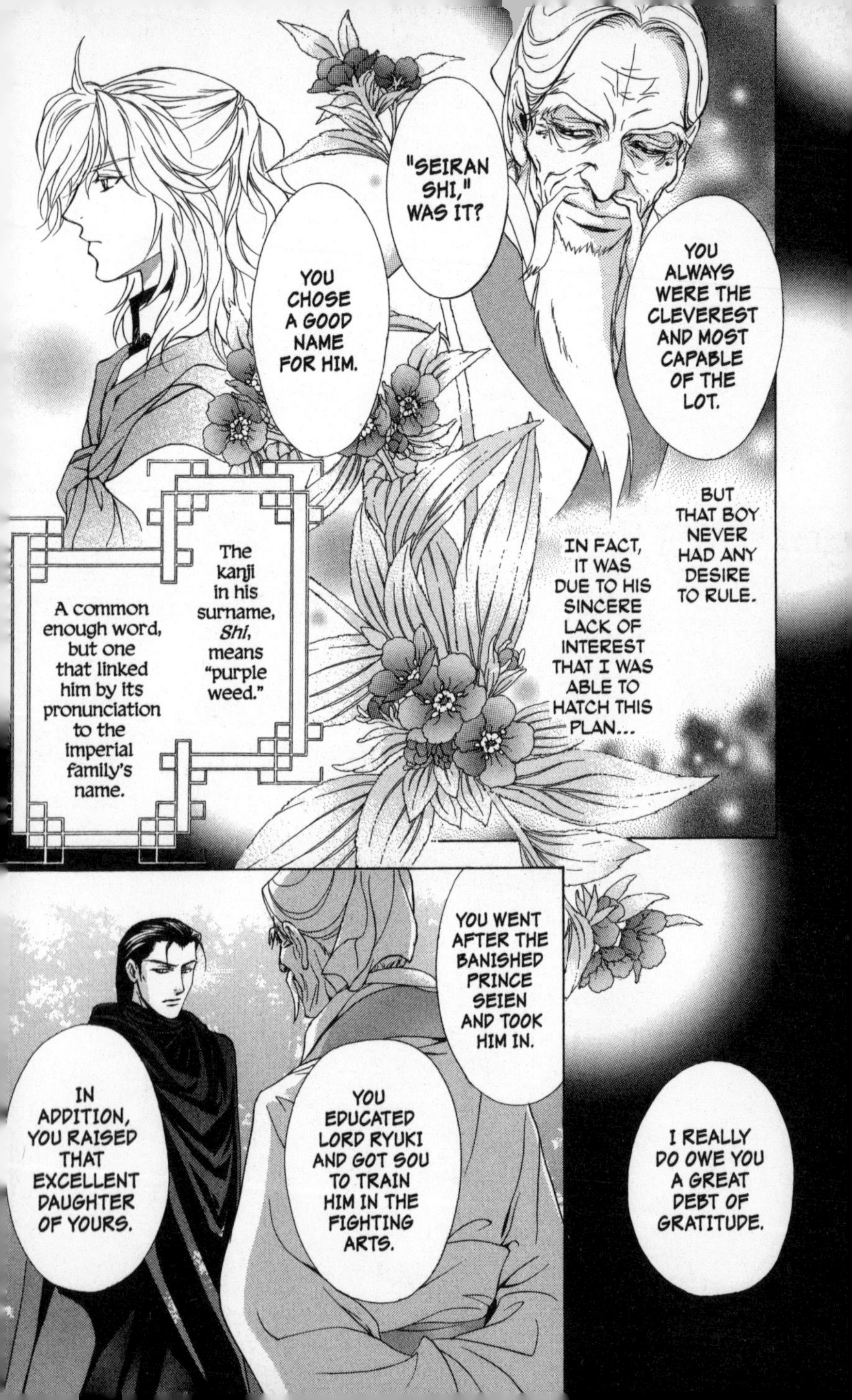
YOU ALWAYS WERE THE CLEVEREST AND MOST CAPABLE OF THE LOT.
BUT THAT BOY NEVER HAD ANY DESIRE TO RULE.
IN FACT, IT WAS DUE TO HIS SINCERE LACK OF INTEREST THAT I WAS ABLE TO HATCH THIS PLAN...
"SEIRAN SHI," WAS IT?
YOU CHOSE A GOOD NAME FOR HIM.
The kanji in his surname, *Shi*, means "purple weed."
A common enough word, but one that linked him by its pronunciation to the imperial family's name.
YOU WENT AFTER THE BANISHED PRINCE SEIEN AND TOOK HIM IN.
YOU EDUCATED LORD RYUKI AND GOT SOU TO TRAIN HIM IN THE FIGHTING ARTS.
IN ADDITION, YOU RAISED THAT EXCELLENT DAUGHTER OF YOURS.
I REALLY DO OWE YOU A GREAT DEBT OF GRATITUDE.

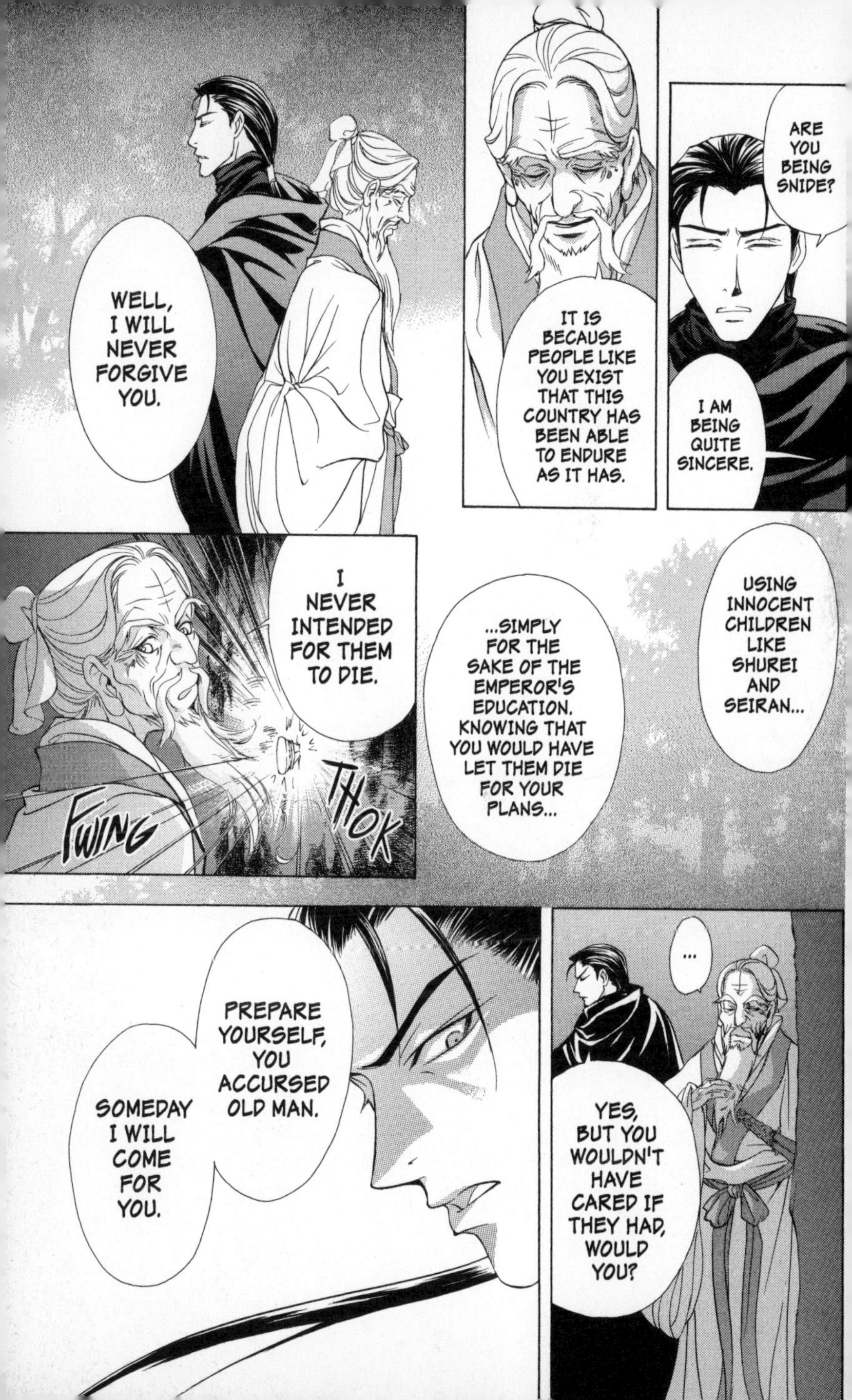
ARE YOU BEING SNIDE?
I AM BEING QUITE SINCERE.
IT IS BECAUSE PEOPLE LIKE YOU EXIST THAT THIS COUNTRY HAS BEEN ABLE TO ENDURE AS IT HAS.
WELL, I WILL NEVER FORGIVE YOU.
USING INNOCENT CHILDREN LIKE SHUREI AND SEIRAN...
...SIMPLY FOR THE SAKE OF THE EMPEROR'S EDUCATION. KNOWING THAT YOU WOULD HAVE LET THEM DIE FOR YOUR PLANS...
I NEVER INTENDED FOR THEM TO DIE.
THOK
FWING
...
YES, BUT YOU WOULDN'T HAVE CARED IF THEY HAD, WOULD YOU?
PREPARE YOURSELF, YOU ACCURSED OLD MAN.
SOMEDAY I WILL COME FOR YOU.

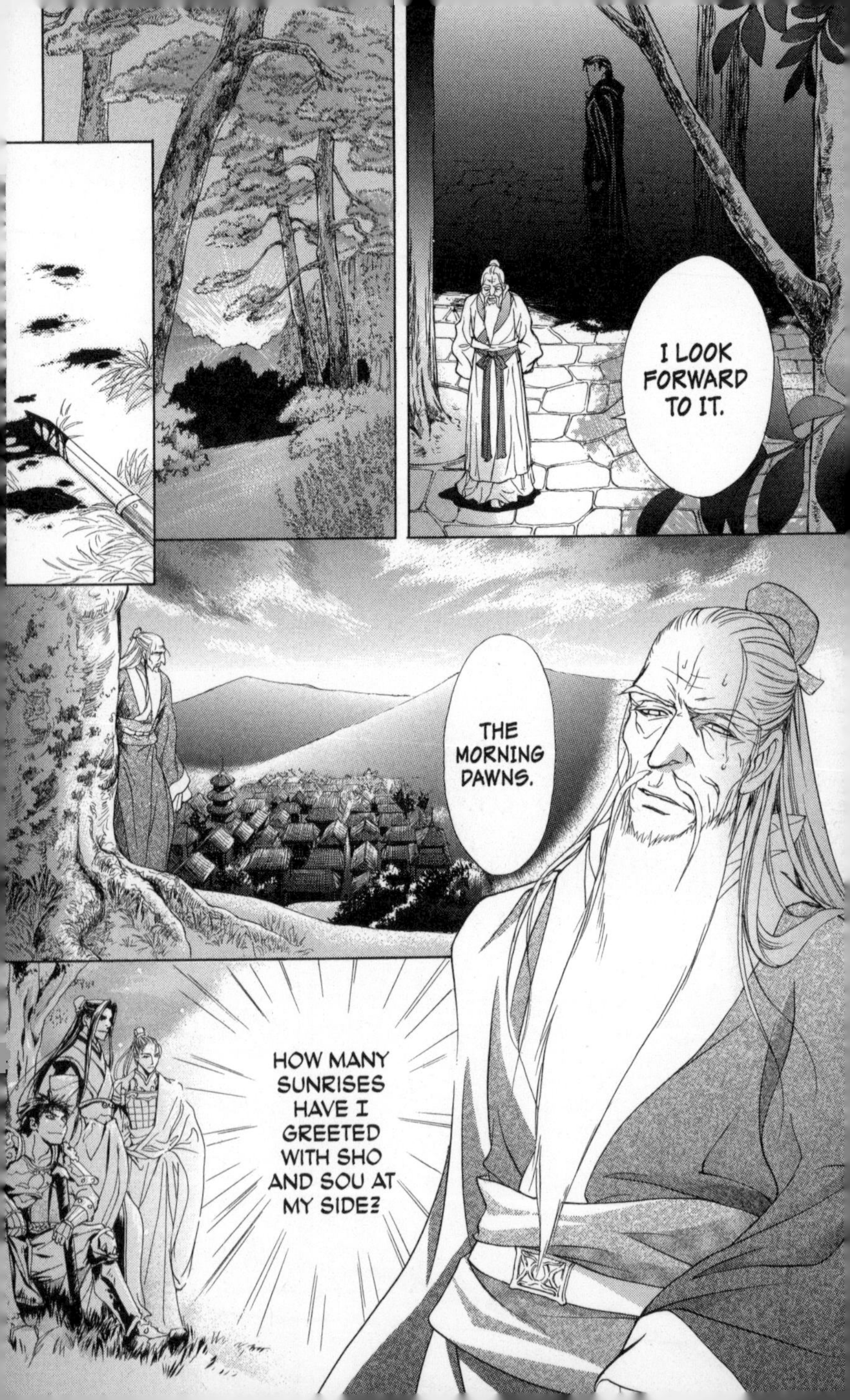
I LOOK FORWARD TO IT.
THE MORNING DAWNS.
HOW MANY SUNRISES HAVE I GREETED WITH SHO AND SOU AT MY SIDE?

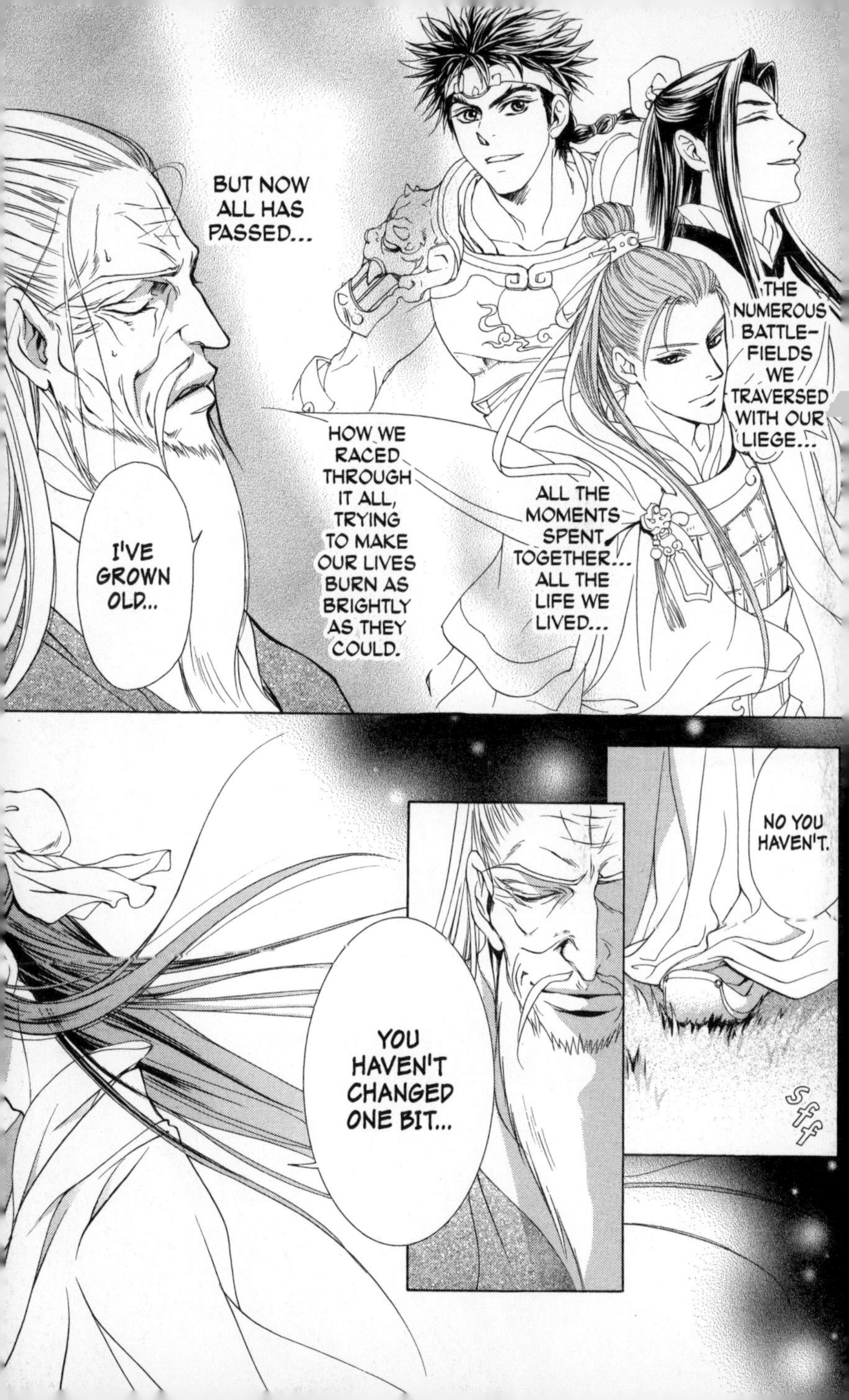
THE NUMEROUS BATTLE-FIELDS WE TRAVERSED WITH OUR LIEGE...
ALL THE MOMENTS SPENT TOGETHER... ALL THE LIFE WE LIVED...
HOW WE RACED THROUGH IT ALL, TRYING TO MAKE OUR LIVES BURN AS BRIGHTLY AS THEY COULD.
BUT NOW ALL HAS PASSED...
I'VE GROWN OLD...
NO YOU HAVEN'T.
SFF
YOU HAVEN'T CHANGED ONE BIT...

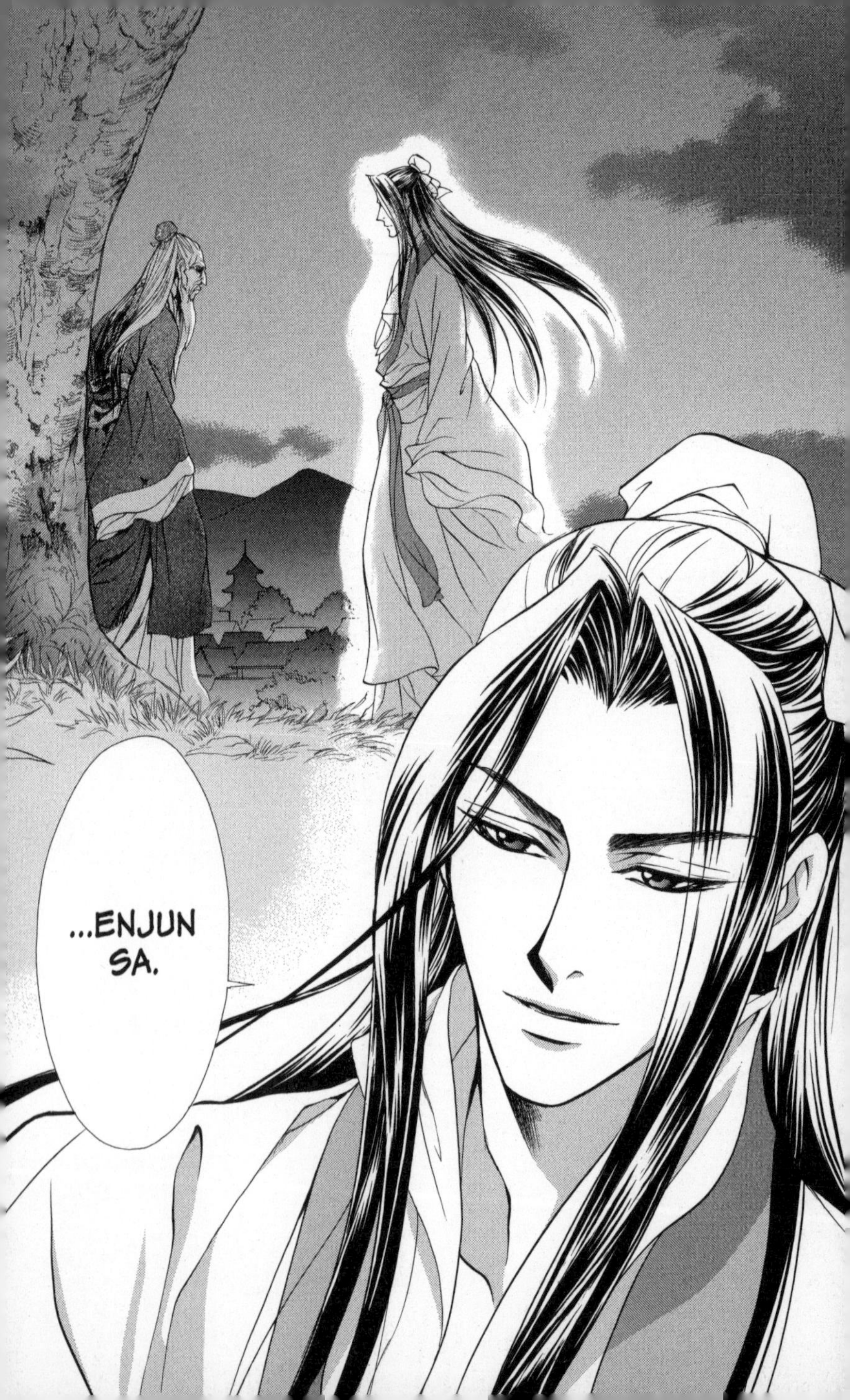
...ENJUN SA.

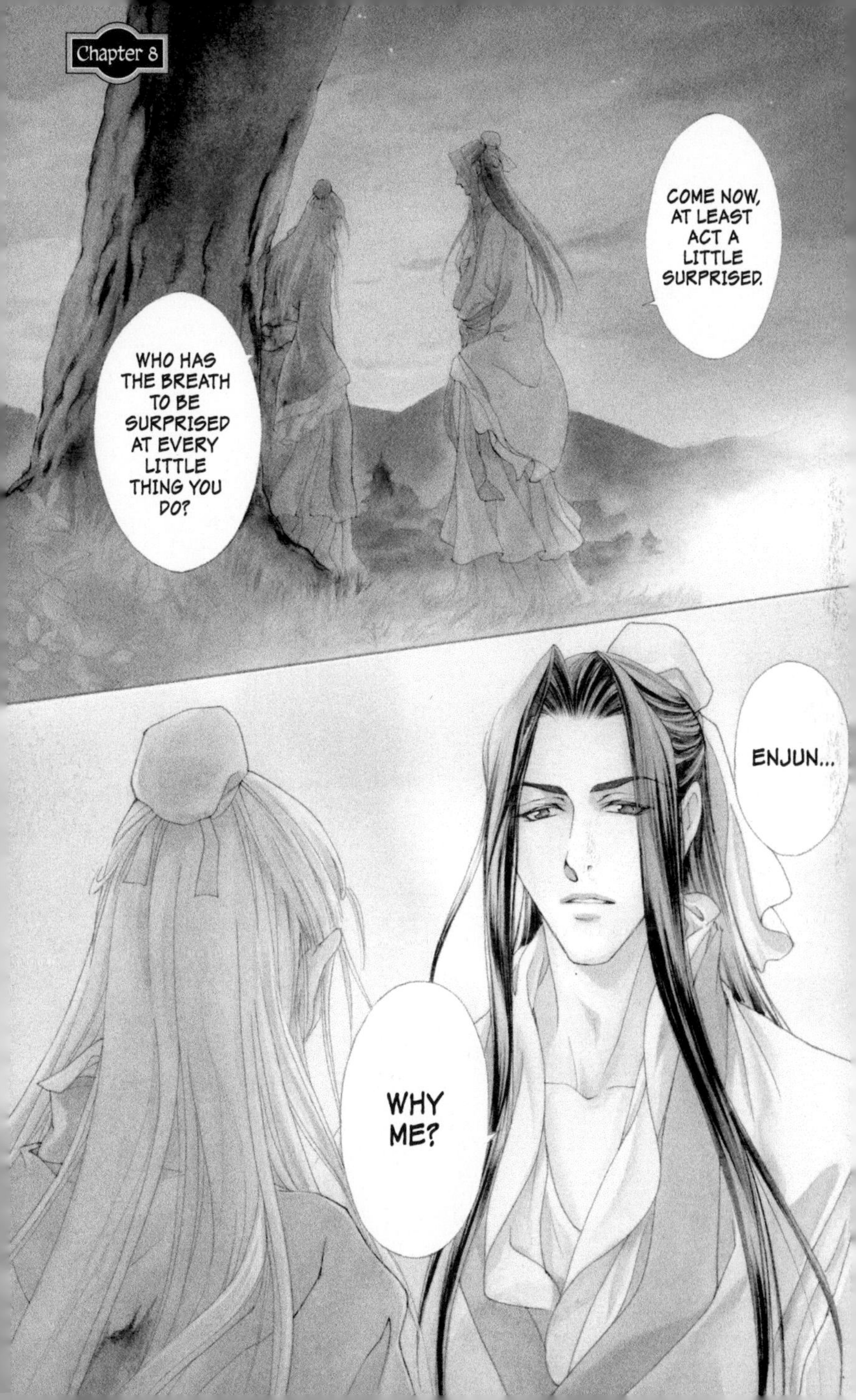
Chapter 8
COME NOW, AT LEAST ACT A LITTLE SURPRISED.
WHO HAS THE BREATH TO BE SURPRISED AT EVERY LITTLE THING YOU DO?
ENJUN...
WHY ME?

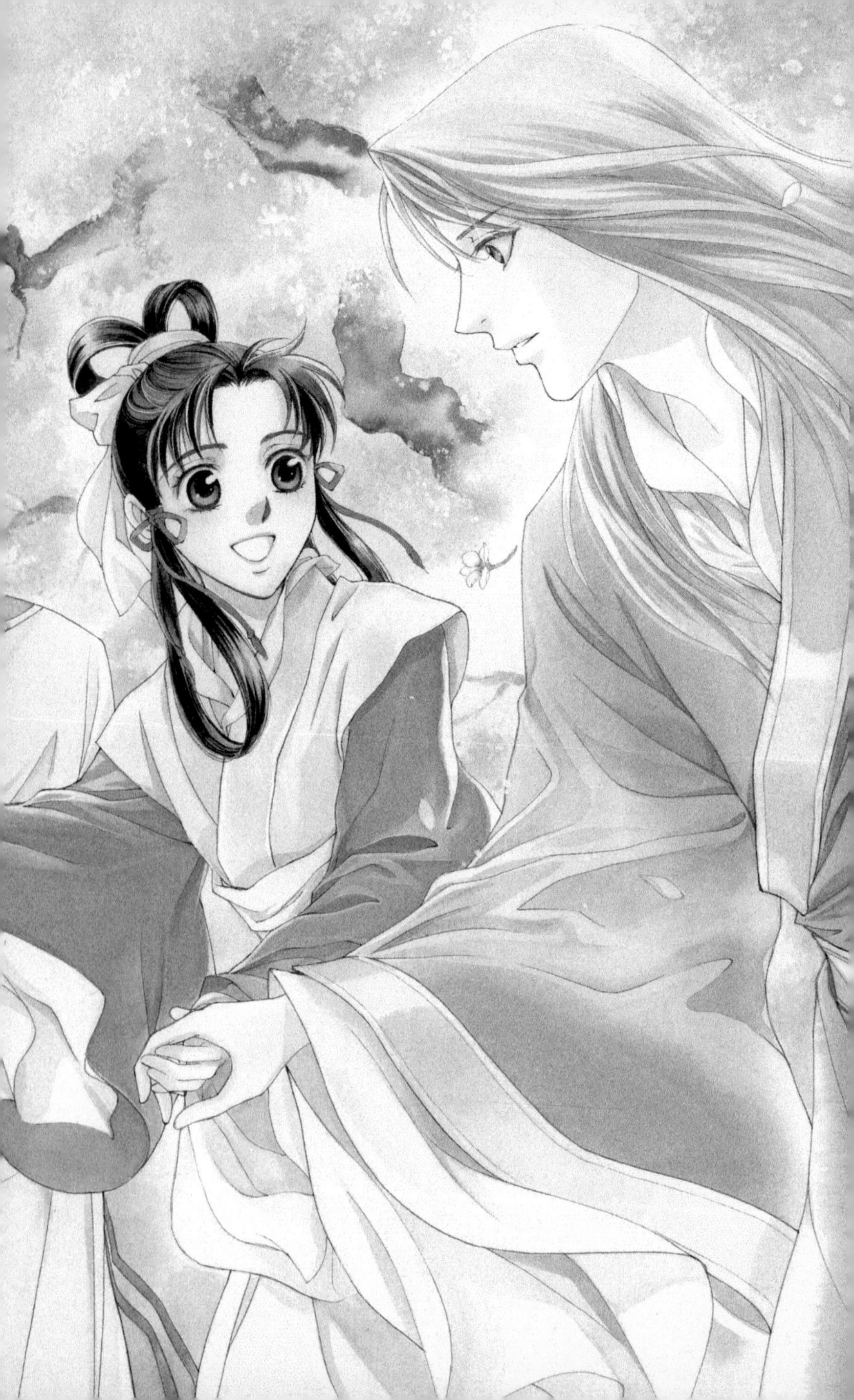

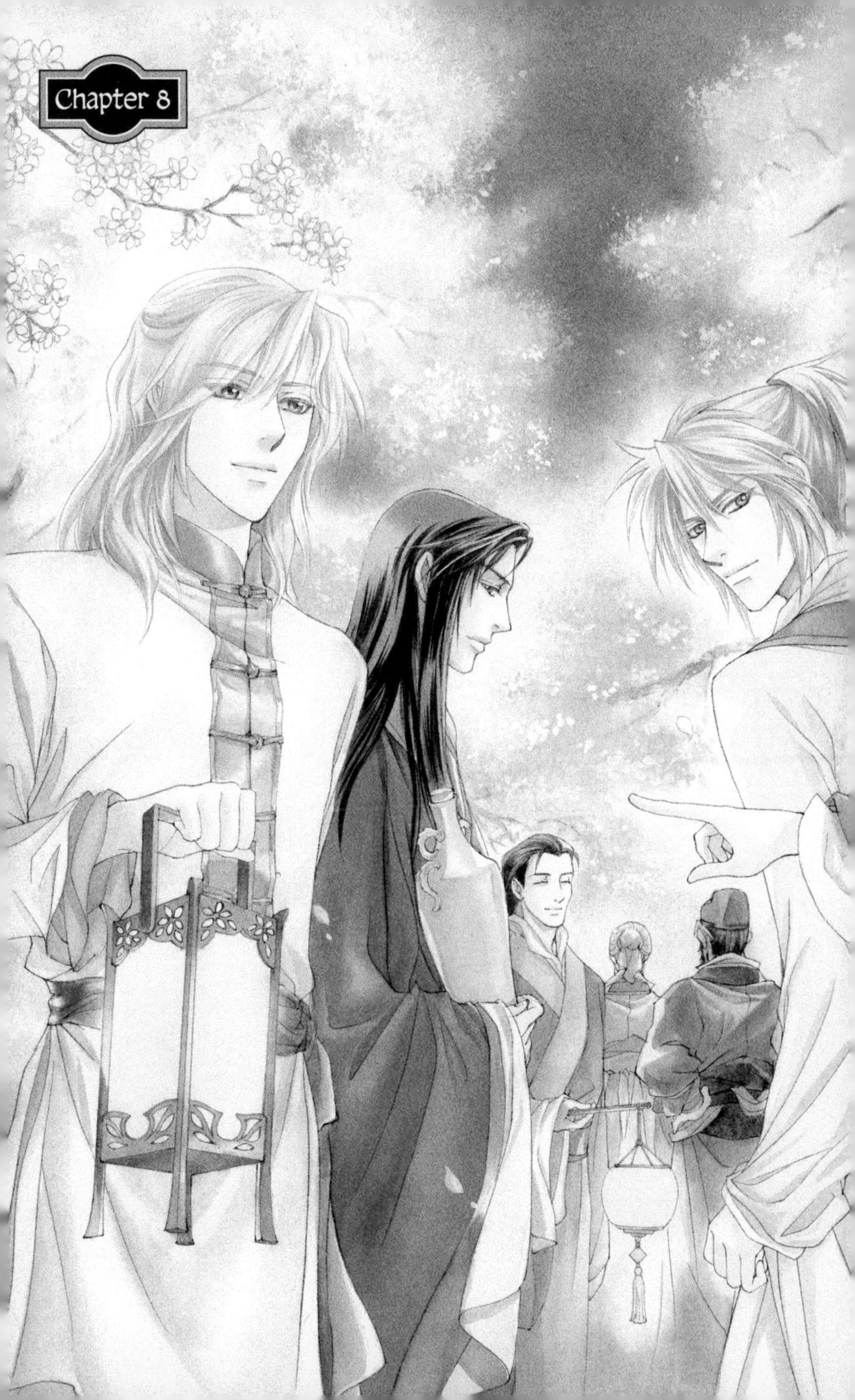
Chapter 8

The Story of
SAIUNKOKU

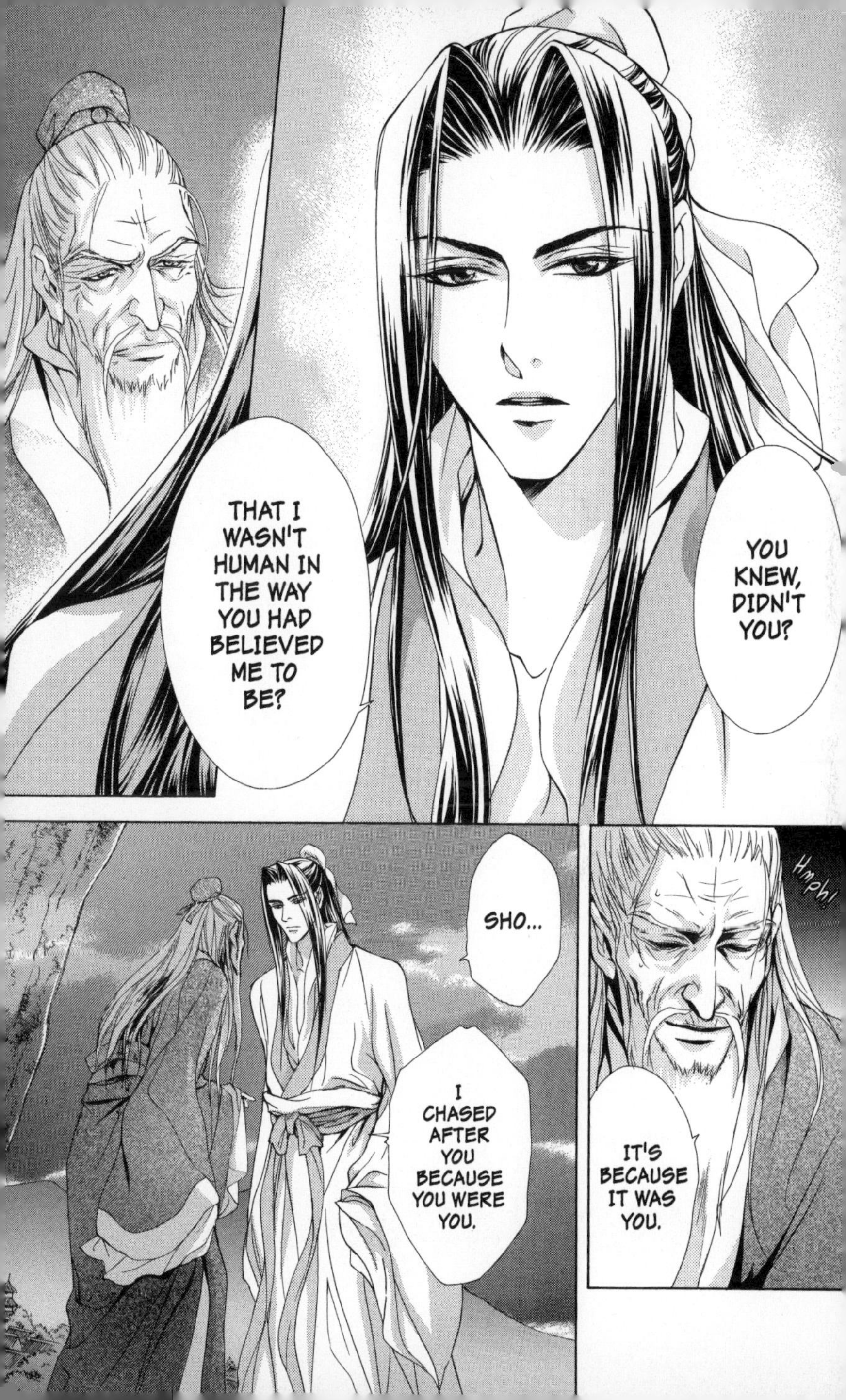
YOU KNEW, DIDN'T YOU?
THAT I WASN'T HUMAN IN THE WAY YOU HAD BELIEVED ME TO BE?
Hmph!
IT'S BECAUSE IT WAS YOU.
SHO...
I CHASED AFTER YOU BECAUSE YOU WERE YOU.

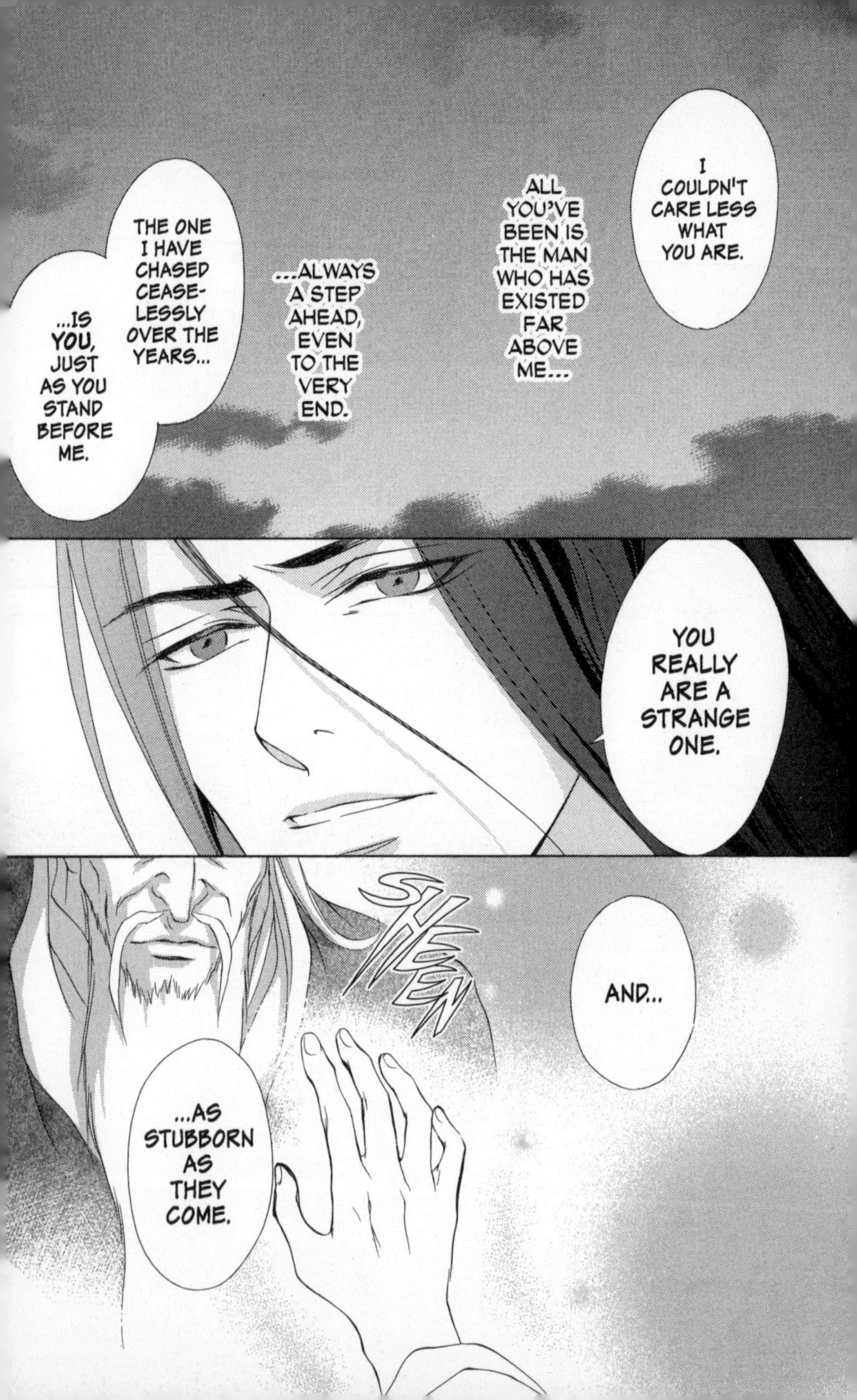
I COULDN'T CARE LESS WHAT YOU ARE.
ALL YOU'VE BEEN IS THE MAN WHO HAS EXISTED FAR ABOVE ME...
...ALWAYS A STEP AHEAD, EVEN TO THE VERY END.
THE ONE I HAVE CHASED CEASE-LESSLY OVER THE YEARS...
...IS **YOU**, JUST AS YOU STAND BEFORE ME.
YOU REALLY ARE A STRANGE ONE.
SHEEN
AND...
...AS STUBBORN AS THEY COME.

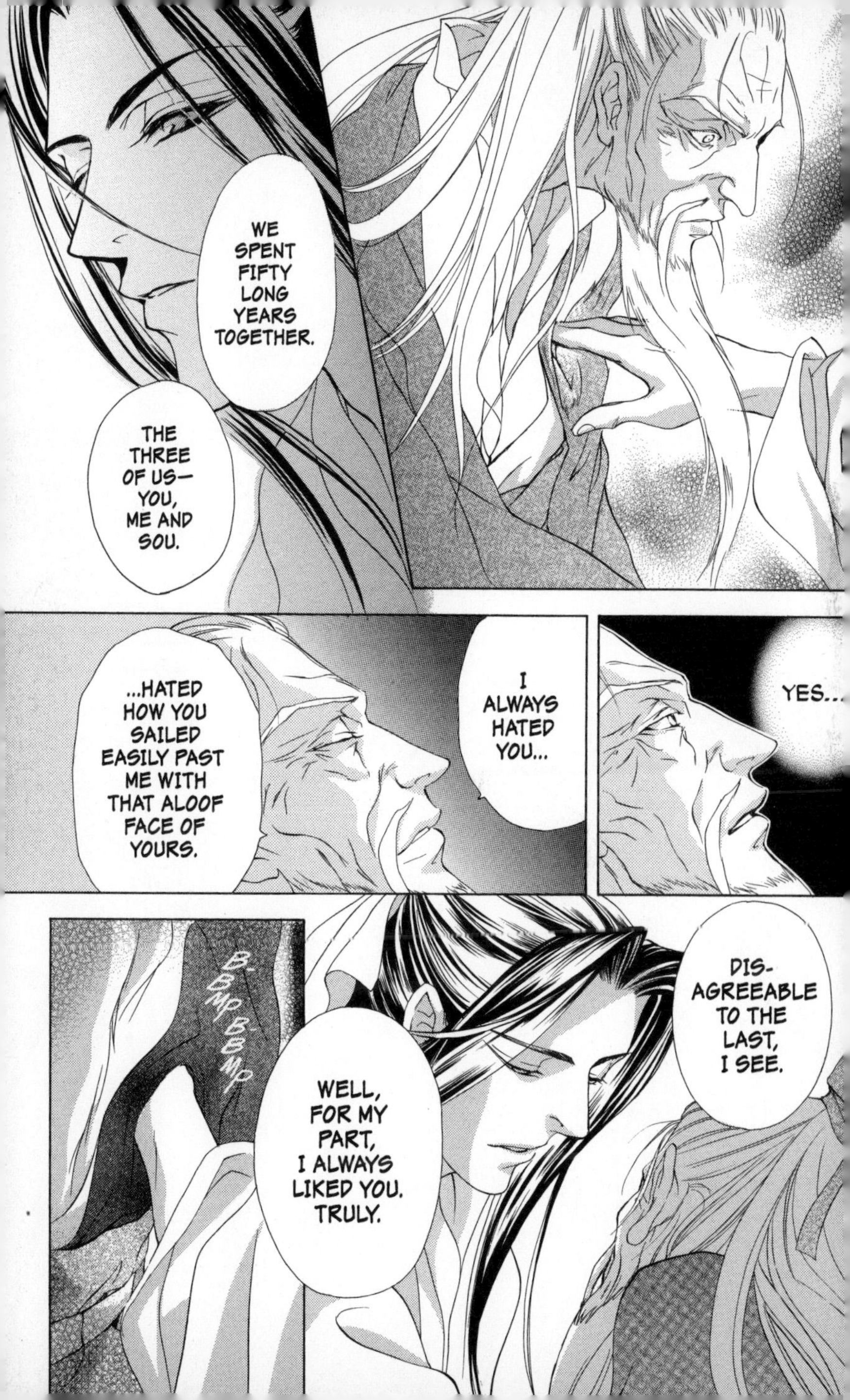
WE SPENT FIFTY LONG YEARS TOGETHER.
THE THREE OF US—YOU, ME AND SOU.
YES...
I ALWAYS HATED YOU...
...HATED HOW YOU SAILED EASILY PAST ME WITH THAT ALOOF FACE OF YOURS.
DIS-AGREEABLE TO THE LAST, I SEE.
WELL, FOR MY PART, I ALWAYS LIKED YOU. TRULY.
B-BMP B-BMP

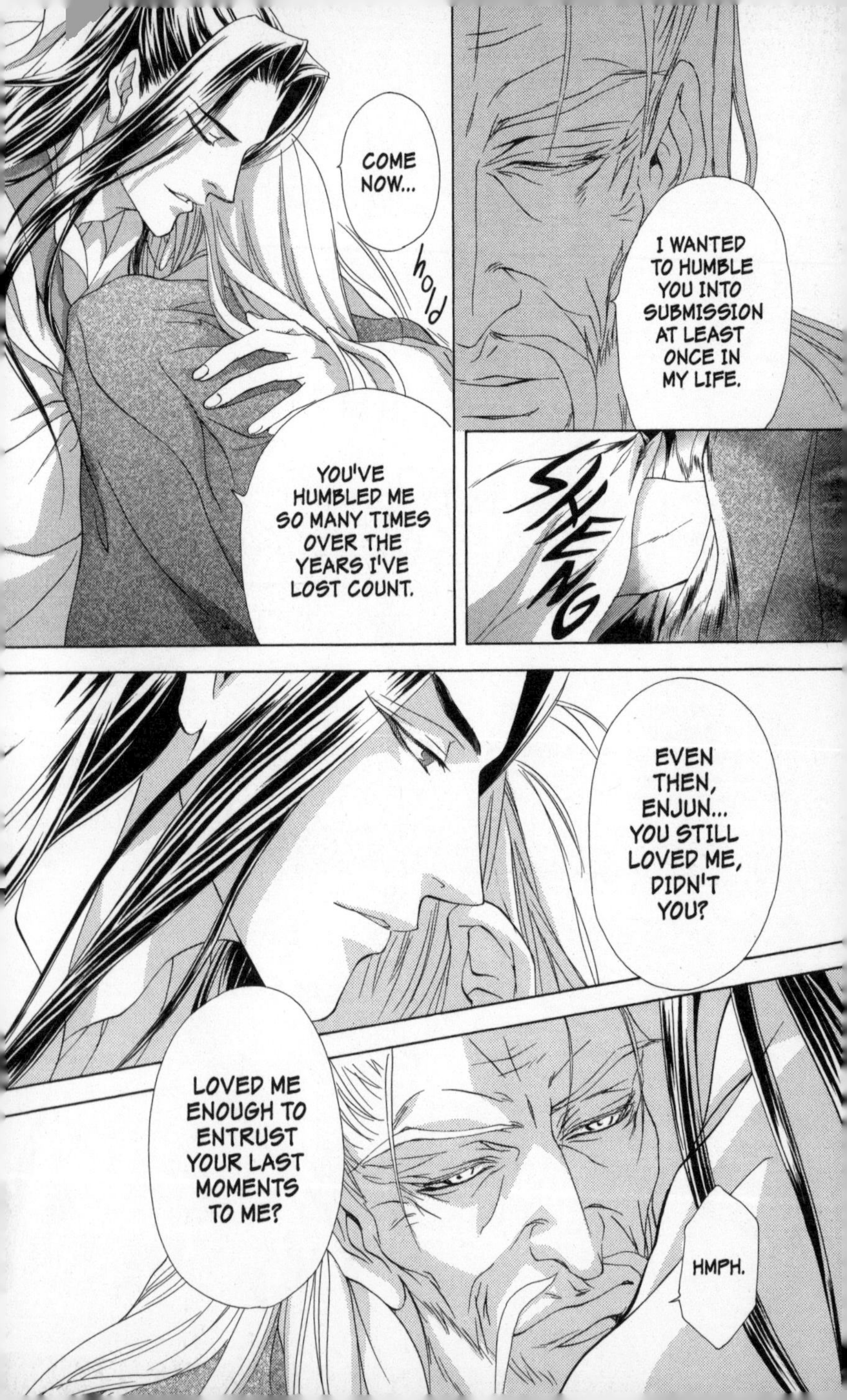
I WANTED TO HUMBLE YOU INTO SUBMISSION AT LEAST ONCE IN MY LIFE.
SHENG
COME NOW...
hold
YOU'VE HUMBLED ME SO MANY TIMES OVER THE YEARS I'VE LOST COUNT.
EVEN THEN, ENJUN... YOU STILL LOVED ME, DIDN'T YOU?
LOVED ME ENOUGH TO ENTRUST YOUR LAST MOMENTS TO ME?
HMPH.

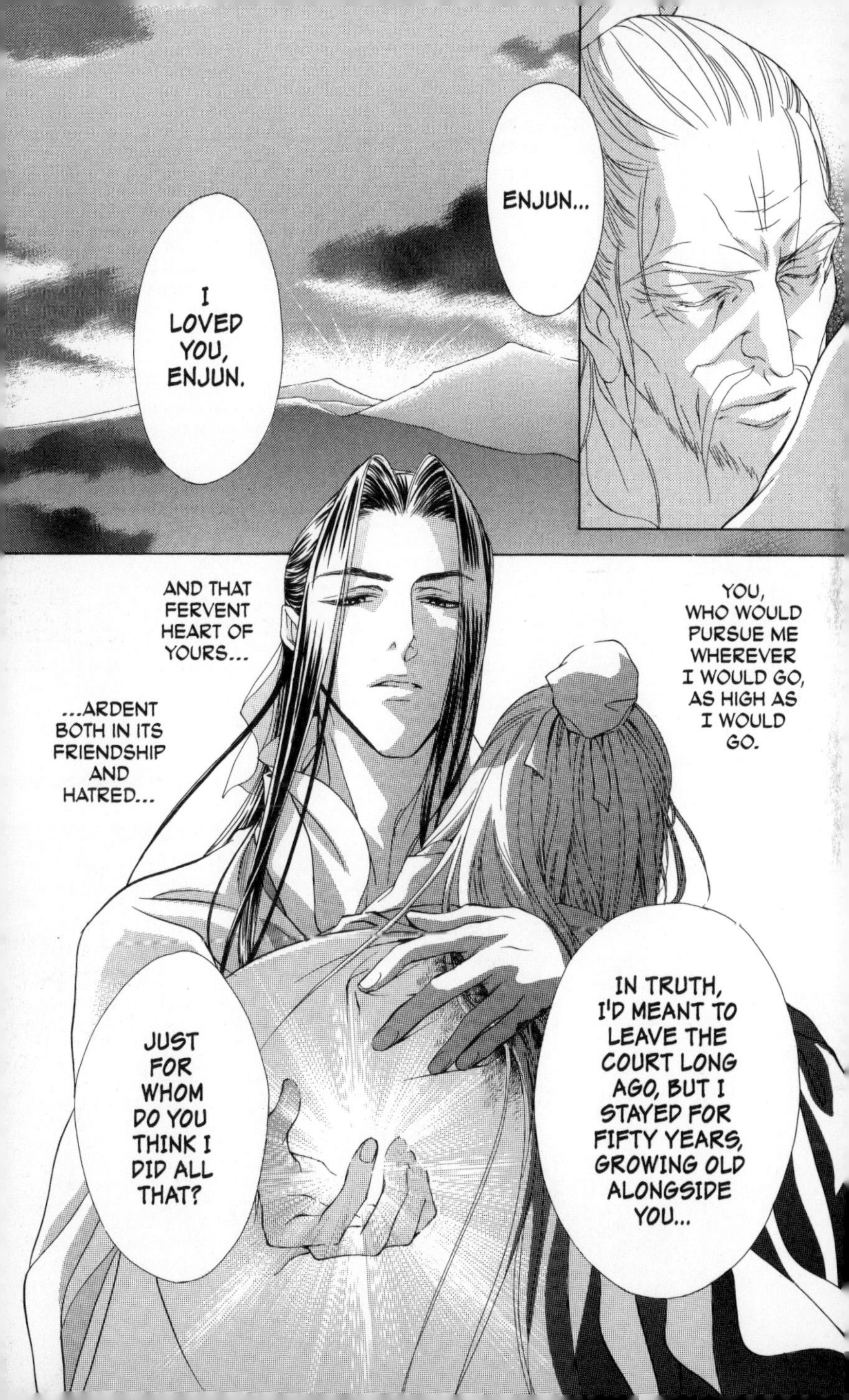
ENJUN...
I LOVED YOU, ENJUN.
YOU, WHO WOULD PURSUE ME WHEREVER I WOULD GO, AS HIGH AS I WOULD GO.
AND THAT FERVENT HEART OF YOURS...
...ARDENT BOTH IN ITS FRIENDSHIP AND HATRED...
IN TRUTH, I'D MEANT TO LEAVE THE COURT LONG AGO, BUT I STAYED FOR FIFTY YEARS, GROWING OLD ALONGSIDE YOU...
JUST FOR WHOM DO YOU THINK I DID ALL THAT?

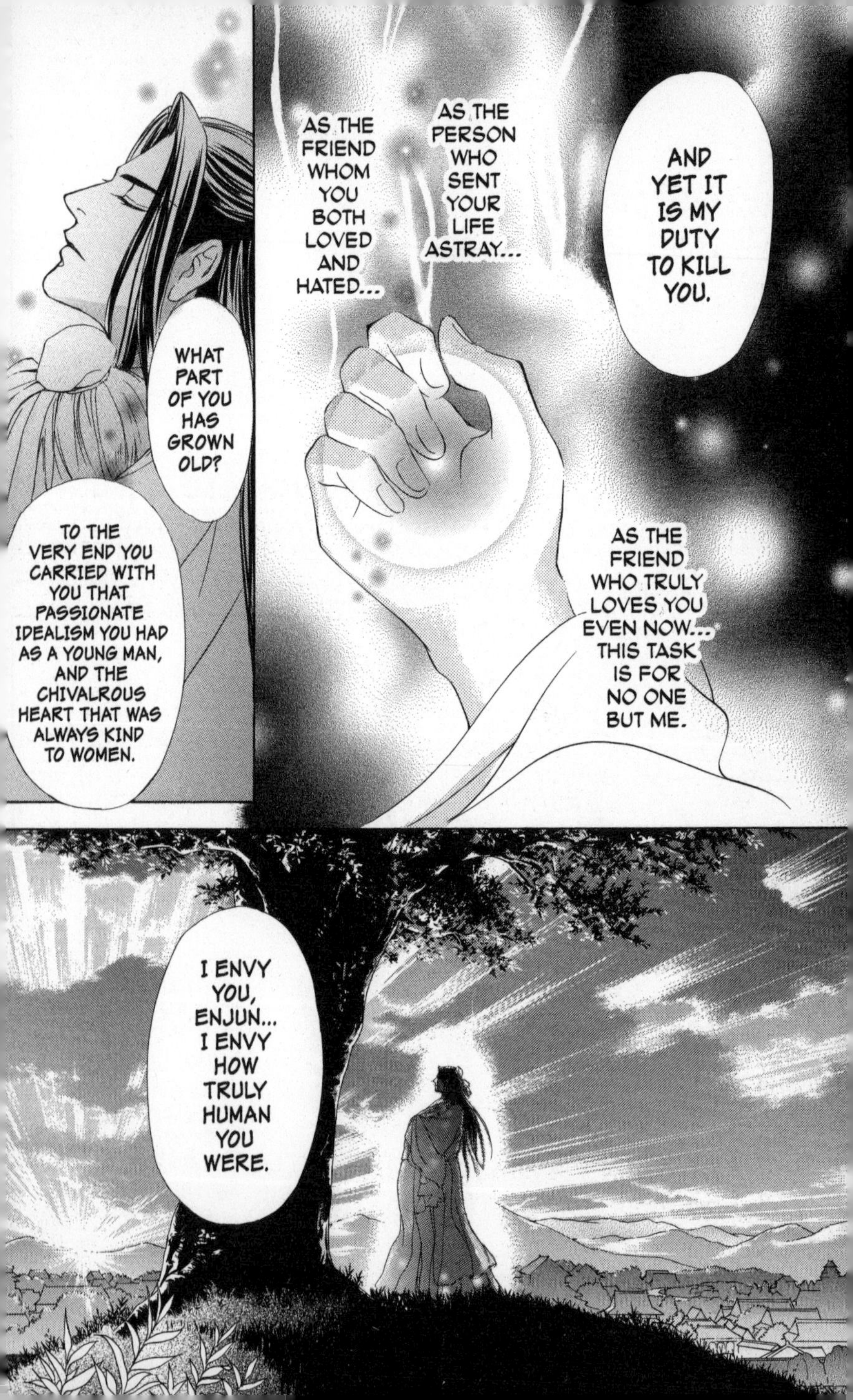
AND YET IT IS MY DUTY TO KILL YOU.
AS THE PERSON WHO SENT YOUR LIFE ASTRAY...
AS THE FRIEND WHOM YOU BOTH LOVED AND HATED...
AS THE FRIEND WHO TRULY LOVES YOU EVEN NOW... THIS TASK IS FOR NO ONE BUT ME.
WHAT PART OF YOU HAS GROWN OLD?
TO THE VERY END YOU CARRIED WITH YOU THAT PASSIONATE IDEALISM YOU HAD AS A YOUNG MAN, AND THE CHIVALROUS HEART THAT WAS ALWAYS KIND TO WOMEN.
I ENVY YOU, ENJUN... I ENVY HOW TRULY HUMAN YOU WERE.

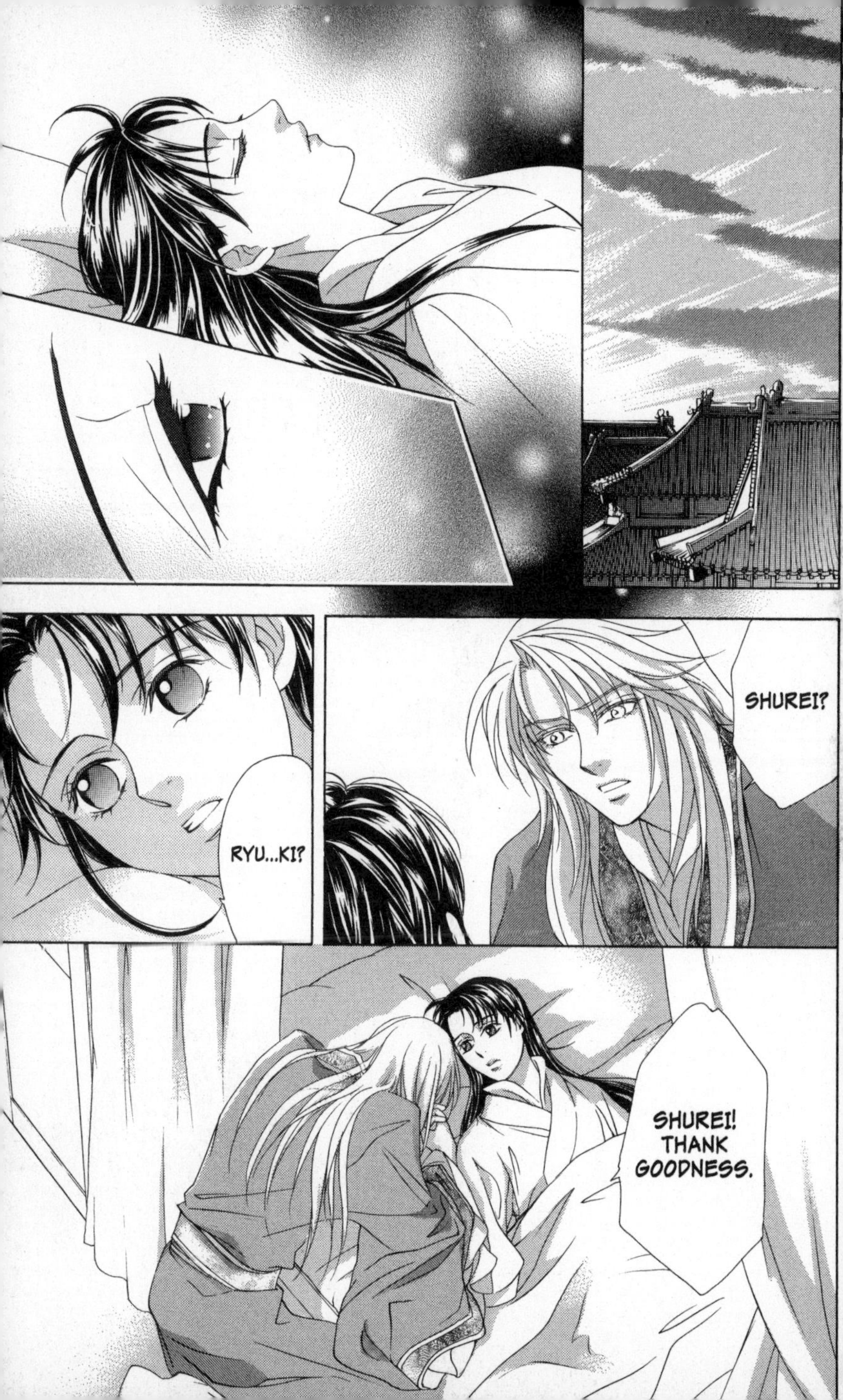
SHUREI?
RYU...KI?
SHUREI! THANK GOODNESS.

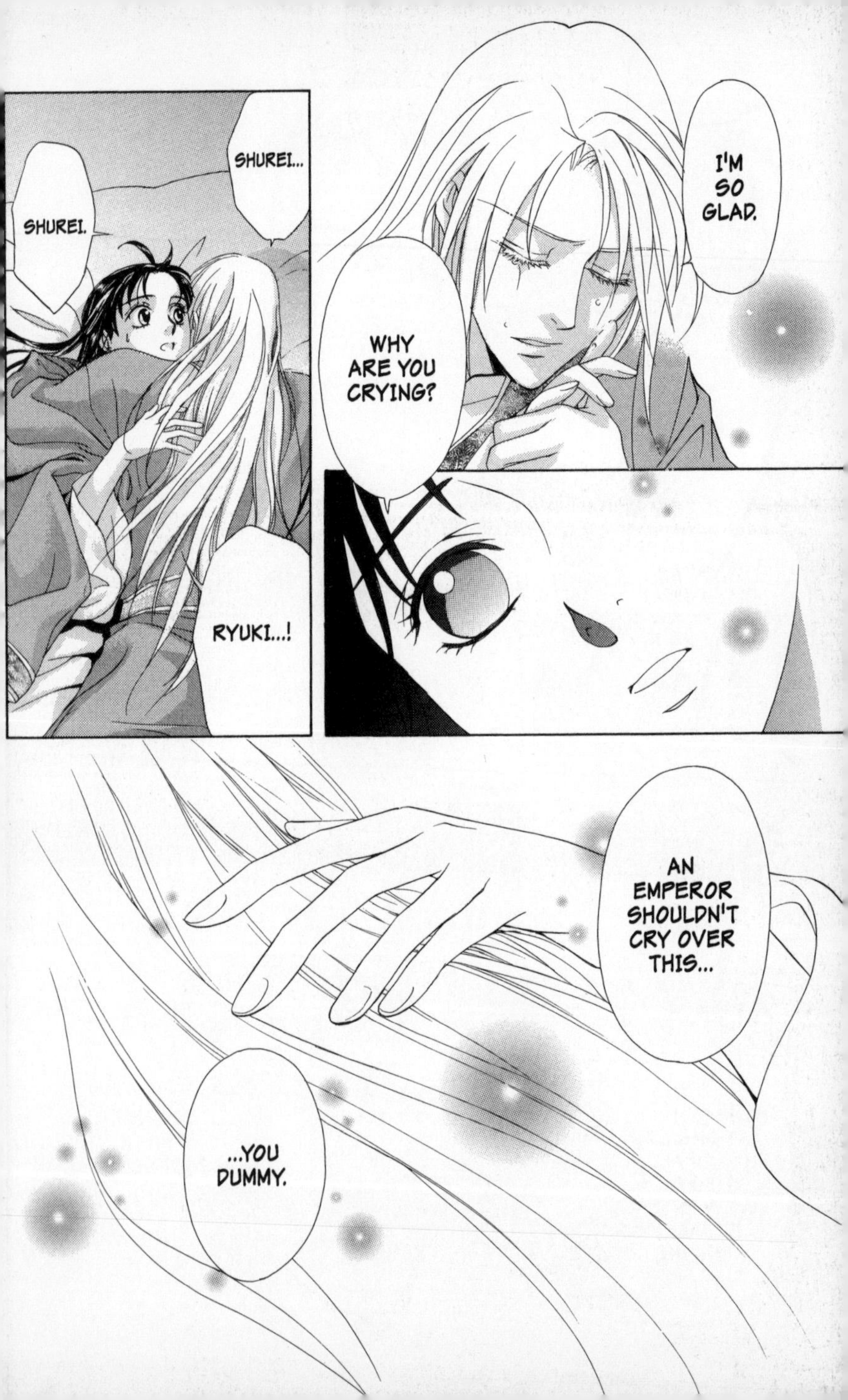
I'M SO GLAD.
WHY ARE YOU CRYING?
SHUREI...
SHUREI.
RYUKI...!
AN EMPEROR SHOULDN'T CRY OVER THIS...
...YOU DUMMY.

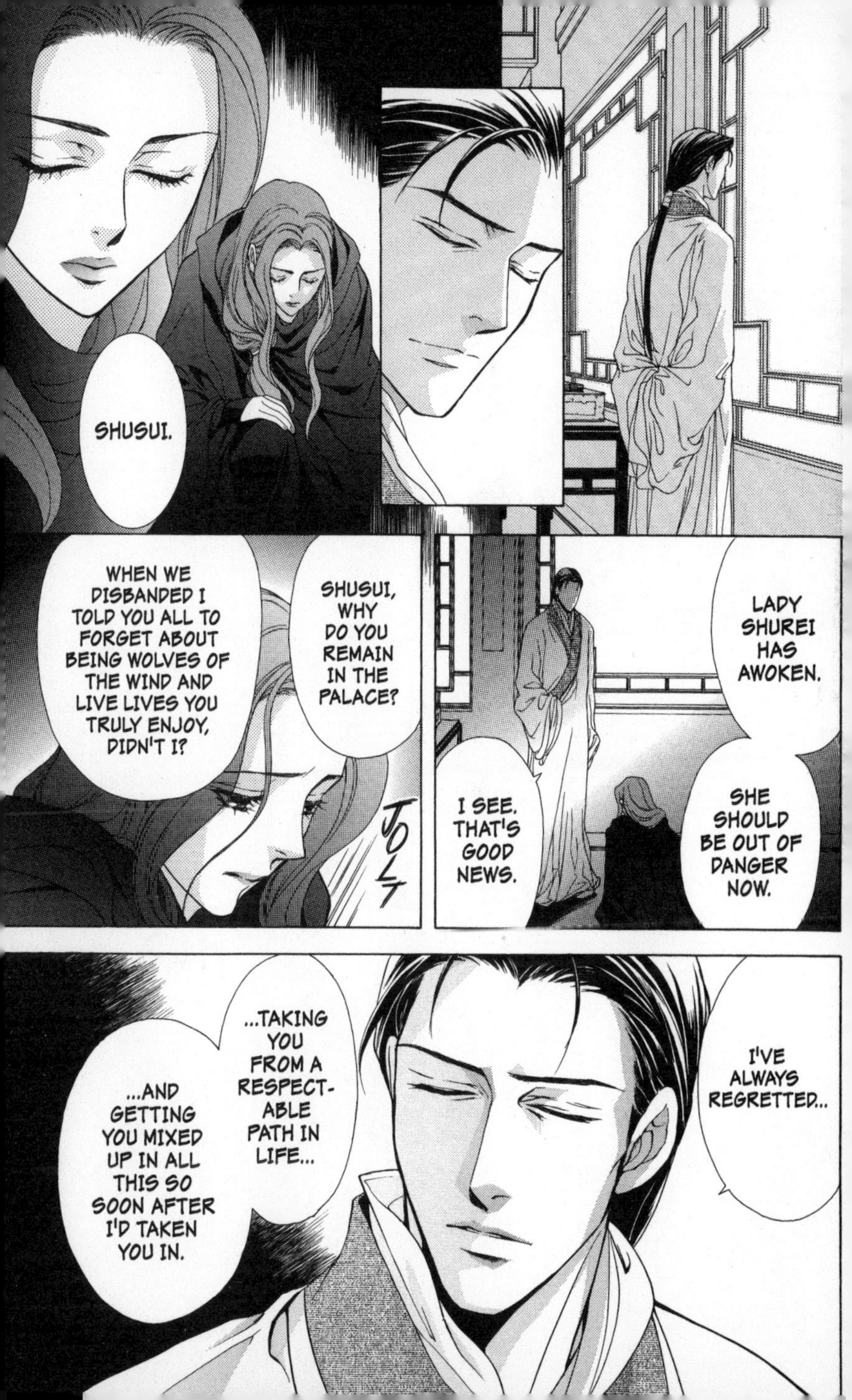
SHUSUI.
LADY SHUREI HAS AWOKEN.
SHE SHOULD BE OUT OF DANGER NOW.
I SEE. THAT'S GOOD NEWS.
SHUSUI, WHY DO YOU REMAIN IN THE PALACE?
WHEN WE DISBANDED I TOLD YOU ALL TO FORGET ABOUT BEING WOLVES OF THE WIND AND LIVE LIVES YOU TRULY ENJOY, DIDN'T I?
JOLT
I'VE ALWAYS REGRETTED...
...TAKING YOU FROM A RESPECT-ABLE PATH IN LIFE...
...AND GETTING YOU MIXED UP IN ALL THIS SO SOON AFTER I'D TAKEN YOU IN.

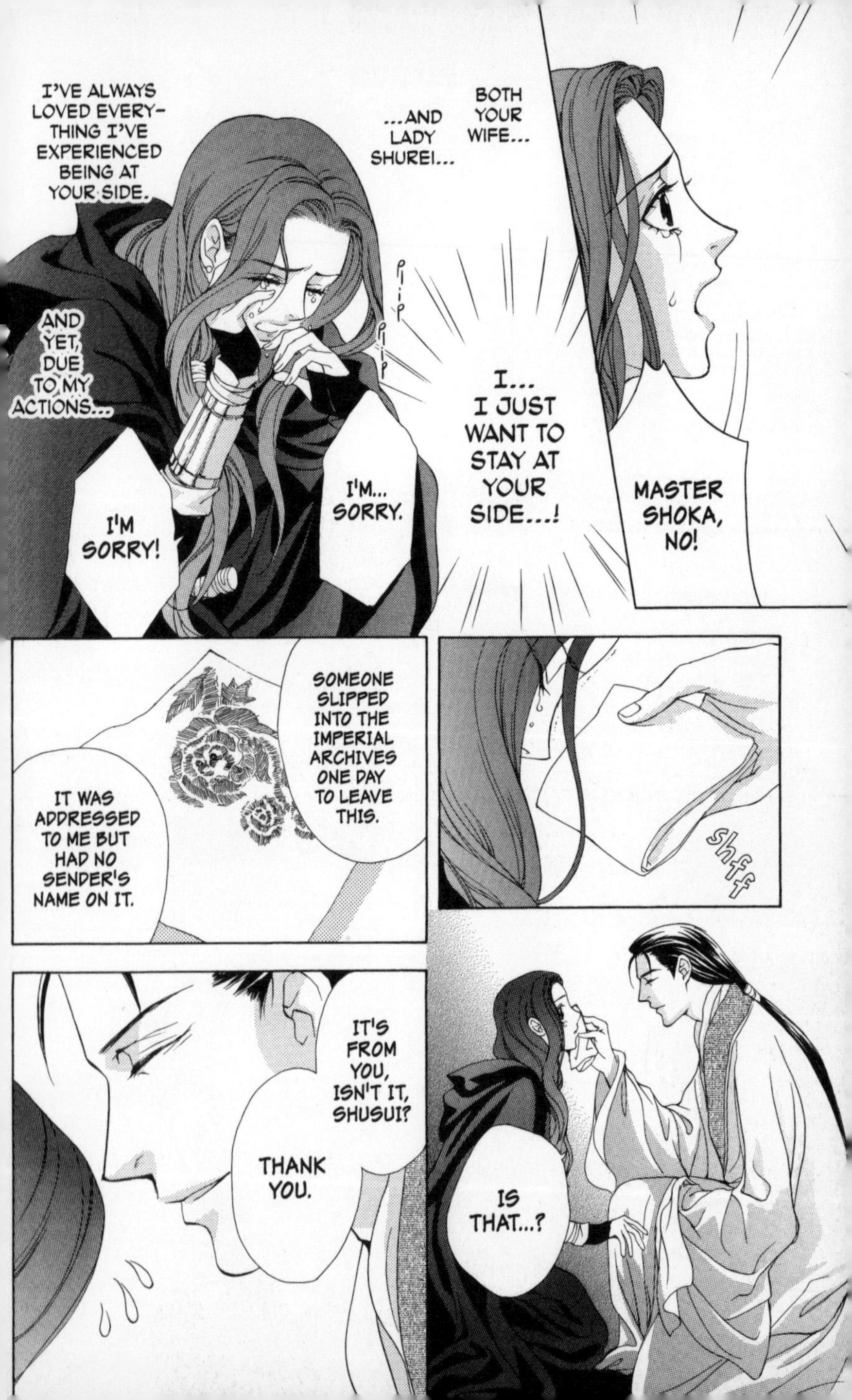
MASTER SHOKA, NO!
I... I JUST WANT TO STAY AT YOUR SIDE...!
BOTH YOUR WIFE...
...AND LADY SHUREI...
I'VE ALWAYS LOVED EVERYTHING I'VE EXPERIENCED BEING AT YOUR SIDE.
AND YET, DUE TO MY ACTIONS...
I'M... SORRY.
I'M SORRY!
shff
SOMEONE SLIPPED INTO THE IMPERIAL ARCHIVES ONE DAY TO LEAVE THIS.
IT WAS ADDRESSED TO ME BUT HAD NO SENDER'S NAME ON IT.
IS THAT...?
IT'S FROM YOU, ISN'T IT, SHUSUI?
THANK YOU.

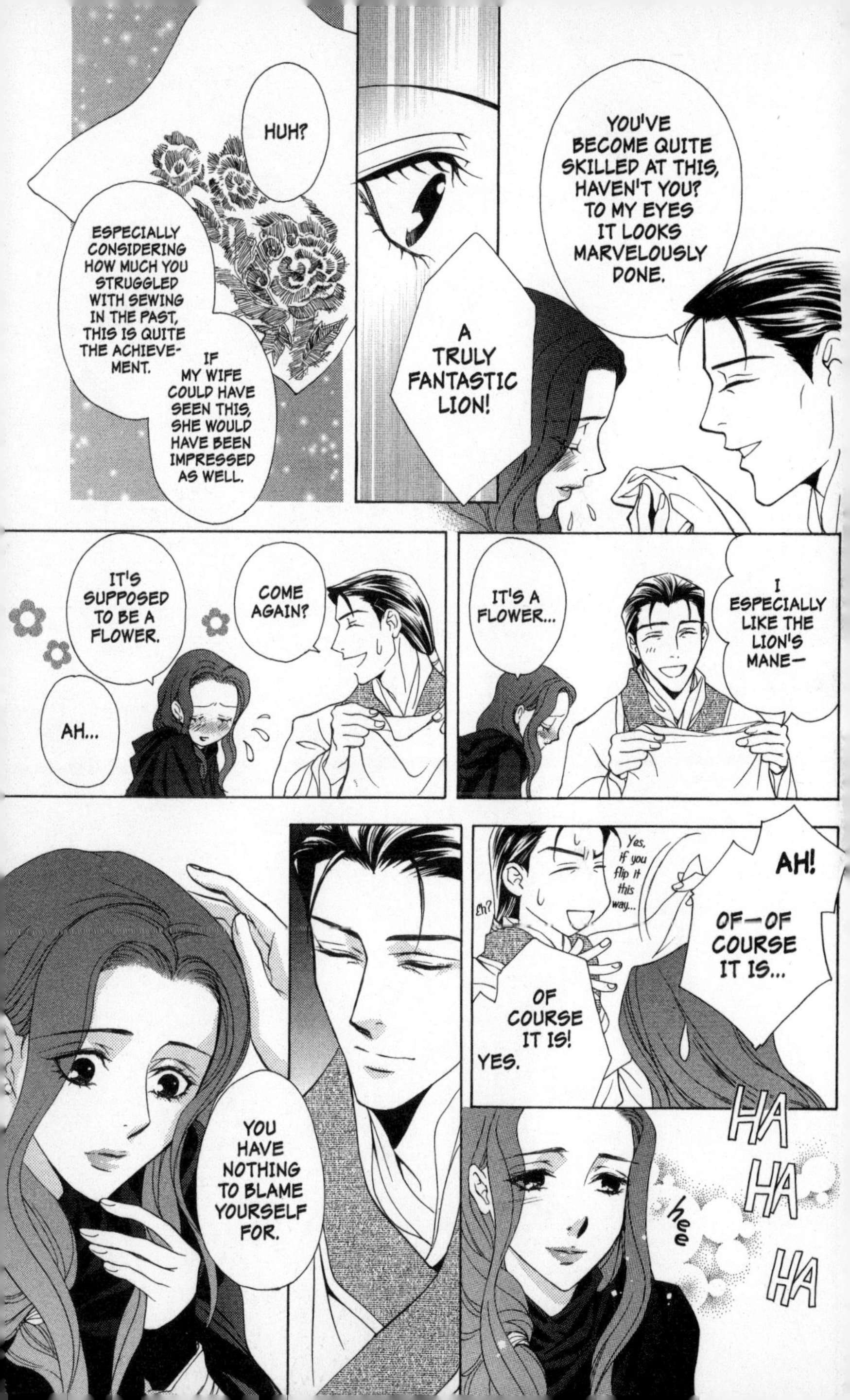
YOU'VE BECOME QUITE SKILLED AT THIS, HAVEN'T YOU? TO MY EYES IT LOOKS MARVELOUSLY DONE.
A TRULY FANTASTIC LION!
HUH?
ESPECIALLY CONSIDERING HOW MUCH YOU STRUGGLED WITH SEWING IN THE PAST, THIS IS QUITE THE ACHIEVE-MENT.
IF MY WIFE COULD HAVE SEEN THIS, SHE WOULD HAVE BEEN IMPRESSED AS WELL.
I ESPECIALLY LIKE THE LION'S MANE—
IT'S A FLOWER...
COME AGAIN?
IT'S SUPPOSED TO BE A FLOWER.
AH...
AH!
OF—OF COURSE IT IS...
Yes, if you flip it this way...
Eh?
OF COURSE IT IS! YES.
HA HA HA
hee
YOU HAVE NOTHING TO BLAME YOURSELF FOR.

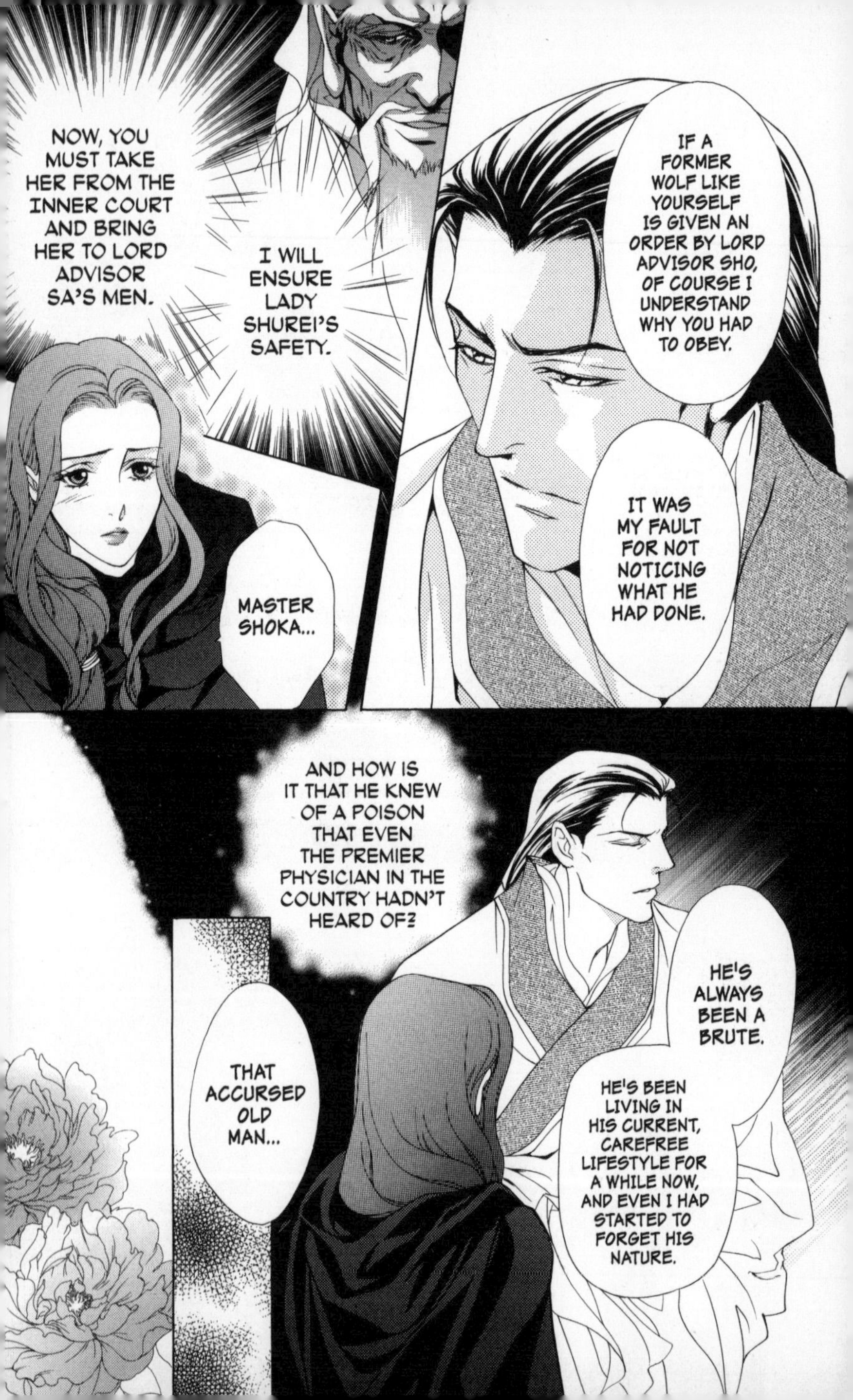
IF A FORMER WOLF LIKE YOURSELF IS GIVEN AN ORDER BY LORD ADVISOR SHO, OF COURSE I UNDERSTAND WHY YOU HAD TO OBEY.
IT WAS MY FAULT FOR NOT NOTICING WHAT HE HAD DONE.
NOW, YOU MUST TAKE HER FROM THE INNER COURT AND BRING HER TO LORD ADVISOR SA'S MEN.
I WILL ENSURE LADY SHUREI'S SAFETY.
MASTER SHOKA...
AND HOW IS IT THAT HE KNEW OF A POISON THAT EVEN THE PREMIER PHYSICIAN IN THE COUNTRY HADN'T HEARD OF?
HE'S ALWAYS BEEN A BRUTE.
HE'S BEEN LIVING IN HIS CURRENT, CAREFREE LIFESTYLE FOR A WHILE NOW, AND EVEN I HAD STARTED TO FORGET HIS NATURE.
THAT ACCURSED OLD MAN...

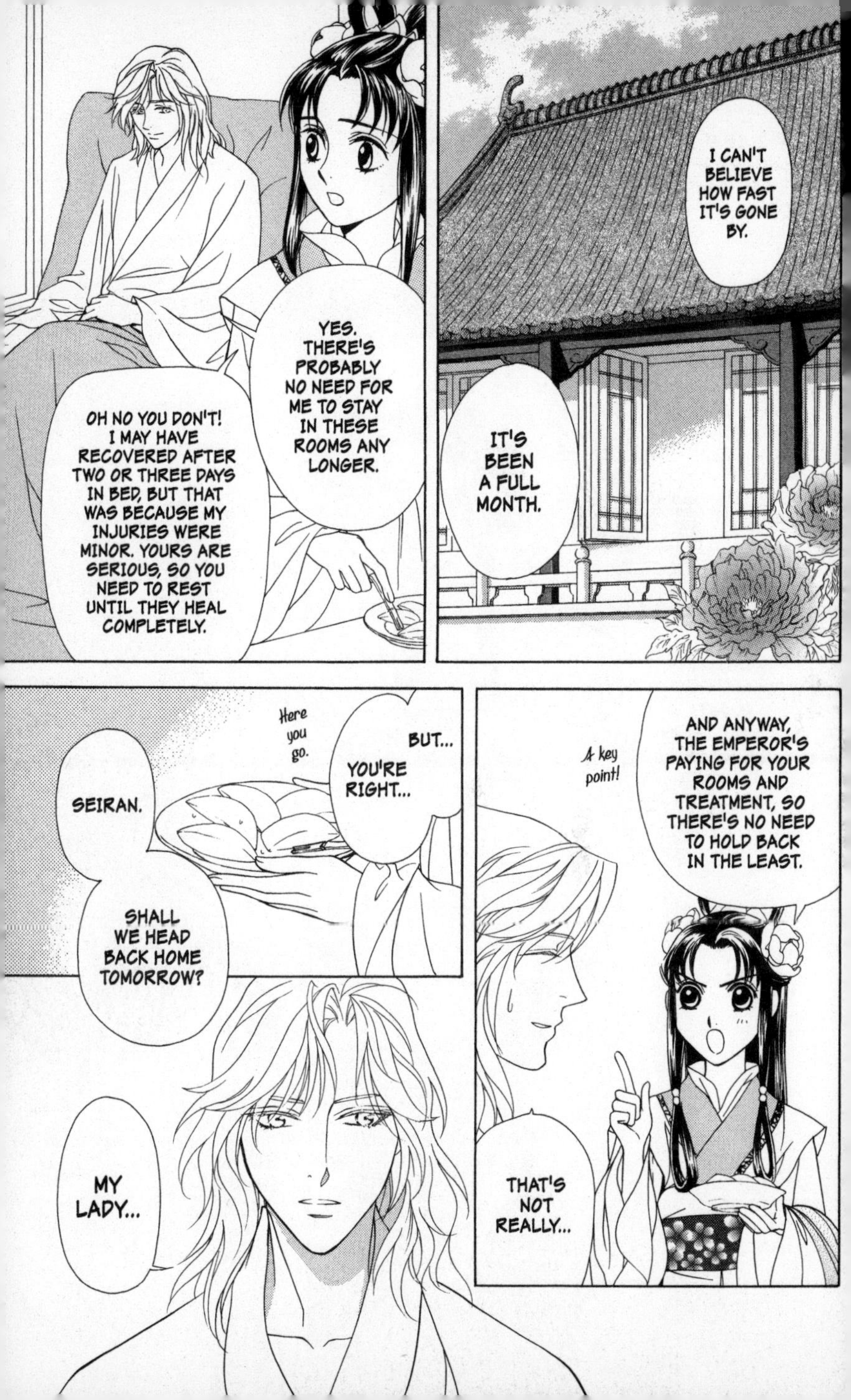
I CAN'T BELIEVE HOW FAST IT'S GONE BY.
IT'S BEEN A FULL MONTH.
YES. THERE'S PROBABLY NO NEED FOR ME TO STAY IN THESE ROOMS ANY LONGER.
OH NO YOU DON'T! I MAY HAVE RECOVERED AFTER TWO OR THREE DAYS IN BED, BUT THAT WAS BECAUSE MY INJURIES WERE MINOR. YOURS ARE SERIOUS, SO YOU NEED TO REST UNTIL THEY HEAL COMPLETELY.
AND ANYWAY, THE EMPEROR'S PAYING FOR YOUR ROOMS AND TREATMENT, SO THERE'S NO NEED TO HOLD BACK IN THE LEAST.
A key point!
THAT'S NOT REALLY...
BUT... YOU'RE RIGHT...
Here you go.
SEIRAN.
SHALL WE HEAD BACK HOME TOMORROW?
MY LADY...

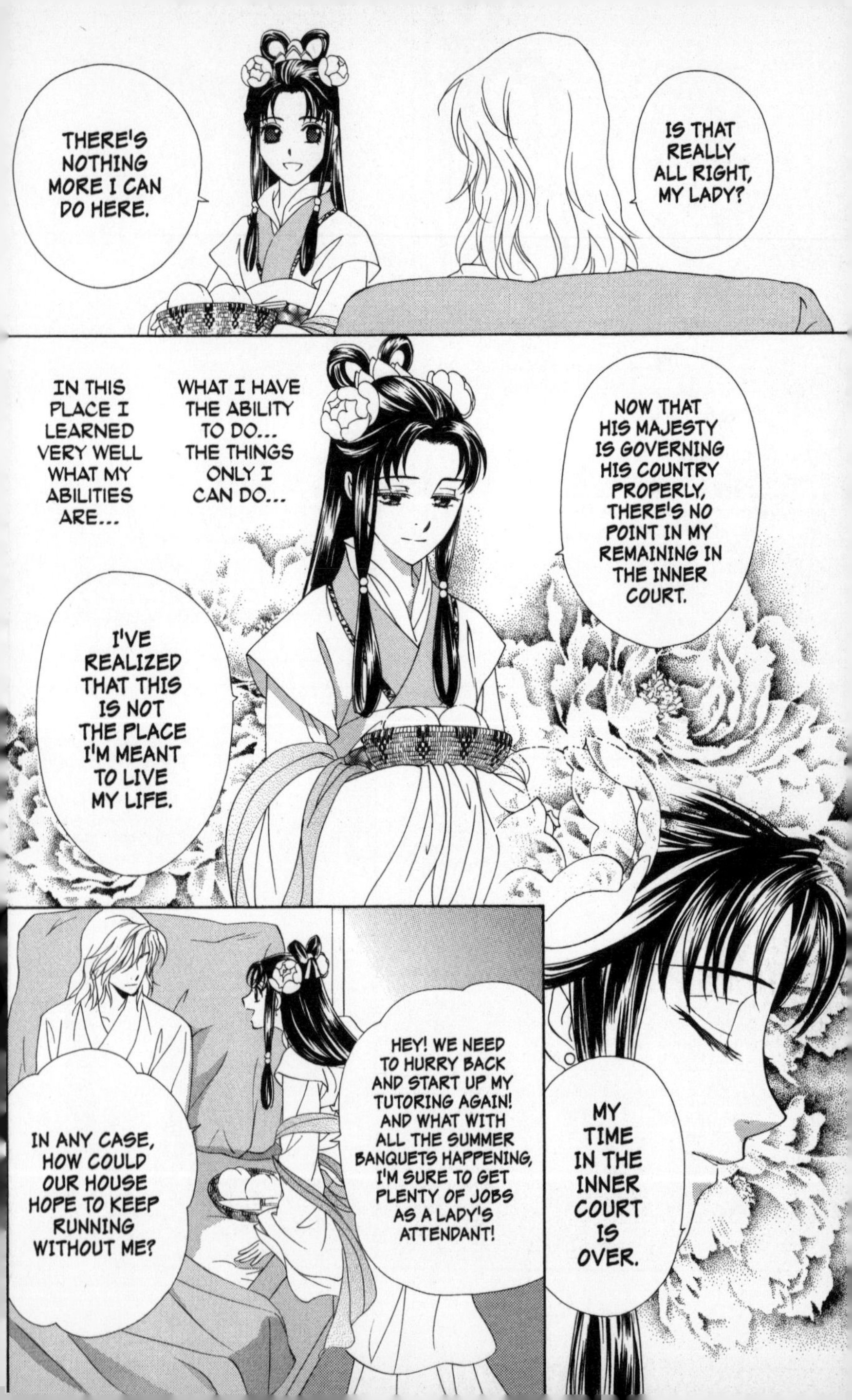
IS THAT REALLY ALL RIGHT, MY LADY?
THERE'S NOTHING MORE I CAN DO HERE.
NOW THAT HIS MAJESTY IS GOVERNING HIS COUNTRY PROPERLY, THERE'S NO POINT IN MY REMAINING IN THE INNER COURT.
WHAT I HAVE THE ABILITY TO DO... THE THINGS ONLY I CAN DO...
IN THIS PLACE I LEARNED VERY WELL WHAT MY ABILITIES ARE...
I'VE REALIZED THAT THIS IS NOT THE PLACE I'M MEANT TO LIVE MY LIFE.
MY TIME IN THE INNER COURT IS OVER.
HEY! WE NEED TO HURRY BACK AND START UP MY TUTORING AGAIN! AND WHAT WITH ALL THE SUMMER BANQUETS HAPPENING, I'M SURE TO GET PLENTY OF JOBS AS A LADY'S ATTENDANT!
IN ANY CASE, HOW COULD OUR HOUSE HOPE TO KEEP RUNNING WITHOUT ME?

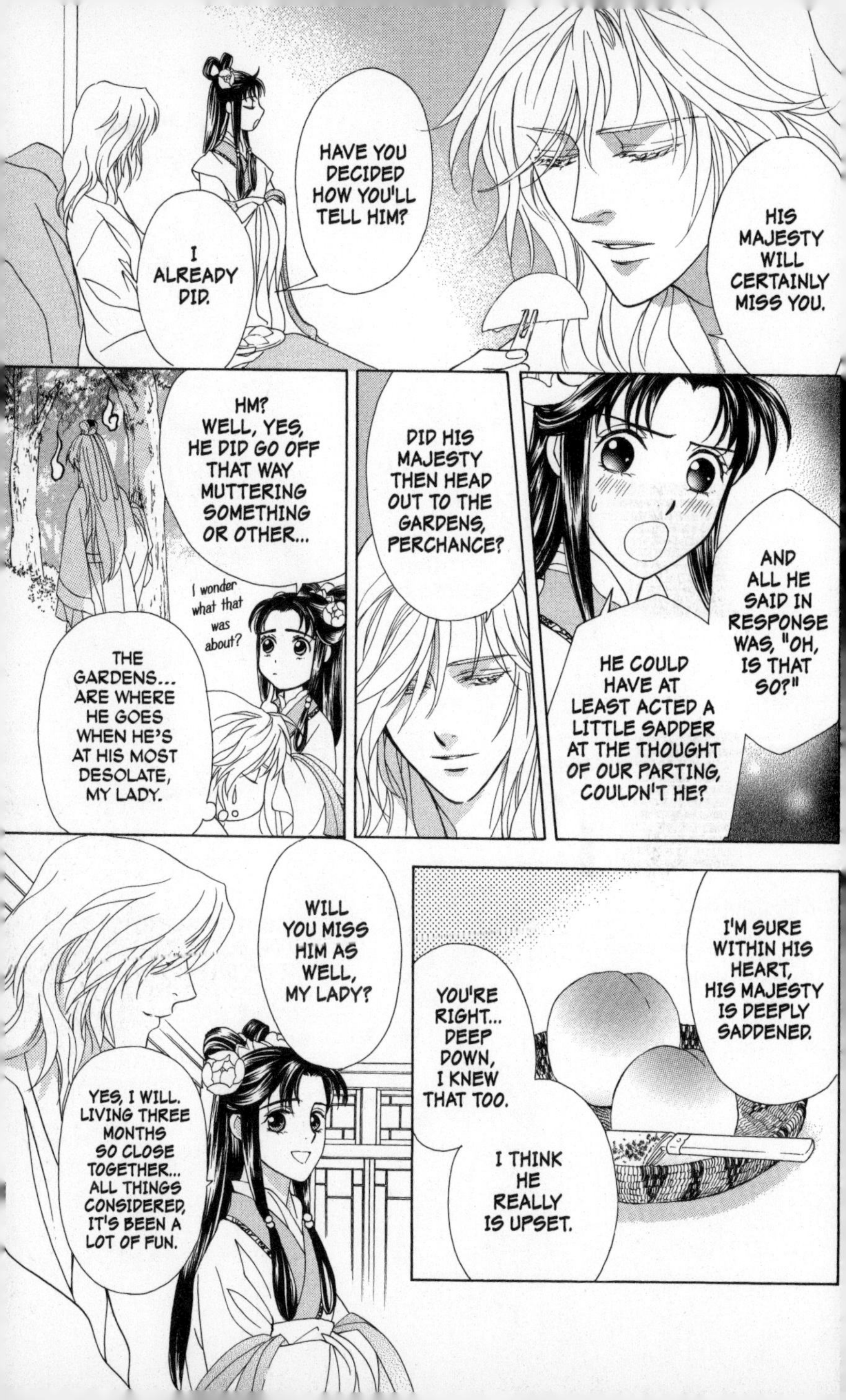
HIS MAJESTY WILL CERTAINLY MISS YOU.
HAVE YOU DECIDED HOW YOU'LL TELL HIM?
I ALREADY DID.
AND ALL HE SAID IN RESPONSE WAS, "OH, IS THAT SO?"
HE COULD HAVE AT LEAST ACTED A LITTLE SADDER AT THE THOUGHT OF OUR PARTING, COULDN'T HE?
DID HIS MAJESTY THEN HEAD OUT TO THE GARDENS, PERCHANCE?
HM? WELL, YES, HE DID GO OFF THAT WAY MUTTERING SOMETHING OR OTHER...
I wonder what that was about?
THE GARDENS... ARE WHERE HE GOES WHEN HE'S AT HIS MOST DESOLATE, MY LADY.
I'M SURE WITHIN HIS HEART, HIS MAJESTY IS DEEPLY SADDENED.
YOU'RE RIGHT... DEEP DOWN, I KNEW THAT TOO.
I THINK HE REALLY IS UPSET.
WILL YOU MISS HIM AS WELL, MY LADY?
YES, I WILL. LIVING THREE MONTHS SO CLOSE TOGETHER... ALL THINGS CONSIDERED, IT'S BEEN A LOT OF FUN.

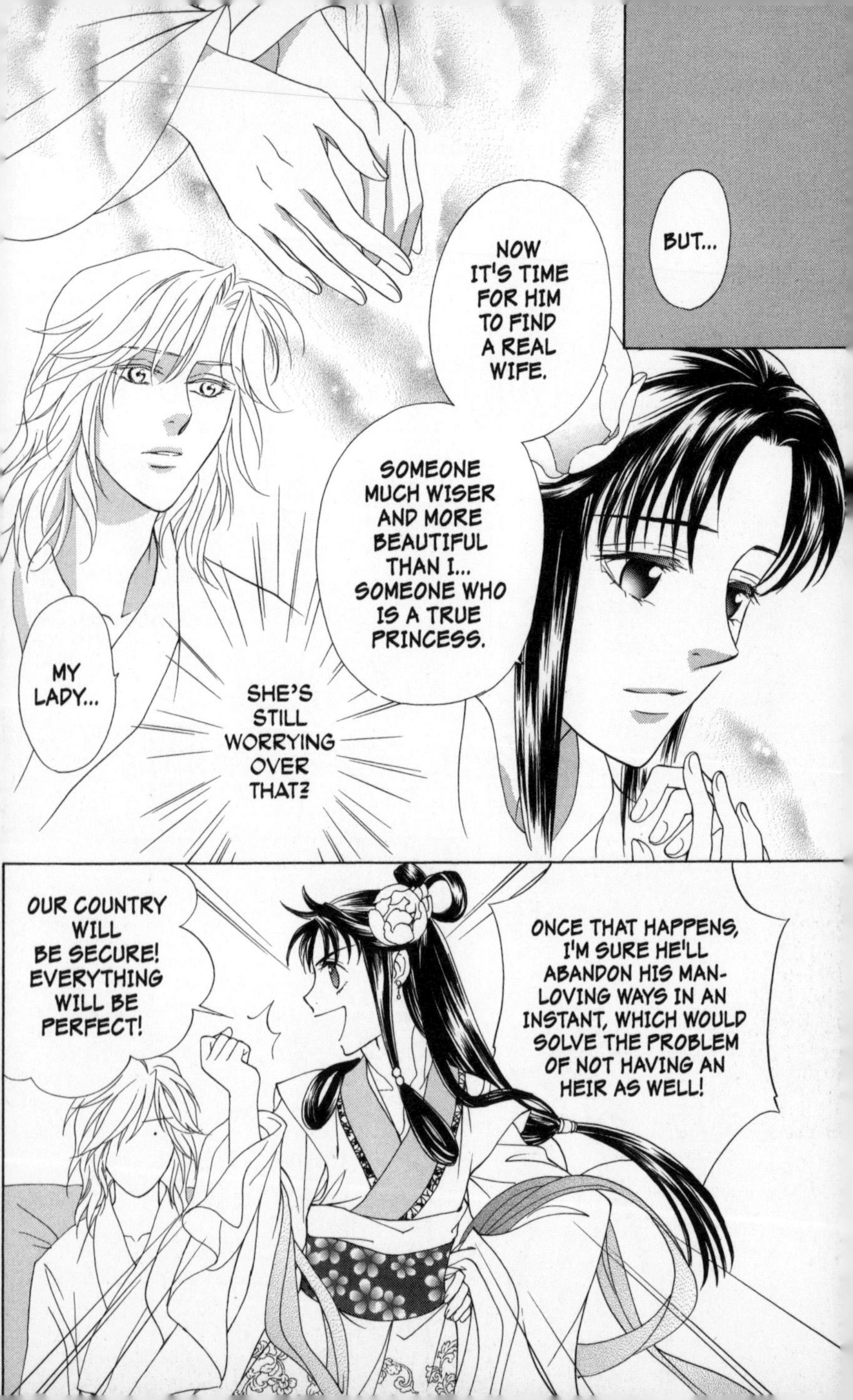
BUT...
NOW IT'S TIME FOR HIM TO FIND A REAL WIFE.
SOMEONE MUCH WISER AND MORE BEAUTIFUL THAN I... SOMEONE WHO IS A TRUE PRINCESS.
SHE'S STILL WORRYING OVER THAT?
MY LADY...
ONCE THAT HAPPENS, I'M SURE HE'LL ABANDON HIS MAN-LOVING WAYS IN AN INSTANT, WHICH WOULD SOLVE THE PROBLEM OF NOT HAVING AN HEIR AS WELL!
OUR COUNTRY WILL BE SECURE! EVERYTHING WILL BE PERFECT!

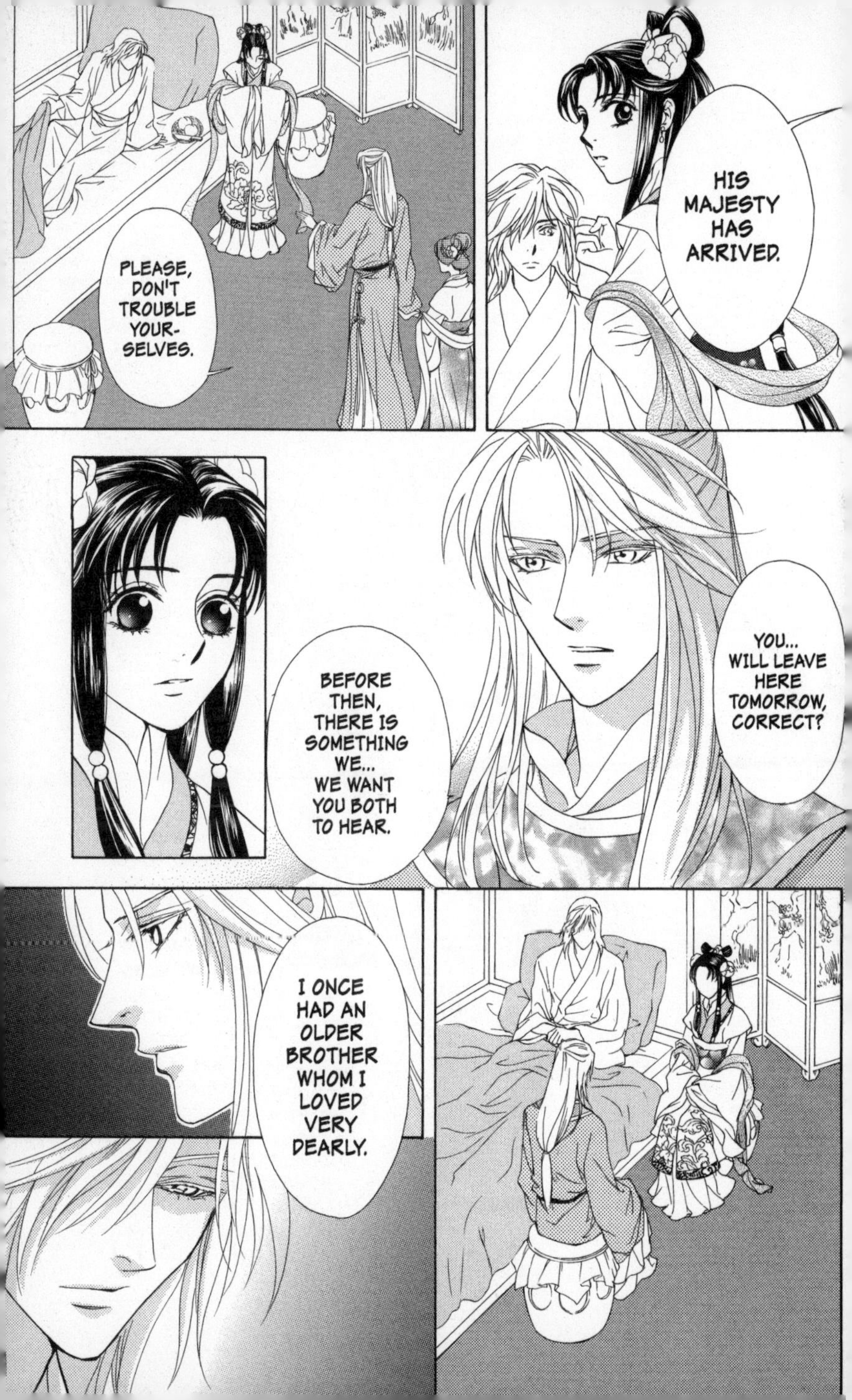
HIS MAJESTY HAS ARRIVED.
PLEASE, DON'T TROUBLE YOUR-SELVES.
YOU... WILL LEAVE HERE TOMORROW, CORRECT?
BEFORE THEN, THERE IS SOMETHING WE... WE WANT YOU BOTH TO HEAR.
I ONCE HAD AN OLDER BROTHER WHOM I LOVED VERY DEARLY.

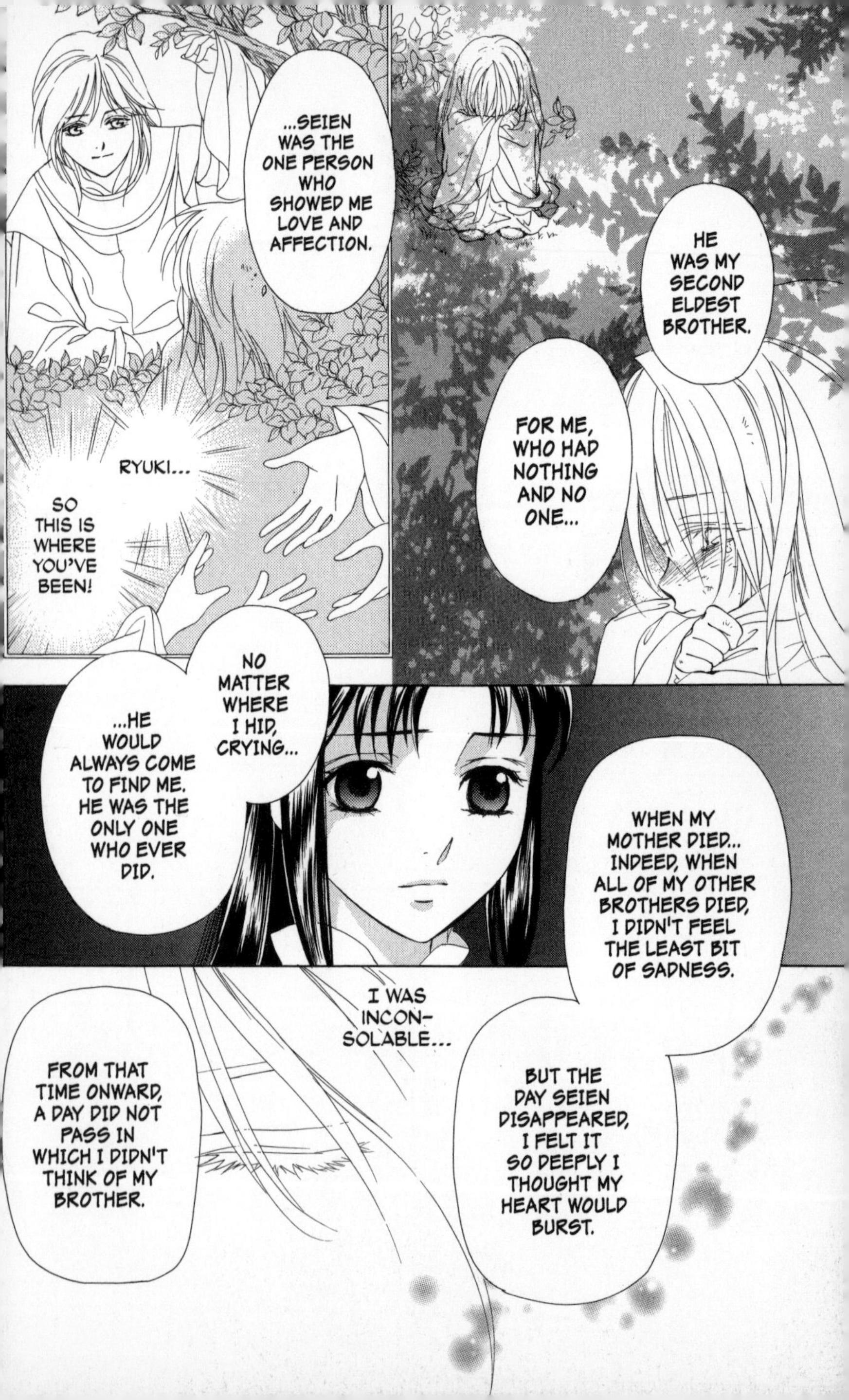
HE WAS MY SECOND ELDEST BROTHER.
FOR ME, WHO HAD NOTHING AND NO ONE...
...SEIEN WAS THE ONE PERSON WHO SHOWED ME LOVE AND AFFECTION.
RYUKI...
SO THIS IS WHERE YOU'VE BEEN!
NO MATTER WHERE I HID, CRYING...
...HE WOULD ALWAYS COME TO FIND ME. HE WAS THE ONLY ONE WHO EVER DID.
WHEN MY MOTHER DIED... INDEED, WHEN ALL OF MY OTHER BROTHERS DIED, I DIDN'T FEEL THE LEAST BIT OF SADNESS.
BUT THE DAY SEIEN DISAPPEARED, I FELT IT SO DEEPLY I THOUGHT MY HEART WOULD BURST.
I WAS INCON-SOLABLE...
FROM THAT TIME ONWARD, A DAY DID NOT PASS IN WHICH I DIDN'T THINK OF MY BROTHER.

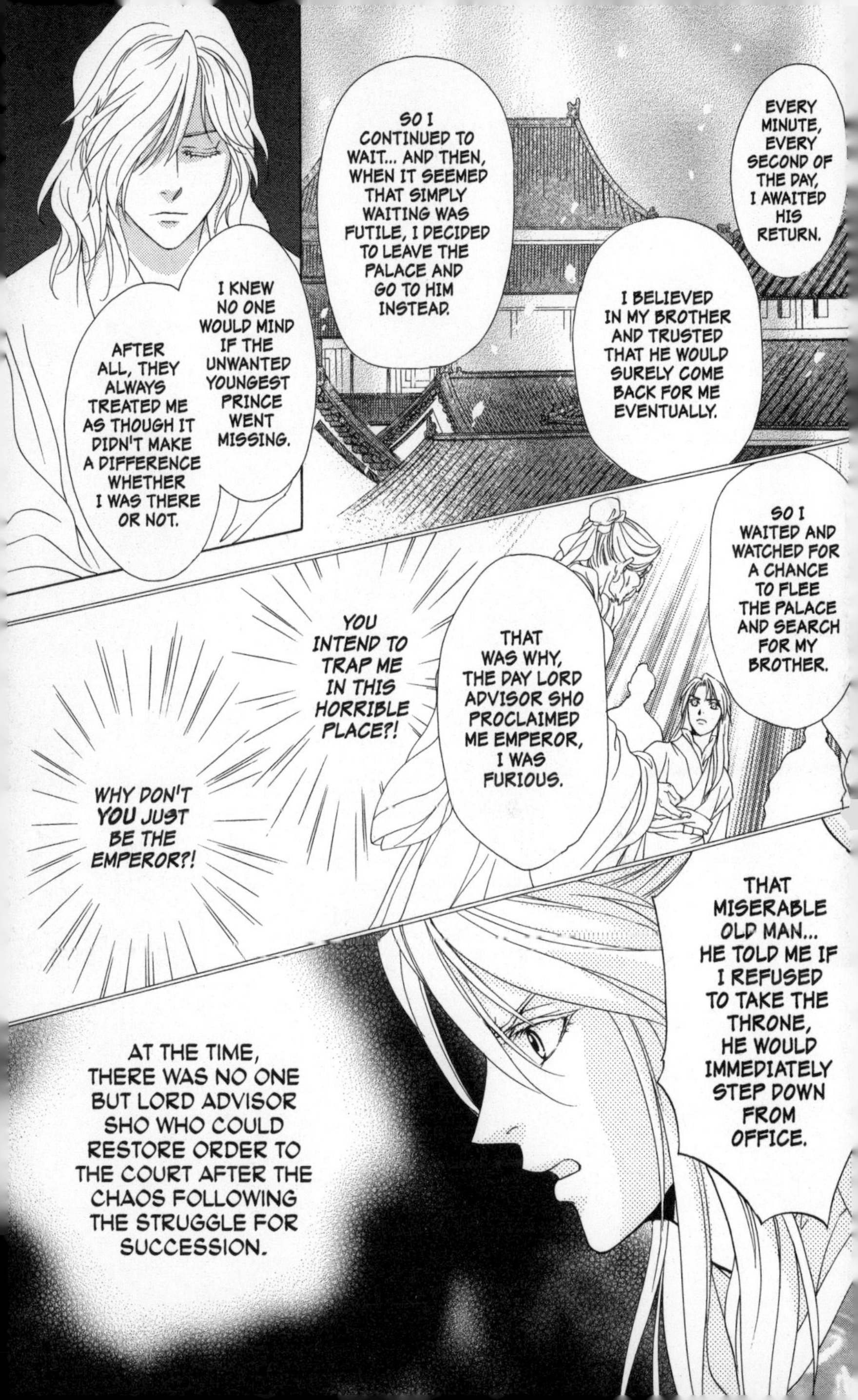
EVERY MINUTE, EVERY SECOND OF THE DAY, I AWAITED HIS RETURN.
I BELIEVED IN MY BROTHER AND TRUSTED THAT HE WOULD SURELY COME BACK FOR ME EVENTUALLY.
SO I CONTINUED TO WAIT... AND THEN, WHEN IT SEEMED THAT SIMPLY WAITING WAS FUTILE, I DECIDED TO LEAVE THE PALACE AND GO TO HIM INSTEAD.
I KNEW NO ONE WOULD MIND IF THE UNWANTED YOUNGEST PRINCE WENT MISSING.
AFTER ALL, THEY ALWAYS TREATED ME AS THOUGH IT DIDN'T MAKE A DIFFERENCE WHETHER I WAS THERE OR NOT.
SO I WAITED AND WATCHED FOR A CHANCE TO FLEE THE PALACE AND SEARCH FOR MY BROTHER.
THAT WAS WHY, THE DAY LORD ADVISOR SHO PROCLAIMED ME EMPEROR, I WAS FURIOUS.
YOU INTEND TO TRAP ME IN THIS HORRIBLE PLACE?!
WHY DON'T YOU JUST BE THE EMPEROR?!
THAT MISERABLE OLD MAN... HE TOLD ME IF I REFUSED TO TAKE THE THRONE, HE WOULD IMMEDIATELY STEP DOWN FROM OFFICE.
AT THE TIME, THERE WAS NO ONE BUT LORD ADVISOR SHO WHO COULD RESTORE ORDER TO THE COURT AFTER THE CHAOS FOLLOWING THE STRUGGLE FOR SUCCESSION.

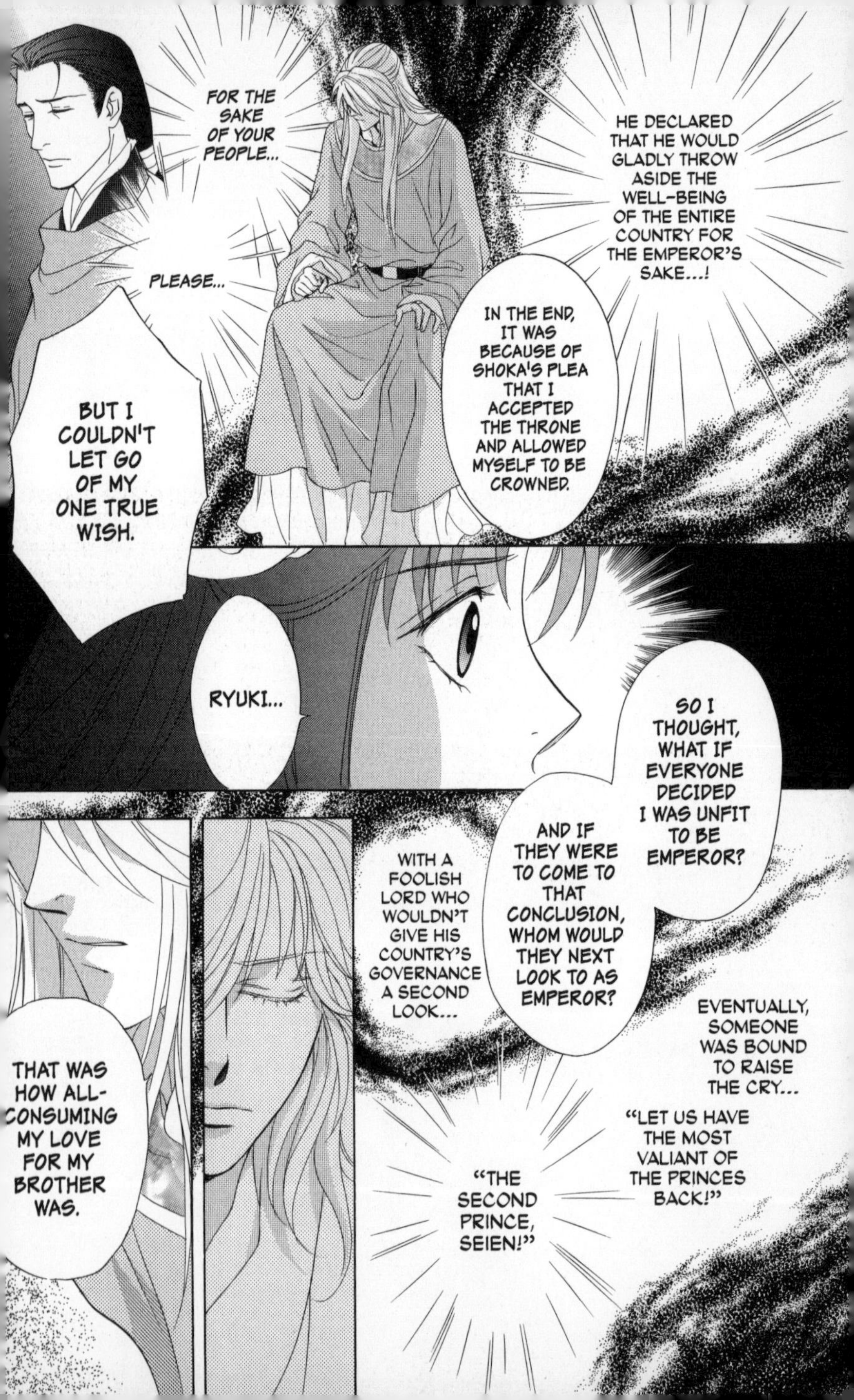
HE DECLARED THAT HE WOULD GLADLY THROW ASIDE THE WELL-BEING OF THE ENTIRE COUNTRY FOR THE EMPEROR'S SAKE...!
FOR THE SAKE OF YOUR PEOPLE...
PLEASE...
IN THE END, IT WAS BECAUSE OF SHOKA'S PLEA THAT I ACCEPTED THE THRONE AND ALLOWED MYSELF TO BE CROWNED.
BUT I COULDN'T LET GO OF MY ONE TRUE WISH.
SO I THOUGHT, WHAT IF EVERYONE DECIDED I WAS UNFIT TO BE EMPEROR?
RYUKI...
AND IF THEY WERE TO COME TO THAT CONCLUSION, WHOM WOULD THEY NEXT LOOK TO AS EMPEROR?
WITH A FOOLISH LORD WHO WOULDN'T GIVE HIS COUNTRY'S GOVERNANCE A SECOND LOOK...
EVENTUALLY, SOMEONE WAS BOUND TO RAISE THE CRY...
"LET US HAVE THE MOST VALIANT OF THE PRINCES BACK!"
"THE SECOND PRINCE, SEIEN!"
THAT WAS HOW ALL-CONSUMING MY LOVE FOR MY BROTHER WAS.

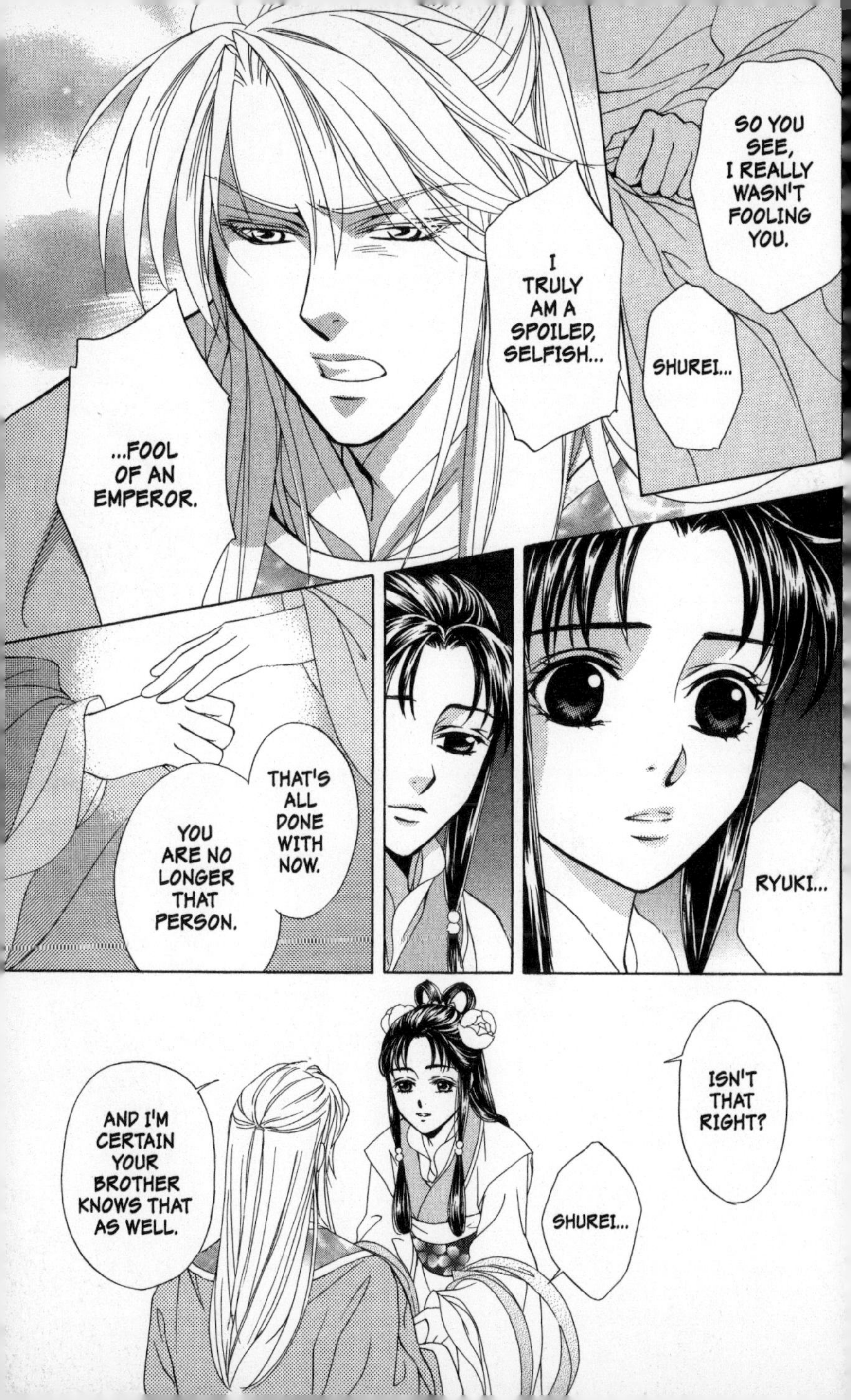
SO YOU SEE, I REALLY WASN'T FOOLING YOU.
SHUREI...
I TRULY AM A SPOILED, SELFISH...
...FOOL OF AN EMPEROR.
RYUKI...
THAT'S ALL DONE WITH NOW.
YOU ARE NO LONGER THAT PERSON.
ISN'T THAT RIGHT?
SHUREI...
AND I'M CERTAIN YOUR BROTHER KNOWS THAT AS WELL.

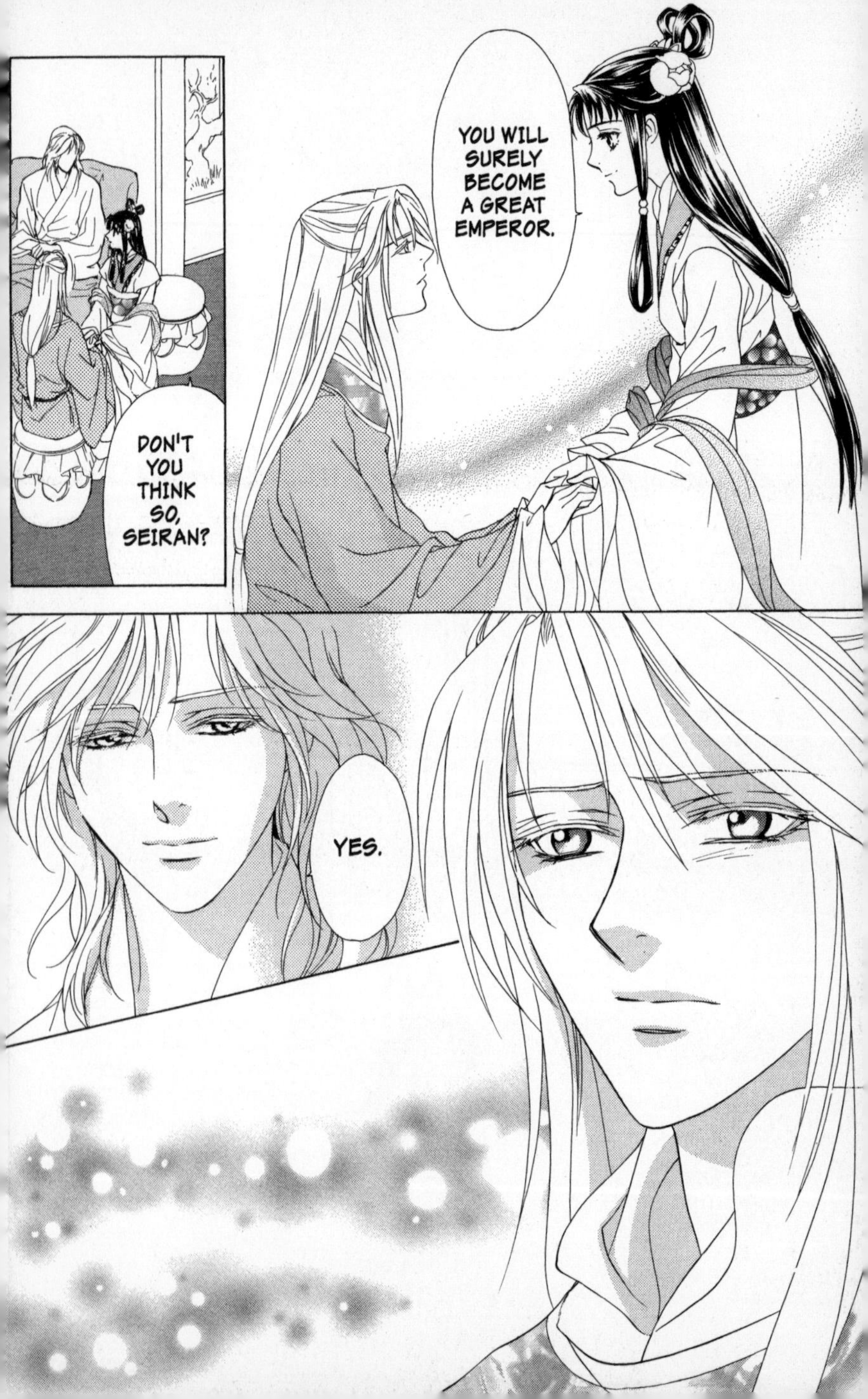
YOU WILL SURELY BECOME A GREAT EMPEROR.
DON'T YOU THINK SO, SEIRAN?
YES.

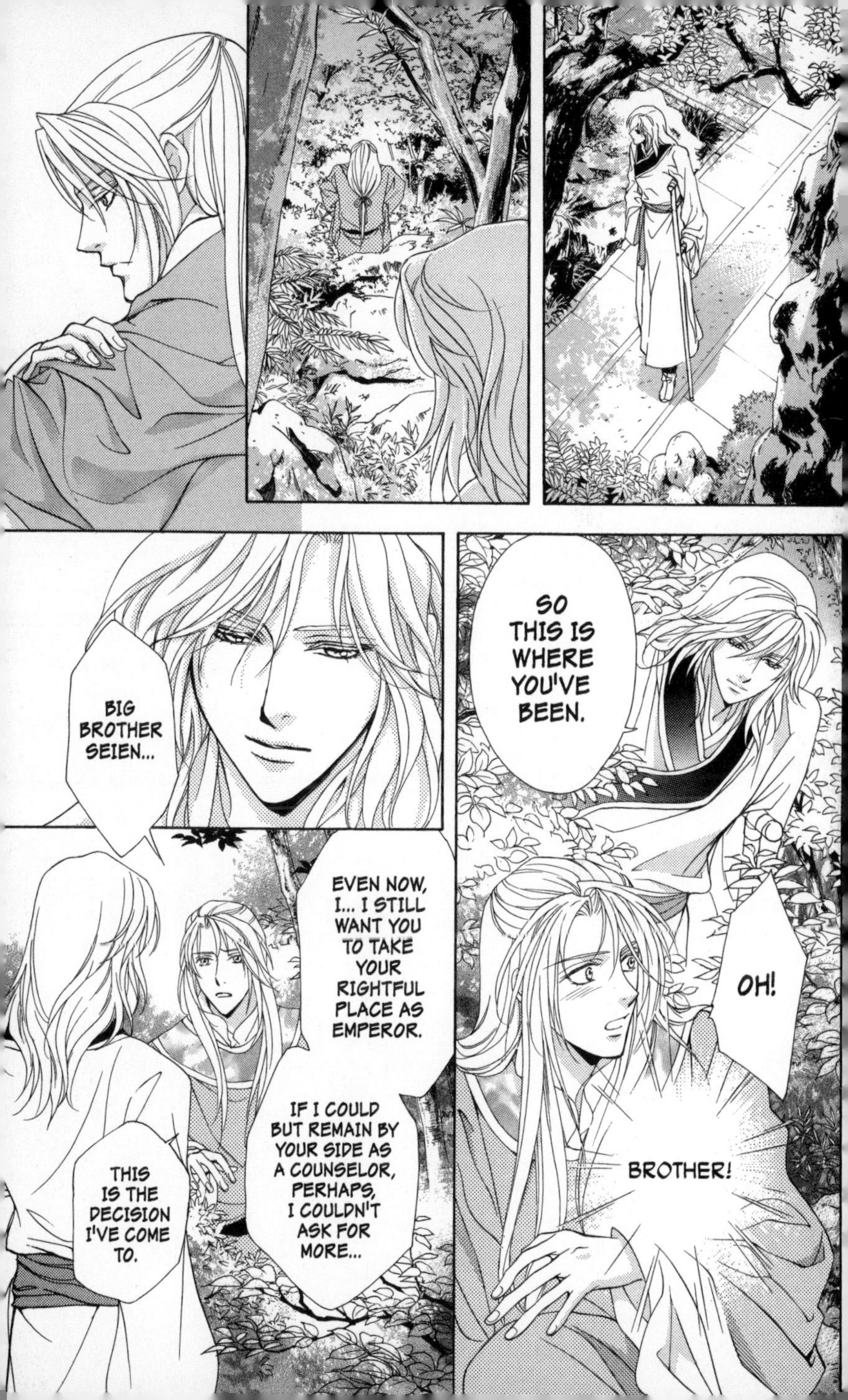
SO THIS IS WHERE YOU'VE BEEN.
BIG BROTHER SEIEN...
OH!
BROTHER!
EVEN NOW, I... I STILL WANT YOU TO TAKE YOUR RIGHTFUL PLACE AS EMPEROR.
IF I COULD BUT REMAIN BY YOUR SIDE AS A COUNSELOR, PERHAPS, I COULDN'T ASK FOR MORE...
THIS IS THE DECISION I'VE COME TO.

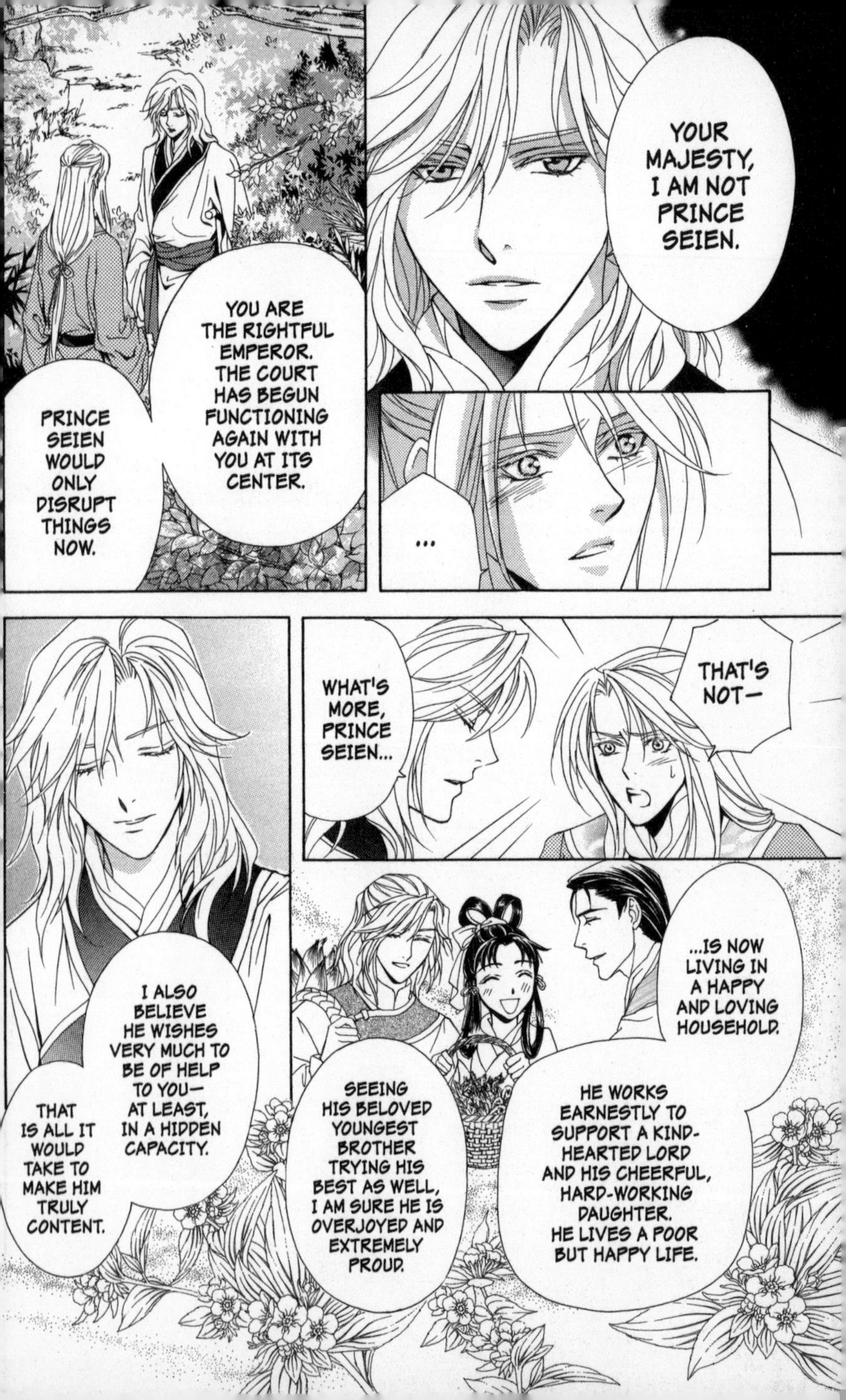
YOUR MAJESTY, I AM NOT PRINCE SEIEN.
...
YOU ARE THE RIGHTFUL EMPEROR. THE COURT HAS BEGUN FUNCTIONING AGAIN WITH YOU AT ITS CENTER.
PRINCE SEIEN WOULD ONLY DISRUPT THINGS NOW.
THAT'S NOT—
WHAT'S MORE, PRINCE SEIEN...
...IS NOW LIVING IN A HAPPY AND LOVING HOUSEHOLD.
HE WORKS EARNESTLY TO SUPPORT A KIND-HEARTED LORD AND HIS CHEERFUL, HARD-WORKING DAUGHTER. HE LIVES A POOR BUT HAPPY LIFE.
SEEING HIS BELOVED YOUNGEST BROTHER TRYING HIS BEST AS WELL, I AM SURE HE IS OVERJOYED AND EXTREMELY PROUD.
I ALSO BELIEVE HE WISHES VERY MUCH TO BE OF HELP TO YOU— AT LEAST, IN A HIDDEN CAPACITY.
THAT IS ALL IT WOULD TAKE TO MAKE HIM TRULY CONTENT.

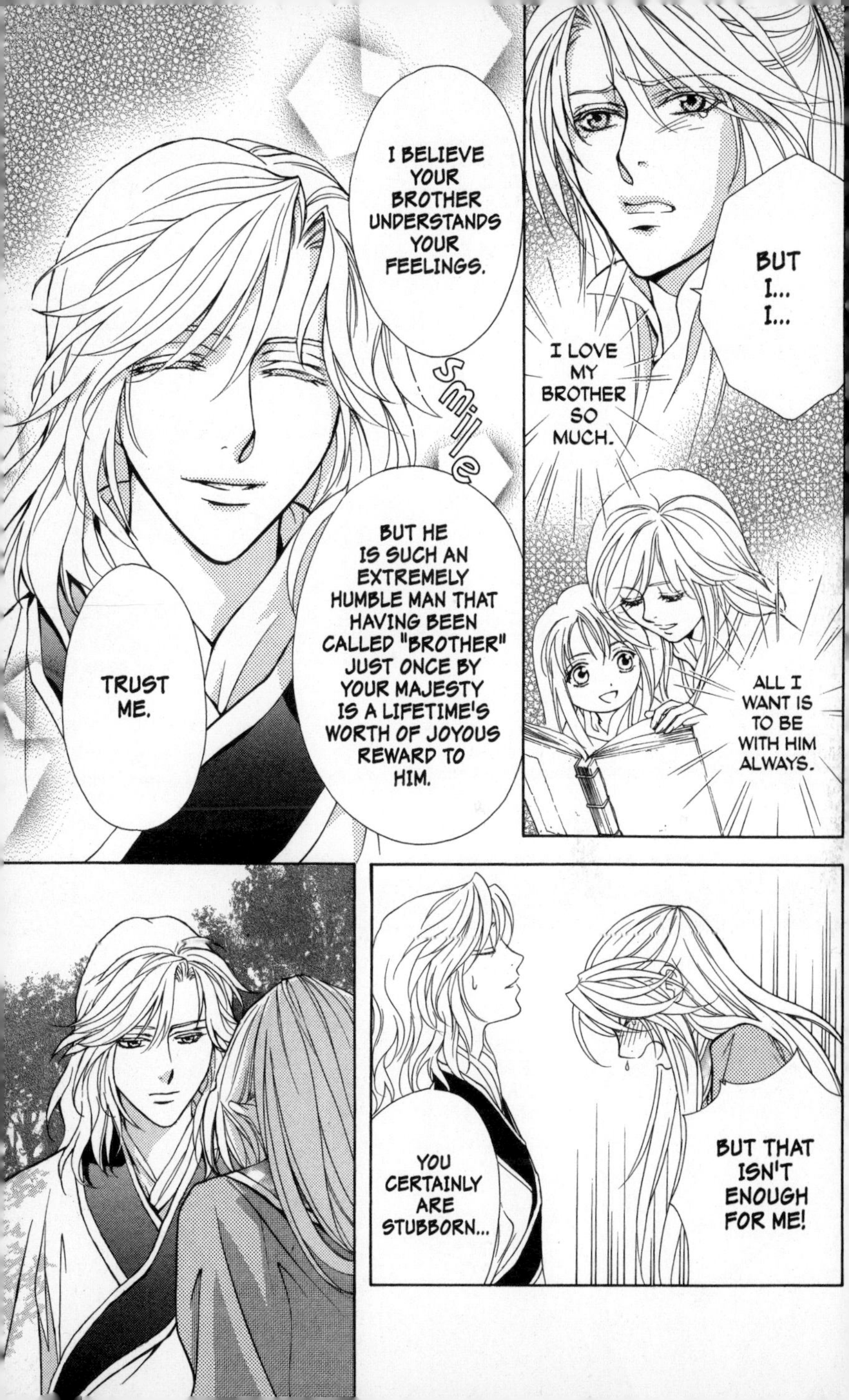
BUT I... I...
I LOVE MY BROTHER SO MUCH.
ALL I WANT IS TO BE WITH HIM ALWAYS.
I BELIEVE YOUR BROTHER UNDERSTANDS YOUR FEELINGS.
smile
BUT HE IS SUCH AN EXTREMELY HUMBLE MAN THAT HAVING BEEN CALLED "BROTHER" JUST ONCE BY YOUR MAJESTY IS A LIFETIME'S WORTH OF JOYOUS REWARD TO HIM.
TRUST ME.
BUT THAT ISN'T ENOUGH FOR ME!
YOU CERTAINLY ARE STUBBORN...

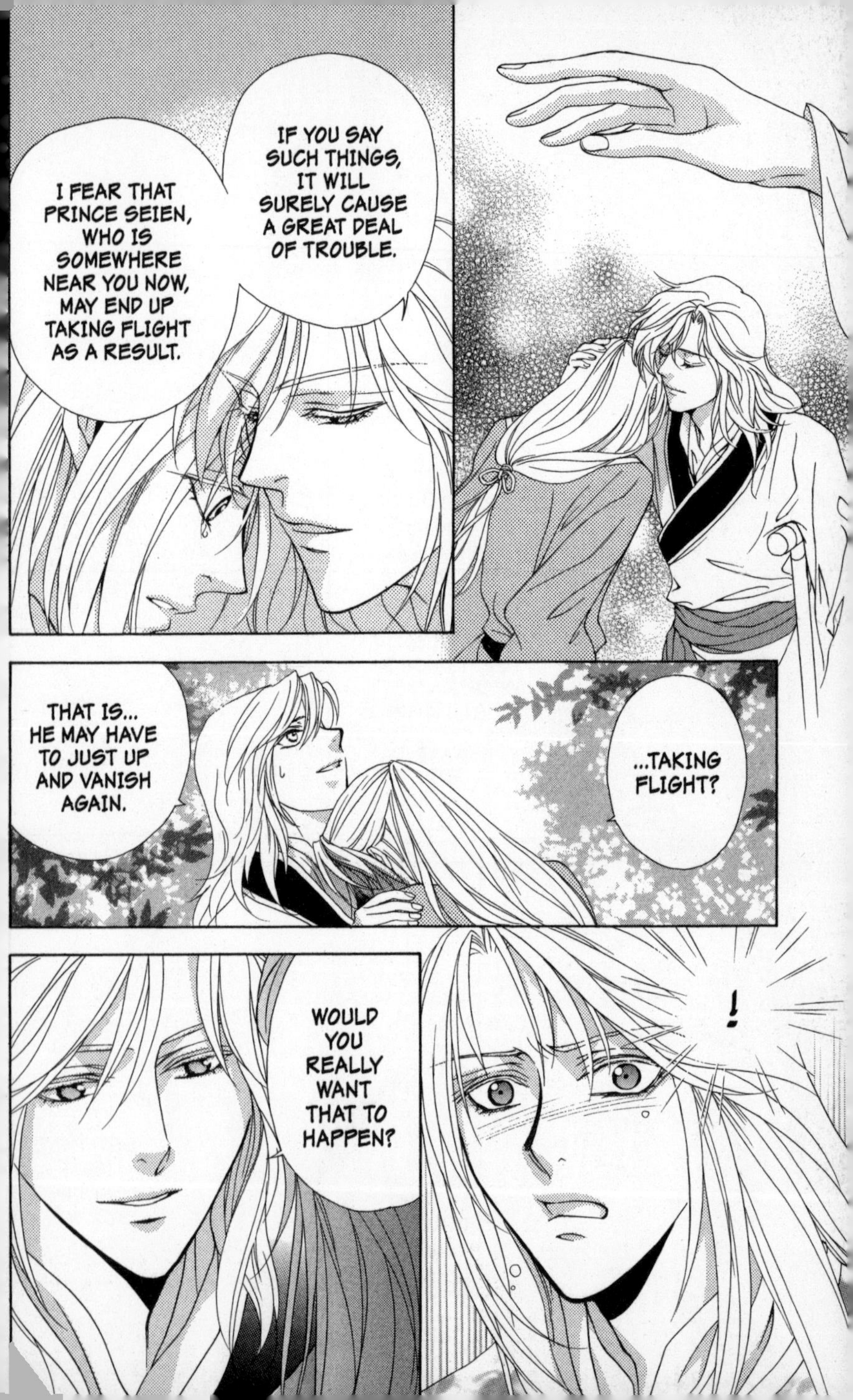
IF YOU SAY SUCH THINGS, IT WILL SURELY CAUSE A GREAT DEAL OF TROUBLE.
I FEAR THAT PRINCE SEIEN, WHO IS SOMEWHERE NEAR YOU NOW, MAY END UP TAKING FLIGHT AS A RESULT.
...TAKING FLIGHT?
THAT IS... HE MAY HAVE TO JUST UP AND VANISH AGAIN.
!
WOULD YOU REALLY WANT THAT TO HAPPEN?

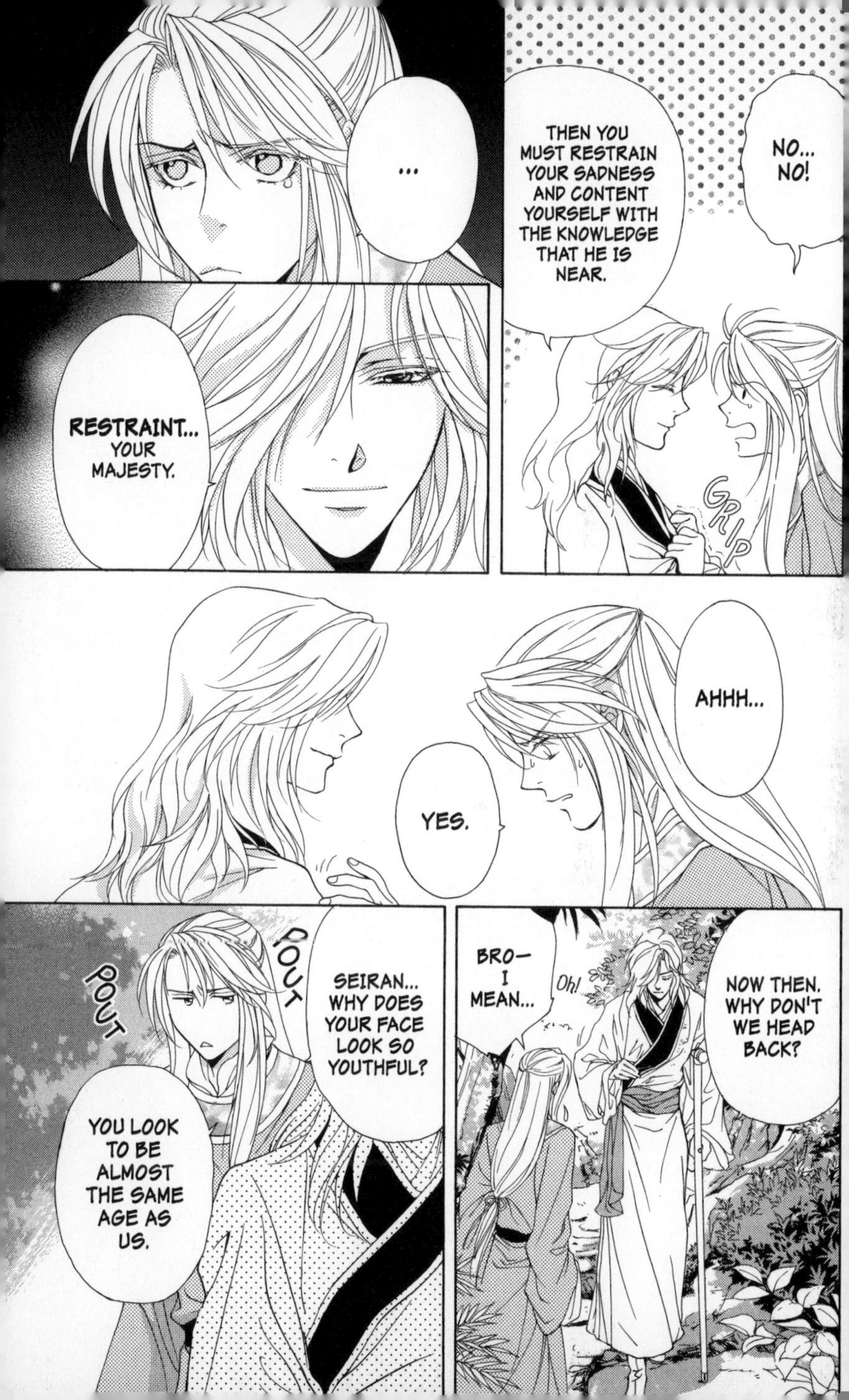
NO... NO!
THEN YOU MUST RESTRAIN YOUR SADNESS AND CONTENT YOURSELF WITH THE KNOWLEDGE THAT HE IS NEAR.
GRIP
...
RESTRAINT... YOUR MAJESTY.
AHHH...
YES.
NOW THEN. WHY DON'T WE HEAD BACK?
Oh!
BRO— I MEAN...
SEIRAN... WHY DOES YOUR FACE LOOK SO YOUTHFUL?
POUT
POUT
YOU LOOK TO BE ALMOST THE SAME AGE AS US.

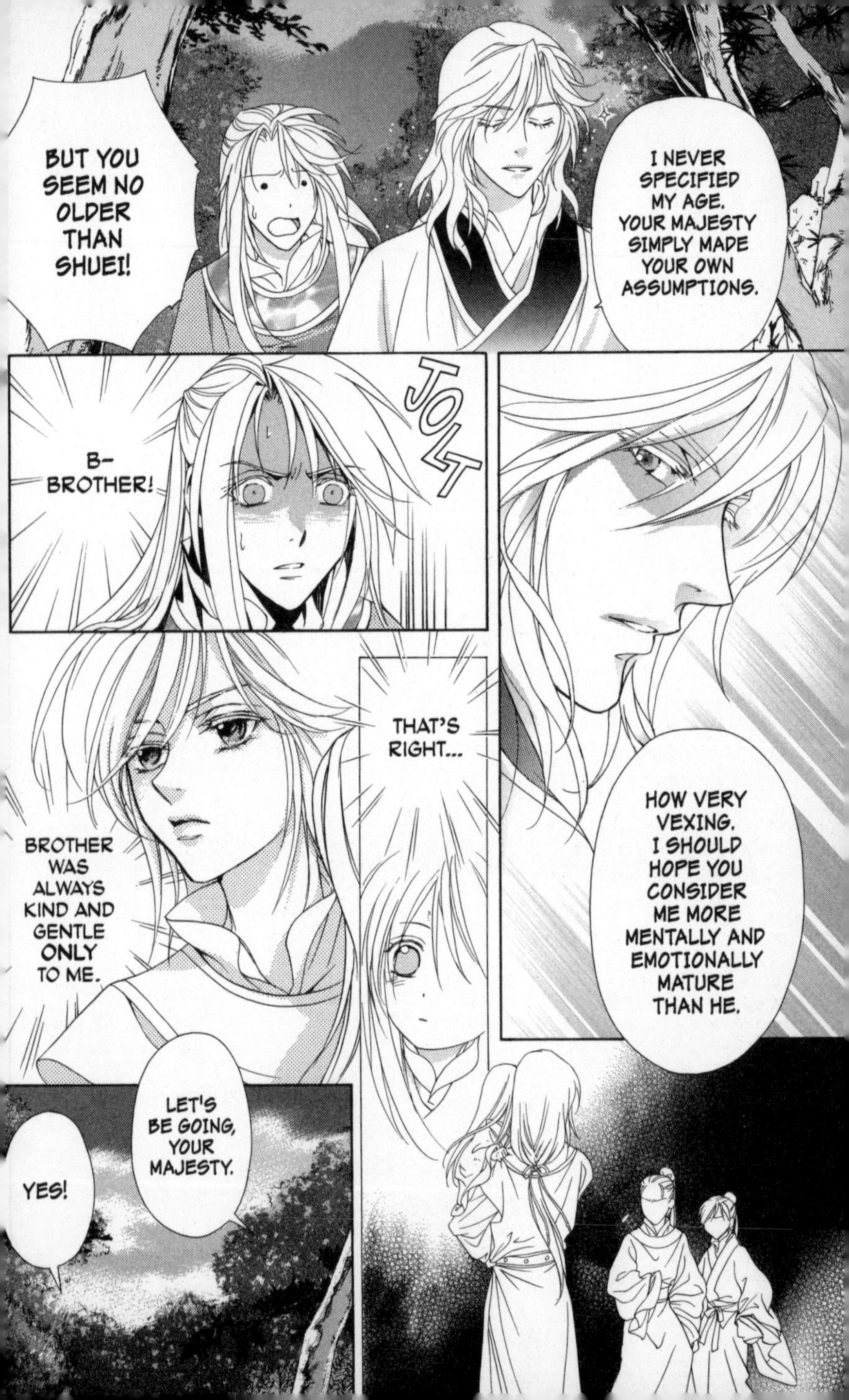

I NEVER SPECIFIED MY AGE. YOUR MAJESTY SIMPLY MADE YOUR OWN ASSUMPTIONS.
BUT YOU SEEM NO OLDER THAN SHUEI!
HOW VERY VEXING. I SHOULD HOPE YOU CONSIDER ME MORE MENTALLY AND EMOTIONALLY MATURE THAN HE.
JOLT
B-BROTHER!
THAT'S RIGHT...
BROTHER WAS ALWAYS KIND AND GENTLE ONLY TO ME.
LET'S BE GOING, YOUR MAJESTY.
YES!

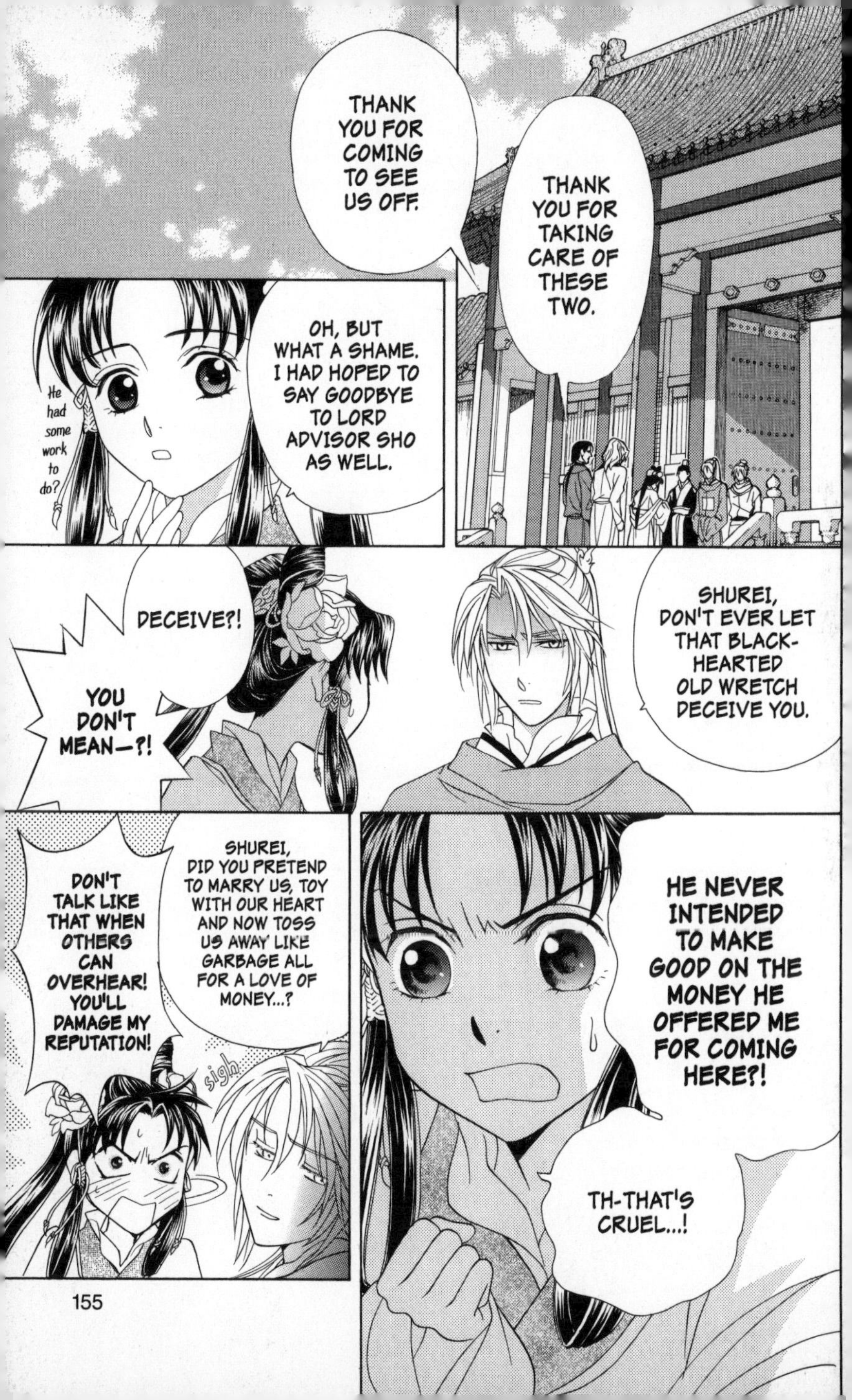
THANK YOU FOR COMING TO SEE US OFF.
THANK YOU FOR TAKING CARE OF THESE TWO.
OH, BUT WHAT A SHAME. I HAD HOPED TO SAY GOODBYE TO LORD ADVISOR SHO AS WELL.
He had some work to do?
SHUREI, DON'T EVER LET THAT BLACK-HEARTED OLD WRETCH DECEIVE YOU.
DECEIVE?!
YOU DON'T MEAN—?!
HE NEVER INTENDED TO MAKE GOOD ON THE MONEY HE OFFERED ME FOR COMING HERE?!
TH-THAT'S CRUEL...!
SHUREI, DID YOU PRETEND TO MARRY US, TOY WITH OUR HEART AND NOW TOSS US AWAY LIKE GARBAGE ALL FOR A LOVE OF MONEY...?
DON'T TALK LIKE THAT WHEN OTHERS CAN OVERHEAR! YOU'LL DAMAGE MY REPUTATION!
sigh

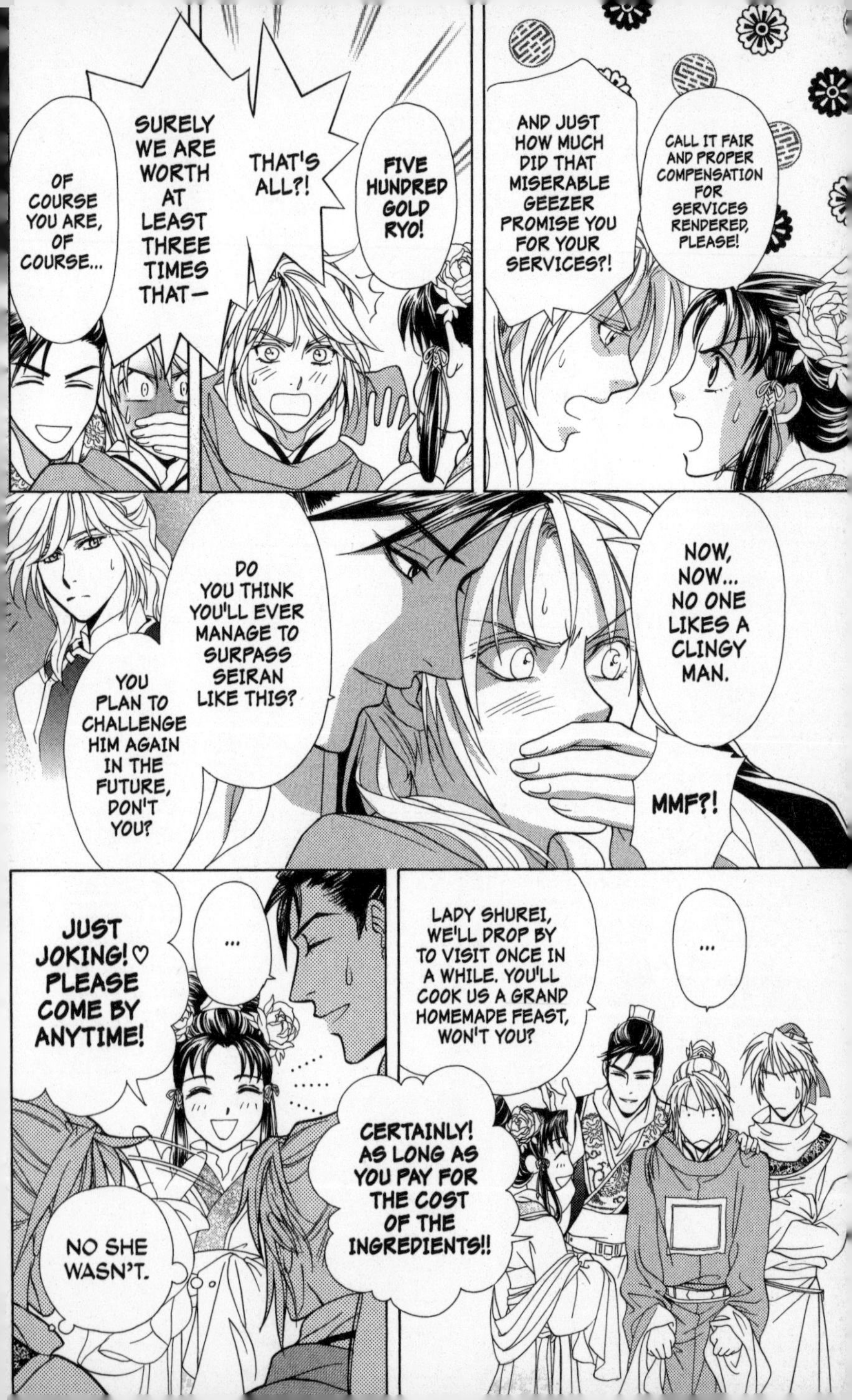
CALL IT FAIR AND PROPER COMPENSATION FOR SERVICES RENDERED, PLEASE!
AND JUST HOW MUCH DID THAT MISERABLE GEEZER PROMISE YOU FOR YOUR SERVICES?!
FIVE HUNDRED GOLD RYO!
THAT'S ALL?!
SURELY WE ARE WORTH AT LEAST THREE TIMES THAT—
OF COURSE YOU ARE, OF COURSE...
NOW, NOW... NO ONE LIKES A CLINGY MAN.
MMF?!
DO YOU THINK YOU'LL EVER MANAGE TO SURPASS SEIRAN LIKE THIS?
YOU PLAN TO CHALLENGE HIM AGAIN IN THE FUTURE, DON'T YOU?
...
LADY SHUREI, WE'LL DROP BY TO VISIT ONCE IN A WHILE. YOU'LL COOK US A GRAND HOMEMADE FEAST, WON'T YOU?
CERTAINLY! AS LONG AS YOU PAY FOR THE COST OF THE INGREDIENTS!!
...
JUST JOKING! ♡ PLEASE COME BY ANYTIME!
NO SHE WASN'T.

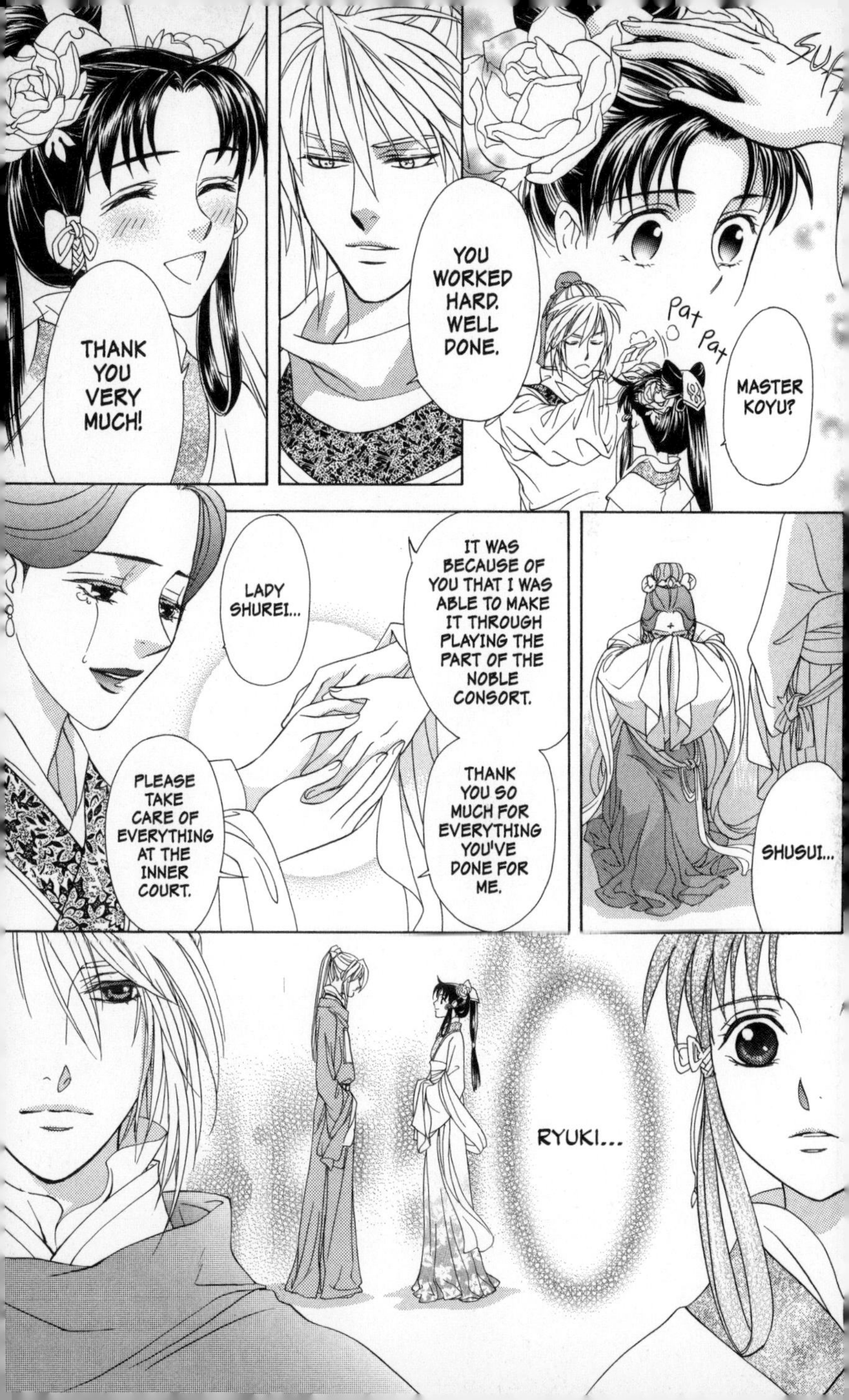
SUF
Pat Pat
MASTER KOYU?
YOU WORKED HARD. WELL DONE.
THANK YOU VERY MUCH!
SHUSUI...
LADY SHUREI...
IT WAS BECAUSE OF YOU THAT I WAS ABLE TO MAKE IT THROUGH PLAYING THE PART OF THE NOBLE CONSORT.
THANK YOU SO MUCH FOR EVERYTHING YOU'VE DONE FOR ME.
PLEASE TAKE CARE OF EVERYTHING AT THE INNER COURT.
RYUKI...

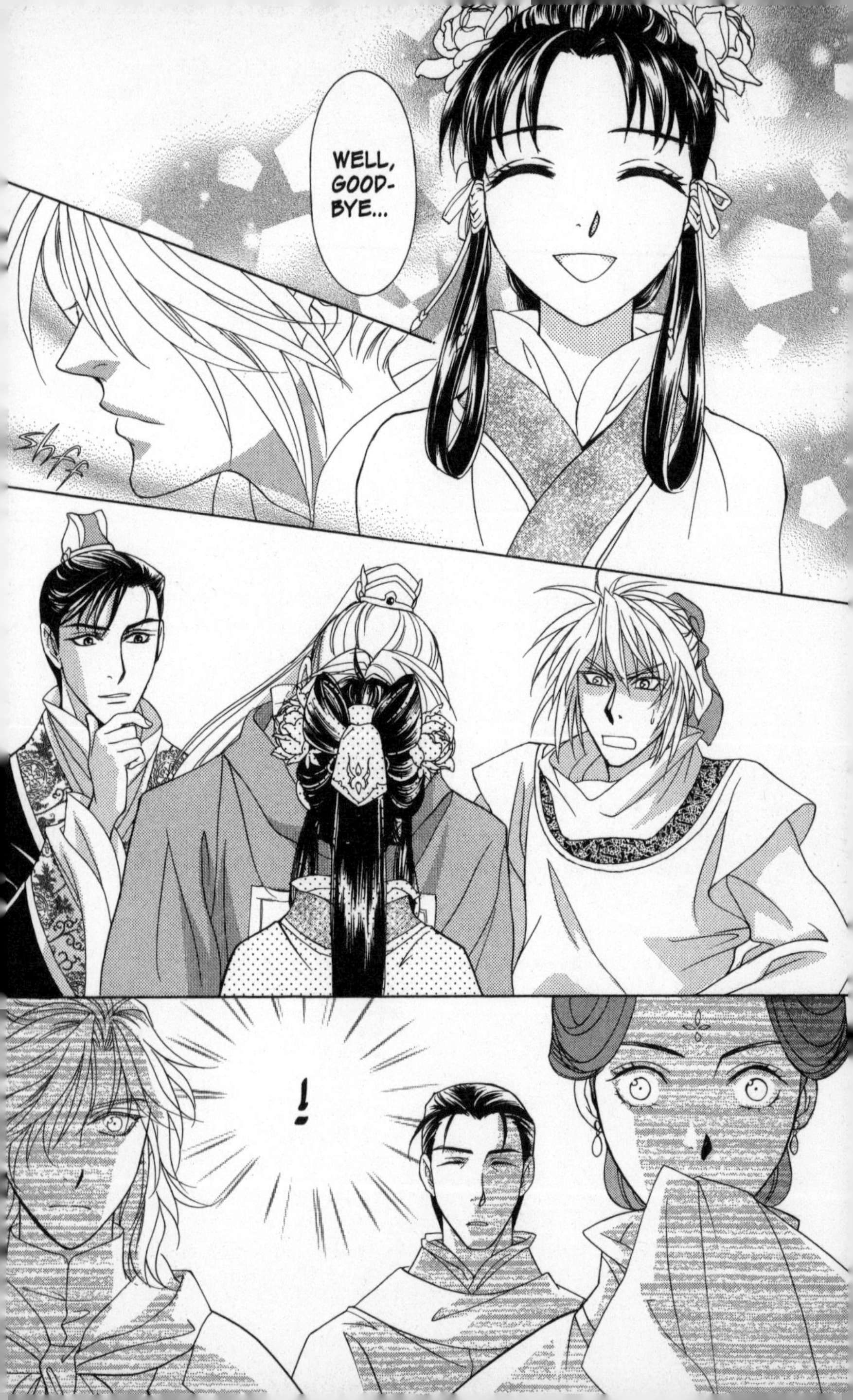
WELL, GOOD-BYE...
shff
!

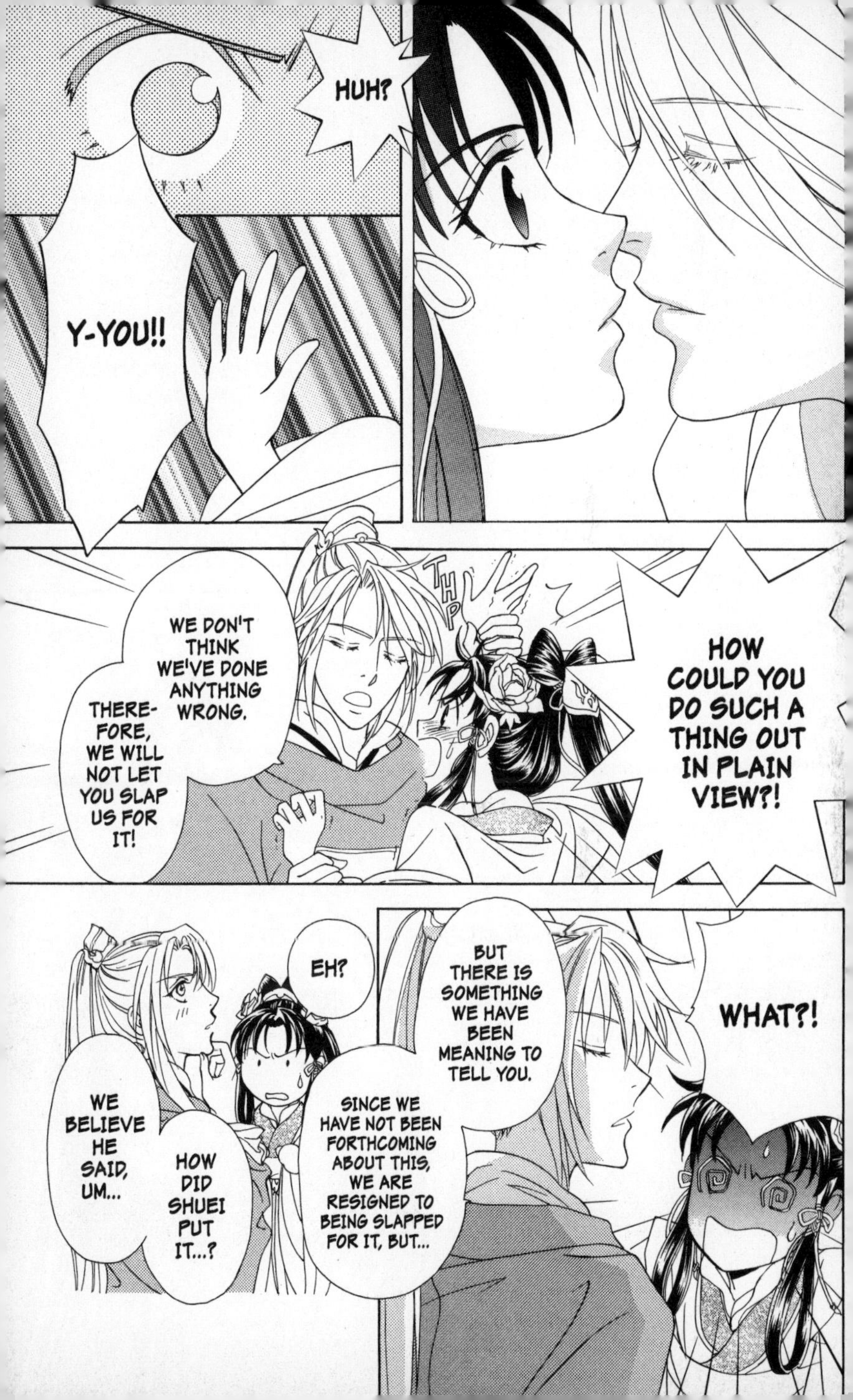
HUH?
Y-YOU!!
HOW COULD YOU DO SUCH A THING OUT IN PLAIN VIEW?!
THP
WE DON'T THINK WE'VE DONE ANYTHING WRONG.
THERE-FORE, WE WILL NOT LET YOU SLAP US FOR IT!
WHAT?!
BUT THERE IS SOMETHING WE HAVE BEEN MEANING TO TELL YOU.
SINCE WE HAVE NOT BEEN FORTHCOMING ABOUT THIS, WE ARE RESIGNED TO BEING SLAPPED FOR IT, BUT...
EH?
WE BELIEVE HE SAID, UM...
HOW DID SHUEI PUT IT...?

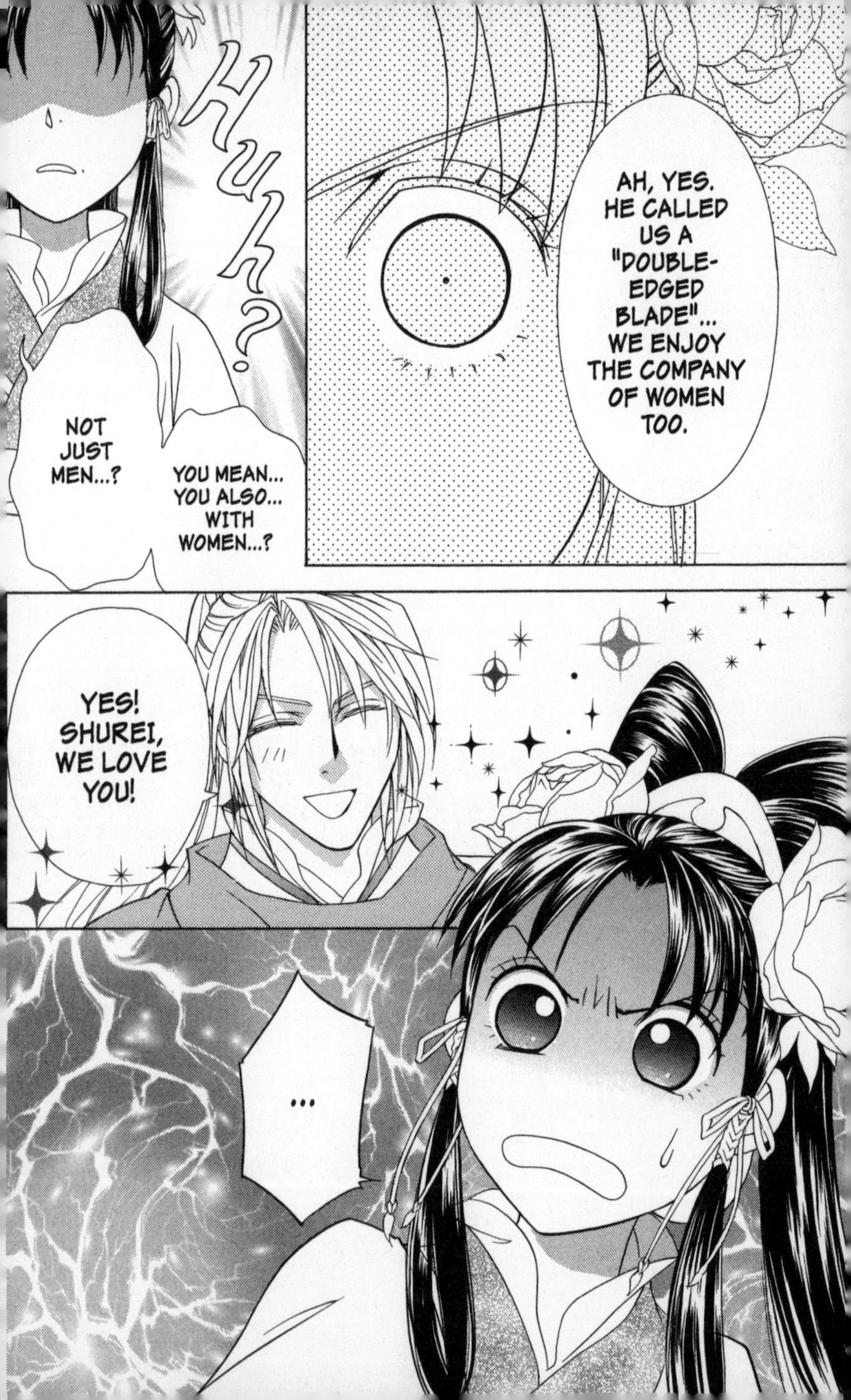
AH, YES. HE CALLED US A "DOUBLE-EDGED BLADE"... WE ENJOY THE COMPANY OF WOMEN TOO.
HUh?
NOT JUST MEN...?
YOU MEAN... YOU ALSO... WITH WOMEN...?
YES! SHUREI, WE LOVE YOU!
...

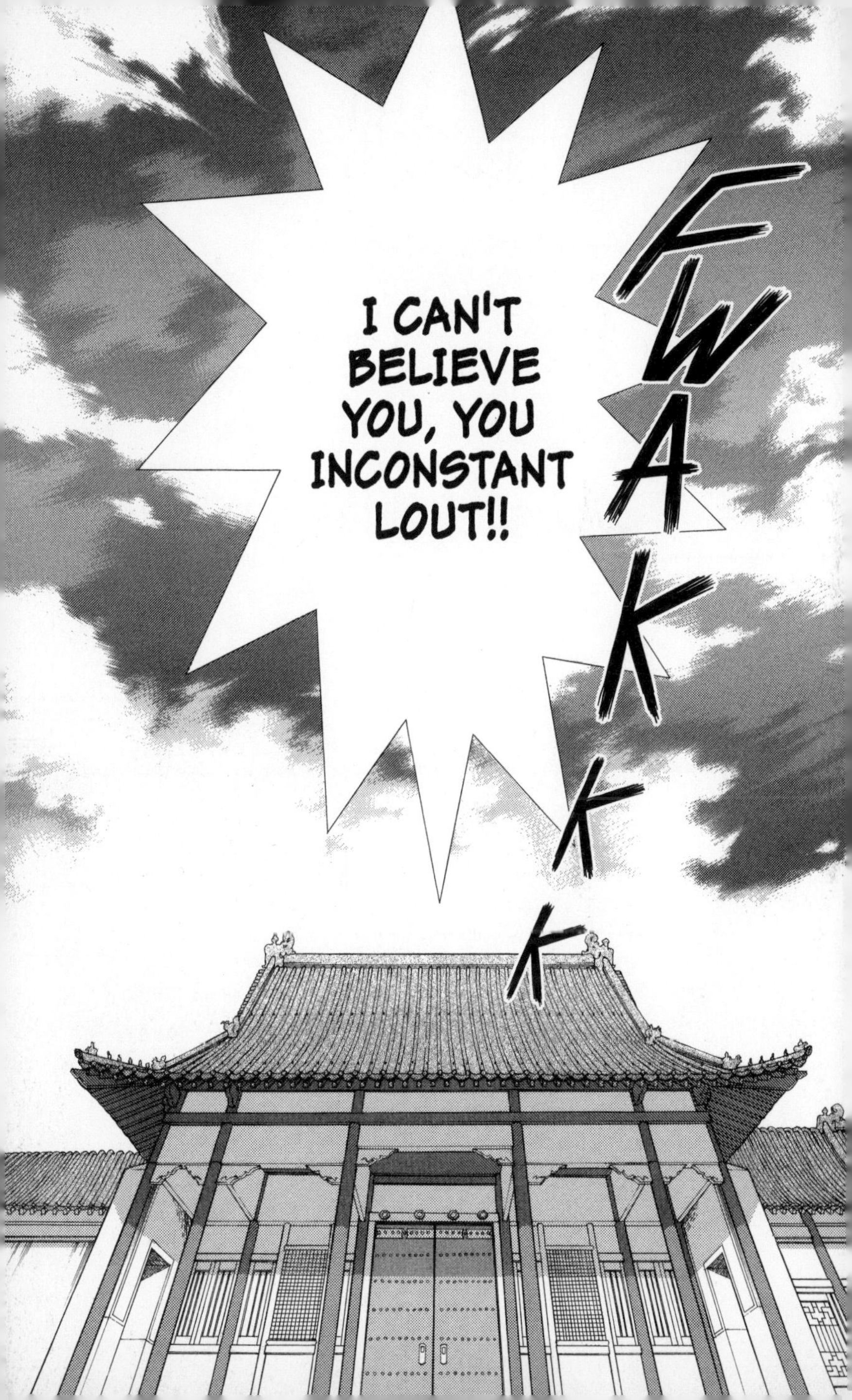
I CAN'T BELIEVE YOU, YOU INCONSTANT LOUT!!
FWAKKK

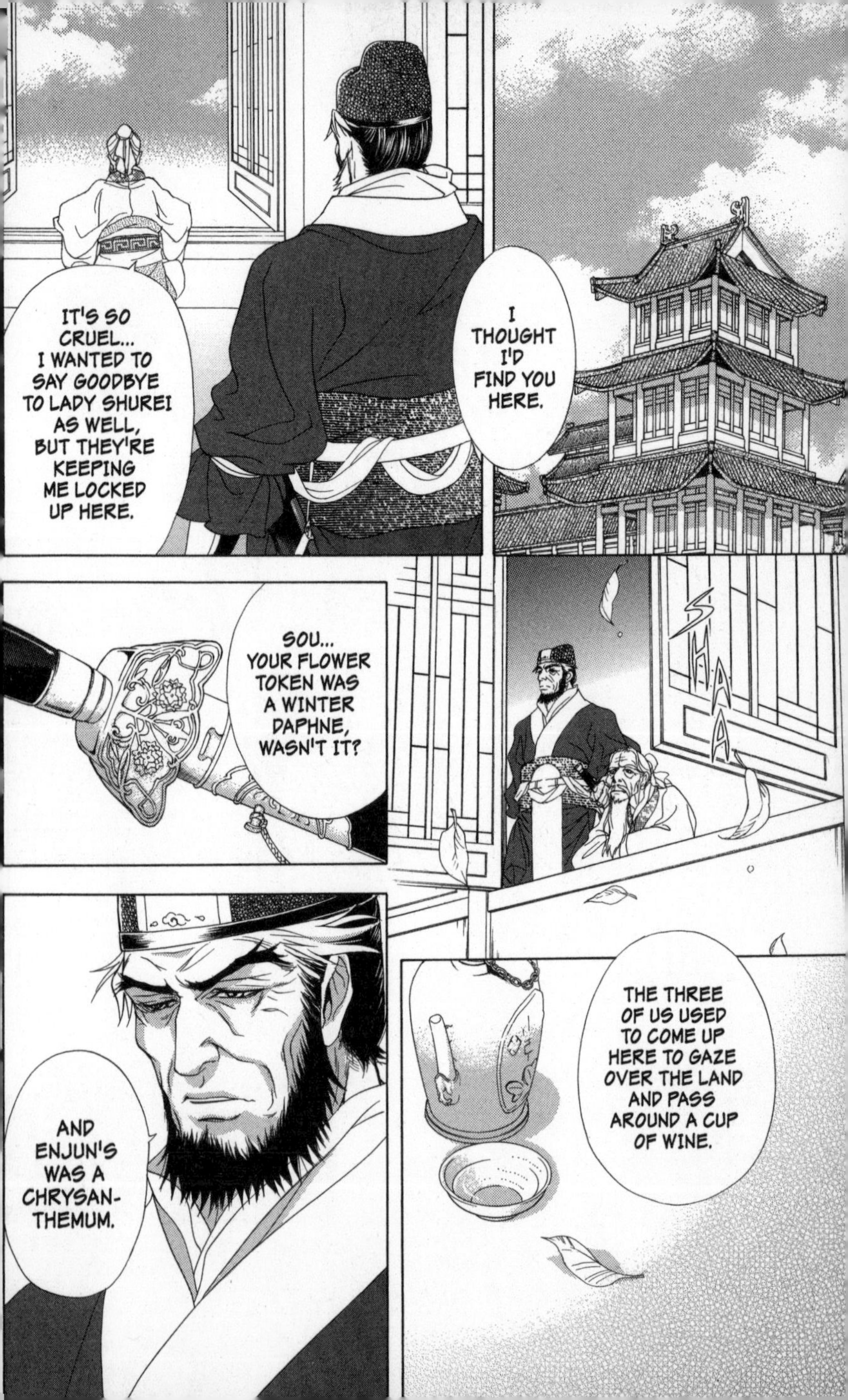
I THOUGHT I'D FIND YOU HERE.
IT'S SO CRUEL... I WANTED TO SAY GOODBYE TO LADY SHUREI AS WELL, BUT THEY'RE KEEPING ME LOCKED UP HERE.
SHAA
SOU... YOUR FLOWER TOKEN WAS A WINTER DAPHNE, WASN'T IT?
THE THREE OF US USED TO COME UP HERE TO GAZE OVER THE LAND AND PASS AROUND A CUP OF WINE.
AND ENJUN'S WAS A CHRYSAN-THEMUM.

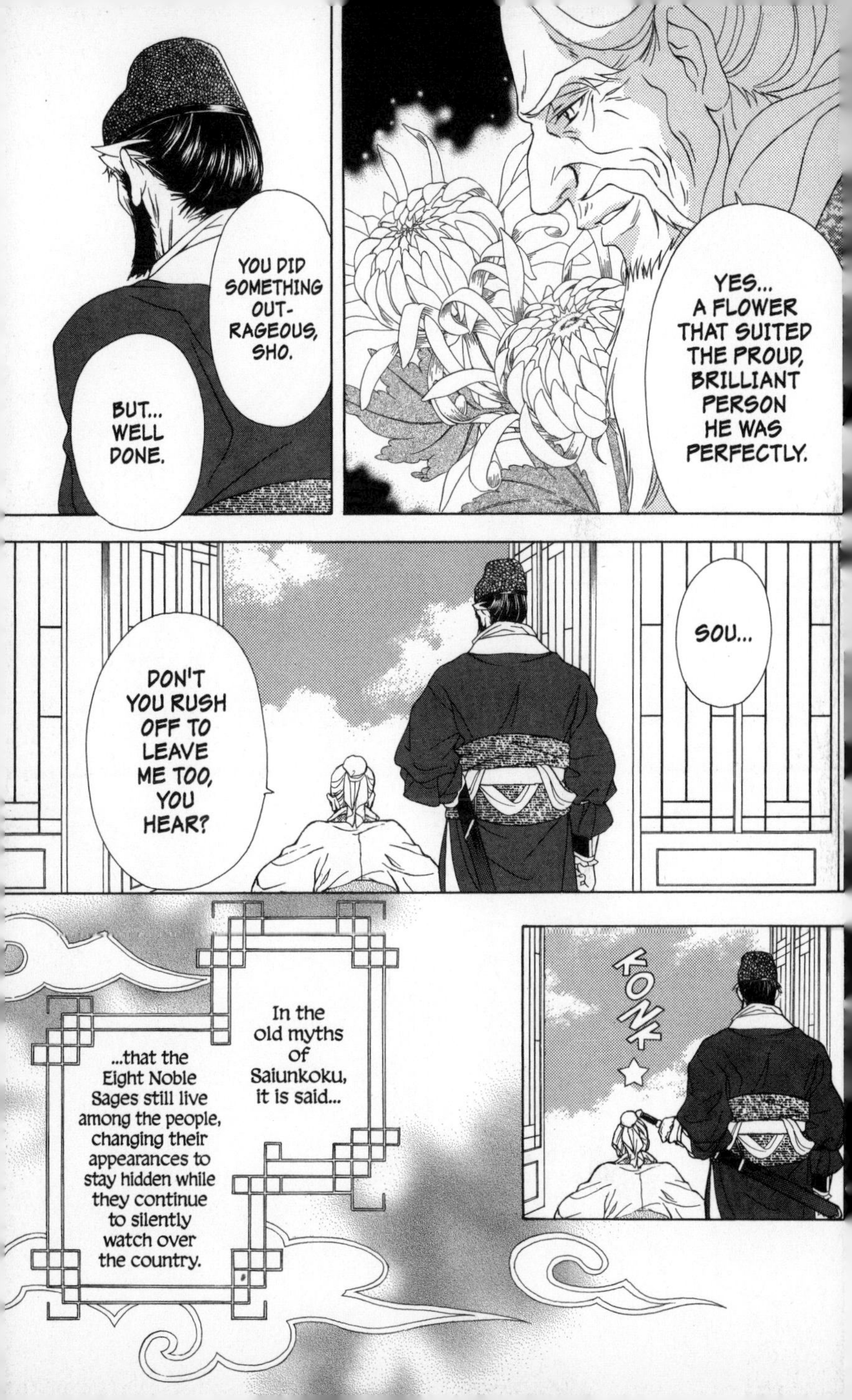
YES... A FLOWER THAT SUITED THE PROUD, BRILLIANT PERSON HE WAS PERFECTLY.
YOU DID SOMETHING OUT-RAGEOUS, SHO.
BUT... WELL DONE.
SOU...
DON'T YOU RUSH OFF TO LEAVE ME TOO, YOU HEAR?
KONK
In the old myths of Saiunkoku, it is said...
...that the Eight Noble Sages still live among the people, changing their appearances to stay hidden while they continue to silently watch over the country.

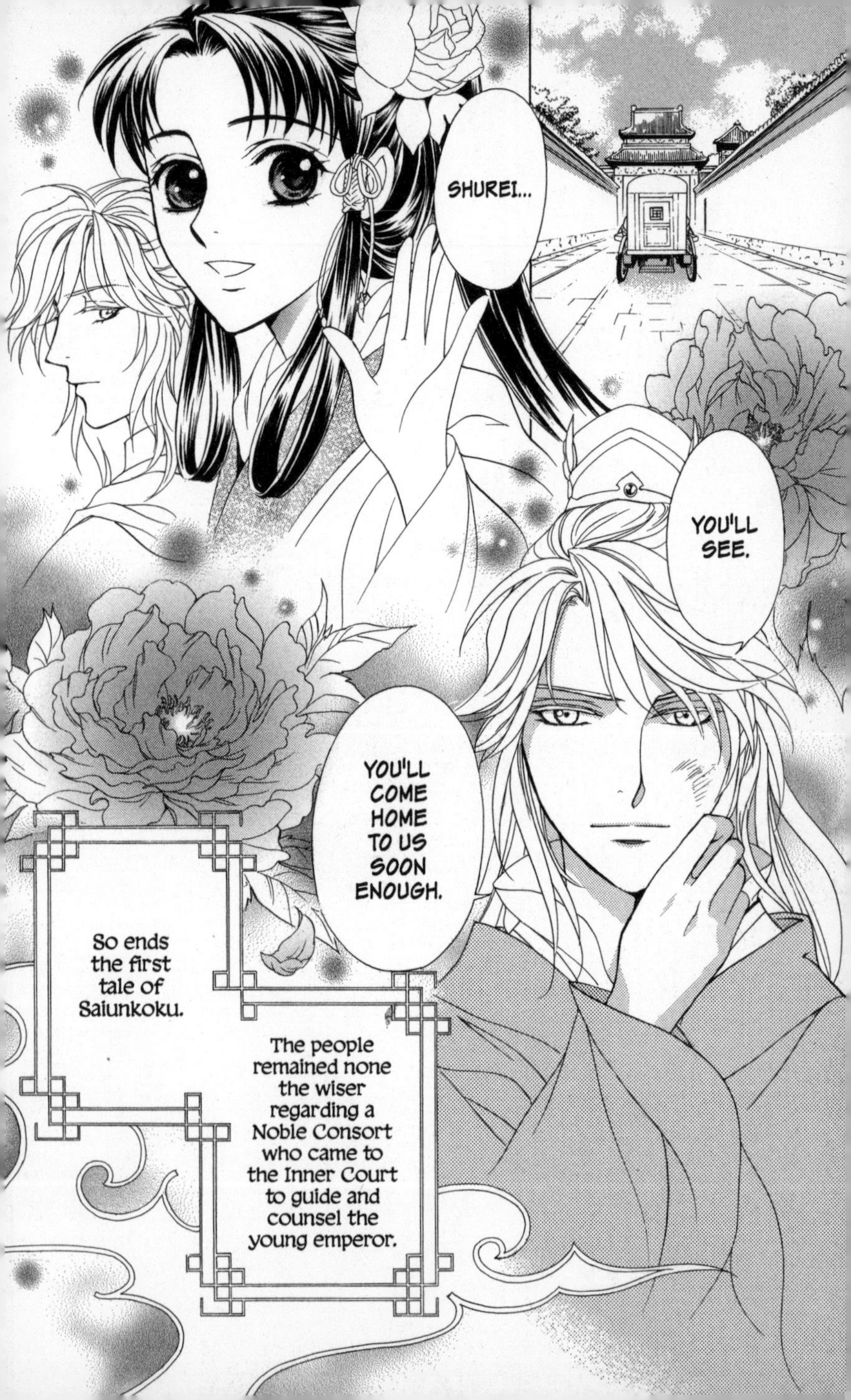
SHUREI...
YOU'LL SEE.
YOU'LL COME HOME TO US SOON ENOUGH.
So ends the first tale of Saiunkoku.
The people remained none the wiser regarding a Noble Consort who came to the Inner Court to guide and counsel the young emperor.

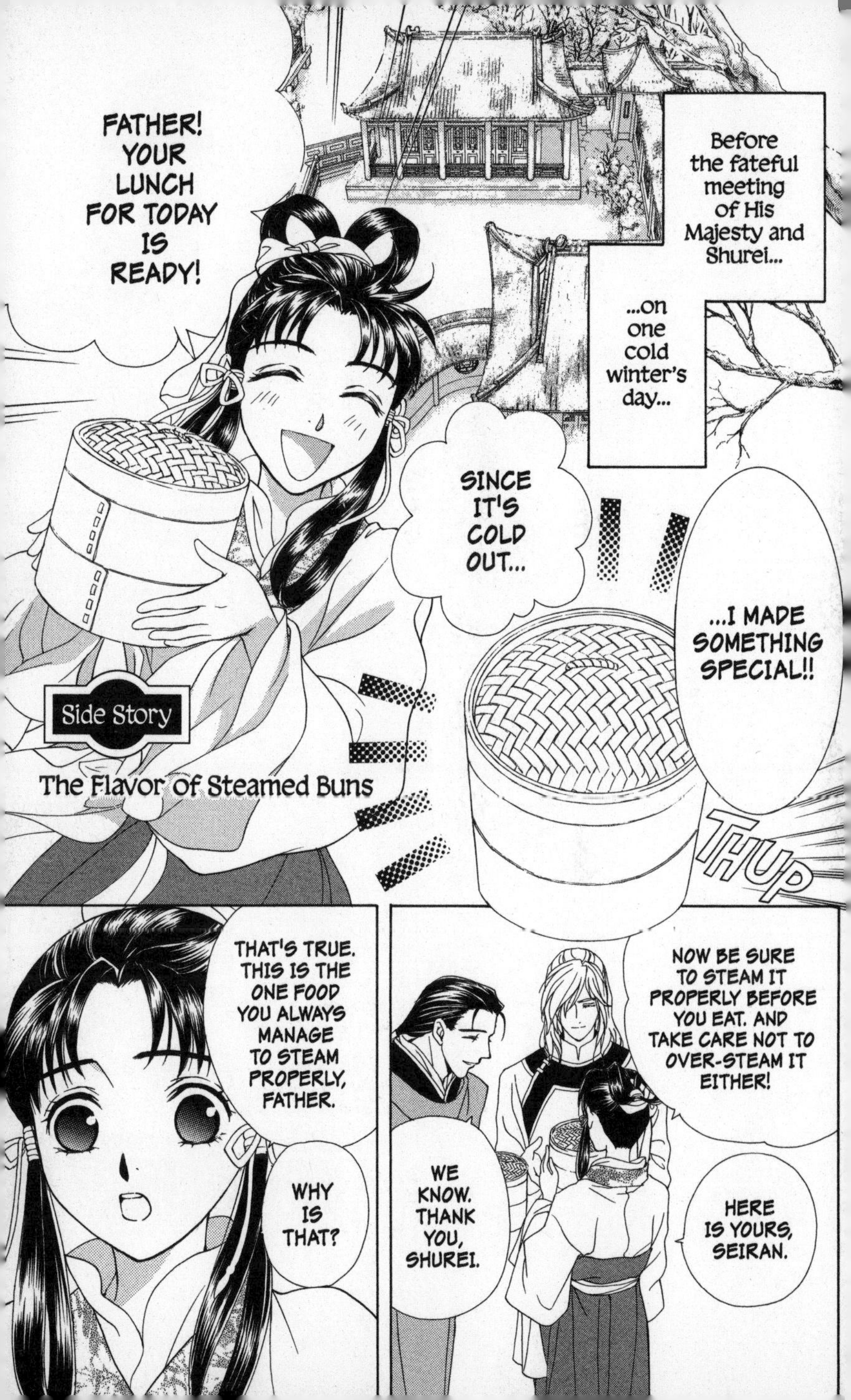

Before the fateful meeting of His Majesty and Shurei...
...on one cold winter's day...
FATHER! YOUR LUNCH FOR TODAY IS READY!
SINCE IT'S COLD OUT...
...I MADE SOMETHING SPECIAL!!
THUP
Side Story
The Flavor of Steamed Buns
NOW BE SURE TO STEAM IT PROPERLY BEFORE YOU EAT. AND TAKE CARE NOT TO OVER-STEAM IT EITHER!
HERE IS YOURS, SEIRAN.
WE KNOW. THANK YOU, SHUREI.
THAT'S TRUE. THIS IS THE ONE FOOD YOU ALWAYS MANAGE TO STEAM PROPERLY, FATHER.
WHY IS THAT?

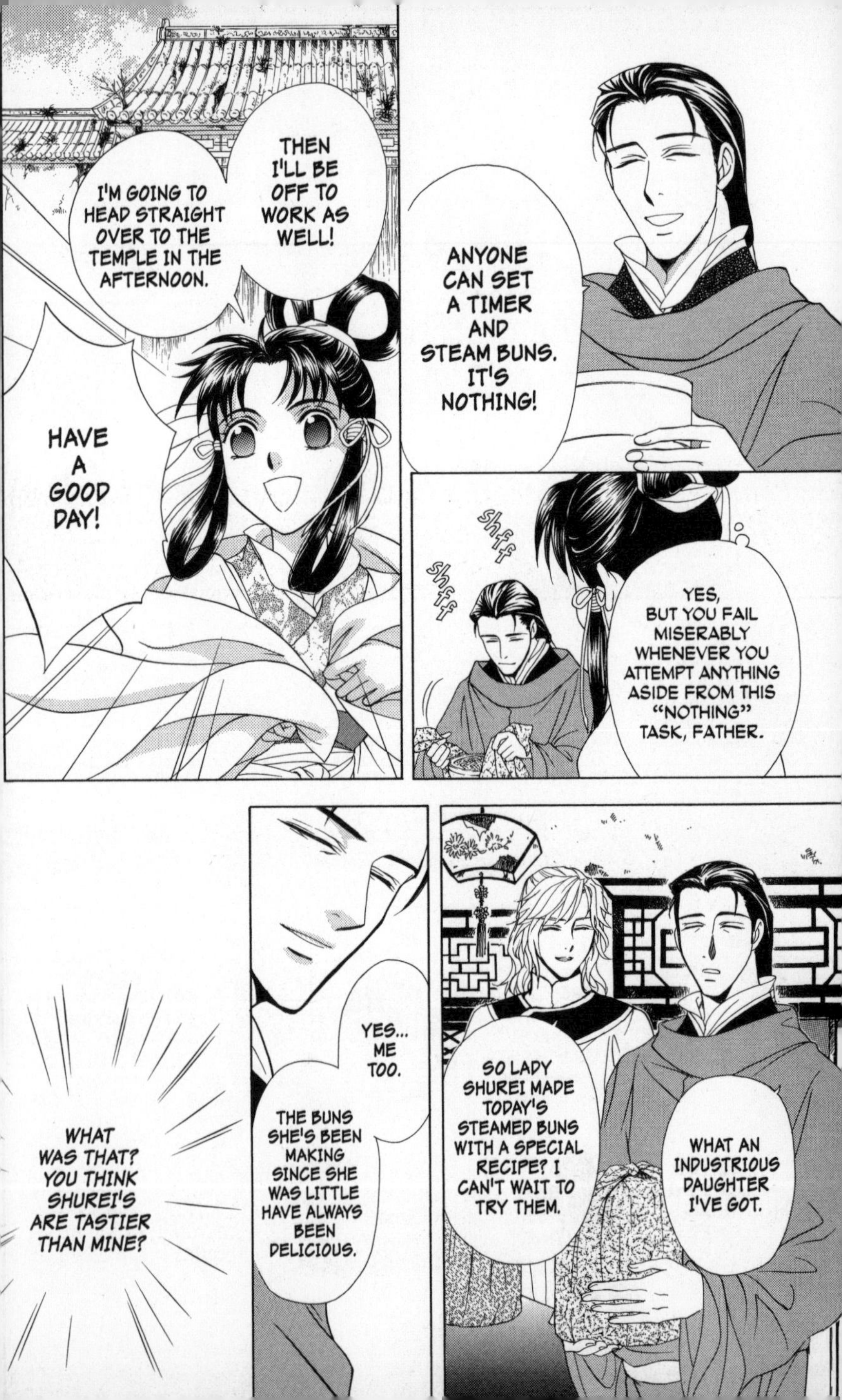
ANYONE CAN SET A TIMER AND STEAM BUNS. IT'S NOTHING!
shff
shff
YES, BUT YOU FAIL MISERABLY WHENEVER YOU ATTEMPT ANYTHING ASIDE FROM THIS "NOTHING" TASK, FATHER.
THEN I'LL BE OFF TO WORK AS WELL!
I'M GOING TO HEAD STRAIGHT OVER TO THE TEMPLE IN THE AFTERNOON.
HAVE A GOOD DAY!
WHAT AN INDUSTRIOUS DAUGHTER I'VE GOT.
SO LADY SHUREI MADE TODAY'S STEAMED BUNS WITH A SPECIAL RECIPE? I CAN'T WAIT TO TRY THEM.
YES... ME TOO.
THE BUNS SHE'S BEEN MAKING SINCE SHE WAS LITTLE HAVE ALWAYS BEEN DELICIOUS.
WHAT WAS THAT? YOU THINK SHUREI'S ARE TASTIER THAN MINE?

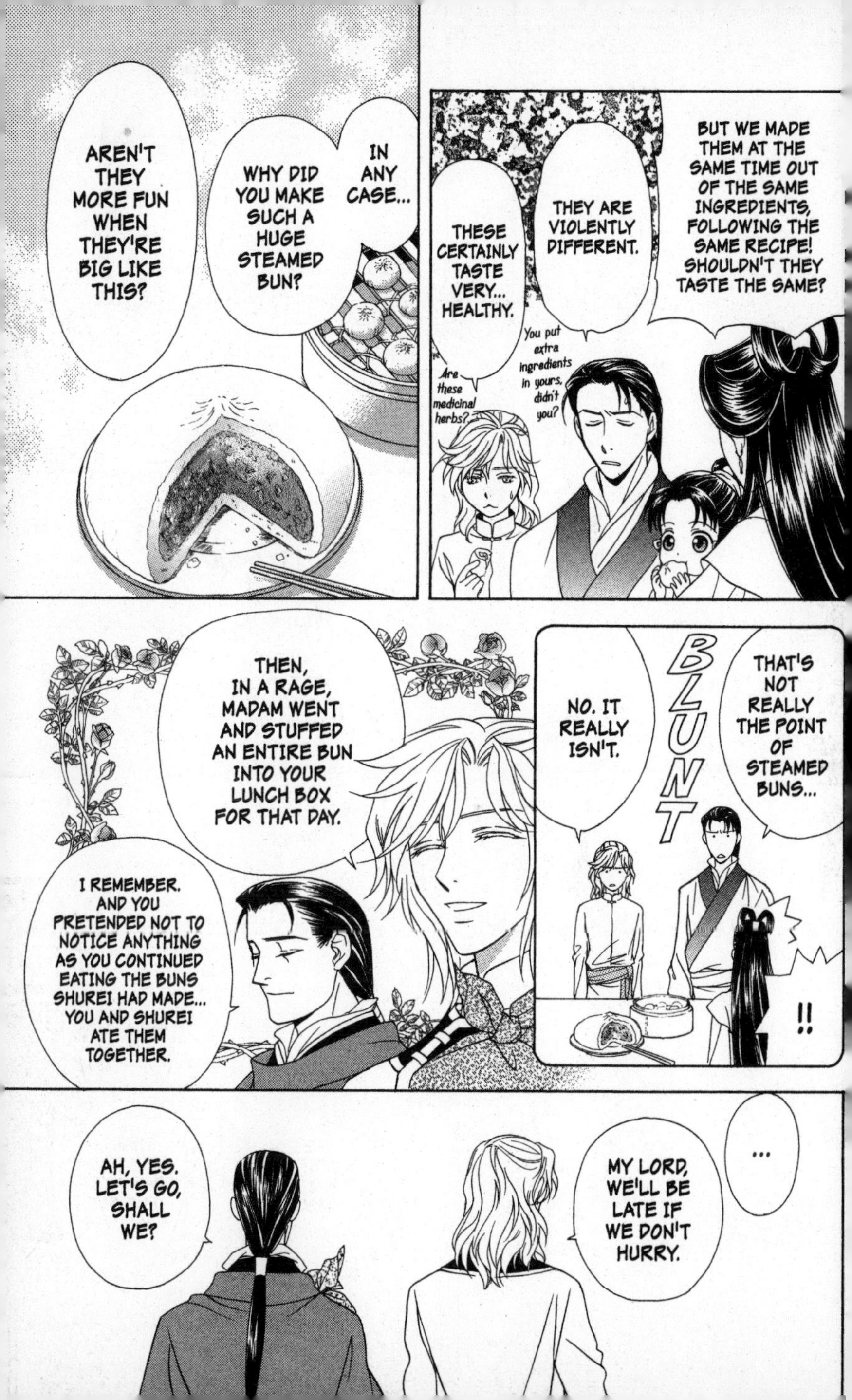
BUT WE MADE THEM AT THE SAME TIME OUT OF THE SAME INGREDIENTS, FOLLOWING THE SAME RECIPE! SHOULDN'T THEY TASTE THE SAME?
THEY ARE VIOLENTLY DIFFERENT.
You put extra ingredients in yours, didn't you?
THESE CERTAINLY TASTE VERY... HEALTHY.
Are these medicinal herbs?
IN ANY CASE...
WHY DID YOU MAKE SUCH A HUGE STEAMED BUN?
AREN'T THEY MORE FUN WHEN THEY'RE BIG LIKE THIS?
THAT'S NOT REALLY THE POINT OF STEAMED BUNS...
BLUNT
NO. IT REALLY ISN'T.
!!
THEN, IN A RAGE, MADAM WENT AND STUFFED AN ENTIRE BUN INTO YOUR LUNCH BOX FOR THAT DAY.
I REMEMBER. AND YOU PRETENDED NOT TO NOTICE ANYTHING AS YOU CONTINUED EATING THE BUNS SHUREI HAD MADE... YOU AND SHUREI ATE THEM TOGETHER.
...
MY LORD, WE'LL BE LATE IF WE DON'T HURRY.
AH, YES. LET'S GO, SHALL WE?

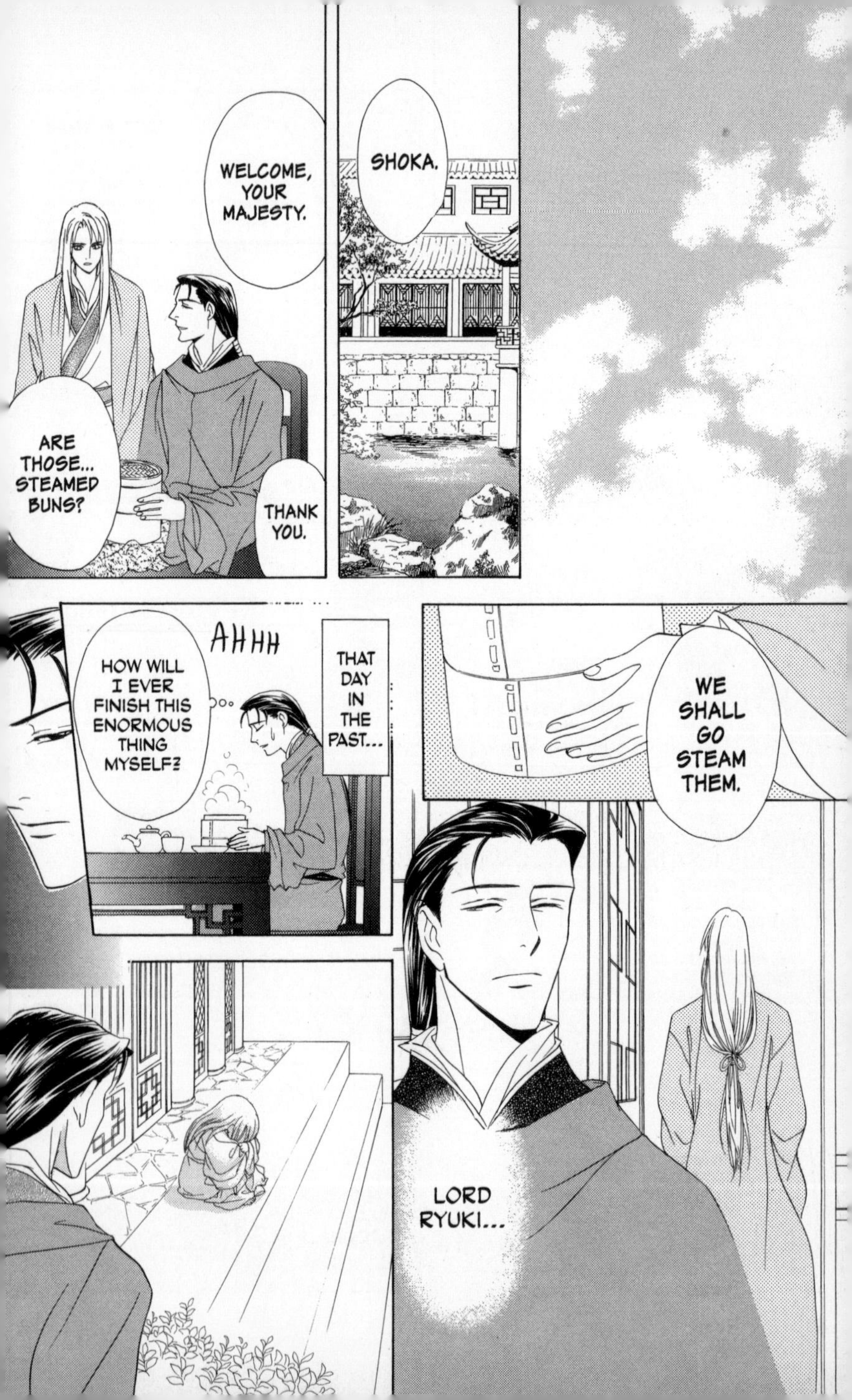
SHOKA.
WELCOME, YOUR MAJESTY.
THANK YOU.
ARE THOSE... STEAMED BUNS?
WE SHALL GO STEAM THEM.
THAT DAY IN THE PAST...
AHHH
HOW WILL I EVER FINISH THIS ENORMOUS THING MYSELF?
LORD RYUKI...

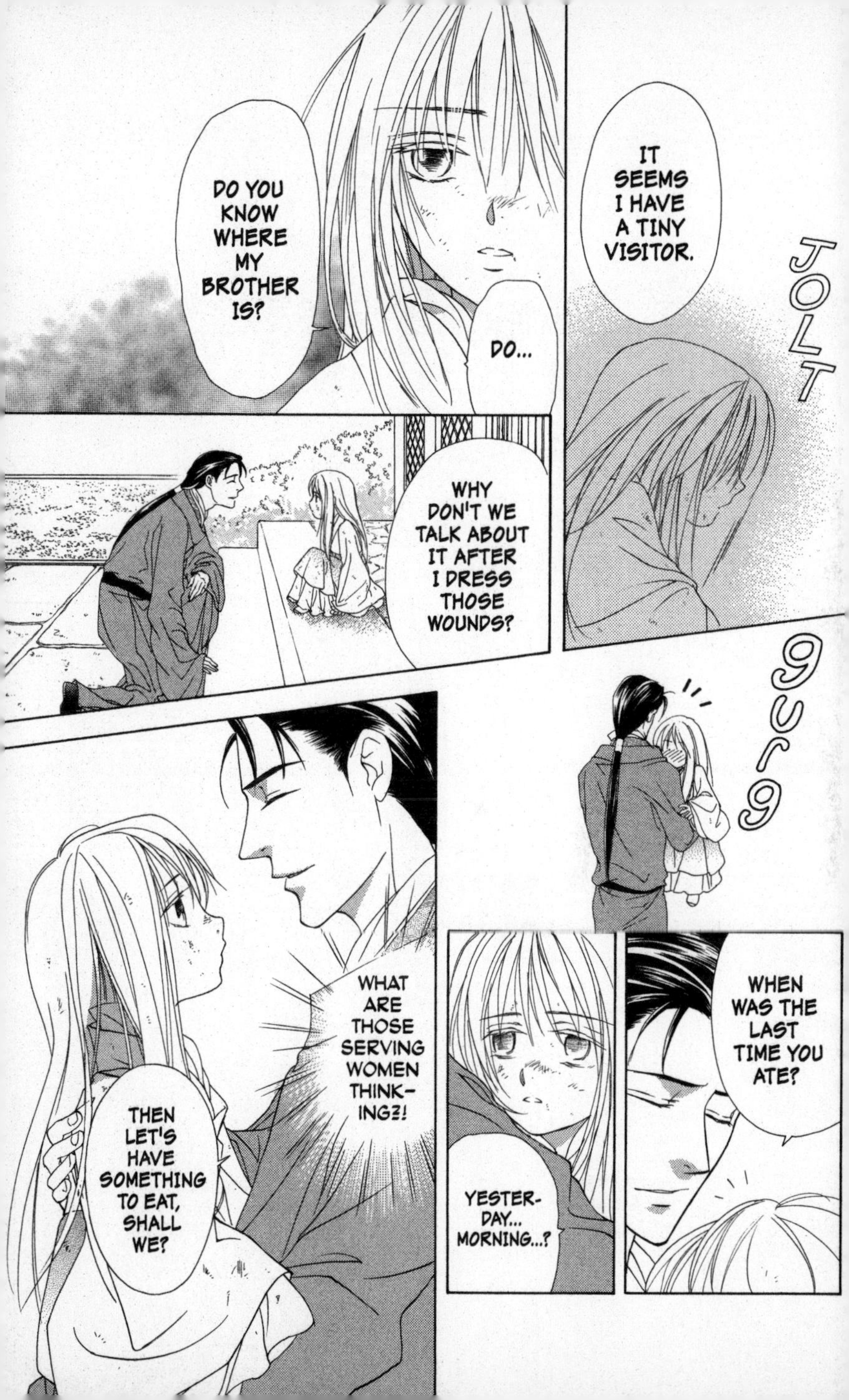
IT SEEMS I HAVE A TINY VISITOR.
JOLT
DO...
DO YOU KNOW WHERE MY BROTHER IS?
WHY DON'T WE TALK ABOUT IT AFTER I DRESS THOSE WOUNDS?
GURG
WHEN WAS THE LAST TIME YOU ATE?
YESTER-DAY... MORNING...?
WHAT ARE THOSE SERVING WOMEN THINK-ING?!
THEN LET'S HAVE SOMETHING TO EAT, SHALL WE?

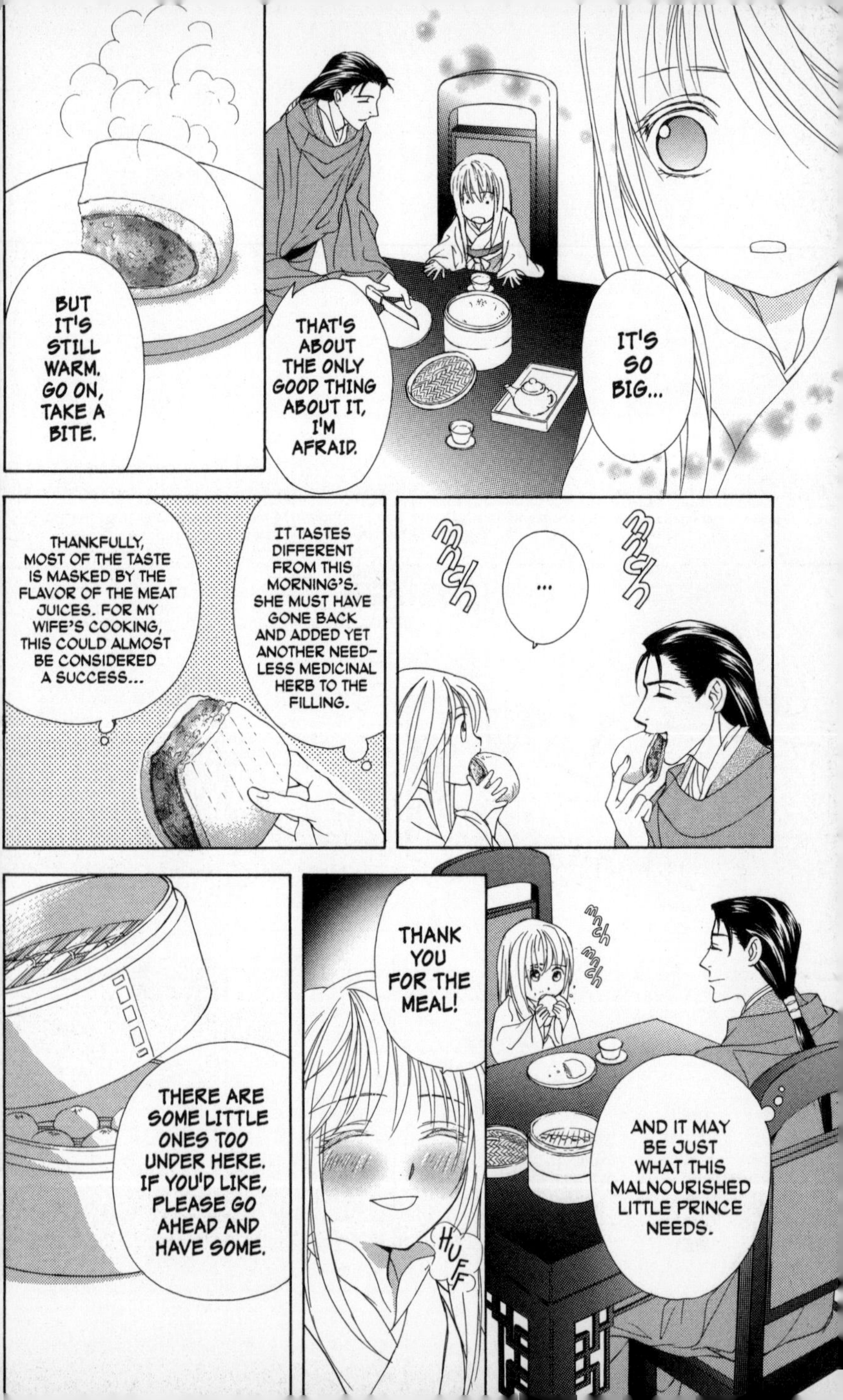
IT'S SO BIG...
THAT'S ABOUT THE ONLY GOOD THING ABOUT IT, I'M AFRAID.
BUT IT'S STILL WARM. GO ON, TAKE A BITE.
MNCH
...
MNCH
IT TASTES DIFFERENT FROM THIS MORNING'S. SHE MUST HAVE GONE BACK AND ADDED YET ANOTHER NEEDLESS MEDICINAL HERB TO THE FILLING.
THANKFULLY, MOST OF THE TASTE IS MASKED BY THE FLAVOR OF THE MEAT JUICES. FOR MY WIFE'S COOKING, THIS COULD ALMOST BE CONSIDERED A SUCCESS...
MNCH
MNCH
AND IT MAY BE JUST WHAT THIS MALNOURISHED LITTLE PRINCE NEEDS.
THANK YOU FOR THE MEAL!
HUFF
THERE ARE SOME LITTLE ONES TOO UNDER HERE. IF YOU'D LIKE, PLEASE GO AHEAD AND HAVE SOME.

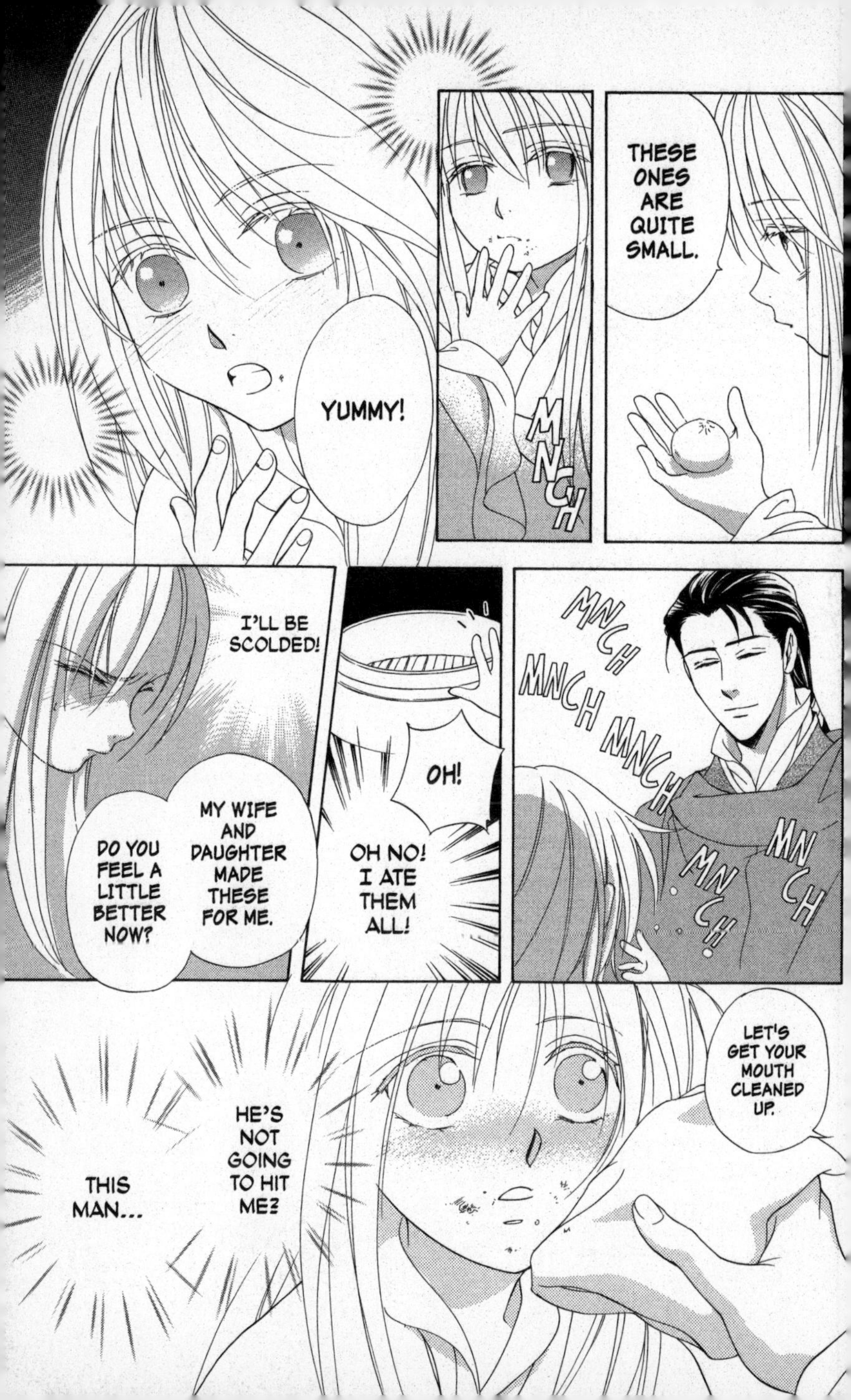
THESE ONES ARE QUITE SMALL.
MNCH
YUMMY!
MNCH
MNCH
MNCH
MNCH
MNCH
OH!
OH NO! I ATE THEM ALL!
I'LL BE SCOLDED!
MY WIFE AND DAUGHTER MADE THESE FOR ME.
DO YOU FEEL A LITTLE BETTER NOW?
LET'S GET YOUR MOUTH CLEANED UP.
HE'S NOT GOING TO HIT ME?
THIS MAN...

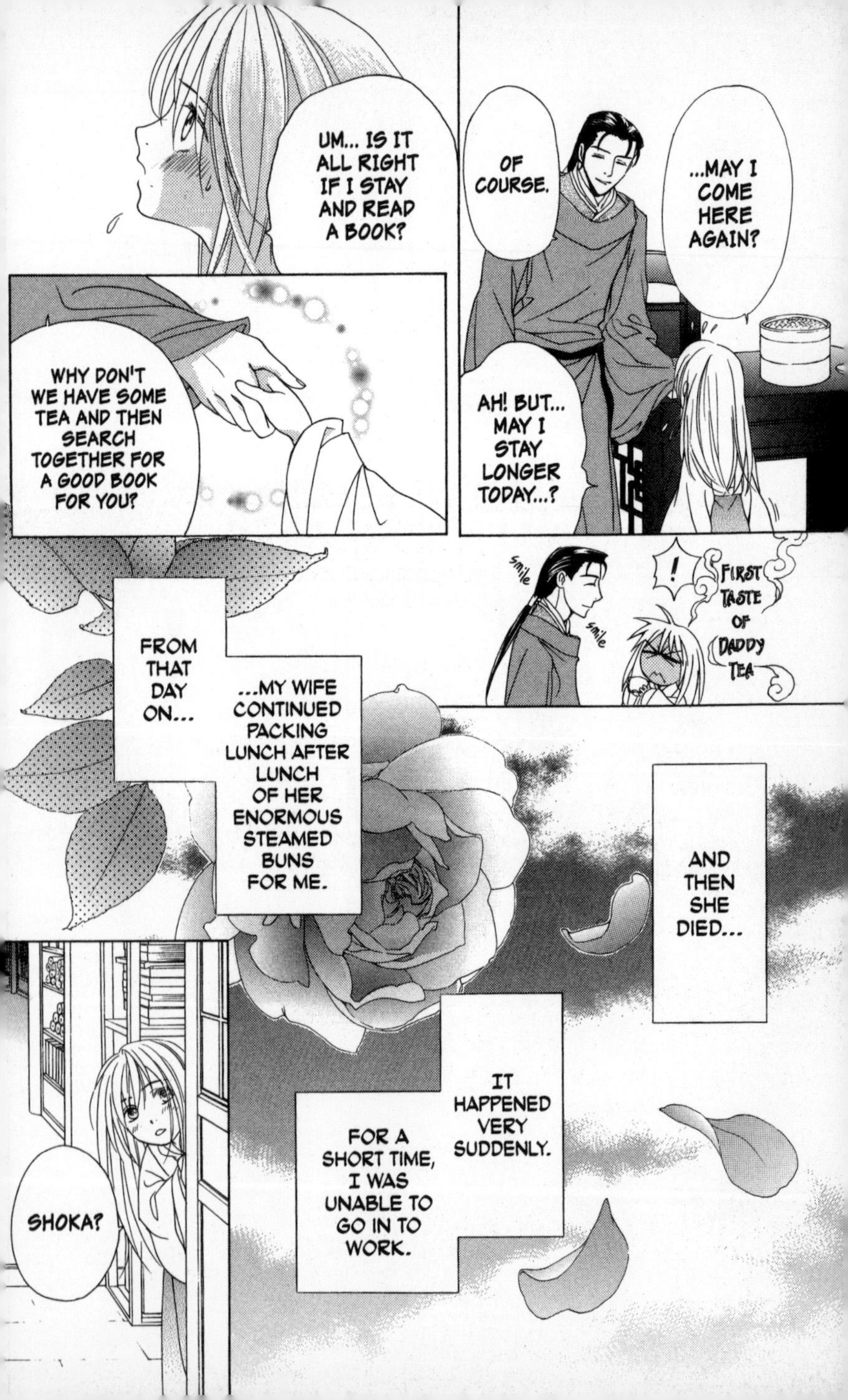
...MAY I COME HERE AGAIN?
OF COURSE.
AH! BUT... MAY I STAY LONGER TODAY...?
UM... IS IT ALL RIGHT IF I STAY AND READ A BOOK?
WHY DON'T WE HAVE SOME TEA AND THEN SEARCH TOGETHER FOR A GOOD BOOK FOR YOU?
!
FIRST TASTE OF DADDY TEA
smile
smile
FROM THAT DAY ON...
...MY WIFE CONTINUED PACKING LUNCH AFTER LUNCH OF HER ENORMOUS STEAMED BUNS FOR ME.
AND THEN SHE DIED...
IT HAPPENED VERY SUDDENLY.
FOR A SHORT TIME, I WAS UNABLE TO GO IN TO WORK.
SHOKA?

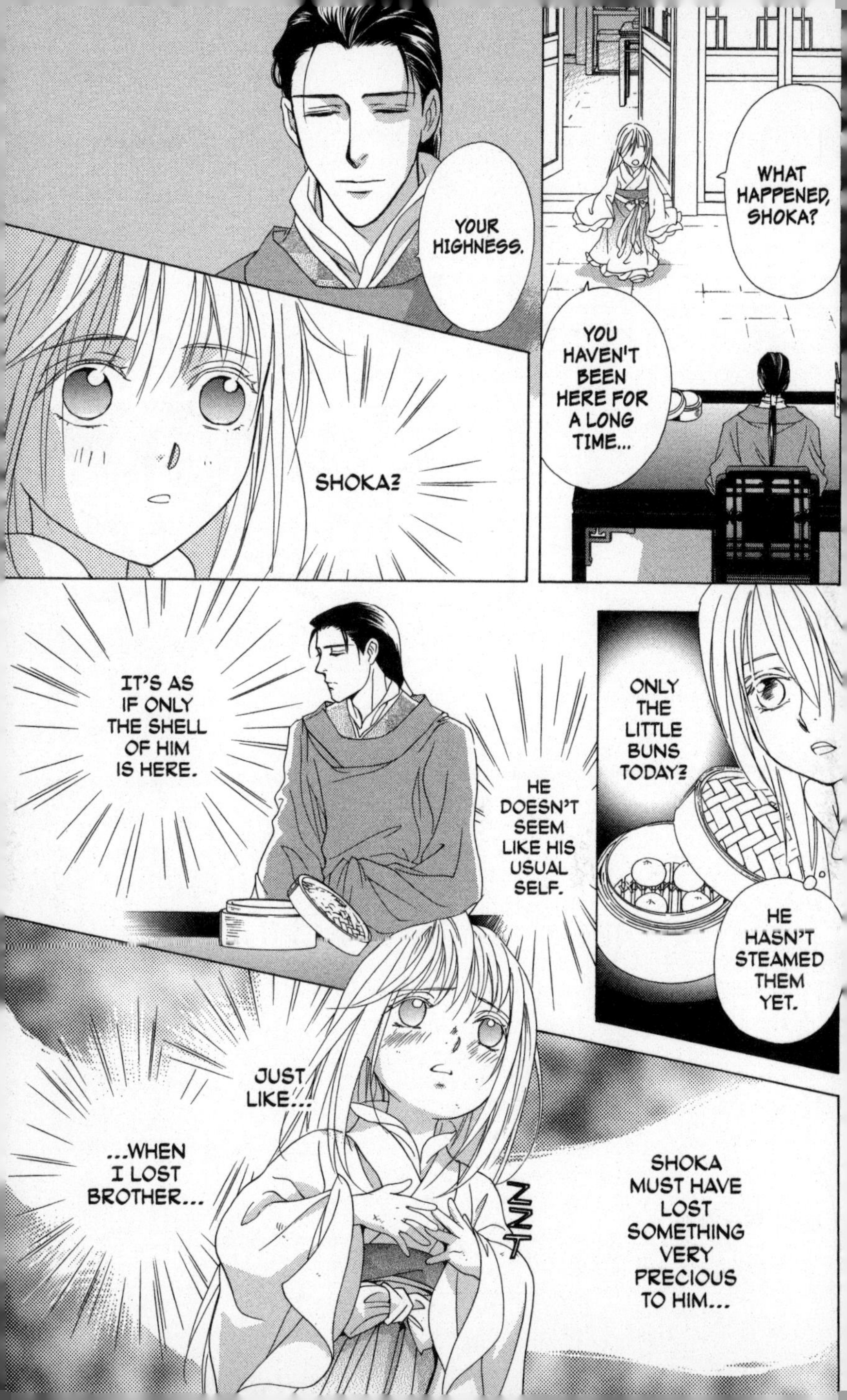
WHAT HAPPENED, SHOKA?
YOU HAVEN'T BEEN HERE FOR A LONG TIME...
YOUR HIGHNESS.
SHOKA?
ONLY THE LITTLE BUNS TODAY?
HE HASN'T STEAMED THEM YET.
HE DOESN'T SEEM LIKE HIS USUAL SELF.
IT'S AS IF ONLY THE SHELL OF HIM IS HERE.
SHOKA MUST HAVE LOST SOMETHING VERY PRECIOUS TO HIM...
ZZT
JUST LIKE...
...WHEN I LOST BROTHER...

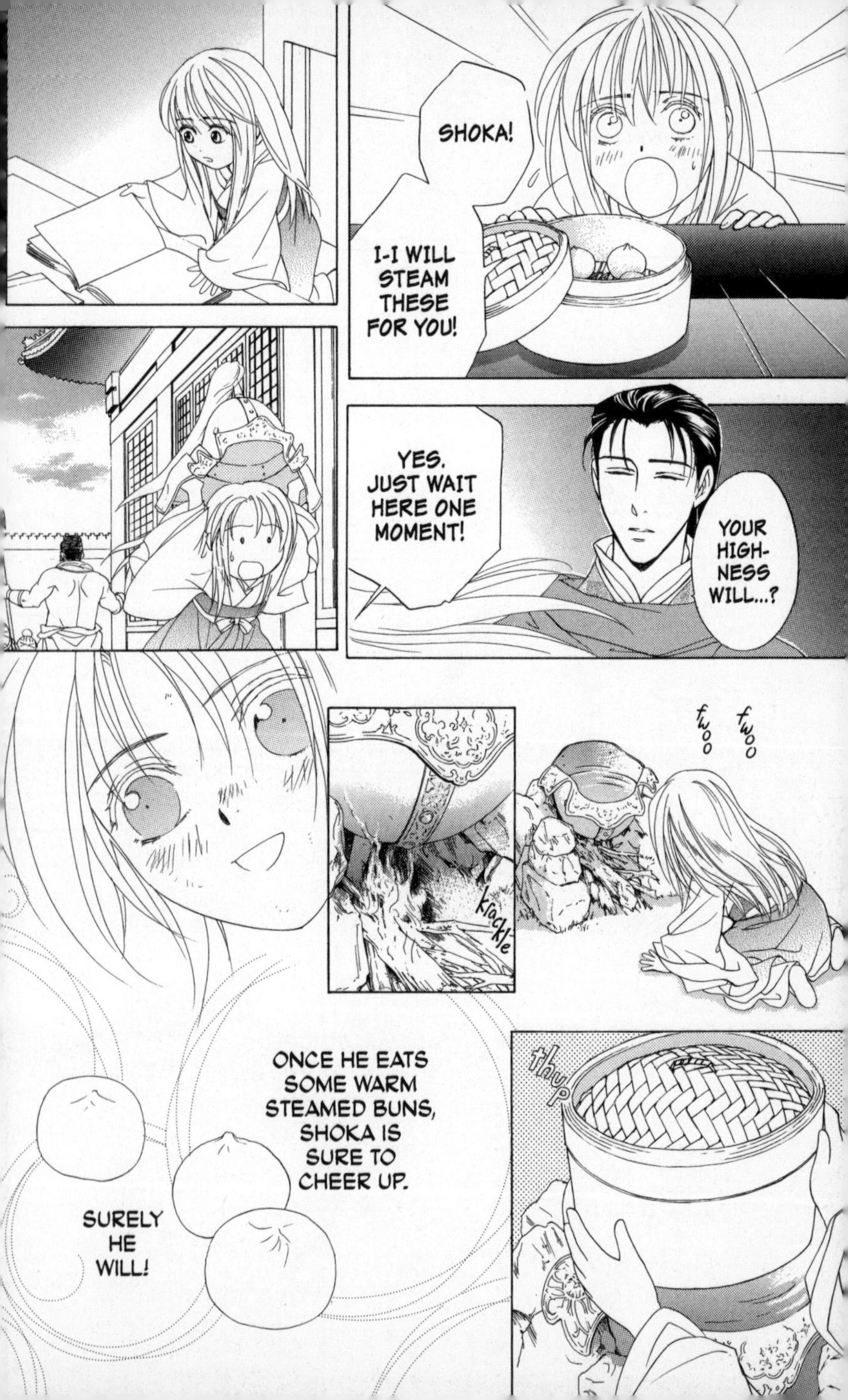
SHOKA!
I-I WILL STEAM THESE FOR YOU!
YOUR HIGHNESS WILL...?
YES. JUST WAIT HERE ONE MOMENT!
fwoo fwoo
krackle
thup
ONCE HE EATS SOME WARM STEAMED BUNS, SHOKA IS SURE TO CHEER UP.
SURELY HE WILL!

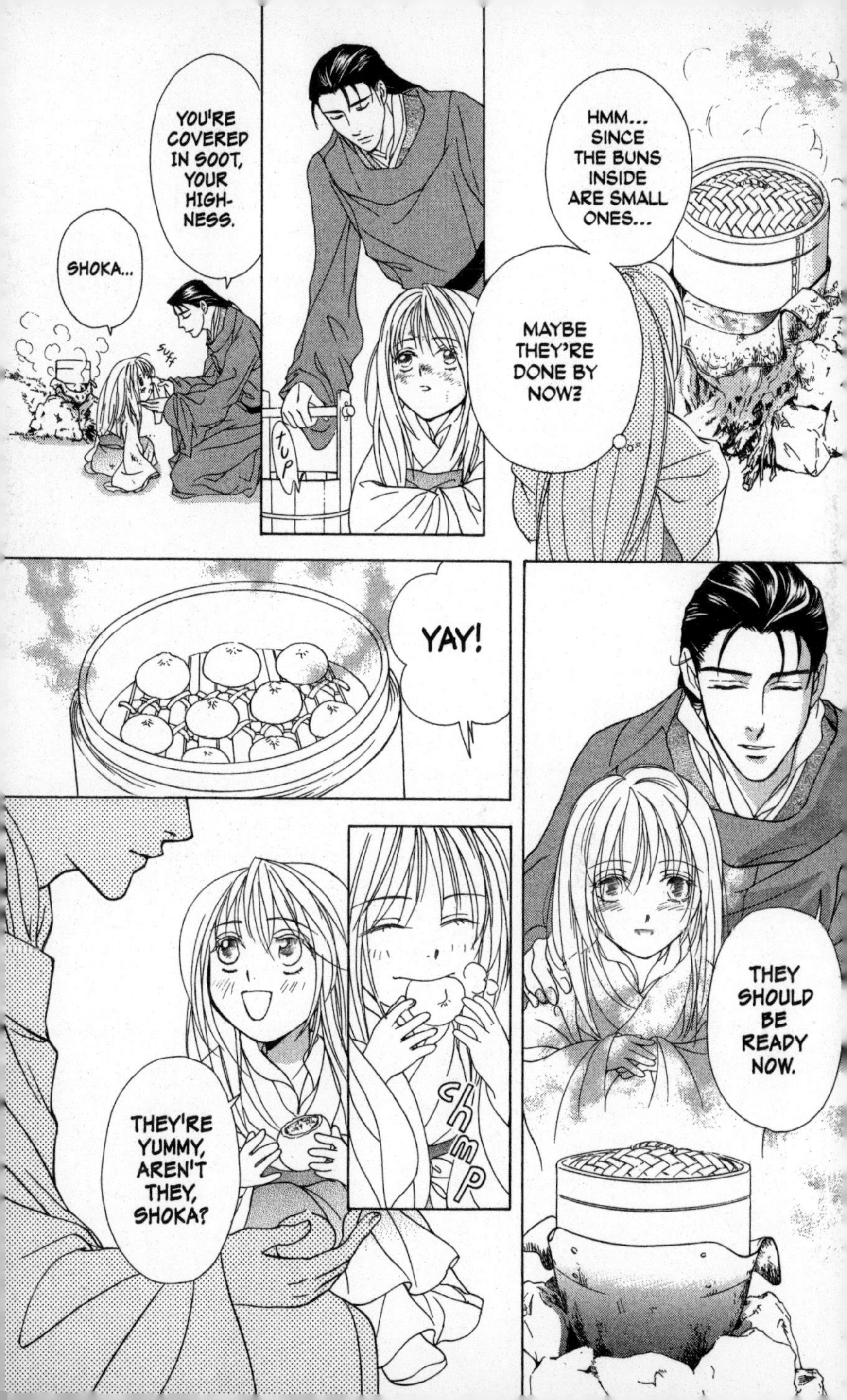
HMM... SINCE THE BUNS INSIDE ARE SMALL ONES...
MAYBE THEY'RE DONE BY NOW?
TUP
YOU'RE COVERED IN SOOT, YOUR HIGH-NESS.
SHOKA...
SUFF
THEY SHOULD BE READY NOW.
YAY!
CHMP
THEY'RE YUMMY, AREN'T THEY, SHOKA?

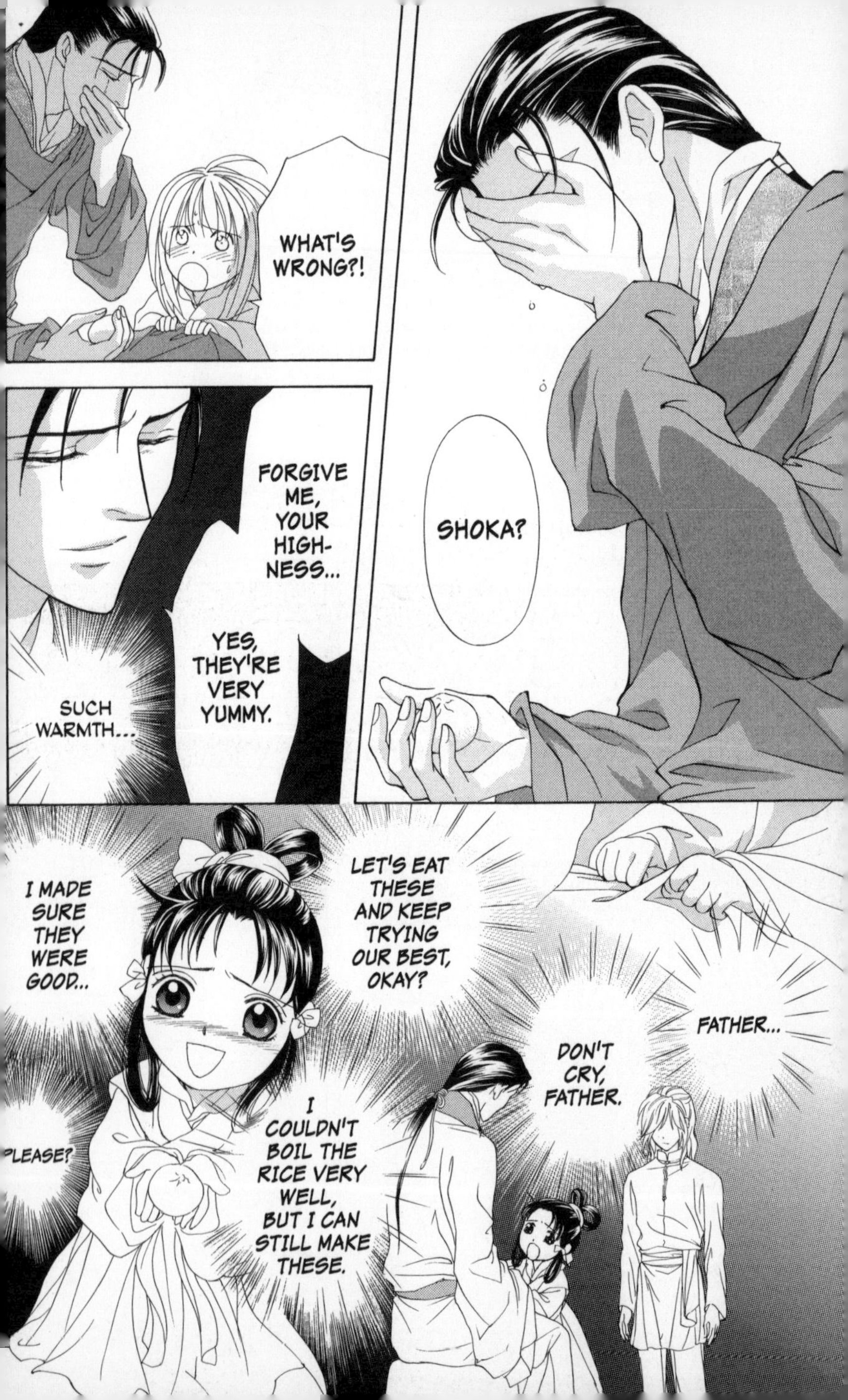
SHOKA?
WHAT'S WRONG?!
FORGIVE ME, YOUR HIGHNESS...
YES, THEY'RE VERY YUMMY.
SUCH WARMTH...
FATHER...
DON'T CRY, FATHER.
LET'S EAT THESE AND KEEP TRYING OUR BEST, OKAY?
I COULDN'T BOIL THE RICE VERY WELL, BUT I CAN STILL MAKE THESE.
I MADE SURE THEY WERE GOOD...
LEASE?

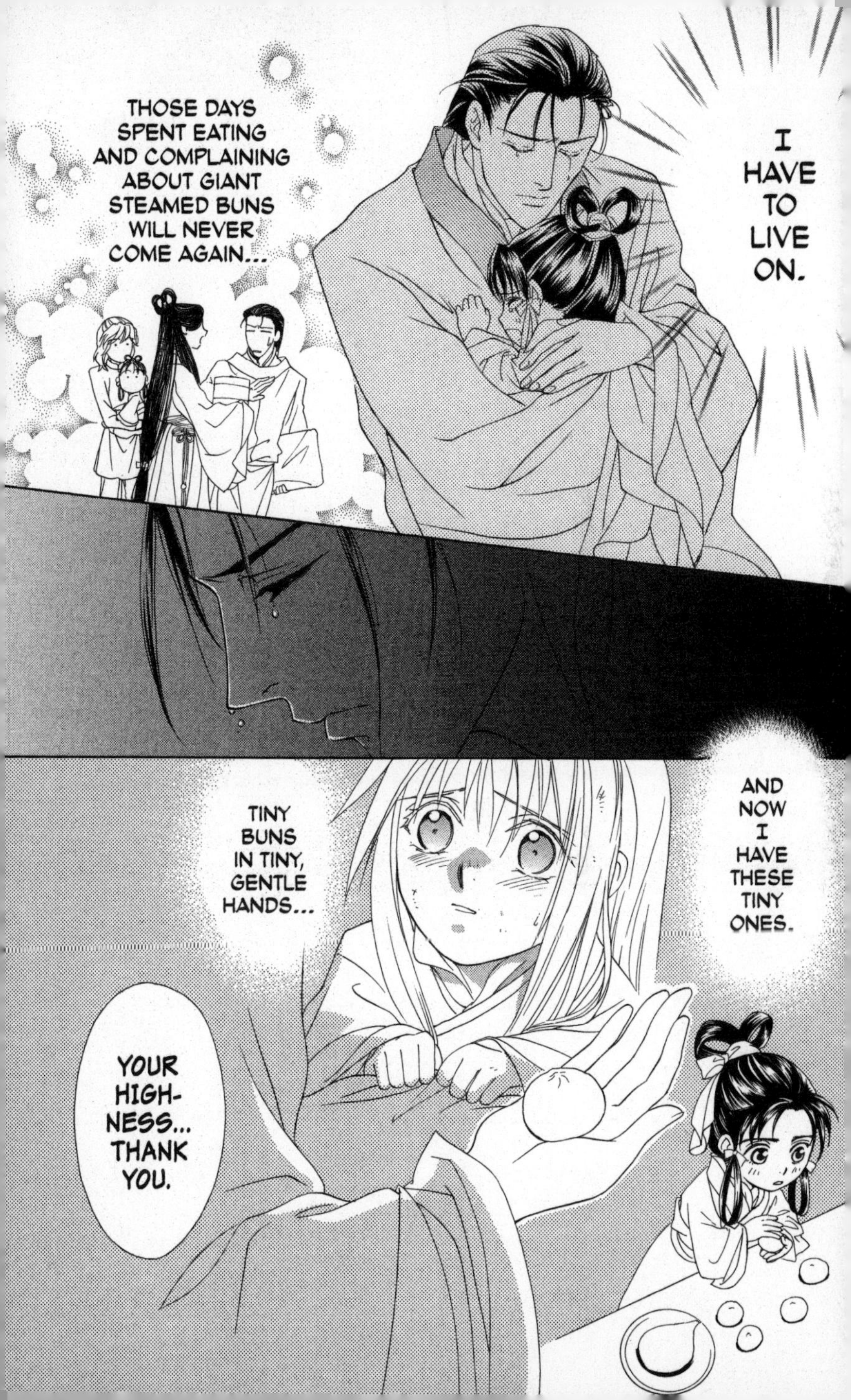
I HAVE TO LIVE ON.
THOSE DAYS SPENT EATING AND COMPLAINING ABOUT GIANT STEAMED BUNS WILL NEVER COME AGAIN...
AND NOW I HAVE THESE TINY ONES.
TINY BUNS IN TINY, GENTLE HANDS...
YOUR HIGHNESS... THANK YOU.

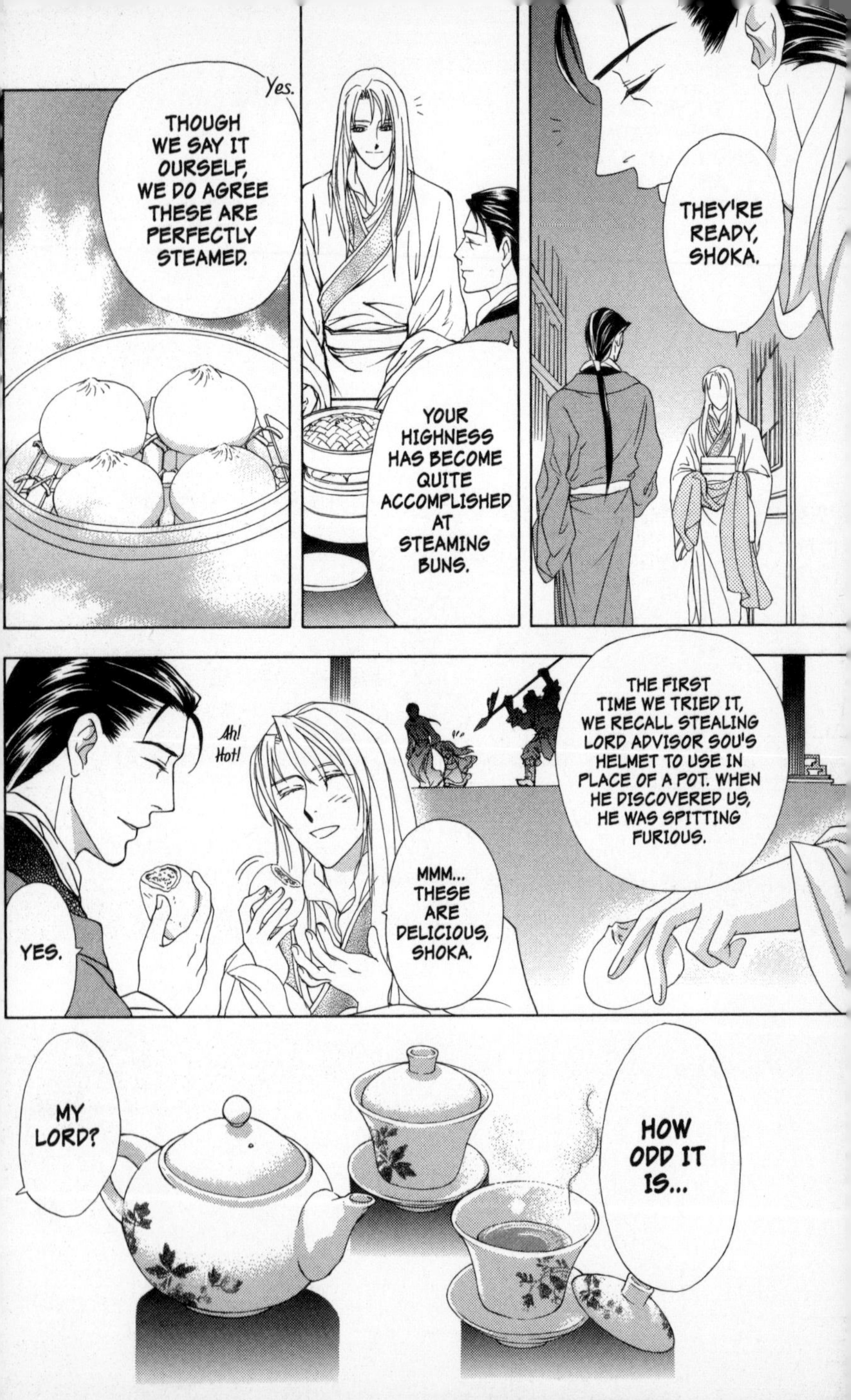
THEY'RE READY, SHOKA.
YOUR HIGHNESS HAS BECOME QUITE ACCOMPLISHED AT STEAMING BUNS.
Yes.
THOUGH WE SAY IT OURSELF, WE DO AGREE THESE ARE PERFECTLY STEAMED.
THE FIRST TIME WE TRIED IT, WE RECALL STEALING LORD ADVISOR SOU'S HELMET TO USE IN PLACE OF A POT. WHEN HE DISCOVERED US, HE WAS SPITTING FURIOUS.
MMM... THESE ARE DELICIOUS, SHOKA.
Ah! Hot!
YES.
HOW ODD IT IS...
MY LORD?

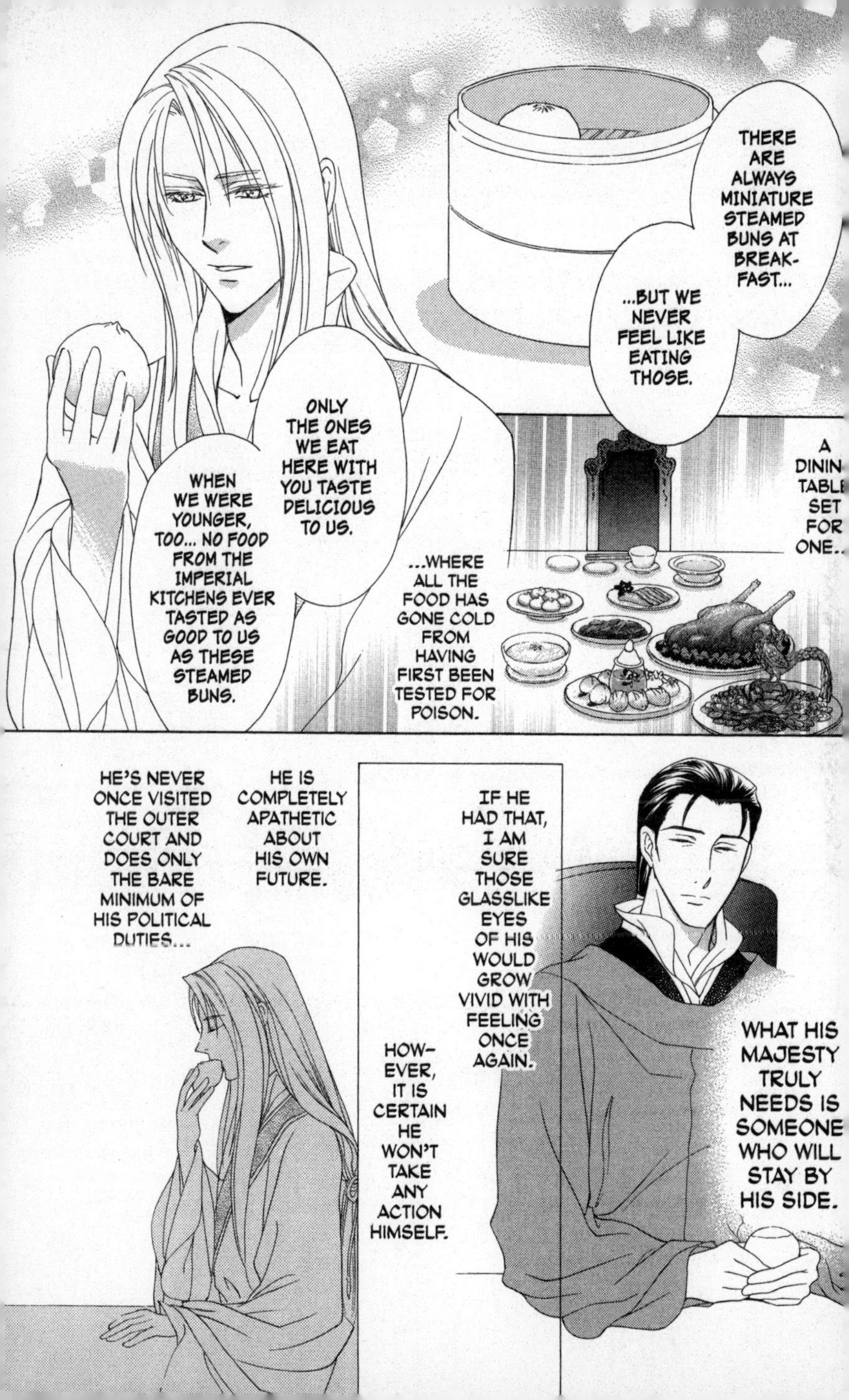
THERE ARE ALWAYS MINIATURE STEAMED BUNS AT BREAK-FAST...
...BUT WE NEVER FEEL LIKE EATING THOSE.
A DINING TABLE SET FOR ONE...
...WHERE ALL THE FOOD HAS GONE COLD FROM HAVING FIRST BEEN TESTED FOR POISON.
ONLY THE ONES WE EAT HERE WITH YOU TASTE DELICIOUS TO US.
WHEN WE WERE YOUNGER, TOO... NO FOOD FROM THE IMPERIAL KITCHENS EVER TASTED AS GOOD TO US AS THESE STEAMED BUNS.
WHAT HIS MAJESTY TRULY NEEDS IS SOMEONE WHO WILL STAY BY HIS SIDE.
IF HE HAD THAT, I AM SURE THOSE GLASSLIKE EYES OF HIS WOULD GROW VIVID WITH FEELING ONCE AGAIN.
HOW-EVER, IT IS CERTAIN HE WON'T TAKE ANY ACTION HIMSELF.
HE IS COMPLETELY APATHETIC ABOUT HIS OWN FUTURE.
HE'S NEVER ONCE VISITED THE OUTER COURT AND DOES ONLY THE BARE MINIMUM OF HIS POLITICAL DUTIES...

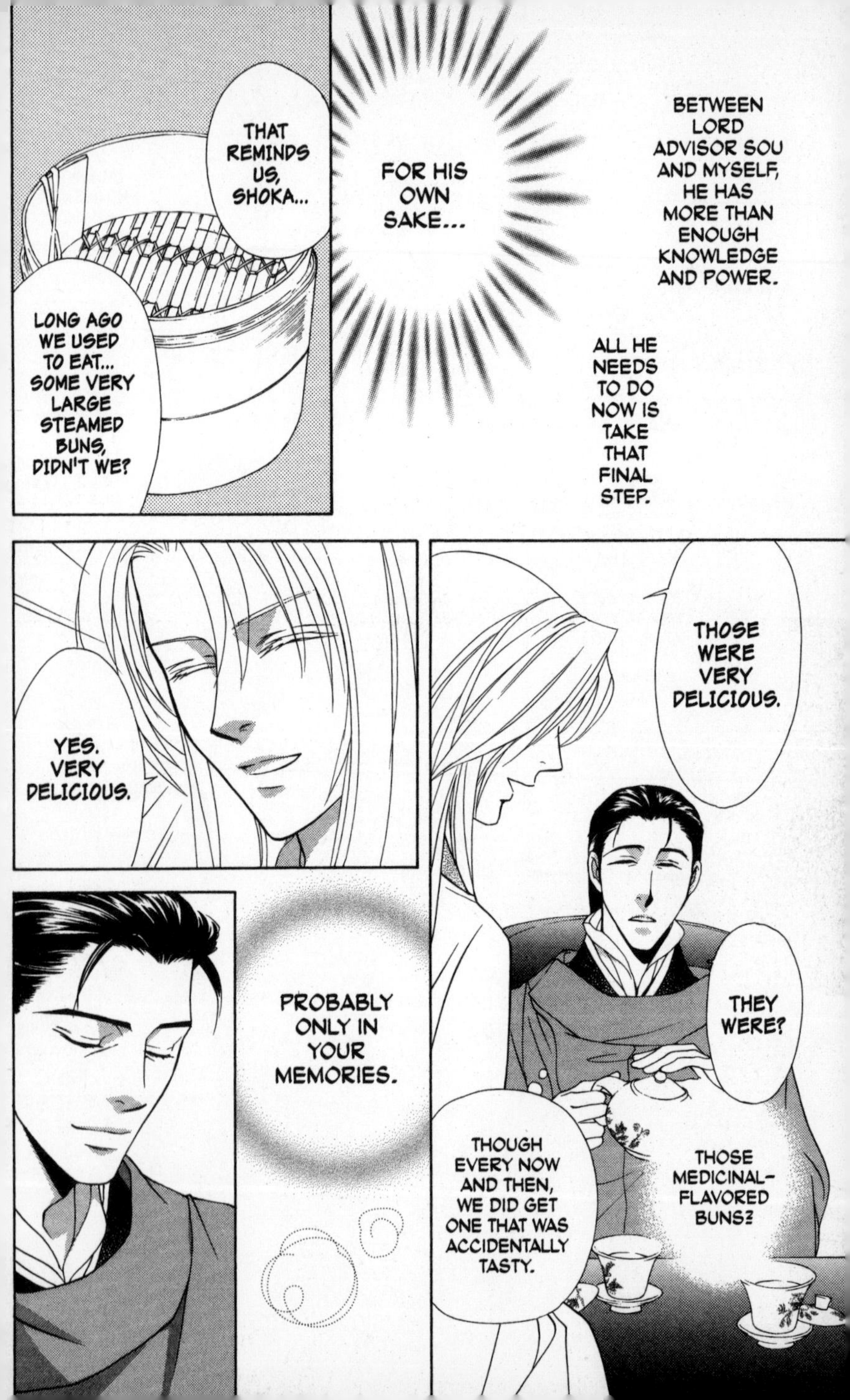
BETWEEN LORD ADVISOR SOU AND MYSELF, HE HAS MORE THAN ENOUGH KNOWLEDGE AND POWER.
ALL HE NEEDS TO DO NOW IS TAKE THAT FINAL STEP.
FOR HIS OWN SAKE...
THAT REMINDS US, SHOKA...
LONG AGO WE USED TO EAT... SOME VERY LARGE STEAMED BUNS, DIDN'T WE?
THOSE WERE VERY DELICIOUS.
THEY WERE?
THOSE MEDICINAL-FLAVORED BUNS?
THOUGH EVERY NOW AND THEN, WE DID GET ONE THAT WAS ACCIDENTALLY TASTY.
YES. VERY DELICIOUS.
PROBABLY ONLY IN YOUR MEMORIES.

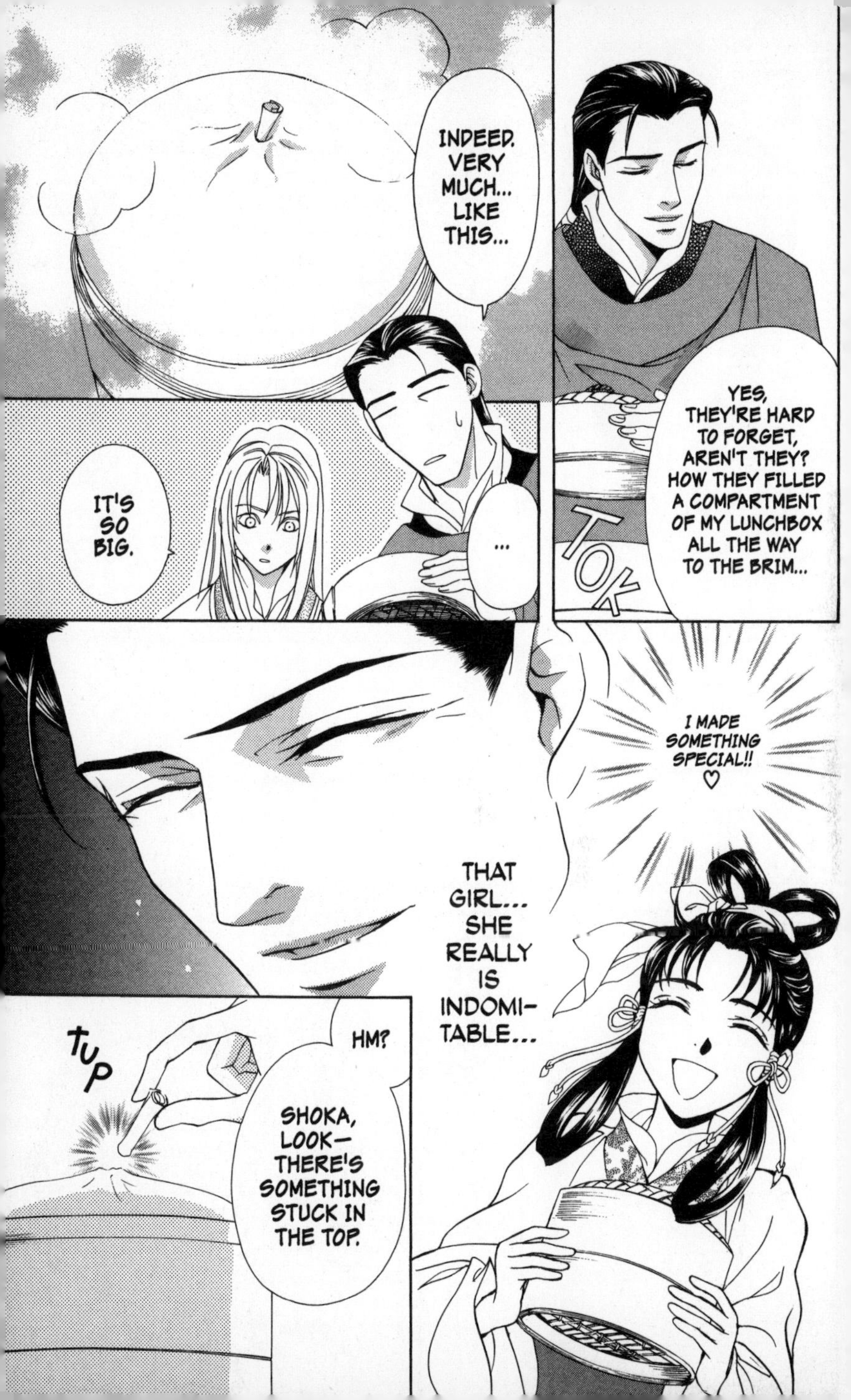
YES, THEY'RE HARD TO FORGET, AREN'T THEY? HOW THEY FILLED A COMPARTMENT OF MY LUNCHBOX ALL THE WAY TO THE BRIM...
TOK
INDEED. VERY MUCH... LIKE THIS...
...
IT'S SO BIG.
I MADE SOMETHING SPECIAL!! ♡
THAT GIRL... SHE REALLY IS INDOMITABLE...
HM?
SHOKA, LOOK— THERE'S SOMETHING STUCK IN THE TOP.
TUP

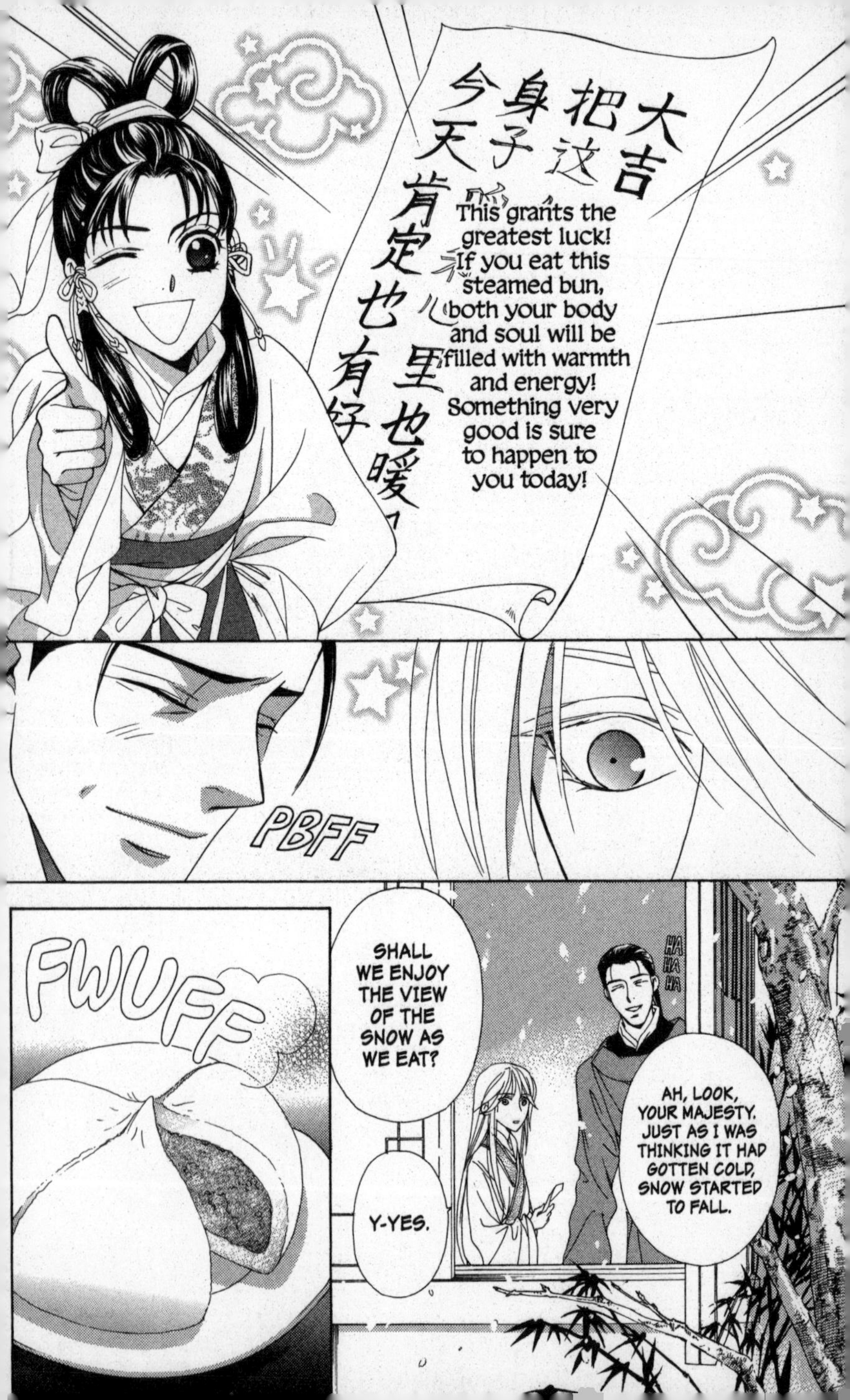
大吉把这身子今天
肯定也有好
里也暖
This grants the greatest luck! If you eat this steamed bun, both your body and soul will be filled with warmth and energy! Something very good is sure to happen to you today!
PBFF
HA HA HA
AH, LOOK, YOUR MAJESTY. JUST AS I WAS THINKING IT HAD GOTTEN COLD, SNOW STARTED TO FALL.
SHALL WE ENJOY THE VIEW OF THE SNOW AS WE EAT?
Y-YES.
FWUFF

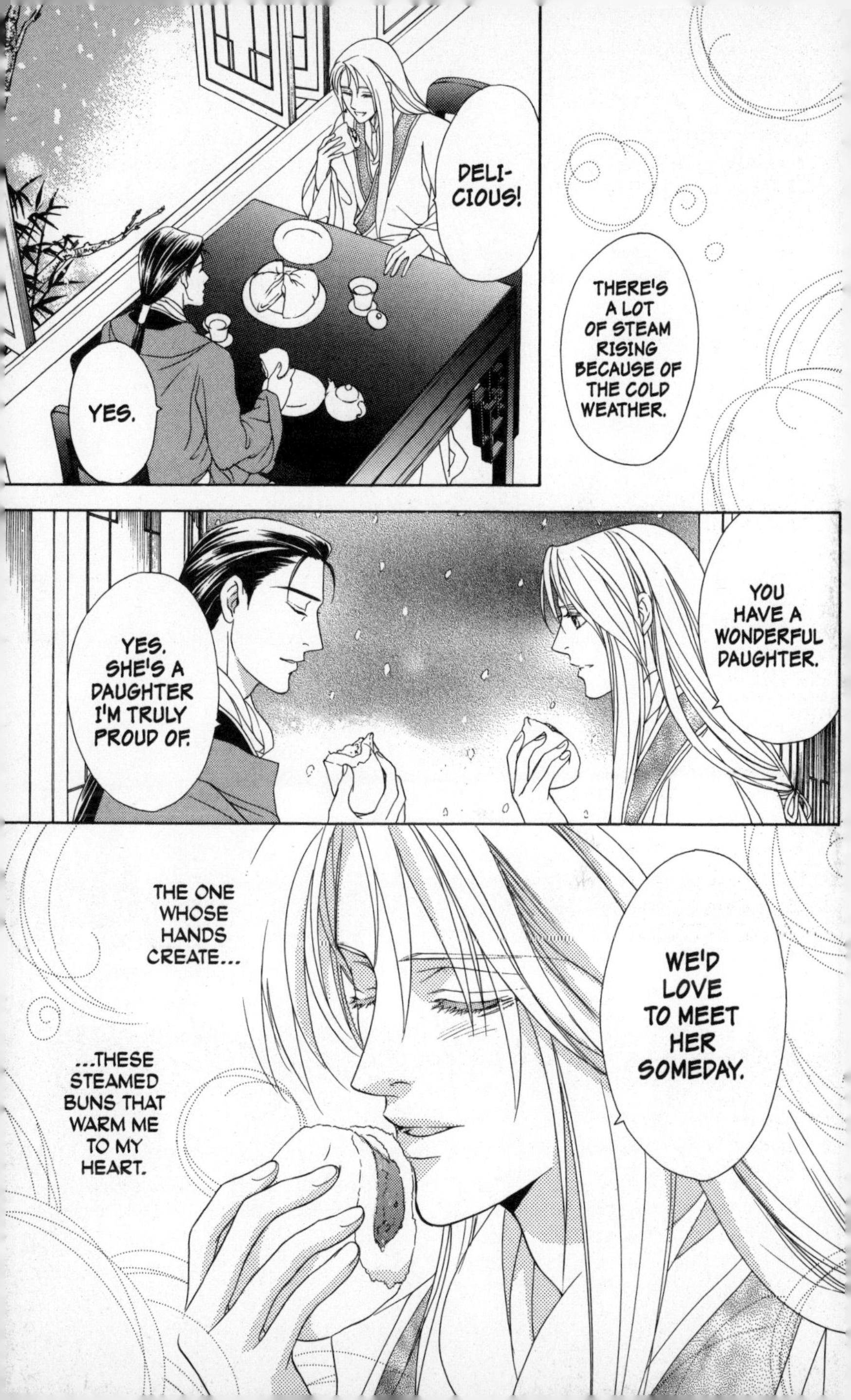
DELI-CIOUS!
THERE'S A LOT OF STEAM RISING BECAUSE OF THE COLD WEATHER.
YES.
YOU HAVE A WONDERFUL DAUGHTER.
YES. SHE'S A DAUGHTER I'M TRULY PROUD OF.
WE'D LOVE TO MEET HER SOMEDAY.
THE ONE WHOSE HANDS CREATE...
...THESE STEAMED BUNS THAT WARM ME TO MY HEART.

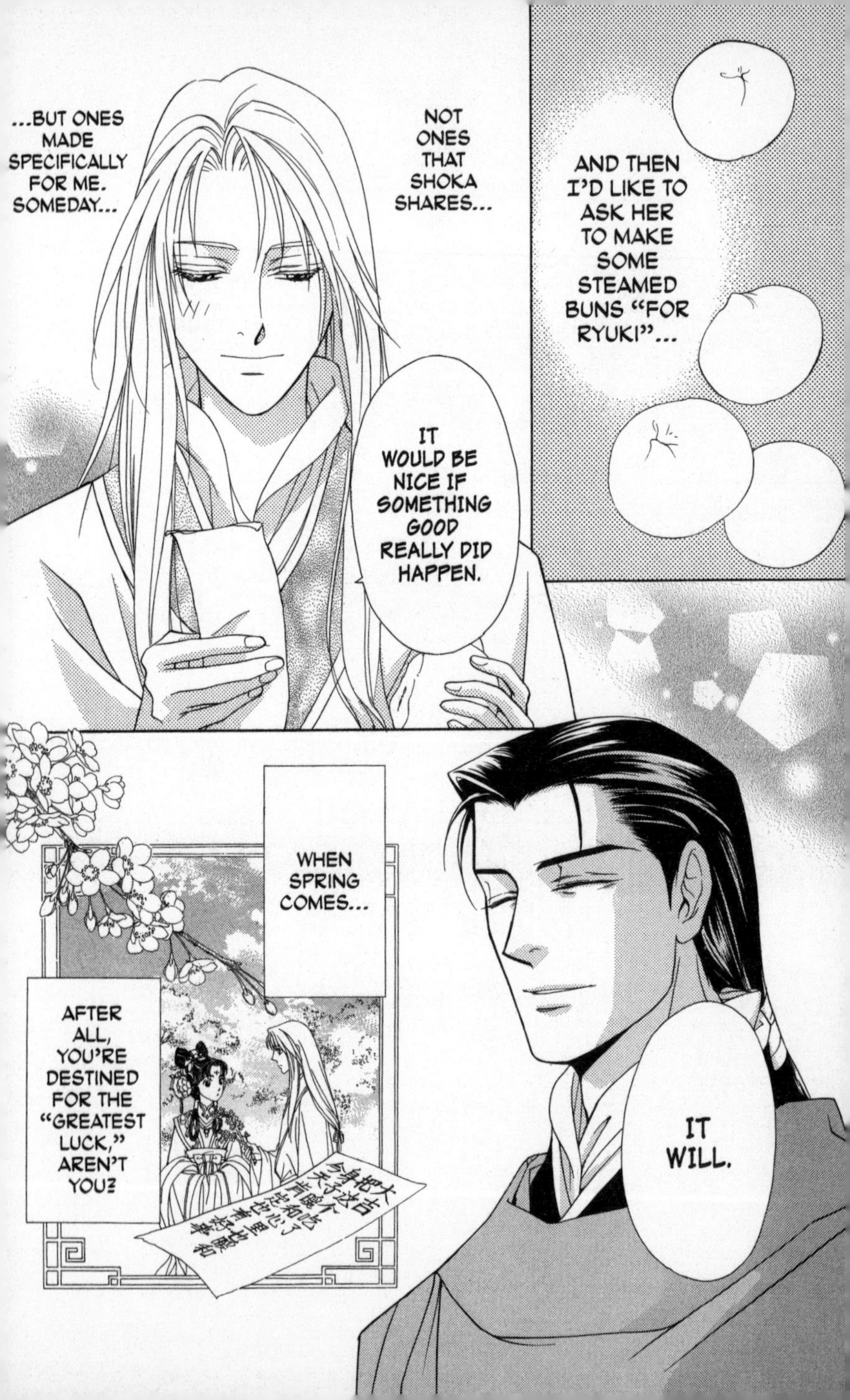
AND THEN I'D LIKE TO ASK HER TO MAKE SOME STEAMED BUNS "FOR RYUKI"...
NOT ONES THAT SHOKA SHARES...
...BUT ONES MADE SPECIFICALLY FOR ME. SOMEDAY...
IT WOULD BE NICE IF SOMETHING GOOD REALLY DID HAPPEN.
IT WILL.
WHEN SPRING COMES...
AFTER ALL, YOU'RE DESTINED FOR THE "GREATEST LUCK," AREN'T YOU?

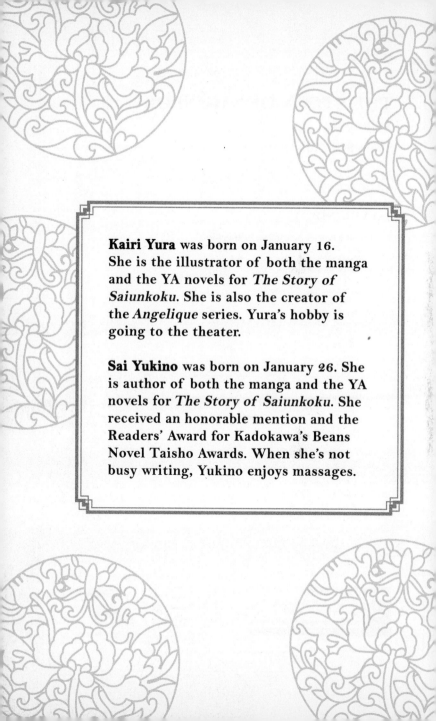

Kairi Yura was born on January 16. She is the illustrator of both the manga and the YA novels for *The Story of Saiunkoku*. She is also the creator of the *Angelique* series. Yura's hobby is going to the theater.

Sai Yukino was born on January 26. She is author of both the manga and the YA novels for *The Story of Saiunkoku*. She received an honorable mention and the Readers' Award for Kadokawa's Beans Novel Taisho Awards. When she's not busy writing, Yukino enjoys massages.

THE STORY OF SAIUNKOKU
Volume 2

Shojo Beat Edition

ART
KAIRI YURA
STORY
SAI YUKINO

Translation & English Adaptation/Su Mon Han
Touch-up Art & Lettering/Sabrina Heep
Design/Yukiko Whitley
Editor/Nancy Thistlethwaite

Saiunkoku Monogatari Volume 2
© Kairi YURA 2007
© Sai YUKINO 2007
First published in Japan in 2007 by KADOKAWA SHOTEN Publishing Co., Ltd.,
Tokyo. English translation rights arranged with KADOKAWA SHOTEN Publishing
Co., Ltd., Tokyo.

Printed in the U.S.A.

Published by VIZ Media, LLC
P.O. Box 77010
San Francisco, CA 94107

10 9 8 7 6 5 4 3 2
First printing, February 2011
Second printing, June 2011

LAND OF *Fantasy*

MIAKA YÛKI IS AN ORDINARY JUNIOR-HIGH STUDENT WHO IS SUDDENLY WHISKED AWAY INTO THE WORLD OF A BOOK, *THE UNIVERSE OF THE FOUR GODS*. WILL THE BEAUTIFUL CELESTIAL BEINGS SHE ENCOUNTERS AND THE CHANCE TO BECOME A PRIESTESS DIVERT MIAKA FROM EVER RETURNING HOME?

THREE VOLUMES OF THE ORIGINAL *FUSHIGI YÛGI* SERIES COMBINED INTO A LARGER FORMAT WITH AN EXCLUSIVE COVER DESIGN AND BONUS CONTENT

EXPERIENCE THE BEAUTY OF *FUSHIGI YÛGI* WITH THE HARDCOVER ART BOOK

ALSO AVAILABLE: THE *FUSHIGI YÛGI: GENBU KAIDEN* MANGA, THE EIGHT VOLUME PREQUEL TO THIS BEST-SELLING FANTASY SERIES

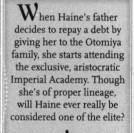

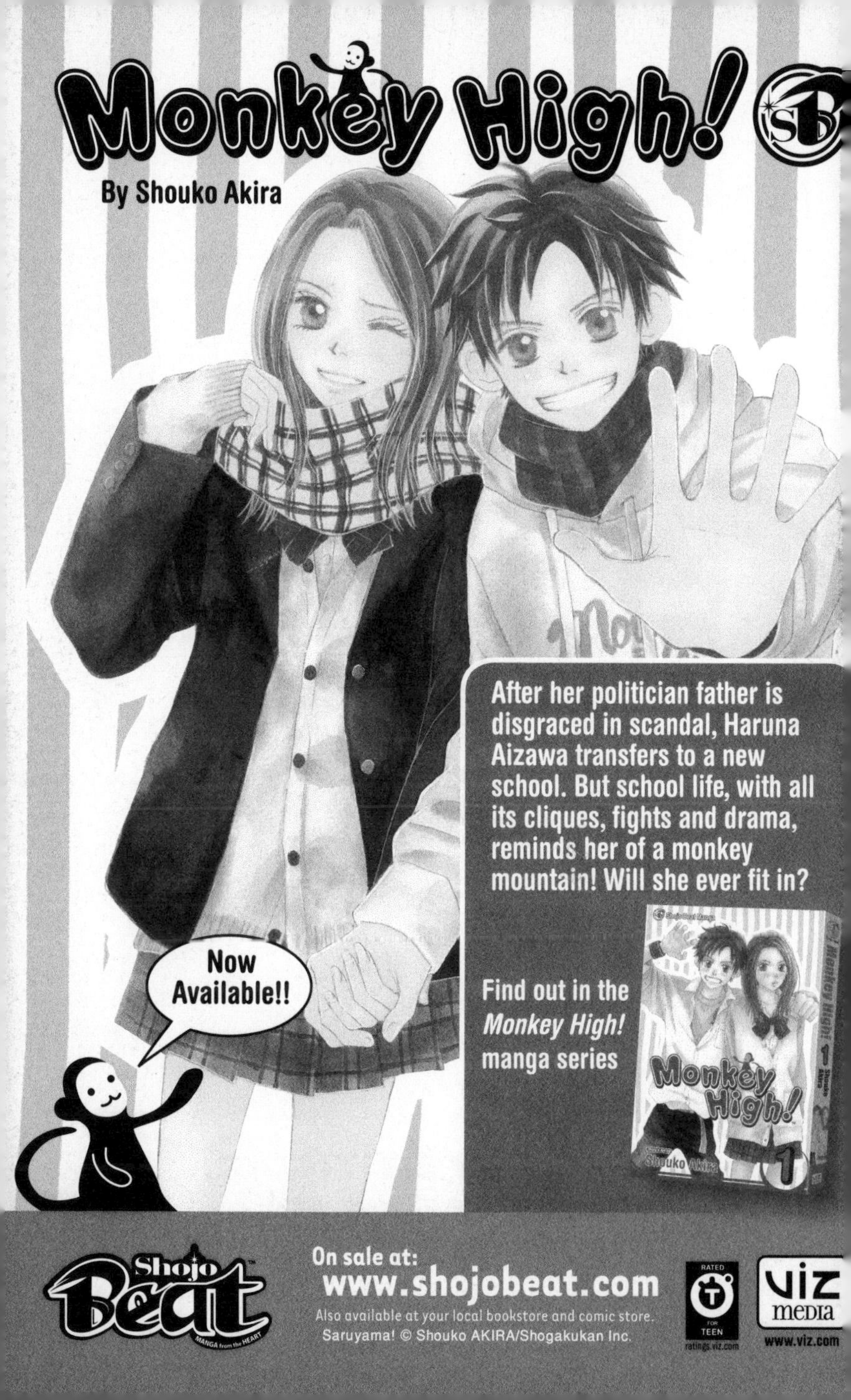
Monkey High!
By Shouko Akira
After her politician father is disgraced in scandal, Haruna Aizawa transfers to a new school. But school life, with all its cliques, fights and drama, reminds her of a monkey mountain! Will she ever fit in?
Now Available!!
Find out in the *Monkey High!* manga series
Monkey High!
Shouko Akira
1
Shojo Beat
MANGA from the HEART
On sale at:
www.shojobeat.com
Also available at your local bookstore and comic store.
Saruyama! © Shouko AKIRA/Shogakukan Inc.
RATED
T
FOR TEEN
ratings.viz.com
VIZ media
www.viz.com

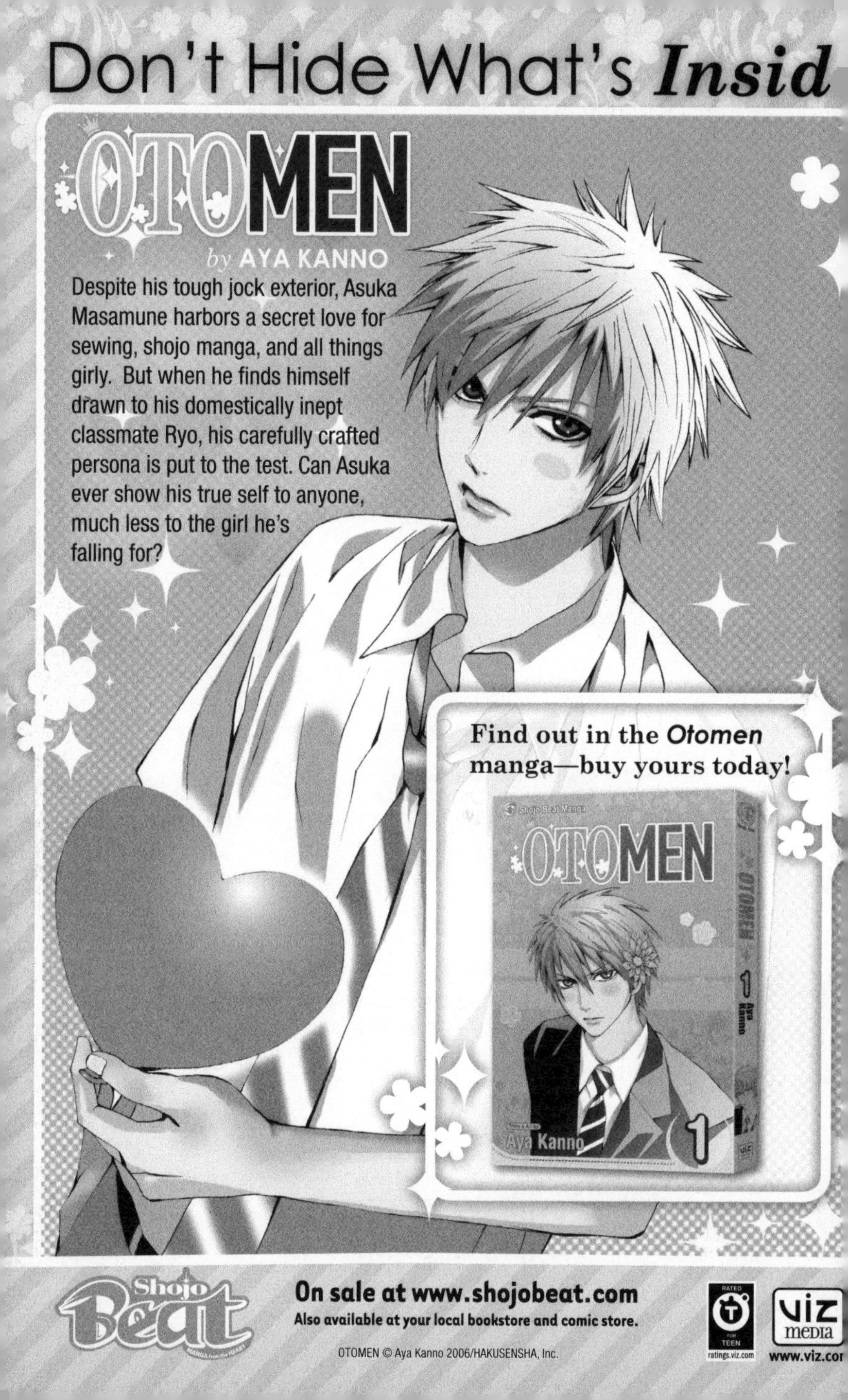
Don't Hide What's *Insid*
OTOMEN
by AYA KANNO
Despite his tough jock exterior, Asuka Masamune harbors a secret love for sewing, shojo manga, and all things girly. But when he finds himself drawn to his domestically inept classmate Ryo, his carefully crafted persona is put to the test. Can Asuka ever show his true self to anyone, much less to the girl he's falling for?
Find out in the *Otomen* manga—buy yours today!
Shojo Beat Manga
OTOMEN
Aya Kanno
1
Shojo Beat
On sale at www.shojobeat.com
Also available at your local bookstore and comic store.
OTOMEN © Aya Kanno 2006/HAKUSENSHA, Inc.
RATED T FOR TEEN
ratings.viz.com
VIZ MEDIA
www.viz.cor